The Holocaust in 100 Histories

The Holocaust in 100 Histories

Paul R. Bartrop

BLOOMSBURY ACADEMIC
LONDON • NEW YORK • OXFORD • NEW DELHI • SYDNEY

BLOOMSBURY ACADEMIC
Bloomsbury Publishing Plc
50 Bedford Square, London, WC1B 3DP, UK
1385 Broadway, New York, NY 10018, USA
29 Earlsfort Terrace, Dublin 2, Ireland

BLOOMSBURY, BLOOMSBURY ACADEMIC and the Diana logo are trademarks of
Bloomsbury Publishing Plc

First published in Great Britain 2024

A catalogue record for this book is available from the British Library.

A catalog record for this book is available from the Library of Congress.

ISBN: HB: 978-1-3504-3511-7
PB: 978-1-3504-3512-4
ePDF: 978-1-3504-3513-1
eBook: 978-1-3504-3514-8

Typeset by Newgen KnowledgeWorks Pvt. Ltd., Chennai, India
Printed and bound in Great Britain

To find out more about our authors and books visit www.bloomsbury.com
and sign up for our newsletters.

For Max, Xavier, and Jack
The Pot of Gold at the End of the Rainbow

CONTENTS

Introduction

As a historian of the Holocaust, I have found across an academic lifetime that my work must always proceed from stories. The Holocaust was not an idea or a theory: it was a vast amalgam of events that happened to real people in real situations. The words of Holocaust survivor and (for many) the voice of all the survivors, Elie Wiesel, ring true here more than in many other contexts. As he wrote:

> Let us tell tales. Let us tell tales—all the rest can wait, all the rest must wait.
>
> Let us tell tales—that is our primary obligation. Commentaries will have to come later, lest they replace or becloud what they mean to reveal.
>
> Tales of children so wise and so old. Tales of old men mute with fear. Tales of victims welcoming death as an old acquaintance. Tales that bring man close to the abyss and beyond—and others that lift him up to heaven and beyond. Tales of despair, tales of longing. Tales of immense flames reaching out to the sky, tales of night consuming life and hope and eternity.
>
> Let us tell tales so as to remember how vulnerable man is when faced with overwhelming evil. Let us tell tales so as not to allow the executioner to have the last word. The last word belongs to the victim. It is up to the witness to capture it, shape it, transmit it and keep it as a secret, and then communicate that secret to others.[1]

In honor of that approach, I would like to offer the following by way of an introduction to this book.

One day in November 1944 several children arrived at Auschwitz. We do not know from where they came, nor what their names were. They were *Jewish* children; that's what mattered. As the truck slowed, one little boy holding an apple jumped off. His intention was not to run away; in his youthful excitement, he simply wanted to be first off the truck so he could eat his apple. One of the SS men standing nearby was Wilhelm Boger, later imprisoned for life for the murder of 114 Jews and as an accessory in at least one thousand other cases. On this occasion, Boger saw the boy next to the truck, enjoying himself. Without warning he went over to the boy, grabbed his legs, and smashed his head against a wall. He then calmly picked up the apple and went back to his office. About an hour later a prisoner, who had seen the boy's murder, was called to the office to assist in a translation issue. There, he saw Boger eating the child's apple.[2]

American sociologist and Holocaust survivor Fred E. Katz, who has commented on this incident, notes that Boger's gruesome killing of this innocent child for the apple had a theatrical quality to it: "He ate the apple in front of a witness to the murderous deed. It was no accident that Boger ate the apple when the witness was there to see it. He was *flaunting* his evil."[3] For that little boy, Boger's act was the supreme example in his short life of what the Nazi new order was. We do not know what experiences the child had already lived through, but there is no doubt that at that moment, in those circumstances, SS officer Wilhelm Boger embodied the full horror of the Holocaust.

Accompanying tales must also be questions, of which there is an unending supply. The doyen of Holocaust scholars, Yehuda Bauer, has spent a lifetime leading the way in this regard, and in 1978 he did so in a public address at the University of Washington:

> I fear we have to delve into the reality of the matter to be able to scale the emotional heights: what were the bases of Nazi Jew-hatred? What in Christian theology, in popular antisemitism, prepared the ground? Who were the murderers? What social strata did they come from? What did they think? When was the mass murder planned and how? How did the bureaucracy work that was able to sit behind their desks and direct the murder? Who built the gas chambers? What was the reaction of the victims? Sheep to the slaughter? Glorious resistance? Was there a way of rescue? What were the relations between Jew and non-Jew in the European countries occupied by the Nazis? What were the demographic, cultural, psychological consequences of the Holocaust?

Other questions followed, including the last: "What is the responsibility of the free world towards this event?"[4] He concluded by saying that "such questions and many others cannot be avoided."[5]

Situated between the telling of tales and the asking of questions, this book is not a standard history of the Holocaust. Organized chronologically by year, each of those years is divided appropriately month by month. It is, in fact, a series of histories, each of which tells an individual story taken from the larger whole—of horror, of tragedy, of resistance, of defiance. The stories here look at ideas, people, movements, and events, embracing social, political, economic, religious, military, and cultural phenomena.

Many thousands of works have been produced on the Holocaust, in myriad languages. As far back as 1966, Israeli historian Jacob Robinson identified the magnitude of the task by showing that while "the usual course of any particular community is even and uneventful," for the most part "little of historical significance takes place, except in those rare times when a peak of military, political, intellectual, and moral activity is reached." The era of Nazi oppression, on the other hand, was quite different. During that period, Robinson wrote, "In the span of only twelve years, every single Jewish community in Europe perforce was faced with the greatest crisis possible to a group—the crisis of existence." What did this mean when translated to day-to-day affairs? For Robinson, it represented nothing less than that every single Jewish community "reached its peak of activity, called upon its deepest spiritual resources, brought forth its ultimate answers to the questions of life and death, of relations between man and God." Given this, he concluded, the task for the historian was "to rescue from oblivion a history as eventful and rich as that of a thousand years."[6]

Bearing in mind that this book is not a history but is, rather, a series of histories, the task I have set myself is to identify a 100 ways of looking at the period of the Third Reich and illustrate how each of them played its part in weaving the broader tapestry that we now call the Holocaust.

Each of these histories can be read on its own, either in sequence or out of order. It is not expected that readers will possess any prior knowledge of the matters under discussion; but if interest is stimulated for those seeking to learn more, a short list of Further Reading accompanies each entry. And not only that, for teachers, students, and those who are neither but aim to reach greater understanding, two Discussion Questions follow each entry, laying down a challenge to think more deeply about the item that has just been read. In every case, it goes without saying that this must merely be the start of a process; the rest is up to the reader to make sense (or not) of the subject at hand.

Why have I taken this approach? Over a career of teaching about the Holocaust and other history, in a variety of educational settings, I have always confronted my students with a question: "How representative of the broader issue is the example you have chosen?" Many of them have not much liked my question, having identified this or that case which (they might inform me) *truly* epitomizes a situation. I know how they felt: I was often of the same view when similarly challenged by my teachers. It is, however, a worthy question, much overlooked or maligned these days by those seeking to make a point and have it accepted unconditionally. It must be emphasized that certain examples simply *do not* exemplify a broader truth, even though some might like them to do so for the sake of supporting an argument. Such stories might stand out, or be amazing and worth sharing, or be the only one of their kind found thus far. But how *representative* are they?

This book makes no claim to being comprehensive, nor does it offer a 100 stories about the Holocaust that will answer (or ask) *all* the questions necessary for illumination. Instead, unlike standard histories of the

Holocaust, it offers its 100 stories as part of a whole not necessarily spelled out within the text.

I came to this project via a monthly column I began writing for the Jewish press in Southwest Florida in 2012. The three newspapers—*L'Chayim* (Lee-Charlotte Counties), *Federation Star* (Collier County), and *The Jewish News* (Sarasota-Manatee Counties)—all took my articles, each of which aligned with an anniversary from the Holocaust coinciding with the month in question. The pieces I have selected for this book come from the much larger collection of all these articles, and choosing which to include was possibly the hardest task of them all.

To encourage further understanding, I have also assembled a collection of documents, composed a glossary, and compiled a chronology after the 100 histories. A bibliography of key reference works and online resources rounds out the volume so that readers can explore topics on their own and thus—hopefully—make their own contribution to the history of the Holocaust.

The Holocaust comprised innumerable individual stories. Consider the mother forced to choose between two children on the ramp at Auschwitz, the adolescent girl torn from the embrace of her little sister because she was old enough to work while the younger girl was not, the old man beaten to death by the side of the road by an SS guard because he couldn't move fast enough when ordered to, or the newlyweds who were forced into the squalor of the ghetto where the bride watched her husband die of starvation and disease only to die herself immediately afterward.

And lest it be thought that we are referring only to German Nazis here, it must be recalled that one did not have to be a German in order to be a Nazi—as witness the experiences Jews had with the Arrow Cross (Nyilas) Party in Hungary, the Hlinka Guard in Slovakia, the antisemitic Poles who denounced Jews to their German occupiers, the Vichy French officials and police, the Ukrainian collaborators, and so on. For many people who never saw a Nazi German, the Holocaust was visited upon them by a wide variety of messengers.

Not every story can be rescued, let alone retold; but a few have been here, in the hope that some measure of enlightenment, empathy, awareness, and reflection might surface as a result of what is an otherwise unorthodox way of chronicling what happened during those awful years between 1933 and 1945.

As mentioned, this book is based on a monthly series of articles that first appeared—in a vastly different format—in the Jewish press of Southwest Florida from 2012 onward. Throughout that period, I was consistently encouraged by the editor of all three newspapers, Ted Epstein, who is to be commended for his unceasing efforts in pulling together each month individual publications serving different disparate communities. Recognition should also be given to the former executive director of the Jewish Federation of Lee-Charlotte Counties, Alan Isaacs, who first invited me to write for *L'Chayim* back in September 2012.

This book would not have seen the light of day without the enthusiasm of my publisher at Bloomsbury, Rhodri Mogford, who, from my first suggestion that "something" could be done with the articles I had been writing for the Jewish press, showed that imagination can sometimes triumph over uncertainty. And at a crucial time, my colleague from Stockton University, Michael Dickerman, stepped in with some important information regarding the document section.

Perhaps my greatest debt of gratitude lies with my students at Florida Gulf Coast University. Although the onset of the Covid pandemic in 2020 forced me to "retire" from teaching—and what a ridiculous concept that is, for a lifelong teacher—my students always challenged me to contemplate and rework my ideas, to argue them through and defend them, and be willing to accept criticism and change when change was necessary. The same is true of the thousands of students I have taught over the past four decades. The cut-and-thrust of the classroom, no less than the conference hall or the pages of an academic journal, must serve as ground zero of scholarly thinking, and I am grateful to every student with whom it has been my pleasure to engage.

As always, my life partner Eve Grimm has been my guiding light throughout the entire process in both an academic and personal sense, and no words on a page can offer her sufficient respect for the guidance and care she has always, with wisdom and without hesitation, provided.

Notes

1 Elie Wiesel, "Art and Culture after the Holocaust," *Cross Currents*, 26:3 (Fall 1976), p. 258.
2 Fred E. Katz, *Ordinary People and Extraordinary Evil: A Report on the Beguilings of Evil* (Albany: State University of New York Press, 1993), p. 88.
3 Ibid. Emphasis in original.
4 Yehuda Bauer, *The Holocaust in Historical Perspective* (Seattle: University of Washington Press, 1978), p. 46.
5 Ibid., p. 47.
6 Jacob Robinson, "Research on the Jewish Catastrophe," *Jewish Journal of Sociology*, 8:2 (December 1966), p. 192.

Part 1

1933

JANUARY 1933

1.1 Hitler Is Appointed

Throughout the year 1932, Germany's Weimar Republic was under siege from antidemocratic forces bent on its destruction. The National Socialist Party and the Communist Party, which both attracted more votes than democratic political parties, were dedicated to overthrowing the republic and establishing their own form of totalitarian rule.

It is often said that Adolf Hitler was elected to office, but in a presidential election in March 1932 he only received 36.8 percent of the popular vote compared to incumbent President Paul von Hindenburg's 53 percent. In the last free election Hitler faced, his share of the popular vote decreased. At elections for the Reichstag in 1932 the Nazis went from 37.27 percent in July to 33.09 percent in December. The longer Hitler went through 1932, the less the German people seemed to want him.

A *New York Times* headline from January 30, 1933, however, carried stark news: "Hitler Made Chancellor of Germany but Coalition Cabinet Limits Power; Centrists Hold Balance in Reichstag." Note the *NYT*'s language: "Coalition cabinet limits power," and "centrists hold balance in Reichstag." In January 1933, there were genuine thoughts that Hitler could be reined in, and that, perhaps, his antidemocratic and antisemitic expressions would settle down now that he had been appointed to high office.

Attempting to bring stability to an otherwise impossibly unstable situation, Hindenburg engaged Hitler in a caretaker capacity until truly democratic elections could be held, in a coalition government where the Nazis held only three cabinet positions. Hitler, it was anticipated, would do the dirty work of getting rid of the communists, and then the traditional order would resume. As one member of an elite family was reputed to have said of Hitler's appointment, in a well-known jibe, "We've hired him."

On the evening of January 30, 1933, Hitler stood at an open window watching a torchlight parade of 25,000 Nazi storm troopers march through the streets of Berlin. Beaming, he is said to have exclaimed, "No power on Earth will get me out of here alive." It was an appropriate comment on how he viewed this supreme success. Within a month he had placed himself in such a position of authority that he was able to suspend the constitution, entrench himself in office (still in an emergency capacity), and, within two months, establish the country's first concentration camp at Dachau. Even then, despite all that and massive voter intimidation, he only attracted 43.91 percent of the vote at new elections on March 5, 1933, still not enough for an absolute majority.

After this, Hitler gave up on asking the German people what they wanted. By March 23, with the help of his Nationalist Party coalition colleagues, he had passed an Enabling Act allowing the Cabinet to enact laws—without the approval of the Reichstag—for an initial four-year period. Within four months, all other parties had been eliminated, and Germany was a one-party state.

Hindenburg's miscalculation in appointing Hitler as caretaker chancellor led to disaster for Germany, for Europe, and for the world—and, of course, for the Jewish people. Things could not have been foreseen that way at the time, though as we know, when we see things with 20/20 hindsight everything becomes much clearer.

Before January 30, 1933, Germany possessed what was, on paper, arguably the most democratic constitution in the world. After then, Hitler managed to destroy that constitution and establish his dictatorship in a matter of months.

Discussion Questions

1. In your view, why was Adolf Hitler appointed to power?
2. Why do you think Germany's existing democratic system was unable to resist Hitler's ascent to office in January 1933?

Further Reading

Barth, Rüdiger, and Hauke Friederichs, *The Gravediggers: The Last Winter of the Weimar Republic*, London: Profile Books, 2019.

Range, Peter Ross, *The Unfathomable Ascent: How Hitler Came to Power*, Cheltenham, UK: History Press, 2020.

Walther, Peter, *Darkness Falling: The Strange Death of the Weimar Republic, 1930–33*, London: Head of Zeus, 2021.

FEBRUARY 1933

1.2 The Reichstag Fire and Its Aftermath

On the night of February 27, 1933, a message was received by the Berlin police that the Reichstag, the home of the German parliament, was on fire. Soon after, a 24-year-old Dutchman, Marinus van der Lubbe, was apprehended and charged with arson. Found carrying an identification card of the Dutch Communist Party, the 29-day-old National Socialist government proclaimed this as proof that communists had launched a revolutionary takeover of Germany.

The fear of communism dominating some sectors of the public now enabled the Nazis to consolidate their newly won political position and establish a totalitarian state. It was to combat communism, after all, that the Nazis were put in power in the first place, appointed by the old order to bring an end to the threat of a proletarian uprising.

The day after the fire, Adolf Hitler persuaded President Paul von Hindenburg to sign a Decree for the Protection of the People and the State, suspending all the basic civil and individual liberties guaranteed under the constitution. It empowered the government to take such steps as were necessary to remove this threat to German society. Significantly, it made no specific references to definite adversaries; while directing itself in this instance toward communism, it contained the menacing portent of later restrictions which might be applied toward other "enemies."

Marinus van der Lubbe was not the only one charged with responsibility for the fire; other arrests also took place in a mass crackdown on all communists and socialists. Hundreds were detained in the first few days, and tens of thousands in succeeding weeks. On March 3, Hermann Göring, as Prussian minister of the interior, instructed the Prussian police that not only communists but "those who work with the communists and who support their criminal objectives, even if indirectly," should also be arrested.

The form of arrest was soon referred to as *Schutzhaft*, or "protective custody." Very few ordinary citizens were aware of what happened to a person taken in. Men who had been imprisoned and then released were cowed into such submission that they refused to discuss their experiences, and the Nazi authorities revealed nothing. Often a man simply disappeared from his home, his place of work, or even from the street, and his whereabouts were not disclosed.

Ignorance of the fate of *Schutzhaft* detainees created a climate of fear among the population. It appeared the authorities were indiscriminately arresting people on the flimsiest of charges, or often for no obvious reason at all. Uncertainties abounded: the motives behind the arrest, the future, treatment at the hands of the Nazis, and the means of avoiding such an arbitrary system of seizure.

The wave of early arrests put enormous strains on the existing prison system, and it was soon clear that such a situation could not continue indefinitely. Moreover, the concept of protective custody, some believed, might become less terrifying if it became known that the detainee had merely gone to prison. An institution was thus needed which would concentrate all the *Schutzhaft* prisoners of a given region within a single, non-penal, nonpublic detention center. There were decided practical and political advantages to the creation of such an institution: it would relieve overcrowding in local prisons, it would assemble all the prisoners in one compound far removed from the prying eyes of civilian prison authorities, and it would give concrete form to the sense of dread accompanying *Schutzhaft* arrests.

The result saw the establishment of "special protective custody quarters" separate from police prisons, with the first of these appearing on March 20, 1933, with the opening of a compound about fifteen kilometers northwest of Munich, on the outskirts of the town of Dachau. Other camp establishments soon followed, among them Oranienburg, Papenburg, Esterwegen, Kemna, Lichtenburg, and Börgermoor.

For the most part, these were rapidly established, highly improvised affairs. Little regard was paid to administration, discipline, or utilization. Some were run by SS officers; many were staffed by SA men, often locals who knew or were known by those they were guarding. They frequently operated without any apparent system or direction and little in the way of planning or procedure. Places of political imprisonment had political aims, and selected their captives using political criteria to remove opposition from the community while at the same time intimidating the population into accepting the Nazi regime. With their creation, however, the foundations of the Nazi concentration camp state were laid.

Discussion Questions

1. Who were the first people to be imprisoned in February 1933? Why?
2. Why were concentration camps established in Germany in 1933?

Further Reading

Hett, Benjamin Carter, *Burning the Reichstag: An Investigation into the Third Reich's Enduring Mystery*, New York: Oxford University Press, 2014.

Kogon, Eugen, *The Theory and Practice of Hell: The German Concentration Camps and the System Behind Them*, New York: Berkley Windhover Books, 1975.

Krausnick, Helmut, Martin Broszat, Hans Buchheim, and Hans-Adolf Jacobson, *Anatomy of the SS State*, London: Collins, 1968.

MARCH 1933

1.3 The Enabling Act

On March 24, 1933, the German Reichstag passed the Enabling Act, a constitutional amendment that gave the German Cabinet—in effect, Chancellor Adolf Hitler—plenary powers to enact laws. It followed one month after the Reichstag Fire Decree, which abolished most civil liberties and transferred state powers to the Reich government. The combined effect of the two laws was to transform Hitler's government into a de facto legal dictatorship.

The final two years of the Weimar Republic were unstable, with frequent political, social, and economic crises. President Paul von Hindenburg issued many emergency decrees and dissolved the Reichstag twice in 1932, during which the Nazi Party transformed from a radical splinter group to a party of government. In the two elections to the Reichstag in 1932, it won the largest share of the vote, though never a majority.

After the Reichstag fire of February 27, 1933, Hindenburg accepted Hitler's demand for a decree suspending all political and civil liberties as a "temporary" measure for the "protection of the people and state." The Reichstag Fire Decree enacted the following day then severely curtailed fundamental rights and subjected the police largely to the control of the national government.

In March 1933 the last parliamentary elections took place. The SA, using violence and intimidation, silenced all other parties. The Nazis polled 43.91 percent of the vote, not enough for a majority but enough to quash any future political resistance.

Hitler then proposed an Act for the Removal of the Distress of the People and the Reich, more commonly known as the Enabling Act (*Ermächtigungsgesetz*), ostensibly to allow him greater time to deal with political unrest. This act, consisting of only five articles, vested the government with almost unlimited powers to enact laws, even in cases where the legislation encroached on core provisions of the constitution.

Just before the vote, Hitler made a speech to the Reichstag in which he pledged to use restraint and to use these powers only insofar as they were essential for carrying out vitally necessary measures. He also promised an end to unemployment and pledged to promote peace with France, Britain, and the Soviet Union. But to do all this, Hitler said, he first needed the Enabling Act.

Since the act amended the Weimar Constitution, its adoption required both a two-thirds majority and the presence in the Reichstag of at least two-thirds of all its members. The prospects of achieving the requisite number of votes were good, since the mandates of the eighty-one deputies from the Communist Party had been rescinded under the Reichstag Fire Decree.

Moreover, many Reichstag members had already fled, been imprisoned, or murdered.

The Reichstag convened in the Kroll Opera House, Berlin. After eliminating the communists, Hitler was still thirty-one votes short. The support of the German Center Party was particularly important to secure the remaining votes. Hitler and his interior minister, Wilhelm Frick, gave the Center Party far-reaching guarantees on the continuing existence of the supreme organs of the constitution and the states, promising to respect the rights of the churches, safeguard fundamental rights, and establish a parliamentary committee to scrutinize legislative bills. With these promises (most of which were never honored), the government gained the parliamentary support it required.

Only the deputies from the Social Democratic Party voted against the bill as a bloc, despite massive intimidation by the SA and SS, whose troops had moved in to surround the Kroll Opera House. Despite the obvious intentions of the act, a mere 94 deputies voted against the bill compared with 444 who voted in favor. The Enabling Act passed on March 24, 1933, and was signed by Hindenburg later that day.

The adoption of the act empowered Hitler's government to enact laws without Reichstag consent, and without the president's countersignature. These extensive powers also applied, almost without restriction, to constitutional amendments and to treaties with other states. The act thus marked the final eclipse of the democratic state based on the rule of law. There would be neither further elections nor a constitution to keep Hitler in check. The Reichstag had, in effect, voted away its power.

All subsequent legislation of the Nazi state was based on the Enabling Act. It served to centralize public administration, the judiciary, the security apparatus, and the armed forces in accordance with the "Führer principle," to standardize political life in accordance with National Socialist principles (*Gleichschaltung*) by banning political parties and mass organizations and to abolish freedom of the press. The concentration of power in the hands of the government, and hence in the person of Adolf Hitler, sealed the transition to dictatorship.

Within a matter of weeks, it had become illegal to criticize the government. A new secret police force, the Gestapo, was established, which immediately began arresting those considered to be "unreliable." Dachau, the first concentration camp, opened, trade unions were banned, and freedom of the press was curtailed. Germany became a one-party state with Hitler its dictator.

The Enabling Act was initially adopted for a four-year period but was extended in 1937, 1939, and 1943. It remained the basis of all legislation throughout the Nazi dictatorship and was finally abolished by Law No. 1 of the Allied Control Council after the Second World War, on September 20, 1945.

Discussion Questions

1. Why do you think Hitler needed an Enabling Act in March 1933?
2. Was the Enabling Act legitimate, according to the constitution at that time?

Further Reading

Broszat, Martin, *The Hitler State: The Foundation and Development of the Internal Structure of the Third Reich*, London: Longmans, 1981.
Evans, Richard J., *The Coming of the Third Reich*, New York: Penguin Press, 2003.
Fritzsche, Peter, *Hitler's First Hundred Days: When Germans Embraced the Reich*, New York: Basic Books, 2020.

APRIL 1933

1.4 The April Boycott

A government-directed economic boycott against the Jews of Germany took place on April 1, 1933. Given the years of antisemitic rhetoric flowing from the Nazis before they assumed power on January 30, 1933, there were intense fears throughout the Jewish world that it was only a matter of time before Germany's Jews would be targeted should the Nazis put their statements into practice. Driven by this anxiety, on March 27, 1933, a series of anti-Nazi protest rallies organized by American Jewish organizations took place in New York, Baltimore, Boston, Chicago, Cleveland, Philadelphia, and seventy other locations across the United States. The New York rally, which took place before a packed house at Madison Square Garden, was broadcast around the world. The result saw several Jewish organizations, among them the American Jewish Congress, American League for Defense of Jewish Rights, B'nai B'rith, the Jewish Labor Committee, and Jewish War Veterans, join in a call for a boycott of German goods in the hope that it would make the Nazis realize that Germany could be damaged economically should any antisemitic measures be introduced. In the United Kingdom and other European countries, a Jewish boycott of German goods was also implemented as a symbol of resistance against the Nazis' policies.

In response, the Nazi leadership decided to stage an economic boycott of their own, now against the Jews of Germany. The avowed reason was to exact revenge against the so-called atrocity stories (*Gruelpropaganda*), which, the Nazis maintained, were being spread about Germany overseas. It was the first avowed government action against Germany's Jews, though as early as the 1920s Nazi newspapers frequently called for a boycott of Jewish businesses, a theme often repeated prior to the Nazis coming to power.

In response to the overseas boycott of Germany by Jewish businesses, Nazi propaganda minister Joseph Goebbels announced that a one-day boycott would take place against Jewish businesses in Germany on April 1, 1933. In announcing the boycott, he stated that any other such measures would only be lifted once anti-Nazi protests overseas were suspended. Threatening the Jewish community in Germany, he declared that if the foreign protests did not then cease "the boycott will be resumed … until German Jewry has been annihilated." Julius Streicher, the viciously antisemitic editor and publisher of the newspaper *Der Stürmer*, was placed in charge of organizing the boycott. He issued a series of orders calling for a nonviolent demonstration to begin at 10:00 a.m. on Saturday, April 1.

That morning, many Jewish shop owners awoke to find the windows of their businesses painted with Stars of David, the word *Jude* (Jew), and antisemitic phrases. Storm troopers stood menacingly in front of Jewish-owned department stores and retail establishments and the offices of professionals such as doctors and lawyers intimidating anyone who dared to walk in. Signs were posted throughout Germany saying, "Don't Buy from Jews" (*Kauf nicht bei Juden!*) and "The Jews Are Our Misfortune" (*Die Juden sind unser Unglück!*). In addition, acts of violence were perpetrated against Jews throughout Germany.

Despite this, many Germans ignored the boycott, preferring to shop in the Jewish-owned stores with which they were familiar. Those customers who defiantly tried to enter Jewish shops were taunted and often verbally abused by Nazis and their supporters outside. Furthermore, numerous Jewish veterans of the First World War stood outside their businesses wearing their medals, eliciting more sympathy from non-Jewish Germans. Perhaps realizing that their measure was called too early to be obeyed by an unprepared public, the boycott was called off after only one day, ending at midnight.

The boycott, though abandoned, at least demonstrated the Nazi intent to undermine the viability of a Jewish presence in Germany. Moreover, it marked the beginning of a nationwide campaign by the Nazi Party against the entire German Jewish population. One week after the boycott, on April 7, 1933, the government passed the Law for the Restoration of the Professional Civil Service, a measure dismissing all Jews from employment in government service; this meant that Jews could no longer be civil servants or employed as teachers in public schools, or, given that lawyers were also employed by the state, in the law. Doctors and hospital employees soon followed.

There were three exceptions: Jews who were veterans of the First World War; those who had been employed in the civil service continuously since August 1, 1914; and those who had lost a father or son in combat in the war. Although they were exempted, this, too, would change over time.

Discussion Questions

1. In your view, why was the Nazi boycott of Jewish businesses unsuccessful?
2. Why do you think that after the boycott the Nazis exempted the three categories of Jews mentioned at the end of the article?

Further Reading

Burleigh, Michael, and Wolfgang Wippermann, *The Racial State: Germany 1933–1945*, Cambridge: Cambridge University Press, 1991.
Friedländer, Saul, *Nazi Germany and the Jews:* volume 1. *The Years of Persecution 1933–1939*, London: Weidenfeld and Nicolson, 1997.

MAY 1933

1.5 The Books Are Burning

On May 10, 1933, throughout Germany, the Nazis engaged in a highly orchestrated campaign of book burning, with university students of the German Student Association (*Deutsche Studentenschaft*) purging some 25,000 titles of what were termed "un-German" books. That night, in university communities throughout the country, students marched in torchlight parades and at given times and locations would consign to the flames such unwanted titles as they found in university libraries. Bands played, speeches were made, oaths were taken, and nationalistic songs were sung. Local Nazi leaders lined up to be heard and seen.

On that awful night, the works of all Jewish and many left-wing authors were burned. These included names such as Walter Benjamin, Ernst Bloch, Bertolt Brecht, Friedrich Engels, Lion Feuchtwanger, Sigmund Freud, George Grosz, Jaroslav Hašek, Franz Kafka, Erich Kästner, Egon Kisch, Karl Kraus, Theodor Lessing, Karl Liebknecht, Georg Lukács, Rosa Luxemburg, Heinrich Mann, Thomas Mann, Karl Marx, Carl von Ossietzky, Erwin Piscator, Erich Maria Remarque, Joseph Roth, Nelly Sachs, Anna Seghers, Arthur Schnitzler, Ernst Toller, Kurt Tucholsky, Jakob Wassermann, Franz Werfel, Arnold Zweig, and Stefan Zweig.

Foreign writers were not exempt: these included Victor Hugo, André Gide, Romain Rolland, and Henri Barbusse (France); Joseph Conrad, D. H. Lawrence, H. G. Wells, and Aldous Huxley (Britain); James Joyce (Ireland); Ernest Hemingway, John Dos Passos, Jack London, and Helen Keller (United States); and Fyodor Dostoyevsky, Maxim Gorki, Isaac Babel, Vladimir Lenin, Vladimir Nabokov, Leo Tolstoy, and Leon Trotsky (Russia).

The works consigned to the flames included those of pacifists, liberals, socialists, communists, and anarchists; those whose writings were viewed as subversive or somehow opposed to Nazism; those considered to be traitors; all historical writing deemed as disparaging to the spirit and culture of the German *Volk*, or antithetical to Aryan racial ideals; writings which praised so-called degenerate art; works relating to sexuality and sexual education opposite to the principles of Nazi racial ideas; literature by Jewish authors, regardless of the field; and many other areas to which the Nazis were opposed.

The works of Heinrich Heine, one of the most significant and beloved German poets of the nineteenth century, who had been born Jewish but converted to Christianity in his late twenties, were also burned. His play *Almansor* (1821) contained words that rang all too true that night: "*Dort, wo man Bücher verbrennt, verbrennt man am Ende auch Menschen.*" In English, this translates to the maxim "Where they burn books, in the end they will also burn people."

In Berlin, live radio broadcasts from the scene brought the excitement of the book burnings into people's homes, so that they could hear the speeches (particularly that of Propaganda Minister Josef Goebbels), that took place before some 40,000 spectators. In thirty-four university towns across Germany, the Nazi book burning—termed an "Action against the Un-German Spirit"—was a great success. Widespread newspaper coverage reported the event over the next few days, perhaps not all that surprising given the degree to which Goebbels underwrote the whole idea.

The campaign continued beyond May 10. In some places where it rained, organizers were forced to postpone their event; in others, local Nazis decided to relocate the occasion to June 21, to accompany celebrations for the Summer Solstice. All this worked to the Nazis' advantage, as it enabled them to keep the issue of book purging in the forefront for longer than originally planned.

Book burning, or libricide, is the practice of destroying books and libraries based on motives that are moral, religious, or political in their origins. It is a clear statement any oppressive regime can make about itself, as it goes about the task of silencing what it considers to be an unwanted aspect of a nation or state's culture. The Nazis were not the first to engage in such practices, nor were they the last. Yet regime-sponsored, ideologically driven, and systemic destruction of books and libraries in the twentieth century often served as a prelude or accompaniment to more sinister and destructive human rights catastrophes.

Discussion Questions

1. In your opinion, was there anything positive to be gained for the Nazis in the book burning campaign? If so, what was it?

2. What do you think was meant by Heinrich Heine's statement about burning books and burning people?

Further Reading

Glickman, Mark, *Stolen Words: The Plunder of Jewish Books*, Philadelphia: Jewish Publication Society of America, 2016.
Knuth, Rebecca, *Burning Books and Leveling Libraries: Extremist Violence and Cultural Destruction*, Westport: Praeger, 2006.
Rose, Jonathan, *The Holocaust and the Book: Destruction and Preservation*, Boston: University of Massachusetts Press, 2001.

JULY 1933

1.6 The Vatican and the Nazis Reach an Agreement

On July 20, 1933, Germany signed an agreement with the Vatican. The French word "Concordat" (from the Latin *concordatum*, to agree) is the term employed to describe a treaty entered between the Vatican and a foreign government, and earlier, in 1929, Pope Pius XI had signed a Concordat with the Italy of Fascist leader Benito Mussolini. For many people, therefore, this new one with Hitler did not come as a complete surprise.

The purpose of both these agreements was to guarantee the rights of Roman Catholics in Italy and Germany, as well as the right of the church within these countries to administer its own affairs and manage its own properties. As it would turn out, neither the Nazis in Germany nor the Fascists in Italy were to uphold their end of the agreements.

Throughout his pontificate, Pius XI spoke out against racism, antisemitism, persecution, totalitarianism, and excessive nationalism. While not a philosemite, he was nonetheless a humanitarian and saw the need to reach an accommodation with both dictators and thereby attain some measure of space within which to mitigate their excesses. He therefore considered the Concordat with the Nazis as an opportunity to protect Catholic rights in Germany. Whatever good might come beyond this, he felt, would be a bonus.

However, this had a negative effect for the Jews of Germany. The Concordat legitimized the Third Reich in the eyes of the German Catholic hierarchy, and congregations all over Germany saw that they could from now on square their consciences with the Nazi regime and at the same time remain good Catholics. The international community, moreover, now had a different lens through which to view Nazism. In this way, the Concordat helped to pave the way for the much fuller Nazi takeover of all facets of German society during the period the Nazis referred to as *Gleichschaltung*, or "coordination."

Pius XI eventually realized what he had unleashed and later condemned Nazism. On March 14, 1937, he issued the papal encyclical *Mit brennender Sorge* ("With Burning Anxiety"). The document condemned the Nazis' excesses, even though it made no explicit mention of the Jews. Five days later, on March 19, 1937, he issued a further encyclical, *Divini Redemptoris* ("Divine Redeemer"), wherein he condemned communist persecutions in the Soviet Union, Spain, and Mexico.

One further encyclical, *Humani Generis Unitas* ("On the Unity of the Human Race") was planned, though it was never promulgated owing to Pius's death on February 10, 1939. It condemned antisemitism, racism, and Nazi persecution of the Jews. Because it never went forward, it is sometimes referred to as "The Hidden Encyclical," and the draft text remained secret until it was unearthed and published in France in 1995. Since learning of the draft encyclical, historians have been left wondering what effect it might have had on Germany's Catholics—and from this on Germany's Jews—if it had seen the light of day before the outbreak of war in September 1939.

History, of course, does not allow any alternatives. After the death of Pius XI, his successor, Eugenio Pacelli—who took the name Pius XII—was to be much less conciliatory toward the Jews. He had earlier served as Papal Nuncio to Germany and negotiated and signed the Concordat of July 20, 1933. Intensely opposed to communism, he was theologically conservative and a Germanophile—hardly qualifications suited to confront the Nazis over their antisemitic persecutions. Controversy continues to surround his pontificate regarding the lack of any public condemnation of the Nazi assault and genocide of the Jews.

Those who continue to defend him argue that the actions of the Vatican during the Second World War to give comfort and succor to Jews, much of it in secret, were done with Pius XII's knowledge, and that, had he chosen to speak out, their fate would have been even worse. Those who attack him for his public silence argue that his failure to speak out, given his position as the acknowledged moral voice of the Western world, could possibly have lessened the tragedy since a worse fate for Jews other than what took place cannot be imagined.

Complicating these issues is an at-times simplistic misunderstanding regarding his concern for the preservation of the Church as well as the fate of Roman Catholics involved in all theatres of war. To this can be added his ongoing antipathy toward communism, which he saw as an atheistic force determined to destroy Christianity. Moreover, his own religious perspective regarding Jews saw them as a people antithetical to Christianity, and as a deicide community they did not deserve any special favors when the struggle against communism was, in his opinion, much more important for the future of humanity.

What was not realized at the time was that Hitler had no intention of adhering to *any* agreements with the Vatican. The Concordat signaled to Hitler that the Catholic Church was prepared to turn a blind eye to his excesses. Ironically for the Church, this was to include the incarceration and murder of large numbers of dissenting Catholic priests at the hands of those same Nazis. The failure, if indeed there was one, could be put down to a severe lack of imagination at least and perhaps outright collusion at worst.

Discussion Questions

1. Did the Concordat show that the Catholic Church approved of Hitler and the Nazis?
2. Were there any fundamental differences between Pope Pius XI and Pope Pius XII regarding the Nazis and the Jews? If so, what were they?

Further Reading

Cornwell, John, *Hitler's Pope: The Secret History of Pius XII*, New York: Viking, 1999.
Passelecq, Georges, and Bernard Suchecky, *The Hidden Encyclical of Pius XI*, New York: Harcourt, 1997.
Phayer, Michael, *The Catholic Church and the Holocaust, 1930–1965*, Bloomington: Indiana University Press, 2000.
Wolf, Hubert, *Pope and Devil: The Vatican's Archives and the Third Reich*, Cambridge, MA: Harvard University Press, 2010.

AUGUST 1933

1.7 The *Haavara* Agreement

On March 24, 1933, in response to German antisemitism, Jewish groups worldwide, but particularly in the United States, France, Britain, and Poland, launched a boycott against German goods. They hoped it would pressure the Nazis to restore Jewish rights. In Germany, this demonstrated the existence of a "world Jewish conspiracy" of which Nazi ideology had been warning for years.

In the summer of 1933, however, the Jewish Agency for Palestine, together with the German Zionist Federation and the German Economics Ministry, drafted a plan allowing German Jews migrating to Palestine to retain some of the value of their property by purchasing German goods for the *Yishuv* (the Jewish area of Palestine), which would be redeemed in local Palestine currency. Under this *Haavara* ("Transfer") agreement, Jewish emigrants had to hand over their possessions before they left Germany and the proceeds used by a company specifically set up for this purpose in Tel Aviv to purchase German goods for sale in Palestine. The proceeds of these sales were then paid in Palestinian currency to the emigrants once they reached Palestine. Agreement was reached on August 7, 1933, and signed on August 25, 1933.

For the Zionist Federation of Germany, it was a way to save Jews from the claws of an increasingly hostile regime and by doing so attract them to Palestine. The head of the Jewish Agency's political department, Haim Arlosoroff, said the agreement facilitated a way for Jews to get their property out before it was forcefully taken and either sold at reduced prices or stolen from them outright. For the Nazis, signing an international agreement was further proof of its legitimacy; it also broke the foreign Jewish boycott of German goods and helped the recovery of German exports at a time when the German economy was still experiencing the Depression. Both sides saw potential benefits in such an arrangement.

Internationally, many Jews were critical. Despite encouraging Jews to emigrate from Germany, one of the objects of the agreement was to fragment the Jewish boycott on German goods. No one doubted the moral weight that breaking the boycott would have for world Jewry. For this reason, the Jewish Agency masked its role until 1935, and the agreement was presented as though between private parties. The Zionist Federation was accused of collaboration with the Nazis because those involved in the boycott intended it to cause Germany to change its policies—but most Zionists considered that the Jewish position in Germany was irrevocably lost and that emigration to Palestine was their only option.

Within Germany, the authorities were criticized by radical members of the Nazi Party for helping Jews when their official policy was to solve the "Jewish question." Though the *Haavara* allowed Jews to transfer people and money to Palestine, National Socialism did not support the creation of a Jewish state, whether in Palestine or anywhere else. Opposition to such a creation was based on the view that a Jewish state would aggravate the danger of global domination by the "international Jewish conspiracy" aiming to destroy Germany. This conspiracy concern came to overshadow the idea of Palestine as a place to which Germany's Jews could be dumped.

As a result of the *Haavara* agreement, German exports to Palestine increased so rapidly that by 1937 Germany had moved into first position among countries exporting to Palestine, greater even than that of Britain, the Mandatory Power. The exported goods included agricultural machinery, cement, steel girders, iron plates, aluminum, brass products, watches, and photographic equipment. Across the period 1933–39, the agreement encouraged and allowed the movement of 60,000 people and about a hundred million marks from Germany to Palestine.

The *Haavara* agreement was the first example of a Nazi program of organized Jewish relocation and acted as the only formal contract signed between Nazi Germany and a Zionist organization. The agreement, which continued until the outbreak of war in 1939, solved the problems of an affluent class of Germans able to move but did not improve the living conditions of the Jews left behind in Germany.

Discussion Questions

1. Do you think the Jewish organizations should have engaged in negotiations, or signed an agreement, with the Nazis in August 1933? Why/why not?

2. In your opinion, did the *Haavara* agreement achieve any positive results?

Further Reading

Bauer, Yehuda, *Jews for Sale? Nazi-Jewish Negotiations, 1933–1945*, New Haven: Yale University Press, 1996.

Black, Edwin, *The Transfer Agreement: The Dramatic Story of the Pact between the Third Reich and Jewish Palestine*, New York: Macmillan, 1984.

Nicosia, Francis R., *The Third Reich and the Palestine Question*, London: I.B. Tauris, 1985.

Part 2

1934

FEBRUARY 1934

2.1 The Women's Führer

In February 1934, a woman named Gertrud Scholtz-Klink was appointed by the Nazi Party as leader of the National Socialist Women's League (*NS-Frauenschaft*). As such, she became the most senior woman in the Third Reich.

She was born Gertrud Emma Treusch on February 9, 1902, into a middle-class antisemitic Christian family in Adelsheim, Baden. Her father died when she was eight, leaving her mother to raise Gertrud and her two brothers. Leaving school in 1918, she worked as a nurse in Berlin during the last days of the First World War. At the age of eighteen she married an elementary school teacher, Eugen Klink, with whom she had six children, one of whom died in infancy. In the early 1920s, they joined the Nazi Party, and Eugen Klink became a Nazi district officer. In 1930 he died of a heart attack at a rally.

During their time together, Gertrud Klink saw her role as one of helping her husband in his Party activities—looking after the organization of Party kitchens during events, sewing, or organizing day care for children of the Party's female members. In 1929 she became leader of the Nazi Party women's section in Baden.

In 1932 she married a country doctor, Günther Scholtz, taking the surname "Scholtz-Klink." They divorced in 1938 because he did not share her passion for Nazi politics, though she retained her married name.

After Adolf Hitler appointed Scholtz-Klink as *Reichsführerin* (Women's Leader) and head of the National Socialist Women's' League, she established one of the largest women's organizations in history. Its fundamental concern was with issues relating to the family, particularly motherhood. A woman's role in Nazi Germany was to be considered sacrosanct; it would be her selfless duty to give birth to as many children as possible, take care of her body to ensure maximum fertility, and to make a good German home for her husband and sons. Presenting a child to the Führer was the greatest contribution a German woman could make to the Fatherland.

In July 1936 Scholtz-Klink was appointed to lead the Women's Bureau in the German Labour Front (*Deutsche Arbeitsfront*), responsible for persuading women to work for the Nazi government. In 1938 she argued that "the German woman must work and work, physically and mentally she must renounce luxury and pleasure." Just as the SS under Heinrich Himmler oversaw the separation of Jews from mainstream German life, so Scholtz-Klink directed the disconnect between women and the daily life of Nazi-dominated male society. She spoke often against women participating in government or public life, saying that "anyone who has seen the Communist and Social Democratic women scream on the street and in the parliament, will realize that such an activity is not something which is done by a true woman." Elsewhere, she alerted her members that they had to "deny the Liberal-Jew-Bolshevik theory of 'women's equality'," as any acceptance of it "dishonours them."

Under the close supervision of Heinrich Himmler, Scholtz-Klink supervised the running of six-week training programs, known as "Nazi bride schools," for young women. The course of instruction ensured that women learned how to become good wives in service to the Nazi state. An important part of the course saw to it that women would acquire detailed knowledge of race and genetics, with instruction provided on how young women could become perfect partners for SS soldiers.

The *NS-Frauenschaft* was thus the breeding ground for the master race. The private sphere of women became inextricably bound up with masculinist Nazi ideology. The state sought strict control over female reproduction, as women's bodies provided the means for engineering racial purity.

Many years later, American scholar Claudia Koonz interviewed Scholtz-Klink about the situation in Nazi Germany regarding the Jews. As this fitted into the male sphere, however, Scholtz-Klink denied any involvement. She knew that Jewish women were denied access to *Frauenschaft* activities, but she did not go out of her way to help any Jews seeking assistance because, she said, she "did not know any." At the same time, she considered the treatment of Jews to be legal and therefore beyond the realm of judgment—particularly by women.

Scholtz-Klink led the *NS-Frauenschaft* from February 1934 to 1945. She divorced Günther Scholtz in 1938, and in 1940 married her third husband, *SS-Obergruppenführer* August Heissmeyer. They combined their families. She had five surviving children, and Heissmeyer had five from a previous marriage. Later, they had another child together. In 1944 the Nazi Party advertised Scholtz-Klink and her eleven children as a "fertility model" for the Third Reich. What it did not add was that Scholtz-Klink and Heissmeyer made frequent trips to visit prisoners in women's concentration camps in line with Heissmeyer's role as Inspector of Concentration Camps.

After the war, Scholtz-Klink and Heissmeyer fled Berlin. Captured in the summer of 1945 and imprisoned in a Soviet prisoner of war camp near Magdeburg, they managed to escape and then lived quietly in the village of Bebenhausen, where Scholtz-Klink spent the next three years under the alias of Maria Stuckebrock. On February 28, 1948, however, she was identified and arrested. A French military court sentenced her to eighteen months in prison on the charge of forging documents, and in May 1950 a reevaluation of her sentence penalized her with an additional thirty months. After her release in 1953, Gertrud Scholtz-Klink settled back in Bebenhausen. She later confirmed her ongoing support for Nazism, beliefs she held through to her death, aged ninety-seven, on March 24, 1999.

Discussion Questions

1. What did Gertrud Scholtz-Klink consider should be the true role of women in German society? How was this to be achieved?
2. Do you think Gertrud Scholtz-Klink bore any responsibility for Nazi racism? Why/why not?

Further Reading

Koonz, Claudia, *Mothers in the Fatherland: Women, the Family, and Nazi Politics*, New York: Routledge, 2012.
Stephenson, Jill, *The Nazi Organisation of Women*, New York: Routledge, 2013.
Stephenson, Jill, *Women in Nazi Germany*, New York: Routledge, 2015.

MARCH 1934

2.2 The People's Court

On April 24, 1934, Nazi Germany's "People's Court" (*Volksgerichtshof*) was established. Adolf Hitler had earlier ordered its formation, in line with the Enabling Act of 1933 that gave him a warrant to establish his dictatorship.

The intention was that the People's Court would operate outside of the existing judicial system, with jurisdiction over a broad range of political offenses. It was also given exclusive control over such offenses as Conspiracy to High Treason, State Treason, Listening to Enemy Radio Broadcasts (from 1939), Criminal Malice, Sedition and Defeatism, and Aiding the Enemy (from mid-1941).

The notion of "political crimes" ranged from minor offenses—trading on the black market, work slowdowns, criticizing Hitler or the government, or protesting about work conditions—through to defeatism, espionage, and sabotage. These offenses were viewed by the Court as being "incapable of a defence" and were accordingly punished with great severity. The Court decided how much evidence to consider, and defense attorneys could not question the charges. Defendants were unable to represent themselves or consult their own attorney.

A case brought before the People's Court would follow an initial indictment in which a state or city prosecutor would forward the names of the accused to the Court for charges that were deemed to be political. Defendants were rarely permitted to speak to their attorneys beforehand, and when they did the defense lawyer would usually simply outline how the trial would proceed and refrain from giving any legal advice. Proceedings began when the accused was led into the dock under armed police escort. The presiding judge would read the charges and then call the accused forward for "examination." Although the Court had a prosecutor, it was usually the judge who asked the questions.

Defendants were often harangued during the examination and were never allowed to respond. After a barrage of insults and condemnation, the order "examination concluded" would be given. The defendant was not permitted to choose defense counsel, who had to be a lawyer approved by the chairman of the Senate. Defenders and defendants were often given only a day (sometimes only a few hours) notice before the trial. Often the lawyer and the accused did not know each other beforehand, nor could contact be made prior to the hearing.

After examination, the defense attorneys would be asked if they had any statements or questions. The judge would then ask the defendants for a statement during which time more insults would be shouted at the accused. The verdict, which was almost always "guilty," would then be announced and the sentence handed down at the same time. In all, an appearance before the People's Court could take as little as fifteen minutes. The death penalty was frequent. There was no possibility of appeal, and verdicts could be carried out immediately.

The Nazi Courts did not employ standard legal procedures or principles such as the presumption of innocence, trial by peers, or the right to cross-examine witnesses. Appointed by Adolf Hitler, judges in the People's Courts were expected to be politically reliable and should be Party members. One man alone often acted as judge and jury.

The conduct of the Courts worsened after the outbreak of the Second World War. The number of death sentences increased dramatically: in 1936, eleven death sentences were issued; the year 1943 saw a total of 1,662 executions, about half of which were indictments from the People's Court. In 1945, approximately 5,200 death sentences were carried out, imposed for offenses such as "disseminating news intercepted on radio," derogatory remarks about Hitler, or doubts about the so-called final victory. After the German defeat at Stalingrad during the winter of 1942–3, the People's Court became far more ruthless and hardly anyone brought before the tribunal escaped a guilty verdict.

Two notorious judges who shaped the People's Court were Otto Georg Thierack, who presided from May 1, 1936, to August 19, 1942; and Roland Freisler, who presided from August 20, 1942, to February 3, 1945.

Some hearings were very rapid. An example of this was the treatment of members of the "White Rose" resistance group. On February 18, 1943, this group of Munich University students was caught distributing antiwar leaflets. On February 22, 1943, three of the White Rose group—Sophie Scholl, her brother Hans, and Christoph Probst—were tried and found guilty in less than an hour. The three were guillotined just six hours after their arrest.

Many of those found guilty by the Court were executed in Plötzensee Prison in Berlin. The president of the Court often acted as prosecutor, denouncing defendants, then pronouncing his verdict and sentence without objection from the defense counsel, who usually remained silent throughout. Being hauled before the Court by this stage was tantamount to a death sentence.

On February 3, 1945, judge Roland Freisler was killed owing to a near-direct hit from US Air Force bombers on the court building. His body was reportedly found crushed beneath a fallen masonry column, clutching files he had tried to retrieve from the court building.

After the war, the only member of the *Volksgerichthof* held liable for his actions was Chief Public Prosecutor Ernst Lautz, who was sentenced at Nuremberg to ten years' imprisonment. He was pardoned after serving less than four years of his sentence and then granted a government pension. Of the other approximately 570 judges and prosecutors who had served the People's Court, none was held responsible for their actions. Many, in fact, went on to have successful careers in the West German postwar legal system.

Discussion Questions

1. How did the operation of the People's Court differ from a regular criminal or civil court?
2. In your view, why was the People's Court so harsh in the punishments it imposed? Could these be justified?

Further Reading

Koch, H. W., *In the Name of the Volk: Political Justice in Hitler's Germany*, London: I.B. Tauris, 1997.
McKale, Donald M., *The Nazi Party Courts: Hitler's Management of Conflict in His Movement, 1921–1945*, Lawrence: University Press of Kansas, 1974.
Miller, Richard M., *Nazi Justiz: Law of the Holocaust*, Westport: Praeger, 1995.

JUNE 1934

2.3 The Night of the Long Knives

On June 30, 1934, an event that became known as the Night of the Long Knives took place throughout Germany, when a series of extrajudicial executions were carried out to consolidate Adolf Hitler's hold on power. Hitler, together with Hermann Göring and Heinrich Himmler, sought to bring the head of the *Sturmabteilung* (SA), Ernst Röhm, to heel; they feared that his huge paramilitary organization of nearly four million members might overthrow Hitler as head of the Nazi Party.

Ernst Röhm was one of the first members of the Nazi Party and was perhaps Hitler's oldest and closest friend. The son of a railway official, he was born on November 28, 1887, in Munich. Joining the army, he was commissioned in 1908 and wounded three times during the First World War, including a serious wound to his face that left him permanently scarred. He was awarded the Iron Cross First Class in 1916, and by 1918 had been promoted to the rank of captain. After the war he remained in the military but soon revealed an interest in politics. Among other things, in April and May of 1919 he helped suppress left-wing movements that sought to install a communist government in Munich.

Shortly after the war Röhm first met Hitler. In 1919 he joined the German Workers' Party, a tiny right-wing fringe party that would soon change its name to the National Socialist German Workers' Party—the Nazi Party. Röhm recognized Hitler's oratorical and leadership skills, and they became close friends. After Hitler rose to power in Germany, Röhm was one of the very few people who called him by his first name.

It was Röhm who protected Hitler in November 1923 during the Beer Hall Putsch in Munich, which attempted to overthrow the Weimar Republic. It was a stunning failure, with Hitler, Röhm, and others arrested and convicted of treason. Although Röhm was not imprisoned, he earned his place in Hitler's inner circle as an "Old Fighter" who had shown his unquestioning loyalty to the future Führer.

During the 1920s and early 1930s street brawls took place between competing German political parties. It was necessary to have groups of men on hand to protect speakers and officials and intimidate the opposition. The Nazis were protected by a paramilitary unit, the *Sturmabteilung* (also known as the Stormtroopers or Brownshirts), founded by Hitler in 1921. Röhm became its leader early in 1930. By late 1933, due in part to his popularity, the organization had become a force of awe-inspiring size, dwarfing the German military. This became a problem for Hitler and the army. Röhm, who saw himself gaining steadily in both power and importance, had big plans for the SA, which ultimately caused an irreparable rift between the two old friends. Röhm's expectation was that Hitler would lead a political revolution leaning more toward socialism than capitalism, a matter of immense concern to Germany's business leaders, including some of the Nazi Party's major financial contributors.

Even as Hitler was shifting some of the Stormtroopers' responsibilities (such as protecting Party leaders) to Heinrich Himmler and the SS, Röhm continued to insist that he and the SA should play a larger role in the Party. Röhm also demanded in early 1934 that the SA should form the core of a new Germany military. This offended the professional officer corps that viewed the SA as a group of undisciplined thugs. Hitler, recognizing his need for the army's support, was unwilling to agree to Röhm's demands.

In addition to rejecting Röhm's power play, the army's officer corps also rejected Röhm's personal habits, finding them to be offensive to the standards of the professional military. Specifically, Röhm was gay and made no efforts to hide the fact. When combined with the image of the SA as little other than thugs and drunks, the military's opposition to Röhm and the SA was complete.

Hitler increasingly saw Röhm and the SA as a threat and became concerned about the possibility of a coup attempt. Tasking Göring and Himmler to draw up a list of SA leaders who should be killed so as to dismantle the SA and integrate it into the German military, Hitler contacted Röhm and ordered him to call all senior SA leaders to a conference that would be held on June 30, 1934. Hitler personally supervised Röhm's arrest. Initially reluctant to kill his old friend, Hitler bowed to pressure from Göring and Himmler, and on July 1, 1934, he had Röhm shot.

The purge, codenamed Operation Hummingbird, solidified the army's support for Hitler and increased Himmler's power within the regime. At least eighty-five people (and perhaps many more) died during the purge, including former chancellor Kurt von Schleicher and leading Nazi Gregor Strasser. More than a thousand others were arrested. German judges hastened to demonstrate their loyalty to Hitler, further legitimating his regime. The Night of the Long Knives was a turning point for the German government, establishing Hitler as the supreme authority in Germany. Hitler's actions were retroactively legalized with the passage of the Law Regarding Measures of State Self-Defense, explaining his actions by reference to the need to protect the state against treason. With this, the Nazi dictatorship was complete.

Discussion Questions

1. Why was Hitler so concerned about the growth of the SA and Ernest Röhm's power?

2. What do you think the overall effect the Night of the Long Knives had on the future of the Nazi regime?

Further Reading

Atcherley, Tony, and Mark Cary, *Hitler's Gay Traitor: The Story of Ernst Röhm, Chief of Staff of the SA*, Bloomington: Trafford, 2007.
Hancock, Eleanor, *Ernst Röhm: Hitler's SA Chief of* Staff, New York: Palgrave Macmillan, 2008.
Maracin, Paul, *The Night of the Long Knives: Forty-Eight Hours that Changed the History of the World*, Guilford, CT: Lyons Press, 2007.

JULY 1934

2.4 The Inspectorate of Concentration Camps

On July 4, 1934, an official body, the Inspectorate of Concentration Camps, was created to coordinate the diverse early camps throughout the Reich. Theodor Eicke was selected by SS chief Heinrich Himmler to serve in the position of Inspector.

Born in 1892, Eicke joined the National Socialist Party in 1928 and was the second commandant of Dachau from June 1933 and one of the prime movers behind the development of the Nazi concentration camp system. While at Dachau, he systematized the treatment, supervision, and punishment of the prisoners, and instilled a new esprit de corps into the SS guard detachments. As commandant, he made Dachau a model for all the other camps, instituting policies regarding discipline, camp organization and hierarchy, rituals concerning reception and orientation, and regulations concerning capital offenses. Eicke composed a set of rules that covered most eventualities, including numerous infractions which could incur the death penalty.

When appointed Inspector of Concentration Camps he set about transforming the whole concentration camp edifice according to the Dachau model, resulting in many of the earlier, more haphazardly built camps, known colloquially as "wild concentration camps" (*Wilde-KZ*), being closed. His mandate was to oversee the entire system and bring Dachau-style order to the varied systems of hit-or-miss administration which until then had characterized the camp network. The treatment of prisoners became standardized: clear delineations were made concerning the camps' direction and administration, and Eicke's routine for Dachau now became the archetype for camps all over Germany. Existing disciplinary and penal codes were altered to stop arbitrary decision-making on the part of local commandants, but once rules had been instituted no limits were set on how they were to be carried out. In matters of prisoner discipline, commandants could instruct their guards to be as imaginative as they liked, in accordance with a set of very stringent general guidelines. The offenses capable of attracting severe punishment were many.

Consolidation of the camp administration meant more than the transfer of all prisoners to a centralized control; it also meant that the concentration camps became institutionalized as part of the Nazi social and political system, and it took little time for most of the smaller camps to be closed and those remaining converted to the Dachau model.

In April 1934 Eicke also created an elite unit of specially trained concentration camp guards, the *SS-Totenkopfverbände* (SS Death's Head Formations). Their essential rationale was to serve as a unit capable of administering the very precise regulations Eicke formulated. They acted with strict adherence to discipline—and, increasingly, brutality—toward the prisoners.

The expansion in the number of crimes for which a German citizen could be arrested from the winter of 1935 onward meant the gradual evolution of a carefully planned Dachau-style camp network. Not only this; the first substantial arrests of prisoners other than avowed political opponents of Nazis began to take place. Jehovah's Witnesses, people charged with "anti-social behaviour," and gay men now began to be taken into custody. These arrests were each justified differently by the Nazis. Jehovah's Witnesses went against National Socialist thinking by spreading pacifist philosophies, and "anti-socials," who could count among their ranks elements as diverse as vagrants, itinerant merchants, and so-called work-shy elements, along with gay men, were classed as damaging to the smooth and well-ordered structure of a disciplined society.

In the push to standardize the camps along Eicke's lines, some sacrifices had to be made, and the rationalization program saw large numbers of prisoners in "protective custody" released as the smaller camps were closed. By the winter of 1936–7 inmate populations reached their lowest total since the camps were originally instituted. The Oranienburg camp had been terminated in 1935 to make way for a new one a few miles away at Sachsenhausen, which opened in September 1936. The month of August 1937 saw the establishment of a large camp at Buchenwald, near Weimar, and for nearly a year thereafter there were just four camps in Germany: Dachau, Sachsenhausen, Buchenwald, and Lichtenburg. The first three camps formed a geographically convenient blanket for most of Germany. Sachsenhausen covered north Germany and Berlin, Buchenwald guarded the socialist heartland of Thuringia, and Dachau served Bavaria and the south. Flossenbürg, in northeastern Bavaria not far from the Czech border, was established in 1938, and Mauthausen (near Linz) was set up immediately after the Nazi invasion of Austria in March of that year. Lichtenburg, in the lower Elbe region, was employed solely as a concentration camp for women from mid-1937, until it was also replaced by another Dachau-style camp, Ravensbrück, in May 1939.

With the outbreak of war in September 1939, Theodor Eicke took a more active command of his SS *Totenkopf* units and moved away from the Inspectorate of Concentration Camps. At this time, they numbered

24,000 members; by 1945, this had increased to 40,000. Much of this growth was because in 1939 it had been formed into a combat division, the *SS-Panzerdivision-Totenkopf*. This, in turn, became one of the foundation units of the *Waffen* (armed) SS, the military wing of the SS. As soldiers, the Death's Head units were notorious for their toughness and cruelty in the field, just as they had been as guards. In combat, Eicke's command of the *Totenkopf* saw the perpetration of war crimes, particularly against British soldiers in 1940, and later on the Russian front. Eicke died of injuries after a plane crash on February 26, 1943, shortly after being promoted to SS *Obergruppenführer*, or general.

Eicke had earlier been succeeded as inspector by his second-in-command, Richard Glücks, in November 1939. Under Glücks, the Nazi concentration camp network expanded considerably. In February 1940, he reported to the head of the SS, Heinrich Himmler, that a site had been found for a new camp close by the Polish town of Oświęcim, which in German translated to Auschwitz. By May 1940, upon his orders, the first commandant of the Auschwitz concentration camp, Rudolf Höss, commenced building what would become the largest of all the concentration camps, and a byword for the Holocaust. Glücks introduced several new measures to the concentration camps under his direction, including the use of foreign forced labor and facilities for medical experiments on camp inmates. The full details of his fate are unclear, though it is believed he committed suicide in Italy in May 1945, to avoid trial at the hands of the Allies.

Discussion Questions

1. Why was there a need to create a full bureaucratic organization to administer the concentration camps?

2. What was the relationship between the Inspectorate of Concentration Camps and the SS, and how did this undergo change over the duration of the Third Reich?

Further Reading

Dillon, Christopher, *Dachau and the SS: A Schooling in Violence*, Oxford: Oxford University Press, 2015.

Kogon, Eugen, *The Theory and Practice of Hell: The German Concentration Camps and the System Behind Them*, New York: Berkley Windhover Books, 1975.

Wachsmann, Nikolaus, *KL: A History of the Nazi Concentration Camps*, New York: Farrar, Straus and Giroux, 2015.

NOVEMBER 1934

2.5 Kurt Daluege and the Nazi Police State

The police state that terrorized Germany after 1933—and then all of Europe progressively after 1939—did not emerge out of thin air. It had to develop, and in November 1934 the immense authority of Kurt Daluege, head of Nazi Germany's uniformed *Ordnungspolizei* (Order Police, or Orpo), was confirmed. Covering all German uniformed police and emergency services, Daluege commanded municipal police forces, the rural gendarmerie, traffic police, the coast guard, the railway police, the postal protection service, fire brigades, the air-raid services, the emergency technical service, the broadcasting police, the factory protection police, building regulations enforcement, and the commercial police. Who was this man who wielded such immense power?

Kurt Daluege was born on September 15, 1897. He completed high school in 1916, joined the German army, and in October 1917 commenced officer training. He was severely wounded in combat, hospitalized, and decorated for bravery.

From 1918 to 1921 Daluege was a member of a German irregular militia unit. After working briefly as a factory hand, he studied civil engineering at the Technical University of Berlin between 1921 and 1924, graduating as an engineer. In 1923 he joined the Nazi Party and in March 1926 became leader of Berlin's Stormtroopers. Then, in July 1930, he joined the SS. The next month, when Berlin Stormtroopers attacked Nazi headquarters in what became known as the Stennes Revolt, Daluege's unit overpowered the attack. In an open letter thanking Daluege for his service, Adolf Hitler declared "SS man, your honour is loyalty," which then became the motto adopted by the SS.

In November 1932 Daluege was elected to the Reichstag, and the following May Hermann Göring moved him into the Prussian Interior Ministry, where he took charge of the regular police force. In this capacity he purged the force of what were termed "social democratic" elements and filled it with SS men. Daluege played a key role in the notorious Night of the Long Knives of June 30, 1934, during which Ernst Röhm and many other leaders of the SA were purged. In August 1934 SS head Heinrich Himmler promoted Daluege to *SS-Obergruppenführer* (lieutenant-general).

In 1936 the entire German police force was reorganized, with administrative functions now placed under the control of the SS. There were two main branches: under Reinhard Heydrich were the political police (Gestapo) and the criminal police (Kripo); and under Daluege was the Orpo, covering the municipal police, the rural police, and the community police.

By 1938 Daleuge had over 62,000 police officers under his command, rising to 244,500 in mid-1940. Many Orpo units were later transferred into the regular army as an essential force for holding down occupied Europe. Daluege also established a unit of police officers responsible for the suppression of internal revolts within Germany.

Daluege was an integral element in the Nazi plans to "cleanse" the Soviet Union of Bolsheviks and Jews, and his police battalions were told to pursue their tasks ruthlessly. During the summer of 1941, mass shootings took place all over the occupied territories, and on July 9, 1941, Daluege congratulated his troops for participating in the defeat of Bolshevism. In one action, at Białystok on July 12, male Jews between the ages of seventeen and forty-five were brought by Daluege's police to a sports stadium. A day later they were taken to dig antitank ditches, and within twenty-four hours about 3,000 had been killed. Shortly afterward, on September 1, 1941, Daluege attended another mass execution of Jews near Minsk, in occupied Belarus. In October 1941 he signed deportation orders for Jews from Germany, Austria, and the Protectorate of Bohemia and Moravia to Riga and Minsk.

He then authorized a new role for the Orpo: they would guard deportation trains taking people to their death. Between fall 1941 and spring 1945, hundreds of trains under Orpo control took German, Czech, and Austrian Jews to camps and ghettos in the East, together with many additional transports from Hungary, the Netherlands, Slovakia, France, Belgium, Greece, Italy, Bulgaria, and Croatia.

After Reinhard Heydrich was assassinated in Prague in May 1942, Daluege was sent there to become Deputy Reich Protector of Bohemia and Moravia. In June 1942 he ordered the villages of Lidice and Ležáky razed to the ground in reprisal for Heydrich's assassination. The destruction of Lidice saw the murder of all 173 male inhabitants, with the village's 198 women and children deported to Ravensbrück concentration camp. Daluege then attended a conference on July 7, 1942, organized by Himmler. This discussed an extension of *Aktion Reinhard*, the Nazi secret plan for the mass murder of Polish Jews. It was to be the ultimate phase of the previously decided Final Solution.

Daluege acted as Deputy Reich Protector of Bohemia and Moravia from 1942 until May 1943, when he suffered a massive heart attack; he resigned in August 1943 and took no further part in the war. In May 1945 he was arrested by British troops in Lübeck. He was interned in Luxembourg and then tried at Nuremberg as a major war criminal. In September 1946, after being extradited to Czechoslovakia, he was tried for crimes against humanity. Throughout his trial he was unrepentant, claiming that he was beloved by "three million policemen," only following Hitler's orders, and had a clear conscience. He was convicted on all charges and sentenced to death on October 23, 1946. Aged forty-eight, Daluege was hanged in Prague the next day.

Discussion Questions

1. How did Kurt Daluege's police organizations differ from the police forces we see in our own society today?
2. Do you think Kurt Daluege should have been executed for crimes against humanity? Why/why not?

Further Reading

Browning, Christopher R., *Ordinary Men: Reserve Police Battalion 101 and the Final Solution in Poland*, New York: HarperCollins, 1992.
Westermann, Edward B., *Hitler's Police Battalions: Enforcing Racial War in the East*, Lawrence: University of Kansas Press, 2005.

Part 3

1935

JUNE 1935

3.1 Genesis of the Nuremberg Laws

The Nuremberg Laws on Race were designed by the Nazis to remove Jews from the mainstream of German life. While these laws are dated most frequently from September 1935, we can, in fact, trace their origin to two earlier pieces of legislation that were passed in June that year. These were, moreover, enacted only two days apart, focusing on an obsession running through Nazi thinking from prior to 1933: the issue of sexuality and identity.

On June 26, 1935, a new law made abortions compulsory for pregnant women who might in some way have a disability, or where it was determined that a fetus was unhealthy in utero. The Nazi view was that this would prevent women from "passing on hereditary diseases." Abortions could be forced to achieve the desired result.

Then, two days later, the Ministry of Justice revised the infamous Paragraph 175, originally enacted on May 15, 1871, criminalizing homosexual acts between males. The revision expanded the range of criminal offenses to encompass any contact between men, whether physical or by word or gesture, that could be construed as sexual. This saw the offense of "lewdness between men," such that "a man who engages as the active or passive partner in lewdness with another man is to be punished by imprisonment." Paragraph 175a continued that "severe lewdness" was when homosexual acts were carried out by force or threats, when such acts were committed between consenting males of over twenty-one years of age, or when male prostitutes engaged in such acts. These revisions had the intention of toughening the penalties for any violations, leading to a systematic persecution of gay men.

The two laws of June 26 and June 28, 1935, were an initial Nazi foray into the private lives of Germany's citizens, involving the most intimate relationships. Others were to follow: of interest is that at this early stage they were not specifically directed toward Jews. This would change within the next three months.

What was called the Law for the Protection of German Blood and German Honor was adopted unanimously on September 15, 1935. The new law consisted of seven sections that operated from the Nazis' concern for "safeguarding" the "purity" of "German blood."

In summary form, the seven sections stated that: (1) marriages between Jews and German nationals or those of "kindred blood" were prohibited; (2) relations outside of marriage between Jews and German nationals or those of kindred blood were forbidden; (3) female German nationals or those of kindred blood under the age of forty-five could no longer be employed in Jewish households; (4) Jews were forbidden to hoist the German flag or "present the colors of the Reich," though they could present "the Jewish colors"; (5) punishment for violations of sections (1) and (2) were to be imprisonment with hard labor, while violations of sections (3) and (4) were imprisonment of one year and monetary fines; (6) implementation and supplementation of this law was the responsibility of the Reich minister of the interior; and (7) the law was to take effect on September 16, 1935, with the exception of section (3) which was to become effective on January 1, 1936.

The legislation was signed into effect at the seventh Party Congress during the Nuremberg Rally of September 1935. The gathering was called the Rally of Freedom, where "freedom" signified the reintroduction of compulsory military service—and thus Germany's "liberation" from the restrictions of the Treaty of Versailles. Introducing the Nuremberg Laws at this time was another indication of "freedom" in accordance with Nazi ideology; from this point onward, it was felt, the German people would be able to dictate the very nature of how their population should be comprised.

And things did not stop there. Later in the year the regime continued its intrusion into the private lives of people—both Jews and so-called Aryans—through the addition of other, similar laws.

On October 18, for example, the Law for the Protection of the Hereditary Health of the German People was introduced, requiring all prospective marriage partners to obtain a "certificate of fitness to marry" from the public health authorities. How this was to be determined meant that those in question had to show that they did not suffer from hereditary illnesses or contagious diseases. Also, unions made in violation of the Nuremberg Laws were forbidden on the grounds of "hereditary health."

Finally, on November 14, 1935, a supplemental decree of the Nuremberg Laws extended their remit in certain areas, such as prohibiting marriages or sexual relations between people likely to produce children deemed "racially suspect." While this was very vague and open to interpretation, it was later set up more formally to mean Roma and Blacks, as well as Jews.

Overall, this was a time in which a policy of legal segregation was implemented across Germany. Where Jews were concerned, the Nazis intended that through measures such as these the Jewish population would see the writing on the wall and realize that there was no longer a future for them in Germany and leave. The tragedy was that most German Jews did not see things this way. For every new measure against them, the general response was that no matter how bad things were, they could not get any worse. As a result, most Jews stayed in Germany, preferring to live in what they still saw as their homeland. Tragically, it would take even more drastic measures in succeeding years before they finally saw that no accommodation, of any kind, could be reached with the Nazis.

Discussion Questions

1. Why did the Nazis introduce laws relating to sexuality and identity in June 1935?

2. To what extent were the laws of June extended and further developed as the year progressed? Why do you think this happened?

Further Reading

Evans, Richard J., *The Third Reich in Power*, New York: Penguin, 2005.
Gordon, Sarah, *Hitler, Germans, and the "Jewish Question,"* Princeton: Princeton University Press, 1984.
Schleunes, Karl A., *The Twisted Road to Auschwitz: Nazi Policy towards German Jews, 1933–1939*, Urbana: University of Illinois Press, 1970.

SEPTEMBER 1935

3.2 Nuremberg Protects Blood and Honor

On September 15, 1935, the Nuremberg Laws on Citizenship and Race became operative in Germany. There were two key laws, both of which were adopted unanimously at the Annual Nazi Party Rally at Nuremberg by Adolf Hitler together with minister of the interior Wilhelm Frick, minister of justice Dr. Franz Gürtner, and deputy Führer Rudolf Hess.

The first, the Reich Citizenship Law, stated that only Germans or those related by blood could be citizens of Germany, thus excluding Jews from citizenship and further defining Aryans, Jews, and *Mischlinge* (i.e., persons of mixed racial stock). The new law was designed to further exclude Jews from all manner of public life. Any previous exclusions existing for Jewish veterans of the First World War were, henceforth, removed. Ultimately, the law paved the way for an expansion of additional antisemitic measures, leading to the infamous *Kristallnacht* pogrom of November 1938 and, eventually, to the Final Solution itself through what historian Karl A. Schleunes referred to as "the twisted road to Auschwitz."

Soon after this, another law was introduced, the Law for the Protection of the Genetic Health of the German People, requiring all those wishing to marry to submit to a medical examination, after which a "Certificate of Fitness to Marry" would be issued if they were found to be disease free. Without this certificate, a marriage license would not be issued. Of course, this did not apply to German Jews, as the state did not make any allowance for their marriage to be legitimized in any case.

After the Nuremberg Laws of September 1935, a dozen supplementary decrees were issued that eventually outlawed the Jews completely, depriving them of their entitlements as human beings and citizens, lowering them to the position of "subjects" with fewer rights, no obligations, and a second-class status in the new Germany. And who, in this new Germany, was a Jew? The Nuremberg Laws made a legal attempt to clarify this, as well as who was not a Jew and who fell in between, in line with the Nazi obsession with "racial purity."

The initial step was one of definition. Thus, those with four Jewish grandparents were "full Jews" and those with three Jewish grandparents were "three-quarter Jews." Persons with two Jewish grandparents were considered *Mischlinge* (i.e., "hybrid," but understood in the Nazi context to mean something like "mongrel," "half-breed," or "mixed breed") of the First Degree, provided they were not identified with the Jewish religion and not married to Jewish spouses; and persons with only one Jewish grandparent were *Mischlinge* of the Second Degree.

One of the authors of this division was a lawyer named Wilhelm Stuckart, who worked in the Ministry of Interior with responsibility for constitutional law, citizenship, and racial legislation. Like many Nazis, he was a young man during the 1930s: when the Nuremberg Laws were passed, he was not yet thirty-three years old. Given the task of cowriting the new laws, he attacked his brief with professional care and imagination. Although an antisemite, he wanted to ensure that his legal drafting was as precise and constitutional as possible.

After the Second World War, Stuckart was arrested and tried by the Allies for his role in formulating and carrying out these laws. He spent four years behind bars until released for lack of further evidence in April 1949. Upon his release, he worked as a city treasurer and state employee. In 1951 he was tried in a denazification court, classified as a "fellow traveller," and fined 500 marks. He died in a car crash on November 15, 1953, one day before his fifty-first birthday.

Discussion Questions

1. Why do you think the Nazis were so obsessed with how Jews were to be identified? Why were there so many categories and definitions?

2. Why was so much care taken with legality to persecute the Jews after September 1935?

Further Reading

Gordon, Sarah, *Hitler, Germans, and the "Jewish Question,"* Princeton: Princeton University Press, 1984.

Schleunes, Karl A., *The Twisted Road to Auschwitz: Nazi Policy towards German Jews, 1933–1939*, Urbana: University of Illinois Press, 1970.

Steinweis, Alan E., and Robert D. Rachlin (eds.), *The Law in Nazi Germany: Ideology, Opportunism, and the Perversion of Justice*, New York: Berghahn, 2013.

DECEMBER 1935

3.3 "Selective Breeding" for a Perfect Race

Lebensborn ("Fountain of Life") was the name given to the Nazi program of selective breeding for the purpose of creating a superior race. Nazism embraced the notion of eugenics, a pseudoscientific idea that humans could be bred to create a purer or more perfect race. The Nazi vision imagined an ideal Aryan who was Nordic, tall, and physically beautiful; had perfect features, including blond hair and blue eyes; was fit; and in perfect health. To achieve this refinement of German "blood," it was deemed necessary to exterminate so-called impure races while encouraging the "racially pure" to multiply.

In Munich on December 12, 1935, therefore, the SS established the *Lebensborn* program. Later, SS chief Heinrich Himmler wrote that *Lebensborn* was created to serve the SS through the selection and adoption of qualified children. Part of the SS Race and Settlement Central Bureau, it was under Himmler's personal direction. He stated that it was the duty of all SS leaders to become members of the organization and that they had to apply to join within the next ten days. By 1939, membership stood at 8,000, of which 3,500 were senior SS officers.

Lebensborn thus formed an integral element of the Nazi racial system. The birthrate of Aryan children, it was argued, had to increase. This was to be achieved through the intensive breeding of German women, who met stringent physical standards of height, weight, blond hair, blue eyes, and athleticism, with SS officers. For this, the couples did not have to be married; their biological aptitude was all that mattered. The officers chosen for this purpose had already asserted their impeccable Aryan ancestry as a condition of their joining the SS.

The women chosen by *Lebensborn* would become impregnated in SS-run "stud farms." These were often luxury hotels and spas, where young women and men would meet prior to retiring discreetly to bedrooms after which they would separate never to meet again. After successful impregnation, the women were sent to special maternity homes where they were cared for until the birth of their children. The *Lebensborn* managers then arranged for the adoption of the children by "racially pure" and healthy families who were known to be thoroughly infused with Nazi ideals.

The Cross of Honor of the German Mother was a medal awarded to women who bore the most Aryan children. Where children were likely to be born with disabilities, the Nazis legalized abortion, though it was strictly punished in the case of healthy pregnancies. The focus of the program was one of pure racial reproduction with Nazi concepts of racial hygiene in the foreground. The sole object was to create pure blooded Aryans for the Thousand Year Reich.

Lebensborn established facilities in several occupied countries, with its activities centered in Germany, Norway, and occupied northeastern Europe. In Norway, children born to Norwegian women and fathered by German soldiers were provided with assistance after they were born. Anywhere between 8,000 and 12,000 children were born in *Lebensborn* homes in Norway.

From 1939, when Germany invaded Poland, the *Lebensborn* program engaged in the kidnapping and transfer of children, mostly orphans with appropriate "racial" features, to politically and racially suitable families in Germany. In other parts of Europe beyond Poland, the Nazis also kidnapped children for the *Lebensborn* program—mainly from Yugoslavia, but including Russia, Ukraine, Czechoslovakia, Romania, Estonia, and Latvia. Himmler was alleged to have said that Nazism sought to "win over any good blood that we can use for ourselves and give it a place in our people." Accordingly, his troops kidnapped an estimated 200,000 blond, blue-eyed Polish children, often from their homes or as they walked to school. They were assigned to Nazi families and brought up as Germans, with little or no memory of their true ancestry.

The SS tested the racial characteristics of the children taken by measuring sixty-two different parts of their body. If the child passed the test, he or she was sent away to be placed with German families for "Germanization." By 1942, the term *Lebensborn* had become a code word for the kidnapping of Polish and other children who met these idealized Nazi racial characteristics.

On May 1, 1945, a day after Hitler's death, American troops entered Steinhöring, the Munich base for the *Lebensborn* program. Here, they found 300 children, aged six months to six years. Most of the mothers and staff had fled. British and Soviet troops also found children at *Lebensborn* homes near Bremen and Leipzig, then either put up for adoption or, if the kidnapped children and their families were known, sent home. Some of the children kidnapped in other countries, who were living with families throughout Germany, were repatriated to their native countries, but many had been "Germanized" to such a degree that they no longer fitted into their country of birth.

During the Second World War it had been deemed honorable for a German woman to be carrying the child of an SS officer. After the war this abruptly turned into a matter of shame. The mothers were discouraged from revealing the facts of their wartime activities. Many of the children had been adopted, and their adoptive parents had no desire to divulge to them the truth about their background. Also, wartime destruction meant that a large quantity of the records relating to such births and kidnappings were lost; thus, no actual numbers can accurately be assessed, nor, in an added tragedy, can the family origins of the children ever be traced.

Discussion Questions

1. What were some of the aspects of *Lebensborn* that were morally questionable?
2. In view of the Nazis' aims, do you see any inconsistencies in the execution of the *Lebensborn* program?

Further Reading

Clay, Catrine, and Michael Leapman, *Master Race: The Lebensborn Experiment in Nazi Germany*, London: Hodder and Stoughton, 1995.
Oelhafen, Ingrid von, and Tim Tate, *Hitler's Forgotten Children: A True Story of the Lebensborn Program and One Woman's Search for Her Real Identity*, New York: Berkley Books, 2016.
Weiss-Wendt, Anton, and Rory Yeomans (eds.), *Racial Science in Hitler's New Europe, 1938–1945*, Lincoln: University of Nebraska Press, 2013.

Part 4

1936

JUNE 1936

4.1 August Landmesser's Very Personal Protest

August Landmesser was a laborer working during the 1930s at the Blohm & Voss shipbuilding and engineering works in Hamburg. He is best remembered for what has become renowned as one of the starkest of all acts of resistance in Nazi Germany, when, among thousands of others with their hands raised in the Hitler salute on June 13, 1936, he was pictured with his arms crossed in direct protest at the Nazi regime.

Landmesser was born on May 24, 1910, the only son of August Franz Landmesser and Wilhelmine Magdalene, *née* Schmidtpott. In 1930 he joined the Nazi Party, thinking it might improve his job prospects at a time when the Great Depression was destroying the German economy. There is no evidence that he was committed to Nazi ideology; in fact, in 1934 he did what no committed Nazi would ever do, when he met and fell in love with Irma Eckler, a young Jewish woman.

Within a year they were engaged; immediately, he was expelled from the Party, and their application to be married was rejected in accordance with the Nuremberg Laws of 1935. The Law for the Protection of German Blood and Honor prohibited Jews from marriage with other Germans: sexual relations were also prohibited under a term referred to as *Rassenschande*, or "race shame." Once the laws began to be applied systematically across Germany, the crime became a capital offense. Nazi ideology held that "race mixing" would weaken the "purity" of the Aryan race, especially if children resulted from the union. It was hardly a surprise, therefore, that when the couple had a baby girl, Ingrid, on October 29, 1935, it alerted the Gestapo to their existence, after which they were watched closely.

It was perhaps with this in mind that Landmesser, who by now must have harbored no little dissatisfaction with the regime, took his famous action at the shipyard on June 13, 1936. The occasion was the launch of a new naval vessel, the training ship *Horst Wessel*, a ceremony filled with significance.

In the presence of Adolf Hitler, his deputy, Rudolf Hess, gave a speech, and the mother of Horst Wessel christened the ship with a bottle of champagne. Wessel, of course, was an SA man who was killed in the early Nazi struggle for power and wrote the song that became the Nazi anthem played or sung on every official occasion after the Nazis came to power.

Refusing to give the Nazi salute was Landmesser's ultimate protest against Nazism. He was probably unaware that his action was photographed, or that he stood out to the extent that he did. Now, more than ever, he was being watched by the authorities. For this single act of resistance, he could well have been arrested; that he was not said much about his luck in snubbing the regime at this time.

In 1937 Irma was again pregnant, and the little family attempted to flee to Denmark. Their flight, however, was unsuccessful, and they were arrested near the border. Landmesser was charged with "dishonouring the race," and in July 1937 he was imprisoned in accordance with the Nuremberg Laws. In the trial that followed, both he and Irma argued that neither of them knew she was Jewish, as she had been baptized in a Protestant church after her mother remarried. Accordingly, on May 27, 1938, Landmesser was acquitted for lack of evidence. He was warned that he would be subjected to very harsh punishment if he was ever again arrested for the same offense.

Almost as if to dare the Gestapo to follow through on their threat, the couple continued their relationship openly. On July 15, 1938 Landmesser was arrested again, and this time he was sentenced to hard labor for two-and-a-half years in a concentration camp. It was to be the last time he saw his family.

Irma was also detained by the Gestapo based on a law that allowed for the arrest of Jewish wives where an Aryan man had "dishonoured the race." She was held for a time at the local prison in Hamburg, Fuhlsbüttel, where she gave birth to a second daughter, Irene. From there she was sent to the concentration camp at Lichtenburg, and then transferred to Ravensbrück. She was compulsorily (and permanently) separated from her two daughters. Letters from her in January 1942 show that she was still alive at that point, but in February 1942 she was relocated to a Nazi "euthanasia centre" at Bernburg, Saxony, where she was gassed to death. She was one of 1,400 women from Ravensbrück murdered in Bernburg by the spring of 1942. In 1949 she was pronounced legally dead.

Landmesser was undoubtedly unaware of this. He had been discharged from prison on January 19, 1941, and sent to work as a foreman for a transport company stationed in the seaside resort town of Warnemünde. In February 1944 he was drafted into a penal unit, the 999th Fort Infantry Battalion, which saw service in Greece and other parts of the Balkans. He was killed during fighting in Croatia on October 17, 1944; at the time he was declared missing in action, but in 1949 he, like Irma, was pronounced legally dead.

After their mother's arrest, Ingrid and Irene were taken to Hamburg's city orphanage. Ingrid was later permitted to live with her maternal grandmother, but the infant Irene was removed from the orphanage and about to be sent to a concentration camp when, at the last moment, she was picked up by someone known to the family and sent to temporary safety in Austria. Upon her return to Germany, she was hidden in a hospital where her Jewish identity was suppressed, and she was able to escape detection until the end of the war. Both children lived with foster parents after 1945. In 1951 the marriage of August Landmesser and Irma Eckler was recognized retroactively by the Hamburg Senate. In the fall of that year, Ingrid took her father's surname, Landmesser, though her sister Irene continued to use the surname Eckler.

The story of August Landmesser's defiant action in the Blohm & Voss shipyard in Hamburg achieved widespread coverage after March 22, 1991, when the German weekly newspaper *Die Zeit* published the photograph taken on June 13, 1936, and Landmesser was identified by one of his daughters. Then, in 1996, Irene Eckler published a book, *Die Vormundschaftsakte 1935–1958: Verfolgung einer Familie wegen "Rassenschande"* (*The Guardianship Documents 1935–1958: Persecution of a Family for "Dishonoring the Race"*), in which she chronicled, with documents, how her family had been destroyed in the aftermath of her father's solitary act of resistance and her parents' love for each other—a love that transcended racial ideology and a brutal totalitarian regime.

Discussion Questions

1. What does the story of August Landmesser tell us about the power of the Nazi state to intrude on people's private lives?

2. In your view, could the tragic fate of the little family have been predicted?

Further Reading

Eckler, Irene, *A Family Torn Apart by "Rassenschande": Political Persecution in the Third Reich: Documents and Reports from Hamburg in German and English*, Horneburg: Horneburg Verlag, 1998.

AUGUST 1935

4.2 The Nazi Games

The games of the XI Olympiad began in Berlin on August 1, 1936. Adolf Hitler used the Games to showcase the Third Reich and conceal his regime's antisemitic and militaristic intentions, attempting instead to portray a peaceful and tolerant Germany to the international community. Berlin had been awarded the Games in 1931, prior to Hitler's ascent to power, but the sixteen-day event quickly and inextricably became associated with the Nazi regime. By the time the Games got underway, 3,963 athletes from 49 nations (the largest number of countries attending up to that point) competed in 129 events, across 19 different sports.

When looked at historically, the Games were controversial, but what many people do not realize is the extent to which they also attracted controversy at the time. From the very start they were marked by racism, with the official Nazi Party paper, the *Völkischer Beobachter*, writing in the strongest terms that Jews and Blacks, regardless of their country of origin, should not be allowed to participate.

Following Nazi demands, the German Olympic Committee denied Jews all opportunity of representing Germany. When the possibility of an international boycott was threatened—robbing Germany not only of the Games but also to showcase the new Germany and deprive it of much-desired foreign currency—there was a token relaxing of the rules: now, one athlete with a Jewish background would be allowed to compete for Germany. Helene Mayer, who had a Jewish father, was a world champion fencer who had already won a gold medal at the 1928 Amsterdam Games. With an eye to the prospect of her winning again, she became the token Jew permitted to compete. As it turned out, she won silver in the Individual Foil event.

The opportunity for other Jewish athletes to compete for Germany was denied, however. Four-time world record holder and ten-time German national champion in shot put and discus throw, Lilli Henoch, was excluded; she was later deported and murdered in the Riga ghetto in 1942. Gretel Bergmann, who was an internationally recognized champion high jumper, was replaced on the German team by Dora Ratjen, who was later revealed to be a male who had been raised as a girl.

In advance of large numbers of overseas guests arriving, local Nazi Party authorities removed street signs bearing such slogans as "Jews not wanted" from Berlin's main tourist areas, while all vagrants and Roma were physically moved on to a specially constructed "holding camp" outside the city at Marzahn.

In view of such developments, there was considerable debate outside Germany over whether a boycott of the Games should go ahead. In some countries, notably Britain, France, Sweden, Czechoslovakia, and the Netherlands, discussion took place over whether the Games should perhaps be relocated, while throughout Europe exiled anti-Nazis kept up the pressure for a boycott. These initiatives did not amount to anything definite, with the excuse always being given that the Games had been awarded to Berlin in 1931 and that it would be wrong to punish the city simply because of a change of government.

Individual Jewish athletes from several countries, on the other hand, elected to take matters into their own hands and refused to attend. In this regard, brave athletes such as the South African Sid Kiel and Americans Milton Green and Norman Cahners should be mentioned.

As one of the world's leading sporting nations, the position of the United States was crucial, and in September 1934 the United States Olympic Committee (USOC) accepted a German invitation to visit on a fact-finding mission. After interviewing German Jews who had been carefully selected by the Nazi regime, USOC president Avery Brundage concluded that he had not found any discrimination against Germany's Jewish population. He then became a major supporter of the Games being held in Berlin, famously arguing that "politics has no place in sport." By 1935 he had convinced the Amateur Athletic Union of the United States that an American team should be sent to Berlin. The American Jewish Congress and the Jewish Labor Committee, on the other hand, supported a boycott but had no say in American Olympic Committee operations.

Most African American newspapers supported participation, arguing that this was an opportunity for Nazi racial theories to be challenged and, hopefully, defeated. And to some degree, they were right: the iconic Jesse Owens won four gold medals in the sprint and long jump events and became the most successful athlete to compete at Berlin.

In the effort to keep sport and politics separate, the Jewish American sprinters Sam Stoller and Marty Glickman were omitted from the 4 × 100 relay team on the day of the competition. The speculation has ever since been that in the aftermath of Owens's victories, Avery Brundage did not want to add to Hitler's embarrassment by having two American Jews win gold medals.

An obvious act of appeasement saw a tortured debate take place within the hierarchy of Britain's BBC over whether to accredit its foremost sporting commentator, the Jewish former Olympic gold medalist from the 1924 Paris Games, Harold Abrahams (whose story was later told in the movie *Chariots of Fire*). It was felt that his presence in Berlin could have been embarrassing to the British government and a slap at Germany. The BBC's Controller of Programs, Cecil Graves, wrote to his colleagues: "We all regard the German action against the Jews as quite irrational and intolerable, but would it be discourteous to send a Jew commentator to a country where Jews are taboo?" After much deliberation, Abrahams was sent to Berlin, with Graves concluding that the BBC should inform the Germans of the BBC decision and "leave them to raise any objections."

Germany was the Games' most successful country, winning thirty-three gold medals and eighty-nine medals overall. The United States came second in the medal tally, with twenty-four gold and fifty-six overall. The Berlin Olympics torch relay from Mount Olympus in Greece was the first of its kind, and the Games were the first to have live television coverage. Despite these advances, they were also to be the final Olympic Games for twelve years owing to the Second World War. Ironically, the next Games, slated for 1940, were to have been held in Tokyo.

Discussion Questions

1. Outline briefly the arguments for and against the 1936 Olympic Games being subjected to an international boycott. With which one would you agree? Why?
2. Could it be argued that the 1936 Olympic Games were a success? On what grounds?

Further Reading

Hart-Davis, Duff, *Hitler's Games: The 1936 Olympics*, London: Century, 1986.
Large, David Clay, *Nazi Games: The Olympics of 1936*, New York: Norton, 2007.
Walters, Guy, *Berlin Games: How the Nazis Stole the Olympic Dream*, New York: William Morrow, 2006.

Part 5

1937

MARCH 1937

5.1 The Pope's Declaration

On March 14, 1937, Pope Pius XI issued a papal encyclical entitled *Mit brennender Sorge* ("With Burning Concern"). Its formal title was "Encyclical of Pope Pius XI on the Church and the German Reich to the Venerable Brethren the Archbishops and Bishops of Germany and Other Ordinaries in Peace and Communion with the Apostolic See." While his message was a condemnation of the Nazis' excesses in Germany, it contained no explicit mention of the Jews. Five days later, on March 19, 1937, he issued a further encyclical, *Divini Redeptoris* ("A Divine Redeemer"), in which he condemned persecutions in Russia, Spain, and Mexico.

Reigning between 1922 and 1939, Pius XI was born Ambrogio Damiano Achille Ratti on May 31, 1857, in Desio, Italy. He was ordained in 1879, thereafter earning three separate doctorates from the Gregorian University of Rome. He then became a professor in a seminary.

He entered Vatican service in 1911, beginning his diplomatic career in 1919 when he was posted as Papal Nuncio to the newly independent Poland. He helped establish a working relationship with the Polish government while also seeking an accommodation with the Bolsheviks in Russia. In 1921 he served as Archbishop of Milan. After Pope Benedict XV died on January 22, 1922, Ratti was elected to the papacy on the fourteenth ballot on February 6, 1922, taking the name Pius XI.

Scholarly and bookish by nature, Pius XI was an activist pope who in many ways embraced modernity and did not shy away from using new media like the radio, with which he broadcast the church's message and teachings to a wide audience. He also greatly accelerated evangelism by sponsoring more missionaries throughout the world and by ordaining more priests and other clerical personnel.

It was in the diplomatic realm, however, that Pius's reign had the most far-reaching effect. Although he deeply distrusted Italian Fascism and eyed Benito Mussolini warily, in 1929 he signed the Lateran Treaty with Mussolini's government. This created an understanding between church and state in which both parties pledged not to interfere in the affairs of the other. In return, Mussolini agreed to recognize Vatican City as a sovereign state within Italy, something that had not existed since the days before Italian unification.

Pius soon ran afoul of Mussolini's regime. In 1931, he authored a papal letter in which he stated that one could not be a Fascist and a Catholic at the same time. Not surprisingly, the Vatican's relations with Mussolini soured. This did not stop Pius from negotiating a second Concordat on July 20, 1933, this time with Adolf Hitler's Nazi regime in Germany. Although later criticized for doing so, the pope's view was that communism was a worse scourge than Fascism or Nazism, thereby seeking to protect Catholics and Catholic clergy in Germany while hoping that Hitler would continue to act as a bulwark against Soviet communism. As it was, Hitler largely ignored the Concordat, and by the late 1930s Pius had begun to denounce Nazi ideology. He also castigated Mussolini for copying the Nazis' antisemitism with Italy's new racial legislation beginning in 1938.

However, the encyclical *Mit Brennender Sorge* showed that Pius was more than concerned with the antihuman ideologies espoused by Nazism. Given the specificity of its focus and the audience for whom it was intended, the encyclical was published in German rather than Latin. In view of a lack of any further statements of condemnation of Nazi actions from the Vatican, it became the greatest papal reproach of National Socialist Germany across the duration of the Third Reich. It was not, however, a condemnation of Nazi racial or antisemitic policies but essentially a document focusing on Hitler's nonobservance of the Concordat, particularly involving those involved in Catholic education—a tactic that would enable Pius to criticize Hitler without entering the sphere of politics.

The encyclical had little direct impact, though thousands of copies were smuggled into Germany, where it was disseminated widely. While *Mit Brennender Sorge* did not deal with Nazi racial practices, a second pastoral letter, *Humani Generis Unitas (The Unity of the Human Race)*, was a direct denunciation of racism and Nazi antisemitism. Prepared one year later, it was never published and became known to history as "The Hidden Encyclical." After this, the Vatican, under Pius XI's successor, Pius XII, retreated into a period of self-imposed silence on the matter of the Jews and the Nazi regime.

Pius XI reigned as pope from 1922 until his death in 1939. Throughout his pontificate, he spoke out against racism, persecution, totalitarianism, and excessive nationalism. He was outspoken in his dislike of fascism, communism, and Nazism, and at the same time he was also the first pope to address seriously the subject of Christian ecumenism. He died in the Vatican on February 10, 1939, only months before the start of the Second World War. Ever since then, two questions have dominated: would the world have been a different place had he lived for just three or four more years, and what sort of world would it have been? We can only speculate.

Discussion Questions

1. Could it be argued that Pope Pius XI was a "good" pope who opposed Nazi treatment of the Jews? Or were other factors at play?
2. Do you think any action on behalf of Jews would have taken place if Pius XI's "Hidden Encyclical" had been published before his death?

Further Reading

Anderson, Robin, *Between Two Wars: The Story of Pius XI*, San Jose: Franciscan Press, 1978.
Passelecq, Georges, and Bernard Suchecky, *The Hidden Encyclical of Pius XI*, New York: Harcourt, 1997.
Phayer, Michael, *The Catholic Church and the Holocaust, 1939–1965*, Bloomington: Indiana University Press, 2000.
Rhodes, Anthony, *The Vatican in the Age of Dictators, 1922–1945*, New York: Holt, Rinehart and Winston, 1973.

Part 6

1938

MARCH 1938

6.1 The *Anschluss* and the Jews of Austria

A Jewish presence is believed to have existed in and around Austria from as early as the Roman Empire. The fate of the Jews there waxed and waned over the centuries, but in March 1938, with the invasion of Austria by Nazi Germany, that presence came to a shuddering halt. At the time, Austria had a Jewish population of some 192,000, representing almost 4 percent of the country's total population. The overwhelming majority of Austrian Jews lived in Vienna, where they comprised about 9 percent of the population.

The term given to the Nazi takeover of Austria, *Anschluss*, is usually understood to mean "linkage," "connection," or "union." Historically, it has come to refer specifically to the annexation of the country by Germany on March 12, 1938. After a prolonged period of authoritarian rule, economic difficulties, and intense localized Nazi propaganda, that morning the German *Wehrmacht's* Eighth Army crossed the border. The troops were not met with any significant military or official resistance but were, instead, greeted enthusiastically by cheering Austrians with Nazi salutes, flags, and flowers. Austria was incorporated into the German Reich the next day.

Shortly thereafter, the Nazi racial laws were instituted against Austria's Jewish population, with some 76,000 (mostly men) arrested in the days following their implementation. Many Jews were sent to the concentration camp at Dachau, which had been established, almost to the day, five years earlier. The full force of what the Nazis had been evolving against the Jews in Germany over that period was now brought to bear against Austria's Jews within a matter of weeks. For example, universities, from which Jews were now banned, lost over 40 percent of their students and professors in a matter of hours, while Jews had their property confiscated and their homes looted or expropriated.

After the *Anschluss*, many Austrian Jews tried desperately to leave, but increasingly their means to do so were blocked by hard-hearted bureaucrats in the countries to which they sought refuge. A lucky few did manage to escape, but this was, sadly, only a minority. Vienna, given its large Jewish population, was particularly hard-hit by the Nazi measures, and the grainy images we have today of humiliated Jews being forced to scrub sidewalks with toothbrushes and prayer shawls are, tragically, all too accurate. Street attacks and brutal persecution became daily occurrences in the lives of Austrian Jews from all social classes. For a time, Vienna became the suicide capital of the world, as, in utter desperation at the speed of the horror, March saw 311 cases of suicide registered in the Viennese Jewish community. The next month, April, saw 267 more take their own lives. Across March and April, at least 4,700 Jews managed to flee Austria.

The response of other European countries to the *Anschluss* was timid. Although the victorious Allies of the First World War had prohibited the union of Austria and Germany, their muted reaction to the *Anschluss* was to a large degree reassuring for the Nazis. The Italy of Fascist dictator Benito Mussolini had already been bought off by Hitler, while France and Britain considered that the action was a fait accompli that in any case could not have been stopped other than by force—something they were not prepared to undertake. From this, Hitler drew the conclusion that aggression would be the new order of the day and would win out.

As for the Jews of Austria, they now had to face the same future that had been confronting Germany's Jews since 1933: namely, that the new order had no place for them, and they would have to find a way to either accommodate themselves to the changes or find a way to leave. Caught between the rock and the hard place of these two options, they looked to countries outside as a source of succor. Tragically, as the events of the next few months would show, none of the nations of the world stepped up to the plate, while the Jews were left to contemplate their future in tears and sorrow.

Discussion Questions

1. Why did the Nazis apply their antisemitic laws so quickly after taking over Austria?
2. Do you think protests by the other countries of Europe would have helped Austria's Jews after the *Anschluss*?

Further Reading

Bukey, Evan Burr, *Hitler's Austria: Popular Sentiment in the Nazi Era, 1938–1945*, Durham: University of North Carolina Press, 2000.
Low, Albert D., *The Anschluss Movement, 1931–1938, and the Great Powers*, New York: Columbia University Press, 1985.
Wagner, Dietrich, and Gerhard Tomkowitz, *Anschluss: The Week Hitler Seized Vienna*, New York: St. Martin's Press, 1971.

MAY 1938

6.2 A Chinese Diplomat Helps the Jews

In May 1938, a Chinese diplomat named Ho Feng-Shan was appointed to the post of Consul General in Vienna. This was to be the start of a remarkable period, in which Ho would become one of the first diplomats to save Jews by issuing them visas to escape the Holocaust. In the two years that followed, he was responsible for saving thousands of Jews in Nazi-occupied Austria.

Ho Feng-Shan was born into a poor family in rural Yiyang, Hunan province, on September 10, 1901. His father died when he was aged seven, and his family was assisted by the Norwegian Lutheran Mission, which enrolled him at its mission school. An excellent student, the grounding he received enabled him to go on to further study—first, at the College of Yale-in-China, after which, in 1928, he was accepted into the University of Munich. By 1932 he had earned a PhD in political economy, graduating magna cum laude.

In 1935 Ho joined the Republic of China's Foreign Service, starting his career as a diplomat with an initial posting to Ankara, Turkey. In the spring of 1937, he was placed as First Secretary to the Chinese legation in Vienna. When Germany invaded Austria on March 12, 1938, and the country became absorbed into the Reich, however, the legation was transformed into a consulate. In the subsequent reorganization, Ho became Consul General, and another officer took the title of Vice-Consul. Together, they formed the consulate's staff.

Ho found the Vienna posting an ideal location. Fluent in both English and German, he was an active participant in the social scene, often called upon to speak in public about Chinese culture and customs. He developed a wide circle of friends and acquaintances, many of whom, given the groups among whom he was associating, were Jewish.

After the *Anschluss*, Austria's Jews became subjected in the space of six weeks to the same antisemitic measures that had befallen German Jewry across the previous five years. Desperate to leave the country, many began looking for any country that would accept them, at a time when few were prepared to. The situation intensified to major crisis proportions after the November pogrom, known as the *Kristallnacht*, of November 9–10, 1938. Ho was shocked by the nature of Nazi violence and experienced something of the Nazis' racism himself when he was at one stage held at gunpoint by Nazis searching for Jews. Observing that Austria's Jews were in extreme danger, he soon realized that he could help them to get out.

The government of China was far from convinced that this was a matter requiring Chinese involvement; in fact, China's leader, Chiang Kai-shek (Jiang Jieshi), flirted with Germany's Nazi government throughout the 1930s. He employed German military advisers in his struggle against both the Japanese invaders and the Chinese communists, in addition to purchasing large quantities of weapons from Germany.

Against this background, it was perhaps not surprising that he wanted to maintain good relations with Germany and did not oppose Hitler's racial policies. Accordingly, the Chinese ambassador to Berlin, Chen Jie, instructed Ho Feng-Shan in Vienna that he was not to issue visas to Jews. Ho, however, acting against these explicit orders, began issuing visas for Jews to travel to Shanghai. Although he did not think that many would actually go there, he knew that possession of such a document was considered sufficient to enable Jews to purchase a travel ticket and thereby leave Austria.

His efforts were assisted by contributions made by American relief organizations, which at that stage were trying desperately to assist Jews to get out. Given that he had been forbidden from helping Jews, Ho was forced to maintain contact with these organizations covertly.

For continuing to issue visas despite a direct order for him not to do so, a black mark, or "demerit," was entered into Ho's personnel file in 1939. He continued supplying visas, however, until he was finally recalled to China, in shame, in May 1940. It is not known how many visas he had authorized prior to then. His 200th visa was issued in June 1938, and he signed number 1,906 on October 27, 1938. There is solid room for speculation, therefore, that in the ensuing months through to his departure from Vienna, many, many more, probably numbering in the thousands, would have been issued.

Ho went on to represent China in other diplomatic posts, in Egypt, Mexico, Bolivia, and Colombia. In 1949 he chose to remain loyal to the Republic of China rather than recognize the newly victorious People's Republic of China. He retired in 1973 and moved to the United States, settling in San Francisco where he became a founding member of the Chinese Lutheran Church. His memoir, *Forty Years of My Diplomatic Life*, was published in 1990. Explaining his actions in helping the Jews of Austria against the explicit orders of his own government, he expressed the view that "I thought it only natural to feel compassion and to want to help. From the standpoint of humanity, that is the way it should be."

On August 7, 2000, he was recognized by Yad Vashem as one of the Righteous among the Nations for his courage in issuing Chinese visas to Vienna's Jews. Ho Feng-Shan died at his home in San Francisco, California, on September 28, 1997, aged ninety-six.

Discussion Questions

1. In your view, should Ho Feng-Shan have continued issuing visas even though he was duty bound when ordered to stop? Why/why not?

2. Was there any indication in Ho's background that might have motivated him to act the way he did? Provide examples to support your answer.

Further Reading

Feng-Shan Ho, *My Forty Years as a Diplomat*, Pittsburgh: Dorrance Publishing, 2010.
Paldiel, Mordecai, *Diplomat Heroes of the Holocaust*, New York: Yeshiva
    University/KTAV, 2007.

JUNE 1938

6.3 Max Schmeling: The Boxer Who Cared

On June 22, 1938, arguably the most famous boxing match in history
took place at Yankee Stadium, New York, when the German heavyweight
champion, Max Schmeling, confronted American hero Joe Louis. The fight
was to have implications beyond a simple sporting contest.

Of modest background, Schmeling was born on September 28, 1905. He
became a professional boxer at the age of nineteen and won the German light
heavyweight title two years later. On June 19, 1927, he won the European
light heavyweight title, and then the German heavyweight crown. Moving
quickly to the world number-two ranking and a shot at the heavyweight
championship, on June 12, 1930, he met Jack Sharkey to settle the title.
Schmeling won when Sharkey was disqualified after delivering a low blow—
the only occasion in boxing history when the heavyweight championship
was won by disqualification.

In April 1933, not long after Adolf Hitler became chancellor of Germany,
he summoned Schmeling for a private dinner meeting with himself and several
leading Nazi officials. He told Schmeling that while in the United States he
should inform the American public that reports about Jewish persecution in
Germany were untrue. When Schmeling arrived in New York he complied,
saying that there was no antisemitism in Germany and emphasizing the
point that his own manager, Joe Jacobs, was Jewish.

Later that year Schmeling suffered defeat at the hands of Max Baer
before a crowd of 60,000 at Yankee Stadium. The loss was deemed a
"racial and cultural disgrace" in Germany, where it was considered
outrageous that Schmeling would even have had to fight a "non-Aryan."
Baer's father was Jewish, and Baer fought wearing shorts emblazoned with
a Star of David.

By this stage Schmeling was viewed in the United States as something of
a Nazi puppet. On March 10, 1935, he fought and knocked out American
Steve Hamas in Hamburg, and the 25,000 spectators spontaneously stood
and sang the *Horst Wessel* (the Nazi anthem), with arms raised in the Hitler
salute. This caused outrage in the United States, with Schmeling now being
publicized throughout Germany as the very model of Aryan supremacy and
Nazi racial superiority, something he would detest all his life.

The American public was desperate for Schmeling to return to the United States for another fight, this time against the young American hero, the "Brown Bomber," Joe Louis. On June 19, 1936, the fight took place at Yankee Stadium. As Schmeling's record of late had not been strong he was a 10–1 underdog, and many people thought that at thirty years of age he was past his prime.

Yet Schmeling had studied Louis's technique closely and found a weakness in his defense. In the twelfth round, he scored what some consider the upset of the century, when he sensationally knocked Louis out. In Germany, the Nazi press—to Schmeling's dismay—boasted that the victory represented white Aryan supremacy. When he returned to Berlin, he was invited by Hitler to join him for lunch.

The rematch, at Yankee Stadium on June 22, 1938, became a cultural and political event. It was billed as a battle of the "Aryan versus the Negro," a struggle of evil against good. Held before a crowd of over 70,000, the match saw a determined and highly motivated Joe Louis knock Schmeling out within two minutes and four seconds of the first round.

Schmeling said later he was relieved to have lost, as the defeat removed Nazi expectations of his abilities. It made it easier for him to refuse to act as a Nazi, and he was shunned by Hitler and the Nazi hierarchy for having "shamed" the Aryan Superman ideal. Hitler never forgave Schmeling for losing to Louis.

On the night of November 9, 1938, as antisemitic mobs were sacking Jewish property throughout the Reich during *Kristallnacht*, Schmeling's opposition to Nazism was tested as never before. One of his Jewish friends, David Lewin, begged in desperation for Schmeling to shelter his two sons, Heinz, aged fourteen, and Werner, fifteen. Without hesitation, Schmeling took them to his room in the downtown Excelsior Hotel and kept them there for three days, telling the desk clerk that he was ill and must not be disturbed. Risking his life to save the two brothers, he then helped them escape Berlin. After things settled down, he drove them to his house for further hiding; waiting another two days, he then delivered them safely to their father. In 1939 Schmeling helped the family to flee the country altogether. They went to the United States where Heinz (now Henri) became a prominent hotel owner in Las Vegas.

During the Second World War, a still enraged Adolf Hitler saw to it that at the age of thirty-five Schmeling would be drafted into the Luftwaffe as an elite paratrooper, where he served during the Battle of Crete in May 1941. It was said that the Führer took a personal interest in seeing to it that the former champion would be sent on suicide missions.

After the war and in retirement, Schmeling became one of Germany's most revered and respected sports figures. He remained popular not only in Germany but also in America. He became friends with many of his former foes, particularly his old opponent, Joe Louis. Schmeling would often help him financially, and their friendship lasted until Louis's death in 1981, when Schmeling, in a final tribute, paid for the funeral.

Max Schmeling was a man in conflict with both the Hitler regime and the racial policies of Nazism. The degree of resistance he showed was built around a sense of what it was to be a decent human being. On February 2, 2005, he died aged ninety-nine, at his home in Hollenstedt, near Hamburg.

Discussion Questions

1. Can you identify two examples of Max Schmeling acting as a resister to Nazism? What were they, and why did you choose these?
2. By not supporting the Nazi government, do you consider Max Schmeling to have been unpatriotic? Give reasons for your answer.

Further Reading

Hughes, Jon, "From Hitler's Champion to German of the Century: On the Representation and Reinvention of Max Schmeling," in Pól Ó Dochartaigh and Christiane Schönfeld (eds.), *Representing the "Good German" in Literature and Culture after 1945: Altruism and Moral Ambiguity*, pp. 66–84, Rochester, NY: Camden House, 2013.
Margolick, David, *Beyond Glory: Joe Louis vs. Max Schmeling, and a World on the Brink*, New York: Knopf, 2005.
Myler, Patrick, *Ring of Hate: The Brown Bomber and Hitler's Hero: Joe Louis V Max Schmeling and the Bitter Propaganda War*, Edinburgh: Mainstream, 2005.

JULY 1938

6.4 The Evian Conference

In March 1938, US president Franklin D. Roosevelt invited the nations of the world to meet to discuss what had by now become a global refugee crisis—the Nazi policy of forcing Jews out of Germany. The president's motives appear to have stemmed from his desire to deflect some sections of American public opinion that were beginning to lean toward a liberalization of immigration regulations. He hoped a new organization could be established to manage refugee resettlement. Inviting the nations of the world to participate in the formation of this organization would also show that the United States was playing a leading role in trying to find a solution to the refugee issue, and that the problem was not to be dumped onto the United States alone. The meeting would not compromise the existing policy of any country, and none of those attending would be obliged to make a commitment to receive refugee Jews. That was the sole condition of their appearance.

Along with the United States, some thirty-two European and Latin American states, as well as Australia, Canada, New Zealand, and South Africa, were invited to meet and consider the refugee crisis. Although Roosevelt had hoped the meeting would take place in Switzerland as a sign of the universality and neutrality of the issue, the Swiss refused; consequently, the next nearest preferred place was chosen, the French resort town of Evian-les-Bains, on Lake Geneva.

The conference was dominated by three men: Myron Taylor from the United States, Edward Turnour (Lord Winterton) from Britain, and Henry Bérenger from France. Each stated that their country was not prepared to do anything to expand Jewish refugee immigration. The United States would not commit to any expansion of its immigration quotas, only a merging of the existing German and Austrian allocations. Britain said it would not attend if there was any mention of Palestine or the colonial empire, and the French argued that since 1918 France had taken in more "aliens" than any other European country and was now "saturated." This gave a lead to all the other countries, as they, too, lined up to make their presentations.

The Europeans expressed hesitation over the possibility of supplanting the League of Nations High Commission on Refugees; hoped that the United States and other countries outside Europe would accept a greater share of the burden; and stated that they would only accept refugees for temporary asylum in a short-term transit capacity.

The largest group of states, the countries of Latin America, recognized that the refugee crisis was a humanitarian disaster but expressed a preference for farmers over "urban-dwelling professionals and intellectuals." They held, moreover that the United States and the European nations should pick up the slack in solving the refugee issue.

The self-governing British Dominions informed the conference that they had no interest in resolving the refugee problem. Canada only wanted farmers; New Zealand did not want foreigners; South Africa, though invited, did not attend; Ireland, which had not been invited but went anyway, declared that it was not an immigrant-receiving country; and the Australian position, expressed by the minister for trade and customs, Thomas White, was that "Australia cannot do more ... [and] as we have no real racial problems, we are not desirous of importing one by encouraging any scheme of large-scale foreign migration."

At the end of the nine-day meeting, no resolution was reached. Except for the tiny Dominican Republic, no other nation agreed to accept refugees, and when the conference broke up on July 15 its main outcome was the establishment of a permanent organization, the Inter-Governmental Committee on Refugees. This convened in London on July 19—and then proceeded to do next to nothing of any substance for the refugees.

Attitudes such as those expressed by Thomas White demonstrated to Hitler that Germany's Jews were unwanted throughout the rest of the world. This is not an argument that can only be discussed with the advantage of hindsight. It was clearly apparent to perceptive observers at the time. The tragedy is that while everyone saw the dangers of inaction, no one was prepared to put their words of sympathy into practice. Evian showed clearly that the nations of the world did not yet fully understand the implications of what was happening in Germany in any terms other than their own. Evian prompted a statement from Dr. Chaim Weizmann, later the first president of Israel, that the world was divided into two places: those where Jews could not live and those where Jews could not enter.

For all that, however, the meeting did serve the purpose of concentrating the minds of government leaders, if only for a short time, on the refugee crisis. It *could* have acted as an occasion for caring administrations to make an announcement that they would agree to an increase in their refugee quotas. None, however, chose to do so, and in this lay Evian's real tragedy. It affirmed for Hitler and the Nazis the unwillingness of the democratic nations to extend themselves on behalf of the Jews. What must be remembered, however, is that at the time of the conference the murder of six million Jews was not foreseen by anyone—and certainly not the Nazis. They were at this time still trying to intimidate the Jews of Europe into leaving Germany rather than killing them.

In one sense it could be said that the Evian Conference achieved what it set out to do, which was, quite simply, to enable the countries of the world to make statements explaining why they could not assist in easing the refugee crisis. Evian was not a meeting that intended to find ways to enable refugee admission. The Jewish response to Evian, therefore—one of disappointment, anger, and a feeling of betrayal—was, quite simply, misplaced. Jewish and non-Jewish refugee organizations around the world genuinely hoped that some good would come from the conference, but this was at no stage a sentiment shared by the countries attending.

In July 1938, we must also remember, the nations of the world were administering refugee and immigration policies, not rescue-from-the-Holocaust policies. The Evian Conference did not lead to the Final Solution. Way too much had to happen before then. We can, however, apply the standards of the time to the issue of Jewish refugee and immigration policy. When we do this, we can then examine the records of the various nations of the world relative to the Jews, and when we do that—sadly and tragically— we will still find them wanting. The immediate results of the conference amounted to nothing of any lasting worth, which was exactly what was anticipated. The assembled countries used the opportunity presented to look good, but the refugees got nothing for it.

Discussion Questions

1. In view of what the organizers of the Evian Conference set out to achieve, could it be said that Evian was a "failed" conference?

2. The word Evian, when spelled backward, is "naïve." Do you think that is a more fitting description for what happened there?

Further Reading

Bartrop, Paul R., *The Evian Conference of 1938 and the Jewish Refugee Crisis*, London: Palgrave Macmillan, 2018.
Breitman, Richard, and Alan M. Kraut, *American Refugee Policy and European Jewry, 1933–1945*, Bloomington: Indiana University Press, 1988.
Sherman, A. J., *Island Refuge: Britain and Refugees from the Third Reich, 1933–1939*, London: Frank Cass, 1994.

AUGUST 1938 (1)

6.5 "Sarah," Meet "Israel"

In Act II, Scene II of William Shakespeare's *Romeo and Juliet*, young Juliet Capulet utters lines that are now immortal: "What's in a name?/that which we call a rose/By any other name would smell as sweet." Perhaps so, but what happens when a name is changed by government order? Does the rose remain a rose? On August 17, 1938, the German government put the question to the test, in the Second Decree Supplementing the Law Regarding the Change of Family Names and First Names.

As the next in what was becoming a long line of Nazi decrees forcibly imposing Aryanization on German society, the Nazis hit on the idea that to enforce the many antisemitic policies that had been introduced since the Nuremberg Laws of 1935, it was necessary for officials everywhere to be able to identify Jews formally. Consequently, the Change of Names decree required that all male Jews would be required to adopt the compulsory middle name of "Israel" and all female Jews to add the name "Sarah." The law became operational on January 1, 1939. From then on, all Jews were required to add the name into their passports and other official documents and to all identity cards. All newly born children were required by law to have these names registered alongside the names given by their parents.

Looking at the wording of the decree, we see not only the explicit statement regarding the middle names (for which the decree has become best known): it also states that after the law came into effect Jews would have to choose names for their children from an official list of approved (and highly conspicuous) "Jewish" first names. This list was formalized in a document called the Guidelines on the Use of Given Names issued by the Reich minister of the interior, who in 1938 was Wilhelm Stuckart, a lawyer who was the principal author of the Nuremberg Laws. The new naming legislation was underwritten by the Reich minister of justice, Dr. Franz Gürtner.

The law was the latest in a long list of measures that sought progressively to push the Jews out of German society. Because of the earlier Nuremberg Laws, Jews could only marry other Jews and attend Jewish schools. Sleeping and dining cars on trains, together with barbershops, hospitals, restrooms, and waiting rooms, all became segregated. The Nazis set curfews and shopping hours for Jews and denied them the use of public telephones. They also removed private phones from Jewish homes.

In October 1938, as an initiative of the Swiss government in negotiations with the Nazis, the letter "J" was then stamped on all German passports, ration cards, and other official documents belonging to Jews. This was to serve the purpose of assisting restrictive immigration policies and regulating the entry of Jewish refugees into countries bordering Germany. Later laws in Germany required "non-Aryans" six years old and older to wear a Star of David on the left breast of their clothing. As a final measure reinforcing the identification of Jewish distinctiveness, on August 17, 1939, the Reich Ministry of the Interior issued a listing of names that would henceforth be permitted for Jewish parents to give their new-born babies.

Discussion Questions

1. Why do you think the Nazi government introduced the Change of Names regulation for all Jews, followed by a list of approved names for newly born children?

2. In your view, were the new rules regarding names positive or negative for the Jews? In what way(s)?

Further Reading

Fischer, Klaus, *Nazi Germany: A New History*, New York: Continuum, 1995.
Koch, H. W., *In the Name of the Volk: Political Justice in Hitler's Germany*, London: I.B. Tauris, 1997.
Miller, Richard M., *Nazi Justiz: Law of the Holocaust*, Westport: Praeger, 1995.

AUGUST 1938 (2)

6.6 A Swiss Hero at the Border

On August 18, 1938, the Swiss government closed its borders to Jewish refugees attempting to flee Nazi Germany. Every movement of Jews crossing into Switzerland was declared by the government to be illegal, and refugees were forced back to Germany or Austria. One man, however, refused to adopt what he considered to be a heartless policy. The subsequent actions of Paul Grüninger, a Swiss border police commander, would save several thousand Jews who otherwise would have been denied sanctuary.

Born on October 27, 1891, in St. Gallen, the son of a cigar shop owner, Grüninger lived a simple lifestyle not especially involved in matters outside of his hometown. During the First World War, when Switzerland was neutral, he served in the Swiss army as a lieutenant. After the war he joined the border police, rising to the rank of colonel, and soon became commander of the border police for St. Gallen Canton.

When the Nazis came to power in Germany in 1933 many Jews fled to neighboring Austria. The German annexation of Austria on March 12, 1938, then saw an immediate start to Jewish persecution there, and Austrian Jews now sought sanctuary in Switzerland. To act as a deterrent, in October 1938 the Swiss government asked Germany to stamp the letter "J" on all Jewish passports so Swiss officials might more easily identify (and thus, reject) Jews. In 1939 Switzerland decided not to admit refugees on religious or racial grounds, thereby further denying Jews access.

It was in this context that Paul Grüninger was approached every day by German and Austrian Jews seeking asylum, and, as he heard their stories, he could scarcely believe his ears. When faced with choosing between following the law or staying true to his moral code, his sense of compassion made it impossible to turn the Jews away. Grüninger realized he would be putting himself at risk by doing what he thought was humane and right but believed that saving lives was far more important than preserving his job.

Following his conscience, he admitted over 3,600 Jews—by falsifying their passports and entry papers or turning a blind eye when necessary. He even used his own money to buy winter clothes for refugees who had been forced to leave all their belongings behind. The new arrivals, treated as legal refugees, would be taken to a camp established at Diepoldsau near the Austrian frontier, where they could await permits for a temporary stay in Switzerland or their final departure elsewhere.

On April 3, 1939, however, Grüninger arrived at work to find a young cadet, Corporal Antón Schneider, standing in front of his office door. Blocking Grüninger's way, Schneider's orders had come directly from the office of the commander-in-chief. Grüninger knew instinctively why he was being stopped. A friend working at a border post in Bregenz, Austria, had informed him that he was on the Gestapo's blacklist due to having helped a Jewish woman, who he had already assisted to escape from Austria, recover her jewels. She had left them at a hotel in Bregenz, and Grüninger contacted Ernest Prodolliet of the Swiss consulate in Bregenz to collect the jewels for her. Prodolliet and Grüninger had worked together on missions like this before. The woman was so grateful for Grüninger's help that she wrote about his kindness in a letter to some friends; the Gestapo intercepted the letter, imprisoned the hotel owner, confiscated the jewels, and began to keep an eye on Grüninger.

Soon after this, the Swiss authorities learned of Grüninger's illegal activities and dismissed him. Placed on trial in proceedings that would last two years, the court found him guilty of a breach of duty; he was imprisoned, had his pension revoked, was forced to pay costs, and fined. Although the court accepted that his actions were honorable, they declared that as a state official he should have followed his orders, refused entrance to Jews, and not falsified official documents.

Grüninger was publicly humiliated and lived the rest of his life with a prison record, making it practically impossible to find steady work. He did not seek redress or recognition for his actions, instead focusing on surviving and supporting his family. In 1954 he claimed: "My personal well-being, measured against the cruel fate of these thousands, was so insignificant and unimportant" that he never even took the consequences of his actions into consideration.

When Paul Grüninger died at the age of eighty-one on February 22, 1972, his family was still living in near poverty. In December 1970 the Swiss government sent Grüninger a letter of apology but at the same time still refused him his pension. Then, a year before his death, Israel's Yad Vashem recognized him as one of the Righteous among the Nations. In 1994 the Swiss government published a Declaration of Honor on his behalf, before finally annulling his conviction. In 1998 the Parliament of St. Gallen Canton agreed to compensate Grüninger's descendants, and his family put the money into the Paul Grüninger Foundation, an organization that works to reward outstanding acts of humanity and courage that align with Grüninger's actions. Although most recognition therefore came after Grüninger's death, his decision to save those in need has served as a model of moral behavior for the world today.

Discussion Questions

1. The Swiss government argued that as a state official Paul Grüninger was obliged to follow his orders, yet he refused to do so on moral grounds. Do you think he should have been punished?

2. Was Paul Grüninger a hero for saving Jews or negligent in his duty by doing so? Why?

Further Reading

Hellman, Peter, *When Courage Was Stronger than Fear: Remarkable Stories of Christians Who Saved Jews from the Holocaust*, Melbourne: Marlowe, 1999.
Press, Eyal, *Beautiful Souls: Saying No, Breaking Ranks, and Heeding the Voice of Conscience in Dark Times*, New York: Farrar, Straus, and Giroux, 2012.

SEPTEMBER 1938

6.7 Munich and the Martyrdom of Czechoslovakia

In September 1938, one of the greatest surrenders to bullying on the international stage took place when Britain and France sacrificed the democratic state of Czechoslovakia on the altar of a policy that became known as appeasement. Their hope was that they could buy off Adolf Hitler and thus avoid having to confront him in a war they were not prepared to fight. By not standing up to him, however, all they did was encourage him to continue with his campaign of intimidation and threats. Every time the Western powers surrendered to some new demand, Hitler was inspired to reach even higher, firm in his belief that he could get what he wanted at no cost to himself.

The Munich Agreement was signed on September 30, 1938, by Germany, Britain, France, and Italy. It permitted Germany's annexation of Czechoslovakia's Sudetenland region, an area populated by about three million German speakers who had, as it turned out, never belonged to Germany. As early as May 1938 it was known that Hitler and his generals had their eyes set on Czechoslovakia, while the Czechs, in turn, relied on alliances with France and the Soviet Union to counter German threats. As the year progressed, however, it became clear that both France and its ally, Britain, were not prepared to defend Czechoslovakia. There was a desperate desire to avoid a military confrontation with Germany—at any price.

To keep the peace, British prime minister Neville Chamberlain made three trips during the month of September to see Hitler: on September 15 he went to the Führer's retreat at Berchtesgaden, on September 22 he went to a second meeting at Bad Godesberg, not far from Cologne, and then, finally, he went to Munich on September 29. In each case, he discussed the situation personally with Hitler, offering whatever concessions it would take to stop Germany from going to war.

The third trip saw a four-power conference convened to settle the issue, and on that final occasion, on September 30, Hitler and Chamberlain, together with Eduard Daladier of France and Benito Mussolini of Italy, came together in Munich. They agreed that Germany would annex the Sudetenland, with an international commission to decide the future of other disputed areas.

The Czech government of Edvard Beneš played no role in these discussions and was simply informed of developments. Two Czech delegates were denied access to the meeting and were kept under virtual house arrest in their hotel until the agreement had been signed. Britain and France then informed the Czechs that they faced two options: they could either resist and fight Germany alone or acquiesce peacefully to the

German invasion of their sovereign territory. So that Britain and France would not have to confront the Nazis, this small democratic nation would have to pay the price they demanded and were left to suffer the ultimate punishment for merely existing, as their country was dismembered in tears and sorrow.

Before returning to London, Chamberlain paid Hitler a personal visit in his Munich apartment. He took with him a short note prepared earlier in London, declaring that the two nations would agree to always resolve their differences through consultation rather than war. Offering this to Hitler, Chamberlain then signed it. Hitler signed too, reputedly telling one of those in his circle later that he was pleased to offer Chamberlain his autograph.

Upon his return to London, Chamberlain was met at Heston Airport by jubilant crowds, relieved that the threat of war had passed. He informed the British public that he had achieved "peace with honour," saying that he believed the settlement would bring "peace for our time." A few months later, on March 15, 1939, the hollowness of this promise was revealed when Hitler marched his troops into what was left of Czechoslovakia and snuffed out the little country without a hand being raised to defend it. It was little wonder that Winston Churchill, then seemingly at the end of his political career (though with his best years still ahead of him), could state that the impact of Munich would not mean peace with honor but war with dis-honor.

For the Jews of Czechoslovakia, none of this passed without chilling fear and apprehension. The Sudetenland was gradually occupied across the period between October 1 and 10, and Jews in the region started feeling the Nazi presence immediately. Persecution began, and synagogues would be burned down during the *Kristallnacht* pogrom of November 9–10, 1938. The full weight of Nazi antisemitic laws was imposed on the Czech Jews, and it took little time for the whole region to become the most actively Nazified area within the Third Reich.

A frantic search for some sort of haven now took place for the Jews of the Czech lands. By this time, however, with the Evian Conference of earlier in the year a bad memory, the doors of entry for Jews were being closed all over the world—a situation that would only get worse in the year after Munich.

Discussion Questions

1. The integrity of Czechoslovakia was the price paid by Britain and France for peace in Europe. Given the high stakes involved, do you think larger nations should be entitled to do this?

2. In your view, were Chamberlain and Daladier naïve to think they could bargain with Hitler successfully at Munich?

Further Reading

Caquet, P. E., *The Bell of Treason: The 1938 Munich Agreement in Czechoslovakia*, London: Profile Books, 2018.

Faber, David, *1938: The Munich Appeasement Crisis*, New York: Simon and Schuster, 2008.

Gillard, David, *Appeasement in Crisis: From Munich to Prague, October 1938-March 1939*, Basingstoke: Palgrave Macmillan, 2007.

Kee, Robert, *Eleventh Hour: The Munich Crisis*, London: Hamish Hamilton, 1988.

Robbins, Keith, *Munich 1938*, London: Cassell, 1968.

NOVEMBER 1938

6.8 *Kristallnacht*: The Point of No Return

In the most extensive act of Nazi persecution against Germany's Jews prior to the outbreak of the Second World War, the night of November 9–10, 1938, saw the event known as *Kristallnacht* take place. The event was dubbed by Nazis as the "Night of Broken Glass," or "Night of Crystals" (*Kristallnacht*). It was a term intended to humiliate the Jews; the term we use today was a Nazi term of derision, introduced by Hermann Göring amid much laughter. The event prompted a desperate search for a haven from Jews remaining in Germany, Austria, and the German-speaking Sudeten areas of Czechoslovakia, as they now realized their time in the Third Reich was at an end.

The event itself was far from spontaneous. The pogrom took place against Jewish stores, synagogues, and community centers in what the Nazis referred to as "retaliation" for the fatal wounding of the Third Secretary of the German Embassy in Paris, Ernst vom Rath, by a sixteen-year-old Jewish youth, Hershel Grynszpan. His parents and sister, originally from Poland, had earlier been forcibly relocated across the border between German and Poland and were living in destitute and squalid conditions in the no-man's land between the two countries. Frustrated and angry to the point of desperation, on November 7, 1938, Grynszpan sought to raise the world's consciousness over the injustice meted out to his family and the 2,000 other Jews who were in the same situation. His action in shooting vom Rath in Paris was born out of despair, with terrible consequences for the Jews of Germany.

The Nazis saw it as a wonderful opportunity to launch an anti-Jewish pogrom, the better to intimidate them into leaving, once and for all. Quickly labeling Grynszpan's act as the work of a criminal Jewish conspiracy, they arranged for the "punishment" of German Jewry through a wholesale pogrom against all Jews in the Reich. The attacks were carefully orchestrated. In twenty-four hours of street violence, ninety-one Jews were killed. More than 30,000—one in ten of all Jews remaining in Germany after five years of Nazi rule—were arrested and sent to concentration camps. Before most of them were released two to three months later, up to a thousand had been murdered, 244 in Buchenwald alone. A further 8,000 Jews were evicted from Berlin: they included children from orphanages, patients from hospitals, and elderly folk from retirement homes. Eight hundred and fifteen shops and twenty-nine major department stores owned by Jews were destroyed, and more than 260 synagogues and cemeteries were vandalized. Many of these were burned. In addition, it has been estimated that more than 7,500 Jewish-owned businesses were attacked. The actual cost of the damages inflicted was more than 25,000,000 Reichsmarks, for which the Jews themselves were held liable by the Nazis, as well as a fine of more than one billion Reichsmarks as "reparations."

The possibility that there could ever be an accommodation reached with Nazism—a hope long held by many Jews—now vanished, and the painful truth which they had for so long tried to avoid broke through: they were being forced to quit the country and would have to leave Germany for other lands. Prior to the *Kristallnacht* many could not face up to that awful reality.

Some have termed the November pogrom "the day the Holocaust began," the day after which nothing could ever be the same again for the Jews of Germany. It was certainly a turning point, a point of no return, following which the Jews could hold no illusions as to how the Nazis viewed the Jewish presence in the Nazi state. They would not be considered as members of the community, were to be isolated, reduced to second-class subjects (not considered as citizens), and encouraged at every opportunity to leave—by force, if need be.

Discussion Questions

1. What was the point of the November pogrom? To "punish" the Jews for vom Rath's death? Or was there a deeper underlying motive?

2. Why do you think this article is called "The Point of No Return?"

Further Reading

Gerhardt, Uta, and Thomas Karlauf (eds.), *The Night of Broken Glass: Eyewitness Accounts of Kristallnacht*, London: Polity, 2012.
Gilbert, Martin, *Kristallnacht: Prelude to Tragedy*, New York: Harper, 2007.
Schleunes, Karl A., *The Twisted Road to Auschwitz: Nazi Policy toward German Jews, 1933–1939*, Urbana: University of Illinois Press, 1970.
Thalmann, Rita, and Emmanuel Feinermann, *Crystal Night: 9–10 November 1938*, New York: Coward, McCann & Geoghegan, 1974.

DECEMBER 1938

6.9 Saving the Children

As a response to *Kristallnacht*, the British government immediately approved the entry of Jewish refugees younger than seventeen, on the proviso that they had a place to stay and landing money of £50 to enable them eventually to return home. On December 2, 1938, the first arrivals of Jewish children arrived in Britain.

Much of the preliminary work was done by Jewish relief organizations in Britain, who planned to rescue these German and Austrian Jewish children in what became known as the *Kindertransport* ("children's transport") program. Ultimately, the initiative would bring some 10,000 unaccompanied children to safety prior to the outbreak of war in September 1939. *Kindertransport* was the informal term used to describe the program (officially, it was the Refugee Children Movement). For the most part, Jewish children from Germany, Austria, Czechoslovakia, and Poland were "resettled" or "relocated" between December 1938 and September 1939. The rescued children were resettled in hostels, foster homes, and sometimes on farms.

On November 15, 1938, in the immediate aftermath of *Kristallnacht*, Jewish leaders in Britain appealed directly to Prime Minister Neville Chamberlain for his help in rescuing Jewish children. Specifically, they asked that immigration requirements be altered so that unaccompanied Jewish children might be allowed into the country on a temporary basis. In short order, Parliament took up the issue and agreed to the request, deciding not to set a limit on the number of children to be admitted. Various Jewish relief agencies swung into action, as did the World Jewish Relief Fund, which worked with British officials in identifying children to be moved and arranging for their transport and resettlement.

Once word was received of the British offer, Jewish community organizations in Germany and Austria planned the best ways to send the children to safety. Parents would send letters through bodies such as the Hebrew Immigration Aid Society (HIAS) to sponsors in Britain; some of these sponsors were Jewish, some not. Within days of the public announcement of the *Kindertransport* program, some 500 British households offered to take in a child (and, sometimes, more than one). Children were sent by train to the Netherlands or Belgium, and then by boat to Harwich in southeast England, where they were oriented and then resettled. They left their homes without valuables, a maximum of ten marks, and one small suitcase. None were accompanied by their parents; a few were babies carried by their older brothers and sisters. Most were marked with a name tag on their clothes for the purpose of identification. The first *Kindertransport* left Berlin on December 1, 1938, bringing 196 children from a Jewish orphanage burned by the Nazis during the night of the pogrom on November 9. It arrived in Harwich the following day.

Most transports left by train from Vienna, Berlin, Prague, and other major cities. Hundreds of children, who did not go straight to Britain, remained in Belgium and the Netherlands, safe for the time being. On one occasion, a Dutch social worker, Geertruida Wijsmuller-Meijer, went to Vienna to see Adolf Eichmann in person, demanding that he permit children to leave for the United Kingdom immediately. After suffering many indignities at the hands of the Gestapo, she was granted permission to take 600 children out of Austria, and the first *Kindertransport* from Austria was able to proceed.

In Britain, hostels were administered by members of the Zionist *Habonim* youth movement to house the children. Many others spent time with sympathetic families in cities or on farms in the countryside.

Later, after the Germans invaded Czechoslovakia, the program was expanded to include Czech Jewish children, in an initiative that lay directly at the feet of a British Jew acting in a private capacity, Nicholas (later Sir Nicholas) Winton. Several groups also came from Poland, especially during the summer of 1939.

The *Kindertransport* program effectively ended in September 1939 when Germany attacked Poland, though one last transport for Britain left from the Dutch port of Ijmuiden on May 14, 1940, one day before the Netherlands surrendered. The eighty children on board had been brought by earlier transports to what was expected to be a haven in the Netherlands.

Despite the remarkable figure of around 10,000 children who were saved and resettled in Britain, there is room for speculation to suggest that had the program commenced earlier, the number would have been much larger. It took the November pogrom, however, for Jewish parents in Germany and Austria to realize the urgency of the situation facing their families.

In 1945, with the end of the war, many *Kindertransport* children attempted to reunite with their loved ones back in Europe. Although some were successful, it was a sad fact that many were unable to do so, as their families had perished in the Holocaust or been killed in other wartime tragedies.

Discussion Questions

1. Briefly describe the motives of the British government in allowing the *Kindertransport* program. Was it a humanitarian gesture, or do you think other factors played a role?

2. The *Kindertransport* program was a private initiative. Why do you think the British government did not undertake these rescues itself?

Further Reading

Byers, Ann, *Saving Children from the Holocaust: The Kindertransport*, Buchanan, NY: Enslow, 2011.

Emanuel, Muriel, and Vera Gissing, *Nicholas Winton and the Rescued Generation: Save One Life, Save the World*, Edgeware: Vallentine, Mitchell, 2001.

Samuels, Diane, *Kindertransport*, London: Nick Hern Books, 2010.

Winton, Barbara, *If It's Not Impossible … The Life of Sir Nicholas Winton*, Leicester: Troubadour, 2014.

Part 7

1939

JANUARY 1939

7.1 Hitler Threatens the Jews

On January 30, 1939, Adolf Hitler presented an address to the Reichstag in which he made the most overt threat yet seen to "world Jewry." Known for his lengthy speeches, this one was no exception; when put to paper, it came to sixty-four single-spaced typed pages. It made for dry and tedious reading and was primarily concerned with the economic, political, military, and diplomatic recovery of Germany in the aftermath of the Nazi political victory in 1933.

The address is not remembered, however, for anything other than two paragraphs three-quarters of the way through. Here, Hitler made an important and often-quoted prophecy that if there should ever be another war (which, in his view, would have been caused by "international Jewish financiers"), it would not result in a Jewish victory but, rather, "the annihilation of the Jewish race in Europe."

To begin with, he spoke about his past record, in which he noted that "in the course of my life I have very often been a prophet and have usually been ridiculed for it." In 1933, however, he achieved power. In view of that, he would once more "assume the part of a prophet." The words that followed have since entered Holocaust iconography: "If the international Jewish financiers within and without Europe, succeeded in plunging the nations once more into a world war, then the result will be not the Bolshevization of the world and thereby the victory of Jewry—but the annihilation of the Jewish race in Europe." He continued that "this problem will be solved—the sooner the better—for Europe cannot rest again before the Jewish problem has been eliminated."

What did all this mean in reality? Amid rising international tensions, Hitler made it clear to both the German public and the rest of the world (and especially, the world's Jews) that the outbreak of war would mean the end of European Jewry. Already his preference for the Jews to leave

Germany had been signaled in no uncertain terms through anti-Jewish boycotts, staged book burnings, and anti-Jewish legislation. Ultimately, on November 9–10, 1938, the nationwide pogrom that the Nazis themselves cynically termed *Kristallnacht* demonstrated that the Jews no longer had a future in Germany.

Prior to the German attack on Poland precipitating war in September 1939, a vast number of events took place that further reduced options for Jews to remain in Germany. Throughout 1938 these included the establishment of a Nazi Office of Jewish Emigration to speed up the pace of Jewish emigration from Germany (August 1, 1938), the requirement that Jewish women add "Sarah" and men add "Israel" to their names on all legal documents (August 17, 1938), the closure of Swiss borders for Austrian Jews seeking sanctuary (August 19, 1938), the Munich Conference in which Britain and France surrendered the Sudetenland regions of Czechoslovakia to Germany by negotiation (September 29–30, 1938), and the compulsory stamping of passports belonging to German Jews with the letter "J" to indicate their identity (October 5, 1938).

This new statement, however, took things up a notch. Hitler's Reichstag statement was made on January 30, 1939, to mark the sixth anniversary of Hitler's ascension to the chancellorship, but here he spoke explicitly for the first time about the complete annihilation of European Jewry. It is not clear whether he believed he could achieve this; if he did, he certainly had no idea how it could be done. It is, rather, more likely that he made this radical statement to ease pressure from even more extreme Jew haters within the Nazi Party. He also knew that this would serve an excellent propaganda purpose internationally and might even drive more Jews out of Germany in fear of their lives.

He repeated his threat about the "annihilation of the Jewish race in Europe" several times in the years that followed. On some occasions during the war years he even deliberately misdated the speech as having occurred on September 1, 1939, the date on which Germany invaded Poland, thereby linking the invasion directly to the reason for why the conflict was being fought.

Indeed, the war would eventually mark a transition in Nazi policies toward Jews and lead inexorably toward genocide. But the Final Solution did not really get under way until the summer of 1941, when the Nazis invaded the Soviet Union. In early 1939, when Hitler made his speech, his regime still hoped the remaining Jews in Germany would emigrate. He was not interested at this time in murdering them, just in removing them from Germany. This, of course, was to change later.

In the end, however, while Hitler's address to the Reichstag in January 1939 might have been a simple case of extreme rhetoric, its effect was to encourage Nazi Party radicals, who now felt empowered to proceed with plans and ideas that in due course resulted in giving concrete form to Hitler's bombast.

The bottom line must be that words matter and that those hearing them are often just as important (if not more important) as those uttering them. The Holocaust did not start in January 1939, but the preconditions leading to it, tragically, received a huge boost at that time.

Discussion Questions

1. Do you think Hitler's speech was simply over-exaggerated to sound impressive for his Party colleagues? Or do you think he meant it? Give reasons for your answer.

2. Could the Holocaust have been foreseen from this very early statement? Or was it, instead, just bluff on Hitler's part?

Further Reading

Fleming, Gerald, *Hitler and the Final Solution*, Berkeley: University of California Press, 1984.
Gordon, Sarah Ann, *Hitler, Germans, and the Jewish Question*, Princeton: Princeton University Press, 1984.
Kershaw, Ian, *Hitler, the Germans, and the Final Solution*, New Haven: Yale University Press, 2008.

FEBRUARY 1939

7.2 Hermann Stöhr, Conscientious Objector

Hermann Stöhr was a German pacifist who resisted Nazism before the Second World War and was executed as a conscientious objector to military service and for his opposition to the Nazi state.

Born in Stettin on January 4, 1898, Stöhr was the child of a conservative family of civil servants. When war broke out in 1914, he volunteered for military service at the age of just sixteen. Upon returning from the trenches his experiences had transformed him into a pacifist. Between 1919 and 1922 he studied economics, law, and social policy at the University of Rostock, from where he earned a PhD in 1922. He then moved to Berlin, where he worked under the guidance of Friedrich Siegmund-Schulze, professor of philosophy at the University of Berlin and a deeply committed Lutheran working for social causes and the peace movement.

Stöhr took a position as a secretary in the German branch of the International Fellowship of Reconciliation, an antiwar peace movement based on a common Protestant Christianity cofounded by Siegmund-Schultze in August 1914. He engaged in various journalistic activities on behalf of his mentor, writing pieces that were published internationally. In 1931, however, he lost his position and moved back to Stettin.

After the Nazis came to office in January 1933, Stöhr decided to take a stand against National Socialist Church policy by calling on the Protestant churches to include victims of political persecution in their prayers of intercession and to show practical solidarity with the Jews. He went public in his opposition to Nazi calls for a boycott of Jewish businesses and swastika flags being displayed in churches. He later joined the Confessing Church, a Protestant movement that arose in opposition to Nazi efforts against Protestantism.

On February 28, 1939, Stöhr received his call-up for military service in the German navy and was ordered to report to naval headquarters at Kiel. He replied immediately that for reasons of conscience he was forced to refuse armed service, though in its stead he requested that he be allowed to carry out labor service. This was declined, and he was then given two further call-up orders, on March 2 and August 22, 1939; on each of these occasions he also refused the call. On August 31, 1939, he was arrested and charged with desertion, and on November 1 a military court martial was held in which he was sentenced to a year's imprisonment. At the end of 1939, while in prison, he refused to swear a compulsory oath to Adolf Hitler and rejected the possibility of any compromises. On January 9, 1940, his case came before another court martial, and on March 16, 1940, he was sentenced to death as a conscientious objector. His case was immediately the subject of a request for clemency from the prison chaplain. It was rejected. When it was asked to intervene, the church said it could not get involved in a case of this kind.

Sitting in the Wehrmacht remand prison in Berlin-Tegel, Stöhr awaited news of the date of his execution. He wrote his final letters to family and friends, at peace with his Christian faith and the teachings of Scripture. When told that the date of his execution had been set for June 6, 1940, he wrote a last letter in which he stated that no one was to be sad about his fate and that he faced "the end in gratitude and joy." As it turned out, his execution was delayed beyond the June 6 date, but he was finally beheaded in Berlin-Plötzensee prison on June 21, 1940. The burial took place in the cemetery of the Protestant St. John's church in Berlin-Wedding. During the funeral service the pastor, closely observed by the Gestapo, was prevented from speaking freely about Stöhr and was interrupted several times. The only invocation he was able to recite was the Lord's Prayer.

Studies undertaken into the fate of those who consistently refused military service show that there were at least seven Catholics, two Quakers, one Mormon, seven Seventh Day Adventists, and about 7,000 Jehovah's Witnesses subjected to various forms of judicial persecution from the Nazi state for their beliefs. Only one Evangelical Protestant, however, was convicted and executed: Hermann Stöhr. In the history of resistance to Nazism and the Holocaust, his life and fate were practically forgotten until a German theologian and writer on religious matters, Eberhard Röhm, published a book in Stuttgart in 1985 entitled *Sterben für den Frieden. Spurensicherung: Hermann Stöhr (1898–1940) und die ökumenische Friedensbewegung* (Dying for Peace. Forensics: Hermann Stöhr (1898–1940) and the Ecumenical Peace Movement). Röhm concluded that Stöhr, like another Protestant resister from the same period, Dietrich Bonhoeffer, "died for peace and justice," presenting an "unambiguous stance of conscientious objector" to the Nazis just at the time when no opposition was permitted.

Possibly on account of Eberhard Röhm's work in raising awareness about Hermann Stöhr, there was an aftermath to his case at the very end of the twentieth century. In December 1997 the Berlin Regional Court (*Landgericht Berlin*) reconsidered Stöhr's case and overthrew his 1940 conviction. The radical Christian loner who refused to bow to the Third Reich, who stood up for the Jews, and who said no when commanded to fight contrary to his most cherished beliefs was exonerated. Since that time, a variety of monuments, streets, and squares have been named in his honor.

Discussion Questions

1. Do you think Hermann Stöhr was unrealistic in his constant refusal to bow the knee to the Nazi state? Why/why not?
2. In your opinion, should conscientious objection be permitted in a time of war? Give reasons for your answer.

Further Reading

Pateman, Colin, *Beheaded by Hitler: Cruelty of the Nazis, Civilian Executions and Judicial Terror, 1933–1945*, Stroud: Fonthill Media, 2014.

MARCH 1939

7.3 The Rape of Czechoslovakia

It might be said that the final countdown to war between Nazi Germany and the Western Allies began on March 15, 1939. The Munich Agreement of the previous September saw Czechoslovakia lose its Sudetenland regions, handed across by Britain and France to Hitler on the ground that they were peopled by German speakers who could be "returned" to the Reich (notwithstanding that the Sudetenland had never belonged to Germany).

At this time the Czechs also lost the backbone of their northern defenses, a carefully constructed state-of-the-art series of mountain fortifications and bunkers. In the same grab for territory, Czechoslovakia's other neighbors, Poland and Hungary, chipped in for their share, helping themselves to parts of the Czech state which they thought should be theirs.

The relative ease with which Adolf Hitler managed to negotiate Czechoslovakia into this position—in which its territorial integrity was compromised impossibly—emboldened him to consider further adventures. While the Munich Agreement removed the immediate threat of war and gave Britain and France a breathing space to hasten their preparation for potential conflict, Hitler's confidence—that he could get what he wanted without war—grew. He had never discussed a complete occupation of Czechoslovakia, though he (and other Nazi leaders like Hermann Göring) expressed continual racial contempt for the Czechs and Slovaks.

However, with the occupation of the Sudetenland, Hitler considered that the rest of what was termed "rump Czechoslovakia" should also be occupied. Over the winter of 1938–9 he became convinced that given their capitulation at Munich, Britain and France would not use force to resist any further German expansion.

The severely wounded Czechoslovak government now began to be undermined from within, through calls for the secession of Slovakia. Slovak People's Party leader and Catholic priest, Jozef Tiso, received aid and encouragement directly from Germany for this purpose. And then, on March 14, 1939, after a period of agitation further undermining central resolve, Slovak parliamentarians voted in favor of a complete break with Czechoslovakia, with Tiso making a public appeal to Hitler to step in and guarantee the defense of what was now essentially a German puppet state.

Under these circumstances, Czech president Emil Hácha had little idea how to deal with the situation. He requested an audience with Hitler, who summoned him to Berlin and then used the opportunity to intimidate Hácha, threatening air attack against Prague if he did not order the surrender of the Czechoslovak army. During the meeting Hácha suffered a heart attack and had to be resuscitated by medical staff. Weakly, he gave in to Hitler's terms of total capitulation. The Czech lands were henceforth to be formed into a new German Protectorate of Bohemia-Moravia. This took place early in the morning on March 15, 1939, with German troops entering what remained of Czechoslovakia.

These actions were all in flagrant violation of the Munich Agreement, but no matter; that evening Hitler made a triumphal entry into Prague and took up temporary residence at the Hradčany Castle, from which he could now look forward to becoming master of Europe. He installed Konstantin von Neurath, the former German foreign minister, as Reich Protector of Bohemia-Moravia. Slovakia became an independent state under the leadership of Jozef Tiso, who established an ethnic nationalist, fascist, authoritarian, one-party dictatorship allied to Nazi Germany.

In Prague, ethnic German citizens turned out and waved swastika flags as German troops and military equipment marched in. For the powerless Czechs, however, the German takeover was as great a tragedy as could be imagined. Many gathered in Wenceslas Square, where they repeatedly sang the national anthem until this was suppressed. A portrait of the founder of the Czech state, Tomáš Masaryk, was placed on the Tomb of the Unknown Soldier; this was later destroyed on German orders.

Hitler had not previously forecast an annexation of the rest of Czechoslovakia. He never mentioned it in *Mein Kampf*, and throughout his political career up to this point he repeatedly affirmed that he was only interested in uniting all Germans in a single Reich, which would, by definition, not include Slavs or other non-Germans. On March 15, 1939, however, Germany conquered seven million Czechs, sending other Europeans into a panic regarding just how far Hitler's appetite extended.

The Western surrender at Munich was supposed to end Hitler's territorial ambitions in Europe and guarantee the future peace. The occupation of Czechoslovakia, however, showed that Hitler's guarantees in fact guaranteed nothing. The invasion made it clear that Hitler could not be trusted to keep his promises, and from this point onward Britain and France, with enormous reluctance, started preparing for war. They now declared that if Hitler set his sights on Poland that they would have little option but to defend it. Convinced—finally—that there were no limits to Hitler's territorial ambitions, they saw no other alternative; they would have to prevent German domination of Europe. And if this had to be through force, then so be it. Appeasement was over, and the road to war lay open.

Established as a new state in 1918, Czechoslovakia managed only two decades of national existence before disappearing from the map. And in the six years that followed the outbreak of war in 1939, of up to 320,000 Czech civilians who died, at least 275,000 were Jewish victims of the Holocaust.

Discussion Questions

1. On what basis do you think Hitler could have justified the invasion of Czechoslovakia in March 1939?
2. Why could it be said that "appeasement was over" as a result of the invasion of Czechoslovakia?

Further Reading

Crowhurst, Patrick, *Hitler and Czechoslovakia in World War II: Domination and Retaliation*, London: Bloomsbury, 2020.

Mamatey, V., and R. Luza (eds.), *A History of the Czechoslovak Republic, 1918–1948*, Princeton: Princeton University Press, 1973.
Mastny, Vojtech, *The Czechs under Nazi Rule: The Failure of National Resistance, 1939–1942*, New York: Columbia University Press, 1987.

MAY 1939

7.4 The Tragedy of the *St. Louis*

On May 13, 1939, a German luxury cruise ship, the *St. Louis*, set sail from Hamburg carrying 937 German Jews who were seeking refuge abroad. The *Kristallnacht* of November 1938 was, for many Jews, the final prod they needed to realize that no accommodation could be reached with Nazism. The inhibitions to successful emigration were many. Visas were practically unattainable, and for those who managed to obtain passage on the *St. Louis* their departure seemed to be not only their best chance to leave Germany but also their opportunity to start a new life in a free country.

When the ship left Hamburg, its destination was Havana, Cuba. Adding to the optimism of those on board, it had been arranged that most of the Jewish passengers would have visas enabling them to land temporarily while they obtained permanent residence elsewhere. Upon their arrival, however, the president of Cuba, Federico Laredo Bru, refused the ship permission to dock; under such circumstances, the passengers would be unable to land. In an attempt at profiting from the refugees' plight, Bru demanded a payment of US$500,000 as an entry fee. After a great deal of hesitation, negotiation, and standoff, only twenty-two Jews were permitted to land.

What made the situation even more intolerable was the fact that some 700 of the refugees possessed US immigration quota numbers that would have seen them eligible for entry to that country at some point within the next three years. Denied entry to Cuba, and with no other alternative, the ship turned toward the Florida coast in a desperate hope that the refugees might perhaps negotiate with American authorities for an earlier entry.

The government of President Franklin D. Roosevelt, however, was adamant: no early admissions, no landing of refugees, and no docking of the *St. Louis*. Some accounts refer to vessels from the US Coast Guard having been ordered to intercept the ship to ensure that it would not enter US territorial waters. However, the Coast Guard had been sent following a request of Treasury secretary Henry Morgenthau, Jr., who, far from seeking to deny entry to the *St. Louis*, was concerned for the passengers' welfare and wanted the ship followed in case a change in government policy would allow it to land. He was practically alone, however, as the government was not about to retreat from its stated position.

American Jewish organizations, such as the Joint Distribution Committee, then worked feverishly on the refugees' behalf. Knowing that a US option was unlikely to be successful, pleas were made to secure admission to any Western Hemisphere country. Again, none of these amounted to anything.

With little other alternative available, and with food stocks and patience dwindling, the ship turned around; first, it left American waters and returned to Cuba, and then, a few days later, the captain, acting on orders from the ship's German owners, made the decision to return to Europe. The *St. Louis* docked at Antwerp, Belgium, on June 17, 1939. After further negotiations involving the Joint Distribution Committee, most of the Jews on board were accepted for temporary refuge by a few countries including Britain (228 refugees), Belgium (214), France (224), and the Netherlands (181).

Of those admitted into Britain, all but one survived the Second World War—a victim of a German air raid in 1940. After the Nazis overran Western Europe, however, many of the others did not share the fate of those who went to the UK. Nearly ninety managed to emigrate before the German invasion of Western Europe in May 1940, but some 532 *St. Louis* passengers were trapped when Germany conquered Western Europe. Of the 254 who were murdered subsequently, eighty-four had earlier been granted refuge in Belgium, eighty-four in Holland, and eighty-six in France. Their heart-breaking fate was to become victims of the Holocaust—a fate they could have escaped had their initial visas been honored and the gates of the refuge they had sought not been barred.

The story of the *St. Louis* has become symbolic of the failure of the countries of the Americas to assist the Jews of Nazi Germany in their hour of need, a symbol brought into even starker relief by the legitimacy of the documentation the refugees possessed. The definitive study of their nightmare, written by Gordon Thomas and Max Morgan Witts in 1974, was entitled *Voyage of the Damned*. Given subsequent events, it might be said that no truer statement, embedded within a book title, could have been made.

Discussion Questions

1. Why do you think the US government refused to allow the passengers of the *St. Louis* to land, or even for the ship to dock in a US port?

2. Do you agree with Gordon Thomas and Max Morgan Witts that those on the *St. Louis* experienced a "voyage of the damned?"

Further Reading

Ogilvie, Sarah A., and Scott Miller, *Refuge Denied: The St. Louis Passengers and the Holocaust*, Madison: University of Wisconsin Press, 2006.

Thomas, Gordon, and Max Morgan Witts, *Voyage of the Damned*,
    New York: Stein and Day, 1974.

AUGUST 1939

7.5 Child Euthanasia in the Third Reich

In August 1939, the Reich Committee for the Scientific Registration of Serious Hereditary and Congenitally Based Diseases was established in Germany. Its object was to remove from German society children and young people who were incurably insane or physically handicapped. The means employed to remove them was murder.

On May 23, 1939, a request came from a German family for the mercy killing of their handicapped child, Gerhard Kretschmar, born earlier that year on February 29. His parents, who lived in Saxony, petitioned Adolf Hitler asking for Gerhard to be "put to sleep" as he was born blind, mentally retarded, lacked one leg, and part of an arm. Hitler approved the request, and carbon monoxide gas was selected as the means of the baby boy's death.

This then served as the pretext for the initiation of a much larger "euthanasia" program. The program's original intention was to kill disabled infants and young children, and Dr. Karl Brandt, a medical doctor and SS officer who served as Adolf Hitler's personal physician, was placed in charge of the program's planning and execution along with Philipp Bouhler, head of the Reich Chancellery. They received a rare explicit authorization from Hitler, allowing them to grant "mercy deaths" to "incurable" patients. Before the program relating to children commenced, however, Hitler authorized its expansion to euthanize adults with disabilities as well.

Accordingly, Brandt and Bouhler organized what became known as *Aktion T-4*, from the address of the administrative offices in Berlin running the program, Tiergartenstrasse 4. Although starting as a program centering on children in August 1939, Hitler's preference to euthanize "life unworthy of life"—men, women, and children deemed mentally and physically disabled—was initiated to cover all categories in October 1939.

In time, after that first child's death, others followed quickly, leading ultimately to the murder of up to 5,000 children in so-called special children's wards. *Aktion T-4* covered two separate euthanasia programs: one dated back to spring 1939, dealing with infants and small children up to three who had physical deformities; and a second included mentally disabled older children and adults.

The child euthanasia program usually murdered its victims through lethal overdoses of medication. Adult patients, on the other hand, were removed from their home institutions and transferred to one of six designated killing centers throughout Germany, where they were murdered in specially designed gas chambers.

Planning the program meant that a departmental infrastructure and bureaucratic guidelines had to be established, and this was initiated in a directive dated August 18, 1939. This specified the groups to be included in the program and was to apply not only to those children who had already been identified as incurably ill or handicapped but also to newborn babies suspected of a range of "congenital disorders" at birth. Brandt would later develop another program of enforced abortions for women classed as "genetically defective," which likewise included those who were physically or mentally disabled.

On October 6, 1939, Hitler ordered Brandt to "relieve through death" those mentally ill individuals who could not "take any conscious part in life." He backdated his signature to September 1, 1939, to highlight the order's connection to the war; his logic was that the life of every dead soldier should be balanced by taking the life of a person "unworthy of life."

It now became the duty of doctors, nurses, and midwives to report to the appropriate health authorities if the case of a child or new-born baby came across their desk with any of the designated conditions, so that further action (that is, their murder) could be undertaken. The registration of potential victims became a crucial determinant of whether a child was to be euthanized, in accordance with a stringent set of conditions.

Three Nazi medical bureaucrats received the relevant registration forms, with comments made by the first two as to the nature of the case to assist the third in making his final determination. Only the reporting form was used in making the decision of life or death; the doctors did not examine the child in person or review previous records. On rare occasions a child might not be condemned if the doctors concluded that he or she could grow up and be a productive member of society. The forms also included a compulsory clause in which those doing the reporting were required to indicate the child's race. This was so that Jewish children could be easily identified, and in these cases death was mandatory.

As precedents were generated, the range of those to be included in the child euthanasia scheme was broadened. What began as an assault against children with psychological and physical handicaps was expanded such that those deemed to be "unfit for society"—those, for example, with behavioral problems—were also listed on registration forms, and many were subsequently assessed negatively and gassed in euthanasia centers. Some children slated for compulsory euthanasia, on the other hand, were reprieved temporarily so that they could be "studied" as objects of medical or scientific research prior to being sent to their death.

The killing centers set up for children as specialized pediatric clinics were a precedent for much larger killing centers catering to physically and mentally disabled adults. Once sent to these clinics, children received lethal injections or were sometimes simply starved to death. Children, therefore—whether Jewish or not—were the first and most vulnerable of Hitler's victims, as they remained throughout the war years and the Holocaust.

Discussion Questions

1. Could it be argued that the euthanasia campaign was part of the Holocaust? How?

2. The Nazis considered that child euthanasia was a moral and valuable act for German society. How do you think this could be explained?

Further Reading

Aly, Götz, Peter Chroust, and Christian Pross, *Cleansing the Fatherland: Nazi Medicine and Racial Hygiene*, Baltimore: Johns Hopkins University Press, 1994.

Freidlander, Henry, *The Origins of Nazi Genocide: From Euthanasia to the Final Solution*, Durham: University of North Carolina Press, 1995.

Weindling, Paul, *Victims and Survivors of Nazi Human Experiments: Science and Suffering in the Holocaust*, London: Bloomsbury, 2015.

SEPTEMBER 1939 (1)

7.6 War Is Declared

On September 1, 1939, Nazi Germany invaded Poland. Two days later, because of that invasion, Britain and France declared war on Germany. Although the conflict that would become the Second World War was, at that stage, still localized to those countries (as well as the countries of the British and French Empires), it carried an awful potential to spiral into something much worse. Germany was already allied to Fascist Italy, and a few days before the invasion, it had signed an alliance with the Soviet Union. For several years prior to this, smaller countries all over Europe had been coalescing into alliances and groupings for their mutual defense in case of the unthinkable. What did this mean for the Jews of Europe?

It is important to realize that the outbreak of war did not coincide with the start of the Final Solution—though it must also be said that severe Nazi anti-Jewish measures in Poland were not long in coming. Indeed, within a month the first ghettos were established, with Germany taking advantage of Poland's conquest to begin persecuting the Jews.

This, however, was a piecemeal persecution. At the beginning of the war the Nazis did not yet quite know what to do with the millions of Jews they had just seized. After all, the previous six years had not seen a complete eradication of Jews from Germany, Austria, and Czechoslovakia, and Jewish numbers in this Old Reich had been substantially fewer than they were in the newly occupied territories. The question of how to deal with the much larger Polish Jewish population was therefore one that made the Nazis pause, though only for a short while. The upshot of the interim measures adopted was the creation of a system of ghettos throughout Nazi-occupied Poland.

Consequently, the key question about the Holocaust should perhaps not be "is the Holocaust unique?" but, rather, turning the issue upside down, "what *is* unique about the Holocaust as a case of genocide?"—in other words, to assume its uniqueness and then move straight away to identifying the feature or features that defined its specific character once war had broken out.

The main tool the Nazis employed to achieve their murderous aims could be found in the wartime death camps, and it is these institutions, thoroughly unprecedented in purpose and design, that make up the starkest feature of the Holocaust. Nothing, either before or since, approximates the Nazi death camps in design, intention, or operation. The outbreak of war in September 1939 did not see the immediate establishment of these camps, though the invasion of Poland generated the circumstances that would allow for them later.

Nowhere has any other malevolent regime introduced establishments like the Nazi death camps of Lublin-Majdanek, Treblinka, Bełżec, Sobibór, Chełmno, or Auschwitz-Birkenau. They were, and remain, thoroughly unmatched in human history. As such, they became the most lucid and unequivocal statement German National Socialism made about itself, demonstrating beyond doubt that it was an antihuman ideology in which respect for life counted for nothing. Put together, all these aspects of what the death camps represented added up to a new dimension of genocide.

This, of course, could not have been foreseen, when war broke out in September 1939. For all the persecution that had thus far taken place in the Old Reich, the Holocaust, as we have come to understand it, had not yet begun. The "ground zero" of the Final Solution—the extermination camps—was still several years away.

Discussion Questions

1. What was the relationship between the outbreak of war and the Final Solution that emerged over the succeeding two years?
2. Was there anything distinctive about Poland being the first location of murderous anti-Jewish measures in the Second World War? If so, what was it?

Further Reading

Carley, Michael Jabara, *1939: The Alliance that Never Was and the Coming of World War II*, Chicago: Ivan R. Dee, 1999.

Overy, Richard, *1939: Countdown to War*, New York: Viking, 2010.
Williamson, David G., *Poland Betrayed: The Nazi-Soviet Invasions of 1939*,
    London: Pen and Sword, 2009.

SEPTEMBER 1939 (2)

7.7 The Prescient Words of Chaim A. Kaplan

On September 1, 1939, Nazi Germany invaded Poland. What did this mean for Poland's Jews? Chaim Aron Kaplan, a Jewish educator and diarist, chronicled the day-to-day events of the Warsaw ghetto, making a record of life there under German occupation. His observations on September 1, 1939, were among the most prescient thoughts offered on what the outbreak of war might suggest.

Kaplan was born in 1880 in Gorodishche (Horodyszcze), a village in Belorussia (Belarus) in the Russian Empire. He was educated at the famous Mir yeshiva and later studied at the Vilna (Vilnius) teachers' college. In 1902 he moved to Warsaw, where he established an elementary Hebrew school; he would remain there as principal for the next forty years. In 1921 he visited the United States, and, in 1936, Palestine, with the idea of joining his two children there. As he saw little economic future for himself there, however, he returned to Warsaw.

Kaplan devoted his efforts to teaching and writing. He began keeping a diary around 1933, and in September 1939, with the outbreak of war, he decided to detail Jewish life in Warsaw and thereby preserve a record for posterity. This was to become Kaplan's *Scroll of Agony*. His first entry, on September 1, 1939, was chillingly prophetic: "This war will indeed bring destruction upon human civilization. … I doubt that we will live through this carnage. The bombs filled with lethal gas will poison every living being, or we will starve because there will be no means of livelihood."

After Warsaw's surrender on September 27, 1939, Kaplan wrote: "The Nazis' objective was to eliminate the Jews physically through a slow choking process." By the time the ghetto was established formally on October 12, 1940, roughly 375,000 Jews (nearly a third of Warsaw's overall population), along with many refugees, were squeezed into an area that took up only 2.4 percent of the city's surface area. To make matters worse, Jews were only allotted one-tenth of the required caloric intake and were subjected to forced labor, disease, and slaughter. Kaplan commented on the frequent murder of Jews and the constant treatment they experienced, explaining that: "The Aryans are put to death after a short period of arrest; the Jews are killed without even a pretence of arrest." He further detailed how the Nazis carried out many of their violent acts: "The murderers burst into a home in the middle of the night and put an end to a life."

Scroll of Agony would become one of the most powerful and inspiring testimonies from the Holocaust period. Kaplan recorded his diary in small notebooks and focused primarily on daily experiences. He attempted to remain objective despite the dire conditions, seeing his mission as preserving a record for posterity, focusing strictly on facts and situations as they appeared. The diary recorded the events and experiences Kaplan witnessed himself or were told to him by members of the ghetto community. He set down his thoughts as well as conversations with friends and with those he met in the streets, tracking down firsthand information to provide immediacy and authenticity.

Keeping a diary or any sort of written testimony created many risks. Kaplan, however, felt that recording his experiences was a responsibility. He expressed continual hope that the diary would be saved, realizing its significance for future generations. As the Nazis intensified their murderous activities he worked faster, often writing several times a day to include every detail of the horror surrounding him.

This sense of duty was emphasized in his entry of January 16, 1940: "Anyone who keeps such a record endangers his life, but this does not frighten me. I sense within me the magnitude of this hour, and my responsibility toward it, and I have an inner obligation that I am not free to relinquish. ... My record will serve as a source material for the future generation." He wrote his diary so that others would someday be able to understand the Holocaust and never forget the Jews' experiences during it. In 1942 conditions in the Warsaw ghetto worsened, as Kaplan wrote: "The Jewish section of Warsaw had become a city of slaughter."

Indeed, Kaplan was less concerned about his own future than he was about the future of the diary. He knew he had to get it out of the ghetto if there was any chance that his observations, so carefully chronicled, would survive. Thus, in late 1942 he gave his diary to a Jewish friend named Rubinsztejn, who did forced labor each day outside the ghetto. Rubinsztejn smuggled the notebooks out and delivered them to a Pole, Władyslaw Wojcek, who lived in the small village of Liw, near Warsaw. In the early 1960s, Wojcek moved to the United States, where he sold the notebooks. Eventually, they were edited, translated, and published, and the diary has since appeared in editions in English, German, French, Danish, and Japanese.

Kaplan's final entry was made on August 4, 1942: "If the hunters do not stop, and if I am caught, I am afraid my work will be in vain. I am constantly bothered by the thought: If my life ends, what will become of my diary?" The diary did survive, but Kaplan and his wife did not. They were deported to Treblinka, where they were murdered in December 1942.

Discussion Questions

1. Do you think anything worthwhile could come from Kaplan's diary writing? What might that be?
2. Why do you think Kaplan valued the diary's survival even more than his own?

Further Reading

Kaplan, Chaim A., *Scroll of Agony: The Warsaw Diary of Chaim A. Kaplan* (ed. Abraham I. Katsh), New York: Macmillan, 1965.

OCTOBER 1939

7.8 *Aktion T-4* Commences

The secret "Euthanasia Program" of the Nazis, codenamed *Aktion T-4* (an abbreviation of the address of the Reich Chancellery office at Tiergartenstrasse-4), involved the murder of Germans considered mentally or physically ill, or disabled. These were considered as *"lebenundwertes Leben"* ("life unworthy of life") and deemed detrimental to the physical and spiritual well-being of the Nazi state and the concept of *Volksgemeinschaft* ("people's community")—not to mention the depletion of economic resources.

Clinical discussions of eugenics and racial hygiene were prevalent in Europe and the United States at the turn of the twentieth century. The notion of eugenics included improving the race by not allowing disabled or mentally ill people to reproduce. Canada, Switzerland, the United States, and Denmark had passed laws enabling forced sterilization. Germany's Law for the Prevention of Offspring with Hereditary Diseases, passed in 1933, set a precedent for the T-4 program, requiring compulsory sterilization for Germans in this category. Over 300,000 people were sterilized under the law. Hitler's "euthanasia" program was a natural extension of Nazi racial hygiene theories and the product of increasingly radical policies.

Started in October 1939 and headed by Reich Chancellery chief Philipp Bouhler and Dr. Karl Brandt, the program's earlier design saw the euthanization of infants and young children with disabilities. Originally based on a couple's request to have their severely malformed baby euthanized, Hitler authorized the program's expansion to euthanize adults. After 1939 the program extended to habitual criminals and other "asocials." The Reich Chancellery established several organizations such as the Reich Committee for the Scientific Registration of Severe Hereditary Ailments and the Reich Cooperative for State Hospitals and Nursing Homes, which provided an outwardly benign façade. Murder by gas chamber originated in this program, with the task of turning on the gas tap assigned to a physician and designated as a medical act.

Questionnaires circulated by various front organizations to public and private clinics and institutions gathered information and functioned as the means of locating victims. For children, killing centers were set up as specialized pediatric clinics catering to physically and mentally disabled adolescents. Once there, children received lethal injections, or were simply starved to death. The Nazi assault on mentally and physically disabled adults began with those already institutionalized. Victims were transferred to one of the six killing centers—Brandenburg, Bernburg, Hadamar, Sonnenstein, Grafeneck, and Hartheim Castle—where they were herded into fake showers and gassed with carbon monoxide. Upon their death, their bodies were immediately cremated, and medical certificates sent to their families, fictitiously indicating a heart attack as the cause of death and the need for cremation due to the threat of disease.

Although T-4 staff worked meticulously to conceal their actions, the rash of mysterious deaths among the mentally disabled rapidly aroused suspicion from affected families. Outrage and protest over these extralegal killings—voiced most famously by Catholic Bishop Clemens August Graf von Galen—gathered tremendous momentum, and in August 1941, Hitler halted the euthanasia program. Unofficially, however, the killings continued until the end of the Third Reich in a decentralized and even more clandestine fashion, with local physicians administering lethal injections.

Much attention was redirected toward Jews, Roma, Poles, and others in conquered territory. Just as the sterilization law was a precursor to euthanasia, *Aktion T-4* was a forerunner of the Final Solution, marking the logical conclusion of Nazi race thinking. The killing centers, gas chambers, and crematoria that became hallmarks of the Holocaust were all developments of Hitler's euthanasia program.

Persecution of the Jews had become a fixed Nazi policy very soon after the outbreak of the Second World War. Because of the urgent need for laborers in Germany, it was decided not to kill Jews who were able to work but, as an alternative, to sterilize them—another aspect of T-4. Forced sterilization would be carried out using massive doses of radiation aimed at prisoners' reproductive organs. In some cases, male prisoners were physically castrated. As many as 4,000 prisoners per day were sterilized between late 1943 and early 1945.

Estimates of Germans who had already been institutionalized and were subsequently murdered by doctors and nurses via lethal injections and gassings after having been already sterilized exceeded 275,000. Of this, at least 5,000 were children.

In December 1946, an American military tribunal at Nuremberg, the Doctors Trial, prosecuted twenty-three doctors and administrators for their role in war crimes and crimes against humanity. These crimes included the systematic killing of those deemed "unworthy of life," including people with mental disabilities and those with physical handicaps. After 140 days of proceedings, including the testimony of 85 witnesses and the submission of 1,500 documents, in August 1947 the court pronounced 16 of the defendants guilty. Seven were sentenced to death.

Discussion Questions

1. Other than killing, what other means were employed to reduce the number of those who came under the jurisdiction of the T-4 campaign?

2. In view of those targeted by the T-4 campaign, do you think the doctors involved were kind or cruel in their actions?

Further Reading

Aly, Götz, Peter Chroust, and Christian Pross, *Cleansing the Fatherland: Nazi Medicine and Racial Hygiene*, Baltimore: Johns Hopkins University Press, 1994.
Freidlander, Henry, *The Origins of Nazi Genocide: From Euthanasia to the Final Solution*, Durham: University of North Carolina Press, 1995.
Peukert, Detlev, *Inside Nazi Germany: Conformity, Opposition and Racism in Everyday Life*, New Haven: Yale University Press, 1989.
Weindling, Paul, *Victims and Survivors of Nazi Human Experiments: Science and Suffering in the Holocaust*, London: Bloomsbury, 2015.

DECEMBER 1939

7.9 Friedrich Übelhör Establishes the Łódź Ghetto

Friedrich Übelhör was a German Nazi Party governor who ordered the construction of a ghetto in the Polish city of Łódź on December 10, 1939. He was born on September 25, 1893, in Bavaria. His father was a professor at the University of Würzburg, the city where Übelhör attended high school until 1913. When war broke out in 1914, he joined an artillery regiment and served for four years, fought on the Western Front, was assigned to the Army High Command, and received various military decorations. He ended the war as a first lieutenant.

After the war, Übelhör served in the *Freikorps* militia of General Paul von Lettow-Vorbeck and took part in suppressing a communist uprising in Hamburg on July 19, 1919. He studied law and political science in Freiburg and Würzburg for five semesters but dropped out and did not complete his degree. He joined the Nazi Party in 1922.

In 1924 Übelhör moved to Naumburg, and on April 4, 1925, married Asta Popperoth, daughter of the former Higher Regional Court vice-president, Ludwig Popperoth. By June 1925 he had become politically active, reorganizing the regional Party structure in Naumburg. In 1931 he became Nazi Party County Leader in Naumburg and was elected to the Reichstag on March 5, 1933.

Poland was invaded in September 1939, and the city of Łódź, second only to Warsaw in population and in the size of its Jewish community, was occupied by the Germans on September 8, 1939. On October 26, 1939, Übelhör was appointed as provisional governor of the Kalisch district, with the rank of *SS-Obersturmbannführer* (lieutenant colonel). On November 9, 1939, Łódź fell under the authority of Arthur Greiser, who sought the rapid and total Germanization of the areas under his command.

It took little time for the Jews of Łódź to be subjected to rigorous legal orders and bans. On November 14, 1939, Übelhör announced additional restrictive measures: Jews were to wear a distinguishing Jewish yellow patch on their clothing, and a curfew was introduced for Jews between the hours of 5:00 p.m. and 8:00 a.m. Übelhör's order to mark the Jews of Łódź was the first of its kind enacted in the Third Reich, having no previous basis in Nazi legislation. The head of the Reich Security Main Office, Reinhard Heydrich, would later promulgate a decree on October 1, 1941, relating to the identification of Jews, but this did not apply to children under the age of six. Übelhör's earlier decree certainly applied to infants; violations were punished by death, thus going well beyond that of his superior.

The Jewish community had their businesses taken away. They were imprisoned in their own apartments, and, prevented from supporting themselves, were left without any means to survive. Many Jews were shot, and many others froze to death. According to Nazi estimates, more than 71,000 Jews either left or were deported from Łódź during the first few months of the occupation.

On December 10, 1939, Übelhör produced a report on the feasibility of establishing an enclosed area for Jews. Estimating that there were some 320,000 Jews in the greater Łódź region, he reported that he would be able to collect all of these into a ghetto. His report set out the boundaries of where the ghetto should be and noted that preparation and execution of the plan would be carried out largely by German officers from different policing agencies. The ghetto would be enclosed in barbed wire and its borders guarded. A Jewish administration would be set up. Food and fuel for the ghetto was to be paid for by an exchange of materials to obtain from the Jews "all their hoarded and hidden items of value." Übelhör thereupon ordered the construction of the ghetto and was instrumental in the destruction of the Jewish population.

The Łódź ghetto was formally established in February 1940, sealed on May 1, 1940, and surrounded by a wooden fence, barbed wire, and armed guards. Bridges were built over city streets that ran through the ghetto, allowing the Jews to move to and from various sections of the ghetto without leaving it. A tram ran through the ghetto, but for non-Jews only, and no stops were made inside. The Łódź ghetto became the longest lasting of all the Nazi-imposed ghettos in Poland, operating for more than four years.

Conditions for the Jews imprisoned inside were terrible. Overcrowding, disease (tuberculosis, typhus, and dysentery, among others), atrocious sanitation, and the absence of electricity and running water were only some of the things that threatened survival. Hunger, leading to death by starvation, as well as contributing to the outbreak of some of the diseases already noted, was perhaps the ghetto's greatest burden. Unlike in some other ghettos, there was virtually no successful smuggling of food into Łódź.

Friedrich Übelhör was dismissed from his post as Łódź governor in December 1942 after being accused of embezzlement. The charges were ultimately unproven, but the suspicion damaged his reputation and halted his advancement in the SS. In the latter days of the war he disappeared and remained unaccounted for until he was declared legally dead by the West German government in 1950. On January 19, 1945, when the Soviets liberated the ghetto, fewer than 10,000 of the 230,000 Jews of Łódź had survived.

Discussion Questions

1. Friedrich Übelhör came from a well-off and educated background: how do you think his descent into becoming a pioneering antisemitic Nazi can be explained?

2. What were some of the ways in which the Jews of Łódź suffered in the ghetto? Why did this happen?

Further Reading

Adelson, Alan, and Robert Lapides, *Łódź Ghetto: A Community History Told in Diaries, Journals, and Documents*, New York: Viking, 1989.
Horwitz, Gordon J., *Ghettostadt: Łódź and the Making of a Nazi City*, Cambridge, MA: Belknap Press of Harvard University Press, 2008.

Part 8

1940

JANUARY 1940

8.1 A Tale of Two Januaries

In 1939, with the outbreak of war, Germany's Inspectorate of Concentration Camps was authorized to examine the possibility of setting up new camps. One of the first of these, located in southwestern Poland near the confluence of the Vistula and Soła Rivers, was to be built just outside the town of Oświęcim. In German the name was Auschwitz. This was initially to be a camp for Polish prisoners of war (POWs).

Auschwitz would ultimately serve as an epicenter of the Holocaust, with more Jews murdered there than in any other location. Since the victims came from every part of Europe, and because Auschwitz operated longer than any other extermination camp, it has come to symbolize the horror of the Holocaust overall.

It was on January 25, 1940, that the SS decided to construct a camp near Oświęcim. Then, on February 21, 1940, the Inspector of Concentration Camps, Richard Glücks, reported to Heinrich Himmler that a group of "former Polish artillery barracks" had been found that were suitable for further development. The town of Auschwitz seemed the ideal location, though it had its objectionable side. Surrounded by open swampy moorland, it remained muddy for most of the year; it was unhealthy and malaria infested, and in winter it turned bitterly cold. Severe winds swept down from the north, unimpeded by any natural obstacles. It was flat, cold, wet, muddy, cheerless, and colorless. There seemed little to recommend the area surrounding the little Silesian town.

Despite this, on May 4, 1940, the first commandant, Rudolf Franz Höss, began his task of constructing the new camp. Employing prisoners from other camps as slave labor, the compound was soon built and received its initial batch of permanent inmates on July 14, 1940.

Understanding the history of Auschwitz is a complex challenge. Initially it was established as a camp for Polish soldiers and political prisoners.

Later, Soviet POWs were included, while Jews were added increasingly from mid-1941 onward. Further, there was not a single Auschwitz, but rather three camps—Auschwitz I, Auschwitz II (Birkenau), and Auschwitz III (Monowitz)—along with approximately fifty satellite camps located over a wide geographical region.

Then, in the winter of 1940–1, the German industrial conglomerate I.G. Farben chose Auschwitz as the site for the construction of a new plant. The availability of a railroad junction and raw material, along with the chance to exploit slave labor, added to its allure. An arrangement was made between I.G. Farben and the SS, whereby the latter would provide the slave labor and I.G. Farben would pay for using the workers. At the same time, SS chief Heinrich Himmler ordered the camp system expanded to accommodate over 100,000 additional inmates. Auschwitz would eventually become a vast complex covering fifteen square miles, in which the SS capitalized on the use of slave labor and made a fortune as a result.

Auschwitz, together with five other camps located by the Germans in Poland (Bełżec, Chełmno, Majdanek, Sobibór, and Treblinka) altered the nature and course of concentration camp development. These were the *Vernichtungslager*, the death (or extermination) camps. Because of their existence, the image of the Nazi concentration camps was irrevocably transformed, such that all camps are now viewed as elaborate and gigantic factories created for the purpose of destroying human lives.

The extermination camps were institutions designed to murder millions of people, specifically Jews, methodically and efficiently, in specially designed gas chambers. At Auschwitz, the Nazis employed crystallized hydrogen cyanide, which, on contact with air, oxidized to become hydrocyanic (or prussic) acid gas, manufactured under the trade name Zyklon B.

January 1940 therefore had a lot to answer for. But as the war progressed, and Soviet armies advanced toward Germany throughout the latter half of 1944, the position of Auschwitz seemed uncertain. In September 1944 Heinrich Himmler ordered Rudolf Höss to oversee the camp's liquidation, followed by a second order on November 26, 1944, when delay threatened and the Soviets drew nearer.

After considerable administrative difficulties, the complete evacuation of the complex was ordered for January 17, 1945. The next day, some 22,000 men and women left the camp in a series of horrendous death marches, and the day after that, a further 3,500 were evacuated. They were about all that was left of a camp complex that at one time could boast a population of up to 200,000. The earliest date of free contact with Soviet forces was January 22, 1945. When the camp was formally occupied two days later, there were only 2,819 survivors left at Auschwitz.

The prisoners had been evacuated in the face of Soviet progress; the Russians were so close while the prisoners were marching away that the sounds of battle could be clearly distinguished. The survivors suffered terribly during the forced marches that took them toward the west, and countless numbers perished.

The name Auschwitz evokes many things. What is often overlooked, however, are the bookend dates—January 1940 and January 1945—that separate what happened in the middle. Simultaneously the world's largest murder site and cemetery, the phenomenon of Auschwitz had to begin somewhere. Fortunately, after a herculean effort, it also ended.

Discussion Questions

1. What was attractive for the Nazis about the location of Auschwitz?
2. Describe the relationship between industry and Auschwitz, explaining why Auschwitz was more than a killing center.

Further Reading

Dwork, Debórah, and Robert Jan van Pelt, *Auschwitz: 1270 to the Present*, New York: Norton, 1996.

Gutman, Yisrael, and Michael Berenbaum (eds.), *Anatomy of the Auschwitz Death Camp*, Bloomington: Indiana University Press, 1994.

Van Pelt, Robert Jan, *The Case for Auschwitz: Evidence from the Irving Trial*, Bloomington: Indiana University Press, 2002.

APRIL 1940

8.2 The Shanghai Ghetto

Shanghai's International Settlement was unique in that its policing and passport controls were implemented by an autonomous board governed by non-Chinese. In this environment, all that was needed for admission to enter was an approved departure visa for residence leading from European ports. As a result, Jewish refugees faced few restrictions upon their arrival in Shanghai.

There were two established Jewish communities there already: a Sephardi community dating to the nineteenth century and a more recent Russian-Jewish émigré community that had been trickling in over the previous three decades or so.

In the aftermath of the Battle of Shanghai between the armies of China and Japan (August–November 1937), the city was occupied by the Japanese army. Large sections fell under direct Japanese control. These neighborhoods included Hongkew, part of the International Settlement.

While Japanese forces occupied much of Shanghai, they did not immediately impose restrictions on Jews residing there. The area of Hongkew, which covered about one square mile, saw an increasing influx of Jews fleeing Nazi persecution.

Most of the Jews who came from the Third Reich arrived after November 1938, and from then on, the pace of Jewish immigration increased dramatically. By 1939, the number of Jews in the International Settlement was about 17,000, with small concentrations of Jews in other parts of the city. Once war broke out in September 1939, the inflow of German and Austrian Jews was increased by Jews from Poland and, eventually, other parts of Nazi-occupied Europe. Between late 1940 and early 1941, some 2,100 Jews from Lithuania also found refuge. The total number of Jews in Shanghai now increased to about 24,000, with a majority living in the International Settlement.

The refugees from Germany and Austria, most of whom came as family groups, were impoverished due to the Nazi practice of extracting exorbitant sums before allowing Jews out. They often faced a difficult time upon arrival. Overcrowding encouraged poverty of a kind many of the refugees had never experienced. This situation only got worse when it became apparent that there were too many people in specialist occupations not conducive to a pioneering lifestyle: doctors, musicians, artists, writers, and "intellectuals" in significant numbers were not what the Jewish communities of Shanghai needed at that time. Further, the resources of these communities were limited, and it became increasingly difficult to sustain those who were not viewed as productive members of society. That harsh reality led to resentments on both sides of the Jewish community—which was far from homogenous to begin with.

Over time, impoverished new arrivals found themselves forced into the destitute Hongkew District because they could not afford to live anywhere else in the International Settlement. With the onset of war in Europe from September 1939 onward, many became dependent on welfare assistance: fortunately, this was forthcoming from organizations such as the American Jewish Joint Distribution Committee. The local Jewish community tried to assist as best it could: aid was provided by two refugee organizations, the International Committee for European Immigrants and the Committee for the Assistance of European Jewish Refugees. But these initiatives, by themselves, were never enough to meet the refugees' needs.

Despite the difficulties they faced, the refugees not only flourished but transformed the city. Viennese-style cafes opened alongside Central European delicatessens and bakeries. A Jewish theatre scene emerged and even thrived for a while until the availability of new scripts dried up and actors were forced to make a living beyond the stage. New synagogues were established, while membership increased in existing ones, such as the Ohel Moshe synagogue (which had served as a religious center for the Russian-Jewish community since 1907). Schools were established; newspapers were published.

In addition to the external factors that presented difficulties for the new arrivals, internal problems militated against a smooth transition or a trouble-free existence. Within the Jewish communities there were divisions between Sephardim and Ashkenazim, religious and secular, Zionists and Bundists, long-term residents and recent immigrants, and German-speakers and Yiddish-speakers (and, increasingly, those who spoke some form of English as a common lingua franca). This was truly a situation of survival, coexistence, and competing identities, to say nothing of the multiethnic dimensions of living in a Chinese city.

Added to this complexity was the fact that Shanghai was under foreign military occupation. The Japanese presence was ubiquitous and always carried the potential for brutality, particularly for the Chinese. With the Japanese attack on Pearl Harbor and British territories on December 7–8, 1941, Jewish refugees in Shanghai suffered additional shortages of food, clothing, and medicine, as the closure of shipping into the city brought an end to the inflow of external funds and goods. Further, after the Pearl Harbor attack hardly any additional Jews were able to make their way to Shanghai.

Although Japan and Germany were allies, the Japanese did not share the same antipathy toward Jews as the Nazis. Most Japanese occupation officials in Shanghai viewed them simply as stateless refugees. Yet as the war progressed, the Germans called for the Japanese to institute draconian measures against Shanghai's Jewish population. While for the most part Japanese officials did not comply, in late 1942 the Japanese rendered Jewish refugees "stateless," noting that Nazi Germany had stripped German and Austrian Jews of their nationality. This led to a requirement that most Shanghai Jews would henceforth be required to live in an area called the Restricted Sector for Stateless Refugees, a place of concentration which would informally be known as the Shanghai Ghetto. The plan was implemented in February 1943 and anticipated that all Jews who had arrived in Shanghai after 1937 would reside there.

Nearly 20,000 were forced into the ghetto. The area was barricaded, and the overcrowding generated significant hardship. To a large degree, the Japanese then left the Jews to administer their own affairs, and the Japanese military treatment of Shanghai Jews was relatively undemanding. Although conditions in the ghetto were not nearly as bad as those in Europe, the Jewish refugees nevertheless found themselves chronically short of food and clothing and forced to reside in primitive living quarters. The Japanese did not erect a wall or fence around the area but did enforce a curfew and required that anyone leaving or entering have a written pass. Native Chinese continued to live among the Jews in the ghetto, which lessened their isolation. The Shanghai ghetto saw the continued maintenance of Jewish education, culture, and religious observances, while the ghetto had its own newspapers, theatres, schools, sports teams, synagogues, and even cabarets. And, as before, each group (German, Austrian, Russian, and Polish) had their own institutions based on language and culture.

In 1944, US Air Force bombers began operations against Shanghai in the final push to defeat Japan and drive its troops out of China. On July 17, 1944, an air raid on Shanghai resulted in the deaths of forty Jewish ghetto residents; it is believed that as many as several hundred Chinese were also killed. This was the only time during the war that Jewish refugees in Shanghai were killed. American troops entered Shanghai and liberated it in September 1945.

Discussion Questions

1. What were some of the obstacles faced by Jewish refugees living in Shanghai?
2. Despite these obstacles, in what ways did the Jewish refugees recreate a European lifestyle in Shanghai?

Further Reading

Bacon, Ursula, *Shanghai Diary: A Young Girl's Journey from Hitler's Hate to War-Torn China*, Milwaukie, OR: Milestone Books, 2004.
Eber, Irene, *Wartime Shanghai and the Jewish Refugees from Central Europe: Survival, Co-existence, and Identity in a Multi-ethnic City*, Berlin: De Gruyter, 2012.
Heppner, Ernest G., *Shanghai Refuge: A Memoir of the World War II Jewish Ghetto*, Lincoln: University of Nebraska Press, 1993.
Kranzler, David, *Japanese, Nazis and Jews: The Jewish Refugee Community in Shanghai, 1938–1945*, New York: Yeshiva University Press, 1976.

MAY 1940

8.3 Hitler Invades France

The German army invaded France on May 10, 1940. On the morning of May 15, French prime minister Paul Reynaud wired his newly installed counterpart in London, Winston Churchill, reporting that "last night we lost the battle. The route to Paris is open." By the end of the month the bulk of the French armies had been sent north to confront the Germans, but most were encircled by the panzer armies of the Wehrmacht. As the French struggled to hold lines that were hopelessly confused and crumbling everywhere, worse was to come on June 10, when Italy declared war and invaded southern France. Although this was to be the only theatre in which the French armies managed some degree of success, the Italians capitalized on the French collapse at the hands of the Germans by getting a seat at the peace table and subsequently occupying the French Riviera.

Immediately afterward, between June 15 and 25, the British Expeditionary Force was evacuated from the beaches of Dunkirk, along with tens of thousands of French soldiers. Churchill, in a last-ditch effort to retain some semblance of unity between the British and French allies, proposed a stillborn case for a federal union of the two countries. On June 16, Reynaud resigned as prime minister and was replaced by Marshal Philippe Pétain, who informed the people of France that the fighting must stop and that he had asked the Germans for an armistice. On June 22, 1940, in the same railway carriage in the forest of Compiègne in which the Armistice was signed in 1918 signaling Germany's defeat in the Great War, France surrendered.

The collapse had enormous consequences for Jewish communities throughout France. In 1939 the Jewish population was estimated at somewhere between 300,000 and 330,000. A year later, it had increased by another 10 percent. Overall, perhaps 90,000 were French born. With the outbreak of war on September 3, 1939, Jews flocked to the colors, and by January 1940 Jews in the French army numbered some 60,000, of whom 16,000 were foreign-born. The defeat was just as disastrous for the Jews of France as it was for everyone else, but for the Jews it had the added significance of being to an avowedly antisemitic enemy. The Nazi conquest would initiate a period of unprecedented persecution for Jews living in France.

When the armistice went into effect on July 25, France agreed to the occupation by Germany of three-fifths of the country north and west of a line running from Geneva to Tours and extending south to the Spanish border; in a clause that would hit Jewish refugees especially hard, all Jews previously granted political asylum in France had to surrender to the German authorities. All occupation costs had to be carried by the French themselves. A small French army of 100,000 men for local policing was to be permitted, and the French navy was to be disarmed.

The two-fifths of the country in the southeast not occupied by the Germans was permitted to remain as a quasi-independent French entity under Pétain, with its capital in the resort town of Vichy. This so-called free zone took as its title *L'État français* (French State), to distance itself from the hated *République française* (French Republic), which was henceforth dissolved.

Pétain's goal was to completely rejuvenate the country, based on the concepts of *Travail, Famille et Patrie* (Work, Family, and Fatherland), core ideas that would inject new life into a France that had been drained of its élan vital. The new regime instituted what became known as the National Revolution, diametrically opposite to the perceived ruin caused by the Third Republic. It was characterized by such features as anti-parliamentarism, a rejection of the notion of separation of powers, xenophobia, antisemitism, the promotion of traditional values, a rejection of modernity, and, above all, a personality cult focusing on Pétain himself. Imbued with such ideals, it was clear that there could be no place for a Jewish presence in the new France, and, even less, for foreign Jews.

Anti-Jewish regulations were issued by the Germans in the occupied zone on September 27, 1940. They imposed restrictions: Jews who moved from the occupied zone to Vichy France were forbidden reentry; Jewish businesses had to be identified by clearly marked signs in French and German; all Jews were to be compulsorily registered; and from this point on they were to carry an identity card with the word *Juif* (Jew) stamped on it.

Then, on October 3, 1940, the French *Statut des Juifs* (Jewish Statute) was introduced at Vichy and set the stage for what was to come. It defined Jews as those who had three Jewish grandparents or two Jewish grandparents if their spouse was also Jewish. It also drastically cut back Jewish involvement in French society: Jews would be forbidden from serving in the military as officers or noncommissioned officers, in senior positions in government administration, or in any role with an influence over public opinion. One day later, on October 4, a second law granted local prefects the authority to intern "foreigners of the Jewish race."

The catastrophic Fall of France in the summer of 1940 saw the start of anti-Jewish measures that would culminate in the deportation of more than 75,000 Jews to death camps, where some 72,500 were murdered. The vast majority of these were identified by French civil servants, rounded up by French police, and "processed" before their deportation by French authorities following the *Statut des Juifs*. Although this is now a well-known story, it is necessary to recount it once more. It is a record which will forever be a stain on French history and must be remembered.

Discussion Questions

1. What did the invasion of France in May 1940 signify for the future of Jews living there?

2. In the aftermath of the German invasion and occupation, what role did French authorities play in subsequent events?

Further Reading

Bloch, Marc, *Strange Defeat: A Statement of Evidence Written in 1940*, New York: Norton, 1946.

Gildea, Robert, *Marianne in Chains: Everyday Life in the French Heartland under the German Occupation*, New York: Metropolitan Books, 2002.

Kedward, Roderick, *Occupied France: Collaboration and Resistance, 1940–1944*, Oxford: Blackwell, 1985.

Laub, Thomas J., *After the Fall: German Policy in Occupied France, 1940–1944*, Oxford: Oxford University Press, 2010.

JULY 1940

8.4 The Madagascar Plan

The Madagascar Plan was an outlandish notion which in July 1940 was nevertheless taken seriously by Germany's Nazi regime as a possible way to rid Europe of its Jews. The idea was to expel the Jews to the large French colonial island of Madagascar, off the coast of Africa. As a plan, it resonates today as another steppingstone on the way to the Final Solution.

Expelling the Jews from Europe to Madagascar was not a new idea. It was proposed in France and elsewhere as early as 1885 and continued to be discussed during the early twentieth century, though the island was hardly a wholesome location in which to send millions of Jews. Situated in the Indian Ocean about 250 miles east of South Africa, it is subject to a six-month rainy season, oppressive heat, and cyclones.

The issue had previously been considered briefly by the Nazi leadership. Indeed, the head of the SD (Security Service), Reinhard Heydrich, ordered and received a report from his Jewish affairs expert Adolf Eichmann as early as December 1938. The idea of sending Europe's Jews to Madagascar, however, only became a serious policy proposal after Franz Rademacher, the head of the Jewish Department of the German Foreign Office, wrote a memorandum on July 3, 1940, suggesting this as a solution to the "Jewish Question."

An avowed antisemite, Rademacher sought to elevate the role of the Foreign Office in Jewish affairs, particularly in finding a way to remove Germany's Jews. It was against this background that he suggested that all Jews falling into the German sphere—which, given the conquest of Poland a few months earlier, had increased considerably—be expelled and deported to Madagascar. Throughout the spring and summer of 1940, Rademacher worked hard to develop his plan, along the way alienating himself from Eichmann, who was attempting to take control of the project himself. The idea spread so quickly within the Nazi leadership that it was not long before Hitler made mention of it, and Heydrich successfully argued that it fell within his remit.

The Madagascar Plan envisioned that the island be transferred from France to Germany as a mandated territory. It would become the site of a colony of Jews under the administration of a German Police governor, in which the Jews would create their own administration, including mayors, police, and so on. They would also be responsible for the economic welfare of the island. Tapping into long-standing antisemitic views regarding Jewish wealth, the plan called for the Jews' "former European financial assets" to be transferred to a European bank that would be specially established for the Madagascar project. This way, the Jews would pay Germany for the value of the land, funded by the sale of their property in Europe.

In addition, given that Madagascar would be a mandated territory, Jews deported there would not be permitted to acquire (or retain) German citizenship while at the same time losing the citizenship of the European countries from which they had been deported. Their new status would be as "residents of the Mandate of Madagascar," as "our German sense of responsibility towards the world forbids us to make the gift of a sovereign state" to the Jews.

Another aspect of Rademacher's proposal would see that a colony in Madagascar would prevent the possible establishment of a Jewish state in Palestine, thereby negating "the opportunity for them to exploit for their own purposes the symbolic importance which Jerusalem has for the Christian and Mohammedan parts of the world."

Finally, the conduct of the Jews in Madagascar would act "as a pledge for the future good behaviour of the members of their race in America." The plan considered that it would also be good propaganda, highlighting "the generosity shown by Germany in permitting cultural, economic, administrative and legal self-administration to the Jews."

Adolf Eichmann eventually took over the project, drafting his own plan for Madagascar on August 15, 1940, in which he proposed that one million Jews would be deported to Madagascar annually over the next four years.

The feasibility of the Madagascar Plan rested on the outcome of two military events. The first had already been achieved when France surrendered to Germany on June 22, enabling Madagascar to be transferred to German control. The second was the Battle of Britain between July and October 1940, in which the Germans held that victory over the Royal Air Force would be the first step toward the invasion and surrender of Britain. The outcome of the battle was relevant to the Madagascar Plan, as a German victory would remove Britain's Royal Navy as a factor inhibiting the transport of Jews to Madagascar and would provide the ships needed to carry out such a massive operation.

Germany's defeat in the Battle of Britain brought an abrupt end to the Madagascar Plan. That it had been considered seriously by Nazi leaders, including Hitler, Heydrich, and Eichmann, provides an insight into Germany's thinking in 1940 regarding Europe's Jews.

Although it was clear to all that the Madagascar Plan—had it gone forward—would have resulted in the death of hundreds of thousands of Jews trying to survive in a police state in a difficult climate, it was also clear that the decision to exterminate every Jewish man, woman, and child in Europe had not, in July 1940, yet been made. Nonetheless, a specific mindset was in train that would see the start of its realization within the next twelve months.

Discussion Questions

1. Do you think the Madagascar Plan was a feasible option in the summer of 1940? Why/why not?

2. Was there a relationship between the Madagascar Plan and the Final
   Solution that evolved one year later? If so, what was it?

Further Reading

Browning, Christopher R., *The Origins of the Final Solution: The Evolution
   of Nazi Jewish Policy, September 1939-March 1942*, Lincoln: University of
   Nebraska Press, 2004.
Jennings, Eric, "Writing Madagascar Back into the Madagascar Plan," *Holocaust
   and Genocide Studies*, 21:2 (2007), pp. 187–217.
Longerich, Peter, *Holocaust: The Nazi Persecution and Murder of the Jews*,
   Oxford: Oxford University Press, 2010.

AUGUST 1940 (1)

8.5 Romania's Anguish

The Holocaust in Romania was an absolute calamity for the country's Jews.
On July 4, 1940, King Carol II appointed a pro-Nazi, Ion Gigurtu, to head
the government and declared an amnesty for Romania's fascist Iron Guard
movement. On August 8, 1940, Girgurtu introduced harsh antisemitic
legislation that framed what the legal status of Jews would be from then on.
Signed by the king, it was drafted by Gigurtu and Ion V. Gruia, minister of
justice and a law professor at the University of Bucharest.

This law excluded Jews from many of the benefits of citizenship granted
to them by the 1923 constitution. It legally and politically distinguished
between "Romanians by blood" (*romani de sange*) and "Romanian
citizens," thereby emphasizing the significance of "blood" and "race" to
the nation and state. Accordingly, it stated, "The concept of the nation
can now be construed less as a legal or political community and more as
an organic, cultural community based on the law of blood, from which an
entire hierarchy of political rights emerges; for the law of blood contains all
cultural, spiritual, and ethical opportunities."

Further, the law stated that "the defence of Romanian blood constitutes
the moral guarantee for the acknowledgement of supreme political
rights." These "laws of blood" referred to ethical, spiritual, and cultural
characteristics, rather than anything physical. The law would now regulate
the legal status of Jews in Romania regarding their participation in religious,
political, and economic life.

The law of August 8, 1940, placed Jews into three categories. The first
included Jews who had entered Romania after December 30, 1918; they
were now subject to major restrictions in all aspects of society. The second
category comprised Jews who had been naturalized before December 30,

1918, who had served in the army in either the 1877–8 war of independence or the First World War, were war orphans, or were descendants of the exempted categories. Those in these categories, however, were not considered to be part of the national community and were subject to restrictions on owning property in rural areas and qualifying for public service jobs.

Most Jews in Romania fell into the third category. These were Jews who had become citizens after 1919. Jews in the first and the third categories were prohibited from taking public service jobs, buying property, pursuing military careers, becoming lawyers or notaries public, being appointed members of a corporate board, and owning businesses in rural areas, liquor stores, movie theatres, publishing houses, and Romanian media outlets.

Moreover, all Jews were prohibited from taking Romanian names, while the Jewish religion was not considered to be part of Romania's religious and spiritual community. Like the Nuremberg Laws in Nazi Germany, Jews were now defined through a merger of the dual criteria of religion and ancestry: a person was a Jew if he or she practiced Judaism or was born to parents of the Jewish faith, even if that person had converted to Christianity or was an atheist. One could be considered Christian only if his or her parents had converted prior to the birth of the child.

On September 5, 1940, soon after the introduction of these laws, Ion Gigurtu resigned as prime minister, and although persecution in Romania took place quickly because of the August laws, violence against Jews increased dramatically once his replacement, Marshal Ion Antonescu and the Iron Guard movement, took control of the country. Army and police personnel began assaulting and killing Jews; they also vandalized, robbed, and seized Jewish-owned businesses. The antisemitic legislation set in place in August began to take immediate effect.

By January 2, 1941, a full-scale pogrom took place in Bucharest. On this most horrific occasion, 200 of Bucharest's most distinguished men and women were taken to the abattoir on the edge of the city, stripped, forced to kneel on all fours, and put through all stages of animal slaughter until the beheaded bodies, spurting blood, were hung on iron hooks on the wall.

Antonescu's position was clearly outlined as soon as he assumed office: "The program I will submit to your collective judgment is rooted entirely in the tenets of integral nationalism." This term, "integral nationalism," meant intolerance of ethnic pluralism and the elimination of "foreigners," especially Jews, from all areas of Romanian society. This, in turn, was the bedrock upon which he rested his policy of "Romanianization." Enforcement of this legislation, it was held, would end the "domination" of the "foreign plague" of Jews in Romanian economic life.

While all this was being played out, other developments were impacting Romania. Throughout the year 1940 the country was forced to cede large portions of its territory to the Soviet Union, Hungary, and Bulgaria. On September 6, 1940, the day after the Gigurtu government's resignation, King Carol was forced to abdicate. He was replaced by Michael, his nineteen-year-old son, who would remain on the throne as a figurehead until 1944.

The territorial losses were partly to blame for this upheaval, but an increasingly fascist-oriented Romania could not for long remain outside the orbit of Germany and Italy. All that remained was for Antonescu to set his country on a formal footing alongside the two larger totalitarian states; with this in mind, Romania formally joined the Axis alliance on November 23, 1940.

The year 1940 was replete with opportunities for states to descend into the quagmire of massive human rights violations, antisemitism, and genocide. Romania was one country among many unable to resist the totalitarian temptation.

Discussion Questions

1. Outline briefly the steps leading toward the role Romania would play in the Holocaust.

2. Why do you think Romania adopted its antisemitic legislation, and what did this mean for the country's Jewish population?

Further Reading

Ceausescu, Ilie, Florin Constantiniu, and Mihail E. Ionescu, *A Turning Point in World War II: August 23, 1944 in Romania*, New York: Columbia University Press, 1985.
Ioanid, Radu, *Holocaust in Romania: The Destruction of Jews and Gypsies under the Antonescu Regime, 1940–1944*, Chicago: Ivan R. Dee, 2000.

AUGUST 1940 (2)

8.6 *Armée Juive* and the Jewish Resistance in France

Abraham Polonski was one of the founders of the French Jewish resistance movement. Born in Russia in 1913, he moved to France before the Second World War and worked as an electrical engineer in Toulouse. In August 1940, after the French surrender on June 22, he and his wife Eugénie, together with Dovid Knut and his wife Ariane, and Lucien Lublin, came together to build a secret underground organization called *La Main Forte* ("The Strong Hand"). Its twofold aim was to establish a movement that would defeat the Nazis and then move on to take control of Palestine and establish a Jewish state.

Polonski (whose resistance code names were "Pol" and "Maurice Ferrer") and the others were committed Zionists. On January 10, 1942 they (and others with an equal commitment) established an underground Jewish militia, the *Armée Juive* (Jewish army, or AJ). The first members of the AJ were recruited from a Torah study group led by Rabbi Paul Roitman. The organization received funds from a refugee group based in Switzerland, the Zionist Organization of France.

Armée Juive activities were directed essentially by Polonski and Lublin and undertaken by the most committed members of the various Zionist youth movements. Through to the summer of 1942, Polonski and Lublin recruited militants from Toulouse, Montpellier, Nice, Grenoble, Lyon, and Limoges. They, in turn, fought in their own cities as well as Paris, attacking informers and Gestapo collaborators.

The oath new members of the *Armée Juive* had to take was straightforward: placing their right hand on the blue and white Zionist flag and the Bible, they would recite:

> *I swear fidelity to the Jewish Army*
> *And obedience to its leaders.*
> *May my people live again,*
> *May Eretz-Israel be reborn.*
> *Liberty or death.*

In May 1942 a new resistance organization, the *Mouvement de Jeunesse Sioniste* (Zionist Youth Movement, or MJS), was created by Simon Levitte and Dika Jefroykin. Together with another member, Leonardo Zupraner, they brought into the *Armée Juive* several new resistance members. Recruitment standards were severe, with secrecy and obedience mandatory. The primary purpose of the organization was to resist when success seemed likely, as well as through rescuing Jews by the provision of false papers, assisting with border crossings, and the like.

During the winter of 1943–4 the escape network of the *Armée Juive* helped around 300 Jews flee successfully to Spain, from where most moved on to Palestine. The *Armée Juive* was assisted substantially by outside bodies such as the Jewish Agency for Palestine and the American Jewish Joint Distribution Committee, with tens of millions of francs being disbursed to help procure arms and border crossings.

The *Armée Juive* later evolved into the *Organisation Juive de Combat* (Jewish Combat Organization, or OJC). At its height, it was believed to have more than 2,000 fighters and other operatives. On May 21, 1944, Polonski entered discussions with the National Liberation Committee (*Comité français de Libération nationale*), which led to the OJC being recognized as an official movement within the French Resistance, with its operational district centered in Toulouse.

In June 1944 Polonski narrowly escaped capture—and possible death—at the hands of a local collaborationist militia group in Toulouse. Although he escaped through the roof of the building where he was located, the assault prevented any activities from the *Armée Juive* that day. Polonski now had to go on the run and moved to Lyon where he maintained operations until August 1944. When the Germans surrendered Paris to the Allies on August 25, 1944, Polonski and several of his fighters were present to help achieve the city's liberation.

After the war, Abraham Polonski went on to become a commander of the *Haganah* in Palestine, with responsibility for assisting illegal Jewish immigrants to make their way from France and North Africa to the Middle East. After the creation of Israel in 1948, he retired to a quieter life.

Overall, the *Armée Juive* carried out almost 2,000 actions against the occupying Germans and their collaborationist allies. Many Jews fought in other units as well, often in leading positions. While Jews comprised just 1 percent of the population, they constituted almost 15 percent of the French Resistance movement.

Discussion Questions

1. Were any features of the *Armée Juive* different from other resistance movements you might have studied? What, if anything, marked out the AJ as distinctive?

2. Which of the following adjectives do you think sums up Abraham Polonsky: heroic, brave, committed, reckless—or none of these? Give reasons for your answer.

Further Reading

Henry, Patrick, *Jewish Resistance against the Nazis*, Washington, DC: Catholic University of America Press, 2004.
Latour, Anny, *The Jewish Resistance in France, 1940–1944*, New York: Holocaust Library, 1970.
Lazare, Lucien, *Rescue as Resistance: How Jewish Organization Fought the Holocaust in France*, New York: Columbia University Press, 1996.
Poznanski, Renée, *Jews in France during World War II*, Hanover, NH: University Press of New England, 2001.

SEPTEMBER 1940

8.7 The Tortured Tale of *Jud Süss*

Jud Süss (*Jew Suss*) is a novel written in Germany in 1925 by Jewish author Lion Feuchtwanger, whose writings had been suppressed during the First World War because of what was held to be their revolutionary content. One of the earliest critics of Hitler and the Nazis, he was forced into exile in London in 1934. In *Jud Süss*, he chronicled the story of a powerful ghetto businessman in eighteenth-century Württemberg, Joseph Oppenheimer, who believes himself to be a Jew. His ruthless business practices result in the betrayal of an innocent girl; for this he is arrested and sentenced to death, the victim of anti-Jewish laws. Rather than turn against the Jews of the ghetto by declaring his non-Jewish identity, which he discovers through a set of letters given to him by his mother revealing that his father was in fact a Christian nobleman, he dies on the gallows with dignity and honor.

Feuchtwanger intended the book to be an attack against antisemitism, an allegory on German society for his own day. It was picked up by the Nazis, however, and transformed into a viciously antisemitic movie directed by Veit Harlan and released on September 24, 1940. The plot was twisted to show Oppenheimer as a real Jew and portrayed according to Nazi stereotypes: greasy hair, hooked nose, unscrupulous, bearded, cowardly, and a rapist. At his arrest and execution, he is seen as screaming and unmanly; by contrast his executioners appear to be upright, solid citizens. After Oppenheimer's execution, the rest of the Jews of the city are driven into exile. As a piece of propaganda cinema, the movie had a powerful effect on its audiences, helping to prepare the German public for further anti-Jewish measures. Many viewed it as though it was a documentary and were driven to acts of violence against Jews in the street after having seen it. After its official release in Germany, Heinrich Himmler, the head of the SS, ordered all members of the various official bodies under his command to see the movie; this extended to local police and concentration camp guards. Its effectiveness as a propaganda tool was thus not limited to the viewing public, as it was employed to achieve specific dehumanizing goals against the Jewish racial enemy and to whip up antisemitic violence. Veit Harlan was later tried for crimes against humanity by the Allies at Nuremberg, but his case was dismissed due to a lack of direct evidence implicating him in the destruction of the Jews.

The actor who played the title role, Ferdinand Marian, was an Austrian theatre and film actor. Born in Vienna as Ferdinand Haschkowetz on August 14, 1902, he came from a musical family; his father was a bass player and his mother an opera singer. He gravitated toward the theatre from an early age, working through his father as an extra at the majestic *Stadttheater Graz*, before developing a career in acting. Seeking to make his own way, he moved to Germany and by 1938 began performing as part of the company with the *Deutsches Theater* in Berlin. Here, his most celebrated performance was as Iago in Shakespeare's *Othello*, a characterization that received a positive review from Nazi propaganda minister Joseph Goebbels.

From 1940 onward he was engaged repeatedly for Nazi propaganda films, certainly because of his drawing power but not least because of his ability to play unsavory characters of the kind useful for the purposes of wartime and antisemitic indoctrination. The most important of these was his portrayal of Joseph Süss Oppenheimer in the title role of *Jud Süss*. Goebbels took a special interest in seeing to it that Marian was cast by Harlan in this role, basing himself on what he had seen of Harlan as Iago years earlier.

Initially Marian was reluctant to take the assignment, but Goebbels wrote in his diary: "Talked with Marian about the *Jud Süss* material. He hesitates to play the Jew. But I will make him play the part." Goebbels is reported to have been a frequent visitor to the set and to have even written, or rewritten, parts of the script.

Whereas Feuchtwanger's novel drew a sympathetic picture of a tragic figure, Harlan and Goebbels created an image of Süss, and the Jews around him, as materialistic, immoral, cunning, and untrustworthy. Indeed, Süss, who shaved off his beard, wore court clothes, and worked on his accent to ensure that he would be able to insinuate himself into gentile society, was considered even more detestable owing to this duplicity. The other "Jewish" actors "looked" alien; Süss, appearing to be German, conformed completely to the Nazi image of the treacherous Jew worming his way into "Aryan" society to destroy it from within. The Nazis were thus able to utilize the Süss story as a parable about the alleged Jewish threat to Germany and why it was good and legitimate to draw out the Jews and destroy their influence wherever possible.

The film became a runaway success not only in Germany but across Europe. Seen by tens of millions of movie goers, it was a huge hit at its premiere on September 8, 1940, at the Venice Film Festival. During the war years it was a favorite among Nazi and Fascist youth groups throughout Europe and was even shown to concentration camp guards and German soldiers at the front. Marian's performance as the evil Jew Süss led to the film becoming arguably one of the most successful antisemitic propaganda movies ever made.

Part of the tragedy of Ferdinand Marian's life is that he was not a Nazi and, in fact, had a daughter from his first marriage to Jewish pianist, Irene Saager. Moreover, his second wife's former husband, Julius Gellner, was also Jewish and was hidden by Marian and his wife in the family home during the war.

On August 7, 1946, he was killed in a car crash near the village of Dürneck, Bavaria, aged forty-six. It was rumored at the time that Ferdinand Marian committed suicide, unable to come to terms with the roles he had taken during the war and suffering from previously unresolved feelings of guilt. Another argument is that he was intoxicated, having celebrated the news that he had been granted denazification papers from the American occupying authorities that would have enabled him to resume acting.

Discussion Questions

1. The case against director Veit Harlan was brought against him for crimes against humanity but dismissed for lack of evidence. Reading

the article and considering the impact of the movie, do you think this was a valid judgment? Why/why not?

2. Much of the success of the film was due to the acting skills of Ferdinand Marian. Do you think he bears any responsibility for the antisemitic actions that followed after audiences viewed the film?

Further Reading

Noack, Frank, *Veit Harlan: The Life and Work of a Nazi Filmmaker*, Lexington: University Press of Kentucky, 2016.
Tegel, Susan, *Jew Suss. Life, Legend, Fiction, Film*, London: Bloomsbury, 2011.

NOVEMBER 1940

8.8 *The Eternal Jew* and Its Creator

The Eternal Jew was one of the most notorious anti-Jewish propaganda movies ever made. On November 28, 1940, the 65-minute-long movie premiered in Berlin. Its director was Fritz Hippler, a German filmmaker who ran the film department in the Propaganda Ministry of Joseph Goebbels. He was born on August 17, 1909, and brought up in Berlin. In 1927 he joined the Nazi Party, became a law student at universities in Heidelberg and Berlin, and by 1934 had earned his PhD.

In 1932 he became a Nazi Party district speaker and was promptly expelled from the University of Berlin for inciting violence. On April 19, 1933, however, the Nazi education minister, Bernhard Rust, overthrew all existing actions against students associated with the Nazi Party, enabling Hippler's return. He then became the district and high school group leader for Berlin-Brandenburg in the National Socialist German Students' League. On May 22, 1933, he led his fellow students in a march from the student house to Opera Square, with a collection of banned books that were then publicly burned.

In 1936 Hippler became an assistant to the artist, photographer, and film director Hans Weidemann. In this capacity he worked on the production of newsreels and learned the techniques behind documentary filmmaking. In January 1939 he took over Weidemann's position, meaning that he now worked directly for Goebbels; by August 1939 he had been promoted to head the film department. Among his tasks he regulated which foreign films would be allowed on German screens and what parts of them would be cut. He also produced movies of his own. In 1940 he directed *Der Feldzug in Poland* (*The Campaign in Poland*), a propaganda film demonstrating the superiority of German arms in the first phase of the Second World War from September 1939 onward.

His best-known creative work was undoubtedly *Der Ewige Jude* (*The Eternal Jew*). The film consisted of documentary footage combined with materials filmed shortly after the Nazi occupation of Poland. Hippler shot footage in the ghettos at Łódź, Warsaw, Kraków, and Lublin, the only such footage shot specifically for the film. The rest consisted of stills and archival material from elsewhere. The film itself covered four essential tropes: "degenerate" Jewish life as seen in the Polish ghettos; the nature of Jewish political, cultural, and social values; Jewish religious ceremonies, worship, and ritual slaughter; and Adolf Hitler as the savior of Germany.

While the film's intention was to prepare the German population for the coming Holocaust (even though the Nazis had not themselves yet decided on mass annihilation as the means to destroy Europe's Jews), the movie did not have the desired impact on the German public owing to the fact that *Jud Süss* had already appeared to rapturous acclaim employing top box-office stars. By contrast, *The Eternal Jew* was a documentary based on limited original footage, still images, and archive film clips.

Unlike *Jud Süss*, therefore, which was a great commercial success, *Der Ewige Jude* was something of a failure at the box office. As a propaganda film it would be shown repeatedly for training purposes to troops fighting on the Eastern Front as well as members of the SS, while several foreign-language voiceovers were made, and the film was exported to countries occupied by Germany. Hippler, for his part, was honored by Adolf Hitler for making the movie. In October 1942 he was given responsibility for the control, supervision, and direction of all German movies, making him second only to Goebbels in the Propaganda Ministry.

Such a career trajectory, though impressive, generated resentment in some quarters—no less than from Goebbels himself. He had long kept a watching brief on Hippler, who he saw as sometimes impertinent, often immature, disorganized, and too fond of alcohol. In June 1943 Goebbels finally dismissed him. Hippler was stripped of his SS rank and a trumped-up accusation was brought against him of having denied that he had a Jewish great-grandmother. He was sent to a replacement battalion and underwent mountain infantry training. Released from active duty, he was then given the task of shooting newsreel footage as a cameraman until February 1945. At the end of the war, he was taken by the British as a prisoner of war.

In 1946 he was tried for directing *Der Ewige Jude* and sentenced to two years in prison. Staging a comeback after his release, he collaborated on documentary movies under another name. In a 1981 memoir he claimed that Goebbels was the real creator of *Der Ewige Jude*, having directed large parts of it himself and giving Hippler the credit. Later, he stated that he regretted being listed as the director of the movie because it unfairly resulted in his unjust treatment after the war. In his opinion he had nothing to do with killing Jews and only shot some footage for a film which Goebbels himself then put together. He claimed further that at the time he had little knowledge of the Nazis' murderous policies toward the Jews and was not aware of the Holocaust as it was taking place. If he was given the chance, he said, he would "annul" everything about the film, which had caused him such personal difficulties in his subsequent life. Fritz Hippler lived in Berchtesgaden, Bavaria, until his death on May 22, 2002, aged ninety-two.

Discussion Questions

1. *The Eternal Jew* was a failure at the box office. Why, then, do you think it achieved such notoriety within the Third Reich?
2. After the war, Fritz Hippler denied responsibility for the film's antisemitic content, yet he was the director. How can you account for this disconnect?

Further Reading

Felix Moeller, *The Film Minister: Goebbels and the Cinema in the Third Reich*, Stuttgart: Edition Axel Menges, 2000.
Rentschler, Eric, *The Ministry of Illusion: Nazi Cinema and Its Afterlife*, Cambridge, MA: Harvard University Press, 1996.
Terry Charman, "Fritz Hippler's *The Eternal Jew*," in Toby Haggith and Joanna Newman (eds.), *Holocaust and the Moving Image: Representations in Film and Television Since 1933*, pp. 85–92, London: Wallflower Press, 2005.

DECEMBER 1940

8.9 The *Oneg Shabbat* Archive

In December 1940, in the Warsaw ghetto, a Polish-Jewish historian named Emanuel Ringelblum began collecting the first items of what he called the *Oneg Shabbat* (or "Sabbath Joy") Archive.

Ringelblum was born in Buchach (then in the Austro-Hungarian Empire) on November 21, 1900. He moved to Nowy Sącz in 1914, and under the influence of two friends, Raphael Mahler and Artur Eisenbach, joined *Poale Zion* ("Workers of Zion"), a Jewish workers' movement established throughout Russia at the start of the twentieth century. After the party split in 1920, he moved further to the left and played a major role in the organization's Yiddish cultural work.

In 1927 Ringelblum earned a doctorate in history from the University of Warsaw and developed a reputation as an expert on early Polish-Jewish history. After completing his thesis, he taught history at *Yehudiya*, a private secondary school for girls, before working for the American Jewish Joint Distribution Committee (JDC).

In November 1938 he was sent by the JDC to the Polish border town of Zbaszyn, where 6,000 Jewish refugees from Germany were huddled with nowhere else to go. They had been expelled from Germany but were forbidden from entering Poland. Ringelblum worked in coordinating relief efforts for these people—a duty that left him with much on which to reflect concerning the nature of good, evil, and helping those in need. He later wrote a book, *Notes on the Refugees in Zbąszyń*, which gave a detailed perspective on the situation there.

After Poland was invaded by the Nazis in 1939, Ringelblum and his family were forced into the Warsaw ghetto. It took him little time to realize what he needed to do; he would collect information in secret regarding every facet of ghetto life to serve as a comprehensive and permanent record of what the Nazis were doing to the Jews of Warsaw. He recruited Jewish writers, scientists, and other citizens to work with him in collecting diaries and documents; he organized studies to be undertaken; and he sent young people out onto the streets to gather posters and announcements pasted around the ghetto.

This all came together under the aegis of the *Oneg Shabbat* Archive, with the first items collected in December 1940. The archive would eventually come to comprise a vast amount of data relating to towns, villages, the ghetto, the resistance movement, other ghettos, the Chełmno and Treblinka death camps, and the effects of hunger and disease.

While engaged in these activities, Ringelblum remained active in the day-to-day life of the ghetto. Working on behalf of Jewish Social Aid, he organized welfare programs and soup kitchens and tried to find other ways in which to help combat deprivation. At the same time, he also cofounded, with Menahem Linder, the *Yidishe Kultur Organizatsye*, a society to maintain and advance Yiddish culture in the ghetto.

Gathering materials for *Oneg Shabbat* continued at least until late February 1943, but after then other events overtook the project. The Jewish resistance movement had already begun to fight back against the Nazis the previous month, and the liquidation of the ghetto seemed imminent. To continue his work, Ringelblum saw that he would have to escape, but before doing so he placed the archive into three large milk cans and several metal boxes, which were then buried around various parts of the ghetto.

In March 1943 he and his family relocated to Warsaw's Aryan side. After the ghetto uprising began on April 19 he returned: captured, he was deported to the Trawniki labor camp, but in August 1943 he managed to escape after having been helped by a Polish man and a Jewish woman. He hid in an underground bunker with his wife Yehudis, son Uri, and thirty-four others. Here, he worked around the clock writing a history of Polish-Jewish relations during the war, together with essays on key members of the Jewish intelligentsia. These writings, now known as *Notes from the Warsaw Ghetto*, survived and were published after the war.

On March 7, 1944, the Germans discovered the hideout and seized all those inside. A few days later Ringelblum, his family, and the other Jews with whom he had been hiding were taken into the ruined ghetto and murdered. Overall, only three members of the *Oneg Shabbat* movement survived the war: Hersh Wasser and his wife Bluma and Rachel Auerbach.

After the war, people searched for Ringelblum's archive in the ruins of the ghetto, with mixed results. In September 1946 ten metal boxes were found, and in December 1950 two of the milk cans were located. Despite repeated searches, the rest of the archive, including the third milk can, was never found.

The Jewish Historical Institute is a research establishment in Warsaw dealing primarily with the history of the Jews in Poland. Created in 1947, it was renamed in 2009 in honor of Emanuel Ringelblum. The centerpiece of the collection, the Warsaw Ghetto Archive, is the legacy of Ringelblum's work with *Oneg Shabbat*, containing about 6,000 documents composed of nearly 30,000 individual sheets. When combined with Ringelblum's own writings, the archive constitutes the most comprehensive repository in existence dealing with the daily experience of the Jews in Warsaw during the Holocaust.

Discussion Questions

1. What use(s) do you think researchers can make of the *Oneg Shabbat* Archive today?

2. Why do you think Emanuel Ringelblum decided to begin collecting the items that grew into the *Oneg Shabbat* Archive?

Further Reading

Gutman, Israel (ed.), *Emanuel Ringelblum, the Man and the Historian*, Jerusalem: Yad Vashem Publications, 2010.
Kassow, Samuel D., *Who Will Write Our History? Emanuel Ringelblum, the Warsaw Ghetto, and the Oyneg Shabes Archive*, Bloomington: Indiana University Press, 2007.

Part 9

1941

JANUARY 1941

9.1 A Brazilian Rescuer

On January 1, 1941, a passenger ship, the *SS Alsina*, set sail from Marseille, France, with hundreds of Jews on board. Almost all were carrying forged visas, the work of a remarkable Brazilian diplomat, Luis Martins de Souza Dantas.

Born in Rio de Janeiro in 1876, Souza Dantas was a career diplomat with a long record of service in France prior to the outbreak of war in 1939. After the Fall of France in 1940 and the establishment of a collaborationist government at Vichy, he was asked to stay on as Brazilian ambassador, even though by then he had formally retired.

Noting the perilous position of the Jews under Vichy rule, he requested permission from the Brazilian Foreign Ministry to issue migration visas to a small number of French citizens, without specifying that they were Jews. This was a breach of existing rules, as Brazil had a closed-door policy regarding Jewish immigration. Despite this, he continued granting diplomatic visas to Jews without official approval while at the same time masking their Jewish identity.

His actions in granting these illegal visas would, as it turned out, save hundreds of Jews from certain deportation at the hands of the Vichy authorities. Moreover, in many cases he predated the visas to ensure that any subsequent ban on their use would be negated.

He applied himself to the task of rescue through subterfuge, granting diplomatic visas to those holding passports without going through the usual laborious application process. He would write on the documents in French rather than Portuguese, to ease their exit at the ports of departure, at the same time following all other official procedures to ensure that the documents would be acceptable. He also assisted with the provision of visas for Jews seeking entry through other embassies, interceding personally to claim Brazilian "citizenship" for those who were refugees.

When the *SS Alsina* departed from Marseille in January 1941 carrying more than 500 refugees, hopes were high that this would not be a repeat of the debacle that took place two years earlier involving the *SS St. Louis*. However, as the ship approached Dakar, Senegal, in French West Africa, it was learned that the Vichy government ruling the territory was going to forbid it from continuing.

Desperate, those on board were at once confused and anxious, fearful that they would be returned to an uncertain future in Europe. With their fate in the balance, the *Alsina* remained anchored for four months in tropical heat, with the Jews on board confined to the cargo hold. Britain's Royal Navy then intervened, and in June 1941 the ship was allowed to proceed to Casablanca, Morocco, where the passengers were interned. Four months later, they were released and put aboard the *SS Cabo de Bueno Esperanza*, bound for Brazil.

By this stage the visas granted by Souza Dantas had expired, but he arranged for them to be renewed. Although the Jews managed to move on to Rio de Janeiro, their visas were rejected once the ship reached port. Fortunately, all managed either to remain in Brazil or to secure a temporary stay while they searched for further refuge.

The actions of Souza Dantas flew in the face of Brazil's dictator Getúlio Dornelles Vargas, whose regime tolerated antisemitism. It was not long, therefore, before he became the object of official inquiries. He knew his actions were illegal, but nevertheless he continued to work on behalf of Jews whenever—and for as long as—he was able. Recalled for disciplinary hearings, he defended himself on the ground that he was motivated by "Christian feelings of mercy" regarding Europe's persecuted Jews.

When the investigation into his behavior was opened by Brazil's Ministry of Foreign Affairs, the charge was one of granting irregular visas. He was found guilty of contravening Brazil's immigration policy but escaped sanction on a technicality: since he was theoretically retired and only working for the government as a special favor during the period in which he forged the visas, he was not bound to the same standards as a fulltime permanent representative. It was a minor point, but it saved him from severe punishment.

After the war Souza Dantas returned to Paris, where he lived out his days in obscurity. His career as a diplomat was long over, all previous honors being withdrawn after his recall. The memory of his actions on behalf of those being persecuted during the Holocaust was forgotten for several decades, recalled only by those whose lives he had saved. He died in Paris on April 14, 1954.

Overall, Luis Martins de Souza Dantas saved the lives of upward of 800 people, including 425 confirmed Jews. In the eyes of some, he became the Brazilian equivalent of the German rescuer Oskar Schindler, though in entirely different circumstances. The most important feature linking the two was the duty each felt toward the saving of human lives, and for this, on

December 10, 2003, Luis Martins de Souza Dantas was recognized by Yad Vashem as one of the Righteous among the Nations.

Discussion Questions

1. In what ways did the experience of those on board the *SS Alsina* differ from that of the *SS St. Louis*, two years earlier? How can you account for this?

2. Should Sousa Dantas have been disciplined for his actions in disobeying official Brazilian policy? Why/why not?

Further Reading

Paldiel, Mordecai, *Diplomat Heroes of the Holocaust*, New York: Yeshiva University/KTAV, 2007.

FEBRUARY 1941

9.2 The February Strike in Amsterdam

It is almost inconceivable to imagine that during the Third Reich's rampage through Western Europe a general strike against the Nazis could have been called in one of the occupied countries. It practically defies belief, furthermore, that this strike should have been called on behalf of Jews and in opposition to the Holocaust. Yet this is precisely what took place in February 1941, throughout Amsterdam in the Netherlands.

Willem Kraan, a road worker with the Amsterdam city council, was a member of the Communist Party of the Netherlands (CPN). Along with his friend Piet Nak, a worker in the sanitation department and a fellow CPN member, Kraan made the decision on Sunday, February 23, 1941, to initiate a protest strike over the German treatment of the Dutch Jews.

In early 1941 the persecution of Amsterdam's Jews had begun to intensify. Already there had been anti-occupation protests, and on February 19, 1941, a group led by Ernst Cahn and Alfred Kohn, two German Jewish émigrés, raised their voice against the Nazis. Arrested for fomenting dissent, Cahn became the first resister executed by the Nazis in the Netherlands, and the February strike that followed was a direct outcome of Cahn and Kohn's demonstration. On Saturday, February 22 the Germans raided Amsterdam's Jewish Quarter, and more than 400 Jews were arrested. A second raid took place the next day. Kraan witnessed at firsthand the Sunday arrests, returning home with tears in his eyes.

Without hesitation he spoke to his friend Piet Nak, and together they decided that strike action was needed to paralyze the city so the arrests and deportations would stop. They began approaching workers on the street and at the docks, pleading with them to go out on strike on behalf of the Jews. They also sought the cooperation of the public transport workers, who, it was anticipated, would strangle the city and stop all movement.

On Monday evening Nak spoke before some 300 to 500 workers at the *Noordermarkt* (North Market). Another communist comrade, Dirk van Nimwegen, also made a speech, in which he emphasized that the Dutch people should not be seen to be behaving like the Germans. Those attending agreed to strike action, and the call then went out. Posters were made and distributed throughout the night, along with thousands of handbills.

By Tuesday, all municipal and government services in Amsterdam and nearby areas were on strike, with tens of thousands not showing up for work. News of the strike spread through the city like wildfire as the only widespread strike against a Nazi antisemitic action became a reality. It lasted a mere two days, however, before it was called off on February 25, 1941.

In response, the Germans introduced draconian reprisals: the mayor of Amsterdam was threatened with punishment and dismissal, four strikers were executed, twenty-two were imprisoned (with another forty taken as temporary hostages), and the city of Amsterdam was fined fifteen million guilders.

The Gestapo then sought desperately to find and apprehend the organizers. Piet Nak was arrested and beaten severely, even though the Nazis were unaware of the extent of his involvement. Upon his release he went underground, but in November he was picked up again and interrogated under torture for the next four months as the Gestapo sought information on the nature and extent of the communist resistance. Eventually he was freed, but in May 1943 he was once more arrested on charges of helping Jews before again being released.

On November 16, 1941, Willem Kraan was also arrested. After a brutal period of imprisonment, he and thirty-two others were executed at the Soesterberg airport on November 19, 1942.

In 1966 a monument to the strike and the memory of Willem Kraan was unveiled in the newly renamed Willem Kraanstraat. The bronze statue was supposed to be of Kraan but was, instead, of an anonymous dock worker. Its appearance caused consternation among many of the survivors, particularly Piet Nak, who emphasized that the strike was organized by municipal workers, not dock workers. The monument—entitled *De Dokwerker*—was cast in 1952 by Mari Andriessen and based on a 1930s volunteer from the Spanish Civil War. Nonetheless the monument, located in Jonas Daniel Meier Square, is the focus of an annual commemoration to the February Strike.

On May 31, 1966, Yad Vashem recognized Willem Kraan and Piet Nak as Righteous among the Nations for their remarkable efforts in resisting the Nazis. Their attempt, of course, did not work; the full-scale deportation of

Jews from the Netherlands began in the summer of 1942, and over the next two years over 107,000 were deported to their deaths, mainly to Auschwitz and Sobibór. Only 5,200 of those sent to these places survived.

Discussion Questions

1. How do you account for the Amsterdam Strike taking place?
2. Ultimately, the actions of Piet Nak and Willem Kraan did not save any Jewish lives. Do you think their actions, therefore, were worthwhile?

Further Reading

Presser, Jacob, *The Destruction of the Dutch Jews*, Boston: E. P. Dutton, 1969.
Sijes, Benjamin Aaron, *De februaristaking: 25–26 februari 1941*, Amsterdam: Becht, 1954.
Warmbrunn, Werner, *The Dutch under German Occupation, 1940–1945*, Stanford: Stanford University Press, 1963.

MARCH 1941

9.3 Hans Calmeyer, the Dutch Schindler

From the moment Hans Calmeyer started work for the Nazi administration in the occupied Netherlands on March 3, 1941, he realized that doing so would afford him the opportunity to help persecuted Jews. Utilizing his position, he later became known in some circles as the "Dutch Schindler." So far as can be ascertained, he had no ulterior motive for saving Jews, only his own moral code of what was the right thing to do. From this, and through working within the Nazi system, he was able to save thousands of Jews during the Holocaust.

Calmeyer was born on June 23, 1903, in the German city of Osnabrück, Saxony. His father was a judge. Relatively little is known of his childhood, though it is recorded that because of his father's profession the concepts of law and justice, as well as notions of morality, were instilled in him from an early age. Inevitably, he studied law, and after qualifying as an attorney he opened his own practice in Osnabrück. His straightforward and contented life began to change after the Nazis came to power in 1933, with his legal practice taking on many cases concerning communists and socialists. This resulted in the regime monitoring his work.

Soon after the passage of the Nuremberg Laws in 1935, one of the many restrictions against Jews in public life saw a rule banning Aryans from employing Jewish assistants. Calmeyer's small practice had only two employees, one of whom was Jewish. When he refused to dismiss her, he attracted the attention of the government, and his license was revoked for a year.

Called up for army service in May 1940, Calmeyer took part in the invasion of the Netherlands, after which a friend offered him a job with the occupation authorities in the General Commissariat for Administration and Justice in The Hague. This involved examining and adjudicating "doubtful" racial cases, ruling on the appropriate classification of each person in question, and declaring them either fully Jewish, partly Jewish, or Aryan. It was here that Calmeyer saw his opportunity to aid Jews, though he knew he would have to avoid arousing any suspicion that he was acting outside the rules. The team he built around him comprised several dependable local lawyers who helped draw up false credentials.

Contrary to the Nuremberg Laws, Calmeyer argued that the legitimacy of Jewish heritage should not be based on a person's membership in the Jewish community but rather determined from other forms of evidence such as birth and baptismal certificates. The distinction made all the difference for Jews on whose cases he was to adjudicate. It created a legal loophole, allowing Calmeyer to save thousands from deportation. Of the 4,787 cases brought before him, he decided that 42 percent were to be considered half-Jews (*mischlinge* first degree), and another 18 percent as one-quarter Jews (*mischlinge* second degree), creating a total of 60 percent who were thereby exempt from immediate deportation.

He referred to his work as "building a lifeboat" not only to help Jewish families remain together but also provide them with a sense of hope. With the help only of his closest and most trusted friends, he turned a blind eye to fabricated baptismal certificates and falsified documents so he could save Jews, or at the very least stall their deportation. Given that he had to be seen as incorruptible, Calmeyer was not personally involved in any of the forgeries. In fact, he sidestepped any personal contact with lawyers who approached his department on behalf of Jewish clients so that he would not be suspected of being overly sympathetic. Further, he did not attempt to intervene personally on behalf of Jews in any official capacity.

The SS leadership was highly suspicious of Calmeyer's work and constantly urged the higher authorities to close his operation. He knew this, and, playing for time whenever possible, continually added more names to his special list while trying always to find ways to extend his field of operations.

In June 1943 Calmeyer's team was put under close inspection after SS Police chief Hanns Albin Rauter asked for a complete reexamination of the "Calmeyer Jews." While Rauter had been suspicious of Calmeyer's work for some time, there had been a series of internal power struggles in the Nazi establishment that had delayed Calmeyer's evaluation. The committee appointed to investigate included a Dutch SS member, Ludo Ten Cate, who had been appointed, in early 1942, to the position of Official Representative for Genealogical Certificates. Eventually, however, Ten Cate became involved in a vehement quarrel with other Nazi experts, leading to his dismissal in August 1944 and his transfer to the Eastern Front. After Ten Cate's removal, the SS continued to investigate Calmeyer's practice and kept a close eye on every document that passed through his hands. The following year Calmeyer was openly confronted about trying to save Jewish lives through swindling and deception. He persevered to the end, however, and through his efforts at least 3,000 Jewish lives were saved, the majority as a clear result of his judicious manipulation of the rules.

Calmeyer died in 1972 at the age of sixty-nine. On March 4, 1992, Yad Vashem recognized him as one of the Righteous among the Nations. He had both the moral determination and a position in the Nazi apparatus that enabled him to bring about real change. His leadership saved thousands of lives in an act of resistance all too rarely replicated during the period of the Third Reich.

Discussion Questions

1. Briefly describe the strategy Hans Calmeyer employed to save Jewish lives. In your view, why did he use his position this way?

2. Why was Calmeyer able to escape punishment from the Nazis for his actions?

Further Reading

Niebaum, Peter, Rolf Düsterberg, Siegfried Hummel, and Tilman Westphalen, *Ein Gerechter unter den Völkern: Hans Calmeyer in seiner Zeit (1903–1972)*, Osnabrück: Edition Rasch, 2001.
Paldiel, Mordecai, *Saving the Jews. Amazing Stories of Men and Women Who Defied the Final Solution*, Rockville, MD: Schreiber, 2000.

APRIL 1941 (1)

9.4 The Holocaust Comes to Yugoslavia

Germany invaded Yugoslavia on April 6, 1941. The kingdom had tried to remain neutral after the outbreak of war in September 1939, but the wider strategic situation drew the country more and more deeply into the German orbit. Adolf Hitler, having made military alliances with Hungary, Romania, and Bulgaria, next put pressure on Yugoslavia to join Germany's Tripartite

Pact, and on March 25, 1941, a deal was struck with Yugoslavia's regent, Prince Paul.

The alliance prompted widespread popular discontent and public protest in Yugoslavia, and a contingent of military officers moved quickly to overthrow the regency in a coup d'état on March 27, 1941. Prince Peter, who was still a minor, was declared to be of age and proclaimed as King Peter II. In his name, the newly installed government repudiated the German alliance.

Upon hearing the news Hitler flew into a rage and by way of response issued Führer Directive 25. This declared that Yugoslavia was to be treated as a hostile state, to be slated for destruction. On April 6 German, Italian, and Hungarian troops invaded, and within two weeks the country was occupied.

Two rival resistance groups arose to oppose the Nazi occupation: the Chetniks (Serbian nationalists) and the Partisans, communists led by Josip Broz Tito. While both groups fought the Nazis, they ultimately had different ideas regarding what a reconstituted Yugoslav state would look like. The Chetniks sought a resumption of Serbian dominance, while the Partisans wanted to establish a communist federation in states divided along ethnic lines.

Yugoslavia's entry into the Second World War provided a breakaway Croatian movement, the *Ustaše*, with the opportunity to establish an independent Croatia. After the Axis invasion of April 1941, they came to power and formed a fascist puppet state ruled by Ante Pavelić. The *Ustaše* pursued a policy of ethnic cleansing against Jews, Roma, Muslims, and Serbs in the territories under its control.

Chetnik and Partisan resistance to the Nazis, followed by brutal forms of repression in response, led to violence on a genocidal scale. While the Germans rounded up Jews and Roma for extermination at Auschwitz, the *Ustaše* murdered their victims in a network of locally constructed concentration camps. The most notorious of these was at a place whose name is infamous in the Balkans to this day; Jasenovac, a hundred kilometers south of the Croatian capital, Zagreb. Jasenovac was not established by the Nazis, but was, instead, set up in August 1941 by the *Ustaše*. Over time, it grew to become a complex of five sub-camps and three smaller compounds, including a camp for children at Sisak and a pitiless camp for women at Stara Gradiska, east of the main Jasenovac complex. Jasenovac would ultimately see the murder of over 100,000 victims, mainly Serbs, Jews, and Roma.

The Nazis were not to be denied their contribution to the suppression of Yugoslavia. Other camps were established at Zemun, Sajmiste, and Donja Gradina. Sajmiste was run by the Nazis as an extermination camp for Serbian Jews, and it has been estimated that anywhere between 4,000 and 8,000 Jews were murdered there, in addition to Serbian resisters and Roma. In total, the combined extermination policies of the Nazis and the

Ustaše were responsible for the death of more than 500,000 Serbs; 20,000 Roma; most of the country's Jews; and untold thousands of political opponents.

By August 1942, the Yugoslavian heartland in Serbia became the first state declared by the Nazis to be "Free of Jews" (*Judenfrei*). By the time Yugoslavia was liberated in 1945, only 14,000 of the prewar Jewish population of 82,500 survived. Within Serbia itself, the figures were even starker, with the Nazis having murdered some 14,500 of the prewar Serbian Jewish population of 16,000. Serbia, moreover, was the only country outside of Poland or the Soviet Union where all Jewish victims were killed on the spot without first undergoing deportation.

Ultimately, by the time Tito's Partisans had gained the upper hand and effectively driven the Nazis out of Yugoslavia, their numbers had swollen to over half a million fighting men and women—the foundation of what would be a communist state in a reconstituted Yugoslavia. The antisemitic and fascist *Ustaše*, on the other hand, was effectively destroyed as a force within Yugoslavia. Many of the leaders managed to flee to safety in Spain or South America. Ante Pavelić himself fled to Argentina, where he reorganized the *Ustaše* in exile.

Against this background, it is indeed ironic that half a century later, during the Bosnian War of 1992–5, the Jews were considered by all sides (Orthodox Serbs, Catholic Croats, and Muslim Bosniaks) to be neutral—one of the very few occasions in the history of European warfare that Jews were left alone and unmolested. Some very brave Jewish leaders, such as Zoran Mandlbaum, were aware of what the Jewish past had been during the Second World War and turned their attention to saving all lives in this new conflict. It was a most remarkable set of circumstances, practically unprecedented over the past millennium of Jewish history—and a fitting coda to the Holocaust years that began back in April 1941.

Discussion Questions

1. Could it be argued that there was in fact a series of conflicts in Yugoslavia taking place at the same time, of which that against the Jews was only one part?

2. How do you account for the large death toll in Yugoslavia from 1941 on?

Further Reading

Greble, Emily, *Sarajevo, 1941–1945: Muslims, Christians, and Jews in Hitler's Europe*, Ithaca, NY: Cornell University Press, 2011.

Mojzes, Paul, *Balkan Genocides: Holocaust and Ethnic Cleansing in the Twentieth Century*, Lanham, MD: Rowman & Littlefield, 2011.
Ramet, Sabrina P., and Ola Listhaug (eds.), *Serbia and the Serbs in World War Two*, New York: Palgrave Macmillan, 2011.
Tomasevich, Jozo, *War and Revolution in Yugoslavia, 1941–1945: Occupation and Collaboration*, Stanford: Stanford University Press, 2001.

APRIL 1941 (2)

9.5 A Pogrom in Antwerp

Antwerp, a city in northern Belgium, had a Jewish population of about 50,000 on the eve of the German invasion in May 1940. Of those, only some 20 percent were Belgian citizens; the rest were either recent immigrants from Eastern Europe or refugees from Nazi Germany and Austria. With the Nazi attack on Belgium, about 20,000 of Antwerp's Jews fled before the advance of the Nazis, the vast majority moving south, though Belgium and into France.

At first, despite the Nazi occupation, daily life in the city continued more or less as it had before, but as time progressed things began to deteriorate for Antwerp's Jewish population. Within days of the occupation the Germans had already begun instituting anti-Jewish measures across Belgium and, from these first days, Jews were subject to a curfew from dusk to dawn and Jewish-owned businesses had to carry special markings. In December 1940 a German decree was issued opening the possibility for foreigners to be removed from certain areas of Belgium. Pursuant to this, the German military administration in Antwerp began expelling foreign Jews who had arrived in Belgium after 1938, with some 3,334 deported by the winter of 1940–1, mostly into rural regions.

Moreover, the Germans were supported in their anti-Jewish measures by local pro-Nazi and antisemitic parties and groups. In Antwerp these collaborationist sectors were both more numerous and radical than in other Belgian cities, especially the *Vlaams Nationaal Verbond* (Flemish National Union, or VNV), *De Vlag* (the Flag), and the *Algemeene-SS Vlaanderen* (Germanic SS in Flanders).

Easter Monday on April 14, 1941, saw Flemish antisemitic attitudes boil over into what became a wartime pogrom against Antwerp's Jewish quarter. A screening of the viciously antisemitic German propaganda film *Der Ewige Jude* (*The Eternal Jew*) saw the various Flemish paramilitary groups (including also the *Volksverwering* and the Anti-Jewish League) launch an offensive directed solely at the Jewish population. In scenes reminiscent of *Kristallnacht* in Germany just two-and-a-half years earlier, some 200 rioters, armed with iron bars, sticks, and other weapons, and spurred on by the German occupation authorities, marched their way down the Oostenstraat, the main street in the Jewish district, where they set fire to the Van den Nestlei and the Oostenstraat synagogues, burned a number of Torah scrolls, smashed windows of Jewish-owned shops, and harassed the Jewish population. They then turned their attention toward the home of Rabbi Marcus Rottenburg, Chief Rabbi of Flanders.

Again, as during *Kristallnacht*, the police (unarmed) and fire brigade were called but were forbidden to intervene by the German authorities. Another attack followed three days later. Appalled, the Antwerp city council, following the lead of a horrified population, assumed responsibility for the attacks and offered compensation to the Jews who had suffered damage. The Germans, however, refused to allow this to be put into place.

Having shown the Jews of Antwerp what they could expect from the Nazi administration and the local Nazis in the vicinity, a few months later the Germans began a process of Aryanization of Jewish property. Soon, all of Belgium's Jews were required to wear a yellow star. Then, during 1942, deportations of Jews began. On August 28, 1942, the first mass arrests of Jews took place: first, foreigners—specifically, Romanian Jews—were picked up and taken to a transit camp in Mechelen (known to French-speaking Belgians as Malines), but soon others were also rounded up. In September 1942 Jews were arrested on the streets, and only those who could prove that they held Belgian citizenship were released. It was a short step from there to arresting all Jews, regardless of nationality. A year later, in September 1943, the Nazis began arresting and deporting Belgian Jews as well.

The Jews of Antwerp proactively tried to save themselves and others, and local Zionist youth groups became active in helping to smuggle Jews to secure hiding places. It has been estimated that perhaps as many as 3,000 Jews managed to hide in the Antwerp area during the war, including some 800 who remained in the city itself.

Antwerp was finally liberated on September 4, 1944. During the war, 65 percent of the city's Jews perished. This was a staggering loss and stands in stark contrast to the Jewish losses in Brussels, where 35 percent were deported and murdered. When reasons are called for to explain the difference, three stand out: the fact that a large proportion of Antwerp's Jewish population was foreign, and not of Belgian nationality; that the city contained very distinct Jewish districts, making it easier for the Nazis to target their victims; and, above all, there was a willingness on the part of some in the Antwerp populace to eagerly assist the Nazis in their murderous aims.

Discussion Questions

1. Why do you think the Jews of Antwerp were targeted in such a vicious manner by their fellow citizens?
2. How, if at all, did the pogrom against the Jews of Antwerp differ from the *Kristallnacht* in Germany in November 1938?

Further Reading

Michman, Dan, *Belgium and the Holocaust: Jews, Belgians, Germans*, Jerusalem: Yad Vashem, 1998.

Szarota, Tomasz, *On the Threshold of the Holocaust: Anti-Jewish Riots and Pogroms in Occupied Europe. Warsaw-Paris-The Hague-Amsterdam-Antwerp-Kaunas*, Frankfurt am Main: Peter Lang, 2015.

JUNE 1941

9.6 Operation Barbarossa

On June 22, 1941, the German invasion of the Soviet Union—a campaign code-named Operation Barbarossa—was set in motion. It was the largest military invasion in history and took place along a 2,900-kilometer front from the Baltic to the Black Sea. Germany's armies numbered 3,200,000 men in 151 divisions, with 3,350 tanks, 7,184 guns, and 1,945 planes. Accompanying them were military forces contributed by Germany's allies, with 40,000 Italian troops alongside of 18 Finnish, 14 Romanian, and 2 Hungarian divisions. This was intended to be the start of a European crusade not only to rid the world of communism but also to reestablish the very foundations upon which European civilization (as understood by Nazism) rested.

Nearly two years earlier, on August 29, 1939, Hitler and Stalin had agreed to a pact of mutual nonaggression, which paved the way for the Nazi attack on Poland on September 1, 1939. That arrangement was now overturned, with the German dictator reinforcing his oft-proclaimed role as the savior of Europe against Bolshevism.

The initial campaign objectives of Operation Barbarossa were soon realized, but the Soviet Union did not suddenly capitulate as Hitler had anticipated. This led to it dragging on beyond the ten weeks originally intended. After this, new campaigns and objectives had to be devised, while at the same time the Nazis had to confront Soviet counteroffensives launched in the midst of much colder weather.

As the year lengthened, German and allied troops were severely hampered by heavy rains in October, which turned the roads to mud. November and December saw severe frosts, and in some places the temperature dropped by thirty-five degrees Fahrenheit. Hitler and his military planners, expecting the campaign to be over before winter, had not provided for adequate winter clothing for the troops, and by the spring of 1942, with no progress made toward victory, Hitler turned his attention away from Moscow to capturing the oil fields in the southeast instead.

In one area, however, progress—if it is not too much of an abuse of language to employ that word—had been made. Prior to Barbarossa, on June 6, 1941,

Hitler issued a proclamation known as the *Kommissarbefehl* ("Commissar Order"), in which he directed that any Soviet cadres and political leaders captured would be summarily executed. By extension, within the Nazi conception of communism, this included all Jews, regardless of age, sex, social position, or political opinion. Those designated to carry out this grisly work were known as *Einsatzgruppen*, or "Special Action Groups." The order's formal name was Guidelines for the Treatment of Political Commissars.

The *Kommissarbefehl* was a clear manifestation of the deeply ideological nature of how the forthcoming struggle with the Soviet Union was to be fought. Its core demand was that German soldiers shoot any Soviet political commissars taken prisoner during and after Barbarossa, as they carried "Judeo-Bolshevik" ideas that were antithetical to everything for which Nazism stood. By extension, those targeted included all Jews.

The *Einsatzgruppen* were SS mobile murder squads that accompanied the German military in its assault on Russia. Divided into four groups—A, B, C, and D—their task eventually became the total annihilation of all Jews in the areas to which they had been allocated responsibility. Group A, the largest with a force of approximately 1,000 men, operated in the Baltic States of Lithuania, Latvia, and Estonia; Group B (650) operated in Belorussia (Belarus) and outside of Moscow; Group C (700) operated in Ukraine; while Group D (600) operated in the Crimea and the Caucasus. Three of the four group leaders had doctorates from respected German universities.

Operating together with members of the German army as well as local collaborators, it is estimated that between 1941 and 1943 the *Einsatzgruppen* murdered more than a million Jews. It is their actions that have since come to be labeled as "the Holocaust by bullets." Various means were adopted for their murderous behavior, but most frequently they are remembered through operations in which they gathered the Jews of a town, village, or locality and machine-gunned them to death in large open pits or through utilizing natural formations such as ravines or valleys. Often, the killing would take an entire day, with whole families forced to await their turn within earshot of the shooting.

This process was often quite inefficient and psychologically disturbing for many of those repeatedly undertaking the murders. To get around this, and in hopes of finding a more clinical way effecting killing on a mass scale, mobile gas vans using carbon monoxide poisoning were eventually introduced both to remove the intimacy of contact and to sanitize the process.

The German invasion of the Soviet Union on June 22, 1941, marked the beginning of what some have termed "the War of the Century." For Hitler, the war against the Soviet Union was not to be a conventional conflict following the usual customs and laws of warfare. Instead, it was to be a "War of Annihilation," a clash between the German and Slavic races and between Nazi and Communist ideology from which there would be only one victor. The nature of the war in the East was to reflect the Nazi policy of *Lebensraum* ("Living Space"), in which the region would become an area colonized by so-called superior Aryan Germans and where members of the local population were expendable, Jews especially so.

On May 6, 1942, less than a year after the start of Operation Barbarossa, the *Kommissarbefehl* was overturned after continued appeals to Hitler from German field commanders. This did not stop the killing, of course; the most intensive murder phase of the Holocaust was by that stage already underway, now as a designated SS operation. What began with the invasion of the Soviet Union in June 1941 developed an irrepressible momentum that would only see an end with the defeat of Nazi Germany and the liberation of the camps from the autumn of 1944 onward.

Discussion Questions

1. Operation Barbarossa was a military campaign. Why did it develop into the wholesale and deliberate slaughter of Jews?

2. How can you account for such a high death toll in view of the fact that the four *Einsatzgruppen* numbered so few men?

Further Reading

Glantz, David M., *Operation Barbarossa: Hitler's Invasion of Russia, 1941,* Stroud: History Press, 2011.

Hartmann, Christian, *Operation Barbarossa: Nazi Germany's War in the East, 1941–1945*, Oxford: Oxford University Press, 2013.

Stahel, David, *Operation Barbarossa and Germany's Defeat in the East*, Cambridge: Cambridge University Press, 2009.

JULY 1941

9.7 Mikhail Gebelev, Hero of Minsk

On July 20, 1941, German forces established a ghetto at Minsk, the capital and largest city in what was then called the Byelorussian Soviet Socialist Republic (modern Belarus). The ghetto was to be managed by a Nazi-appointed Jewish Council (*Judenrat*). It was one of the largest in Eastern Europe and was certainly the largest in the parts of the Soviet Union then occupied by the Germans. It ultimately accommodated nearly 100,000 Jews, most of whom would perish in the Holocaust.

One of those caught in the Nazi net was Mikhail Gebelev, who became an anti-Nazi resistance leader in the Minsk ghetto. Born on October 15,

1905, in the Jewish *shtetl* (village) of Uzliany, he later moved to Minsk and worked there as a clerk and civil servant. After Germany invaded the Soviet Union and occupied Minsk on June 28, 1941, Gebelev went into hiding. He had good reason. Within days of the occupation, 2,000 Jewish leaders and intellectuals were massacred by *Einsatzgruppen* squads; additional murders of Jews henceforth became a daily occurrence. Within the first few months of the German occupation, at least 20,000 Jews from Minsk were slaughtered.

At this time, the total population of the ghetto was about 80,000, of which some 50,000 were prewar inhabitants; those remaining were refugees forcibly resettled by the Germans from smaller villages nearby. In August 1941 activists led by Isay Pavlovich Kazinetz, a Jewish engineer, established an underground group that forged documents, set up a radio receiver, and aided Soviet resistance in the area. This was one of the earliest expressions of Jewish resistance after the invasion of the Soviet Union.

Having escaped the clutches of the Nazis, Gebelev contacted Kazinetz, who appointed him as liaison officer between the communist resisters on the Aryan side of the ghetto and the ghetto fighters inside, whose leader was a Polish Yiddish writer from Białystok, Hersh Smolar.

Together with another resistance leader, Matvey Pruslin, Gebelev quickly emerged as the informal head of the ghetto underground due to his charisma and ingenuity, and he played a key role in Kazinetz's plans to stage large-scale simultaneous uprisings throughout Minsk to drive the Germans out and hold the city until the Red Army arrived. These uprisings would be conducted by communists, ghetto fighters, and Soviet prisoners of war incarcerated in the city.

The proposed rebellion did not take place, however, owing to its plans being leaked to the Nazis. Kazinetz was among those ultimately hunted down. Before he was taken, he shot two Germans; wounded and captured, under torture he then held out and refused to reveal any names or information, even after one of his eyes had been put out. On May 7, 1942, Isay Kazinetz and twenty-eight other underground fighters were publicly hanged in the center of Minsk. It is recorded that his defiant last words were "Death to the Nazis!"

Despite this huge setback, the resistance movement in the ghetto remained largely intact due to Gebelev's leadership and support from the head of the *Judenrat*, Moshe Yoffe. In the period that followed, Gebelev organized mass escapes from the ghetto to the forests outside Minsk, where they formed (or joined) partisan units. The underground's main objective was to save as many Jewish lives as possible, realizing that all were condemned to death in any case. At night, under extremely dangerous conditions, couriers led small groups of prisoners out of the ghetto. There were as many as 300 active members of Gebelev's underground organization, and through their efforts perhaps up to 10,000 Jews achieved their objective of escaping the Minsk ghetto, with many joining the partisans.

It was said of Gebelev himself that on the numerous occasions he was encouraged to flee his reply was always that "I am here in the line of duty!"

In August 1942, however, he was arrested by local collaborators as he was preparing the escape of a group of Soviet prisoners of war. He was handed over to the Gestapo, and, like Kazinetz before him, brutally tortured while at the same time refusing to provide any names or information. On August 15, 1942, he was hanged in the Nazi prison in Minsk.

The ghetto itself was liquidated on October 21, 1943. Those Jews remaining in the city at this time, including Moshe Yoffe and Mikhail Gebelev's eighty-year-old father Liev, were murdered, with most being deported to the extermination camp at Sobibór. Several thousand were massacred at a camp that had been established on the outskirts of Minsk, Maly Trostenets. By the time the Red Army retook the city on July 3, 1944, there were only a handful of survivors left.

Hersh Smolar did manage to escape just prior to the final liquidation of the ghetto, and in 1946 produced a memoir of Minsk, *Fun Minsker geto* (published in English in New York in 1989 as *The Minsk Ghetto: Soviet-Jewish Partisans against the Nazis*). In this, he described Gebelev's role in the resistance movement in some depth, highlighting both his initiatives and his heroism in the face of immense obstacles and constant danger.

There is much to recall in the story of Mikhail Gebelev's heroic acts in and around Minsk during the Holocaust. Perhaps the most important of these is that he was more concerned with saving Jewish lives than with taking German ones.

Discussion Questions

1. What was Mikhail Gebelev's role in the Minsk resistance movement?
2. In what way, if at all, was the resistance at Minsk effective? Explain your answer with examples.

Further Reading

Epstein, Barbara, *The Minsk Ghetto, 1941–1943: Jewish Resistance and Soviet Internationalism*, Berkeley: University of California Press, 2008.

SEPTEMBER 1941

9.8 Babi Yar: The Fatal Ravine

Babi Yar, also spelled Babiy Yar or Babyn Yar, is the name given to a large ravine on the northern edge of Kiev in Ukraine. Across the two days of September 29–30, 1941, it was where SS and German police divisions murdered a large segment of the Jewish population of the city. As captive Jews from the city moved into the ravine, *Einsatzgruppen* units from *Sonderkommando 4a* under SS-*Standartenführer* Paul Blobel shot them in small groups. According to reports back to headquarters, 33,771 Jews were massacred in this two-day period. This was one of the largest mass killings at an individual location during the Second World War.

Before the German army invaded Kiev on September 19, 1941, some 160,000 Jews, about 20 percent of the city's population, lived in Kiev. Around 100,000 of them fled before the assault on the city, and during the ensuing battle Axis forces killed or captured more than 600,000 Soviet soldiers, most of whom never returned alive. Kiev was incorporated into *Reichskommissariat Ukraine*, controlled by fanatical East Prussian Nazi district leader Erich Koch.

Immediately following the German takeover, two big explosions, supposedly detonated by Soviet military engineers or the NKVD (*Naródny komissariát vnútrennih del*, or People's Commissariat for Internal Affairs), destroyed German field headquarters and much of central Kiev. The Germans used this incident as a convenient justification to murder Kiev's remaining 60,000 Jews, comprising women, children, the old, and the sick.

After discussions between Blobel, SS-*Brigadefuhrer* Otto Rasch, and Major General Kurt Eberhard (the German field commander in Kiev), Kiev's Jews were ordered to gather with their possessions—including money, valuables, and warm clothing—near the Jewish cemetery no later than 7:00 a.m. on Monday, September 29. They were told they would be relocated, and that disobedience would be punished by death. The assembled Jews were then marched to the ravine at Babi Yar. There, following standard procedure used by *Einsatzgruppen* since late June 1941, SS and police forced the Jews to strip, dispossessed them of their belongings, and shot them into the ravine in groups of thirty to forty people.

The Jews, in their thousands, were steered into barbed-wire areas at the top of the ravine, which were secured by Germany's Ukrainian allies. There they undressed, were beaten, and escorted in groups down the gorge. The initial groups were forced to lie on the ground, face down, and killed by German machine guns. The bullet-riddled bodies were covered thinly with earth, the next group was ordered to lie on top of them, and the process was repeated. The hasty murder of so many people within two days did not assure that all the victims had died, even though shots continued to be fired into bodies. A few managed to survive and though gravely wounded managed to crawl from under the corpses and seek a hiding place.

In the months following the massacre, German authorities stationed at Kiev sporadically reused the ravine as a killing site. They murdered several thousand more Jews, as well as an untold number of non-Jews including Roma, communist officials, Soviet prisoners of war, and Soviet civilians. It is estimated that over the entire period in which German forces occupied Kiev, some 100,000 people were murdered at Babi Yar.

In July 1943, after Soviet forces seized the military initiative, Germany launched *Aktion 1005* to dispose of evidence of their crimes in the Soviet Union. Blobel, who had been discharged from his duties as commander of *Sonderkommando 4a* in early 1942 and transferred to Berlin, returned to Kiev, where he supervised works to eliminate evidence of the murders at Babi Yar. Throughout August and September 1943 his men and enslaved concentration camp prisoners reopened the mass grave, crushed bones, and burned the remains of the dead. When the concealment work was done, almost all the prisoners were killed. However, on September 29, 1943— two years to the day of the massacre—some twenty-five managed to escape under cover of darkness. Fifteen survived to tell what they had seen. Other evidence of the massacres remained, discovered by Soviet forces after the liberation of Kiev in November 1943.

The Babi Yar Massacre of late September 1941 was one of the largest mass killings at any single location during the Holocaust. The horrendous numbers killed were surpassed only by the massacre in October 1941 of 50,000 Jews at Odessa by Romanian (and some German) units and by the two-day *Aktion Erntefest* (Operation Harvest Festival) in early November 1943, which claimed 42,000–43,000 Jewish victims.

In 1959, the novelist Viktor Nekrasov appealed in the pages of *Literaturnaya Gazeta* for a memorial to be established at Babi Yar. The poet Yevgeni Yevtushenko followed this up with a famous poem, "Babi Yar," in the same journal on September 19, 1961. The poem was an open attack upon antisemitism and drew attention to Jewish martyrdom. The composer Dmitri Shostakovich then set Yevtushenko's lines to music in his 13th Symphony, performed for the first time in December 1962. Yevtushenko was publicly denounced by Premier Nikita Khrushchev in *Pravda* on March 8, 1963, but the details of the massacre would not remain censored. Details resurfaced in 1966 in a novel focusing on Babi Yar written by Anatoly Kuznetsov.

After the breakup of the Soviet Union in 1991 the Ukrainian government acknowledged the specifically Jewish nature of the site, and an appropriate rededication was held.

Discussion Questions

1. Why do you think the Nazis went to such lengths to cover up the massacre at Babi Yar later, in 1943?

2. The Nazis used an excuse to begin the mass murder of the Jews of Kiev at Babi Yar. In your opinion, why do you think they did this? Give reasons for your answer.

Further Reading

Arad, Yitzhak, *The Holocaust in the Soviet Union*, Lincoln: University of Nebraska Press, 2009.
Dobroszycki, Lucjan, and Jeffrey S. Gurock (eds.), *The Holocaust in the Soviet Union: Studies and Sources on the Destruction of the Jews in the Nazi-Occupied Territories of the USSR, 1941–1945*, New York: Routledge, 1994.
Khiterer, Victoria, "Babi Yar, the Tragedy of Kiev's Jews," *Brandeis Graduate Journal*, 2 (2004), pp. 1–16.

OCTOBER 1941

9.9 The Martyrdom of Lubny

The small city of Lubny is located in the Poltava Oblast of central Ukraine. It is reputed to be one of the oldest cities in Ukraine, allegedly founded in 988 by Prince Vladimir the Great of Kiev. The first written record concerning Lubny dates from 1107. Jews settled in Lubny in the first half of the seventeenth century. In 1939, on the eve of the Second World War, the Jewish population numbered 2,833, about 10.5 percent of the total.

In October 1941, the Jewish community of Lubny was obliterated by the Nazis. After the launch of Operation Barbarossa in June 1941, the residents of Lubny became immediately vulnerable to German attacks, even though the city itself was not occupied until September 13, 1941. Lubny and its surrounds became a major resistance center, and partisans fought the Nazis outside of the city. With the German takeover, all Jews were immediately registered. The Nazis counted around 1,500 Jewish residents of the city, though this did not consider those from outlying villages who had come in looking for refuge.

On October 10, 1941, the occupying authorities sent an order out to the Jews of Lubny that they were to gather in nearby Zasule for resettlement, making sure to take with them warm clothes and valuables. The "resettlement" was to take place a few days later, on October 16, 1941.

On the appointed day, the Jews of Lubny gathered at Kirov Square, the main market square of the city. Unknown to them was the fact that *Sonderkommando 4a*, one of the units of *Einsatzgruppen C* under the command of Colonel Paul Blobel, had also received orders: to effectuate the liquidation of the entire Jewish population of Lubny. Blobel was one of the SS officers who had organized the massacre at Babi Yar in late September 1941, when 33,771 Jews were murdered in the space of two days. Later, in November 1941, Blobel would receive and put into operation the first gas vans in Ukraine.

Directed by Blobel's unit, all the Jews of Lubny were then herded just outside the city. They never made it to the village of Zasule: instead, they were shot in small batches into the Zasylskiy ravine. As many members of the population as could be located were killed: men, women, children, babies, and the elderly. On that day, 1,865 Jews were murdered; not just the Jews of Lubny but also those from Shtalag-328, a makeshift concentration camp that had been established earlier in Lvov (Lviv) and the areas around Babi Yar.

The Nazis did not stop the killing there; in second half of November 1941, they found and killed another seventy-three Jews, missed in the first sweep. Those who, despite all this, still managed to survive as skilled laborers in demand for the German military, were killed during April and May of 1942.

Overall, therefore, across the period from October 1941 to May 1942, approximately 2,000 Jews were murdered in Lubny. Their fate would have been largely forgotten were it not for the fact that photographs were taken by the SS themselves during the killing process. One photographer in particular, Johannes Hähle, took twenty-nine color photos of Babi Yar and Lubny, though he could not bring himself to make them public or deliver them to his unit. At Lubny, he documented the concentration of the population, their waiting to be murdered, and then the killing itself. Although Hähle died during the Normandy landings in June 1944, his widow kept the photos safe and sold them to a Berlin journalist after the war. The original color photos only surfaced in the year 2000, when they were acquired and placed in the archive of Hamburg's *Institut für Sozialforschung* (Institute for Social Research).

The Holocaust was visited upon the small Jewish community of Lubny as a totality. It was always intended that there would not be any survivors, as subsequent efforts by the Nazis showed. All men, all women, all children; everyone was murdered. The enormity of the Holocaust was such, however, that these 2,000 deaths are hardly ever recorded in histories of the *Shoah*.

The fate of the Jews of Lubny is just one of countless massacres that took place in the wake of the German invasion of the Soviet Union. Though overshadowed by much larger events, it was, for that small community, on October 16, 1941, the epicenter of the Holocaust.

Discussion Questions

1. Why was the massacre at Lubny relatively unknown until the year 2000?

2. Could it be argued that what happened at Lubny was part of a wider campaign that included Babi Yar—or were the two events separate?

Further Reading

Arad, Yitzhak, and Shmuel Krakowski, *The Einsatzgruppen Reports: Selections from the Dispatches of the Nazi Death Squads' Campaign against the Jews, July 1941-January 1943*, New York: Holocaust Library, 1990.

Rhodes, Richard, *Masters of Death: The SS-Einsatzgruppen and the Invention of the Holocaust*, New York: Random House, 2002.

NOVEMBER 1941

9.10 A Meeting of Like Minds

In Berlin on November 28, 1941, Adolf Hitler entertained Haj Amin al-Husseini, the Grand Mufti of Jerusalem, who pledged to cooperate with him in the extermination of the Jews. In doing so, he offered to enlist Arabs to fight for Germany. Who was this man, so admired by Hitler?

Mohammed Amin al-Husseini was a Palestinian Arab nationalist and Muslim leader in Mandate Palestine. Born in Jerusalem in 1895, he was the scion of a family of wealthy landowners claiming direct descent from the grandson of the Prophet. He received an education in an Islamic school, an Ottoman school (where he learned Turkish), and a Catholic school (where he learned French). Sent to Cairo for his higher education, he studied Islamic jurisprudence at Al-Azhar University and then at the Cairo Institute for Propagation and Guidance. He went on to the College of Literature at Cairo University and then the Ottoman School for Administrators in Istanbul, which trained future leaders of the Ottoman Empire. In 1913 he made a pilgrimage to Mecca, earning his honorific "Haj."

On the death of the then Mufti of Jerusalem on March 21, 1921, elections were held to choose a successor. Although al-Husseini only came fourth in the votes, the British governor, Sir Herbert Samuel, seeking to maintain the balance of power between the rival elite Husseini and Nashashibi clans, appointed al-Husseini as the new Grand Mufti.

On March 31, 1933, soon after Hitler's ascent to office in Germany, al-Husseini met with the German consul general in Jerusalem, who advised Berlin that the Mufti would make an excellent ally in Palestine. He identified that the Mufti aimed to terminate Jewish settlement in Palestine, and that, allied with Nazi Germany in a holy war, he would remove the Jewish problem everywhere.

By 1937 al-Husseini had organized a youth group, the Holy Jihad, inspired by the Hitler Youth. British police were sent to arrest al-Husseini in July 1937 for his part in the Arab rebellion, but he managed to escape to the sanctuary in the Muslim area on top of the Western Wall.

In a letter to Hitler dated June 21, 1939, al-Husseini wrote of Arab readiness to rise against the Jewish enemy; once war broke out, he went to Iraq on October 13, 1939, and set up his base of operations there. On April 4, 1941, he attempted a takeover of the Iraqi government with Nazi support. In the resultant pogrom 600 Baghdadi Jews were killed, 911 Jewish houses were destroyed, and 586 Jewish businesses ransacked. When Britain suppressed the takeover, al-Husseini blamed the failure of the takeover on the Jews. On

November 28, 1941, he met with Adolf Hitler, concluding afterward that Nazis and Arabs were engaged in the same struggle to exterminate the Jews.

From the mid-1930s al-Husseini had been friends with Adolf Eichmann. When he visited Eichmann in January 1942 he discussed the formation of a German-Arab military unit, and an *Einsatzgruppe Ägypten* (Egypt) was created and readied for deployment to Palestine in the event of a German victory in North Africa. At the same time, he was briefed on the Final Solution, visited Auschwitz and Majdanek, and was on close terms with Auschwitz commandant Rudolf Höss. He also organized antisemitic Arab radio propaganda and espionage in the Middle East. He had at his disposal six long-range radio stations for his broadcasts (Berlin, Zeissen, Bari, Rome, Tokyo, and Athens), from which he urged Muslims to kill Jews.

In the spring of 1943, al-Husseini learned of negotiations involving the International Red Cross to transport 4,000 Jewish children to safety in Palestine. Seeking to prevent this rescue operation, he directed protests toward the Germans and Italians, as well as at the governments of Hungary, Romania, and Bulgaria. Demanding that the operation be scuttled, he suggested that the children be sent to Poland where they would be subject to "stricter control" (i.e., exterminated). They were duly sent to a concentration camp, meeting al-Husseini's demand that they be killed in Poland rather than transported to Palestine. In September 1943, further negotiations to rescue another 500 Jewish children from the Arbe concentration camp in Italy collapsed due to al-Husseini blocking their departure to Turkey because they would end up in Palestine.

In 1943 he organized a chemical attack on Tel Aviv, but the five parachutists sent to complete the mission were captured near Jericho before they could complete their task. Their equipment, found by the British, included enough toxin to kill 250,000 people through poisoning the water supply. Al-Husseini also tried to convince the Nazis to bomb Tel Aviv and Jerusalem. Concerned over the turning tide of the war, he wrote to Heinrich Himmler on June 5, 1944, and July 27, 1944, asking that he do all he could to complete the extermination of the Jews while there was yet time.

After the war, Britain, France, and the United States refused to prosecute the Mufti as a war criminal. Taken into custody at Konstanz on May 5, 1945, by French troops, he was transferred to Paris on May 19 and placed under house arrest. He received sanctuary from Egypt's King Farouk on June 20, 1946, and his last public appearance came in 1962 when he delivered a speech to the World Islamic Congress in which he called for the ethnic cleansing of the Jews. Haj Amin Al-Husseini, a true bedfellow with Adolf Hitler, died in Beirut, Lebanon on July 4, 1974.

Discussion Questions

1. Why do you think the Allies refused to prosecute Haj Amin Al-Husseini after the war?

2. Do you see any connection between the Second World War, the
   Holocaust, and conflict in the Middle East? If so, what is that connection?

Further Reading

Dalin, David, and John Rothman, *Icon of Evil: Hitler's Mufti and the Rise of Radical Islam*, New York: Random House, 2008.

Litvak, Meir, and Esther Webman, *Empathy to Denial: Arab Response to the Holocaust*, New York: Columbia University Press, 2009.

Patterson, David, *A Genealogy of Evil: Antisemitism from Nazism to Islamic Jihad*, New York: Cambridge University Press, 2011.

DECEMBER 1941

9.11 Days of Infamy

The morning of December 7, 1941 (Hawaiian time), saw a Japanese air attack on the United States at Pearl Harbor, in what President Franklin D. Roosevelt referred to as a "Day of Infamy." The event itself did not automatically lead to the United States entering the Second World War, and for a few short days this new conflict saw the United States in a war with Japan only. America did, however, have an ally in this conflict, because simultaneously with the Japanese attack on Pearl Harbor came attacks on British Hong Kong and Malaya, drawing the British Empire into war with Japan.

Then, inexplicably in the eyes of some at the time, on December 11, 1941, German dictator Adolf Hitler and Italian dictator Benito Mussolini declared war on the United States. In Washington, President Roosevelt asked Congress for a counter declaration of war on Germany and Italy, saying that "never before has there been a greater challenge to life, liberty and civilization."

Almost immediately, the president pledged the United States to a "beat Hitler first" strategy that saw the United States commit to focus on the European theatre prior to turning toward the Japanese enemy in the Pacific. Eventually, by war's end, nearly 90 percent of America's military resources were devoted to defeating Hitler.

While all this was being played out, other "days of infamy" were taking place regarding the Holocaust. On December 8, 1941, near the city of Łódź in Nazi-occupied Poland, Chełmno, a new extermination camp designed specifically for murdering Jews, became operational. Jews taken there were placed in mobile gas vans and driven to where they would be buried, while carbon monoxide from the engine exhaust was fed into the sealed rear compartment. All inside were gassed to death. Early in the New Year, these vans gave way to fixed gassing installations at Chełmno, the first of what became known as "extermination camps."

As if to underscore these new arrangements, on December 16, 1941, the Nazi governor of occupied Poland, Hans Frank, declared during a cabinet meeting of his senior advisers: "Gentlemen, I must ask you to rid yourselves of all feelings of pity. We must annihilate the Jews wherever we find them and wherever it is possible in order to maintain there the structure of the Reich as a whole." With this, the worst phase of the killing during the Holocaust was about to begin. At the start of 1942, 80 percent of all Jews in the Nazi occupied areas were still alive; one year later, 80 percent of all those to be murdered in the Holocaust were already dead.

Earlier that same week, on December 12, 1941, the *Struma*, a small ship carrying 769 Jews desperate to leave Europe for safety in Palestine, departed the Romanian port of Constanța and ventured into the Black Sea. The waters off Constanța—the biggest port on the Black Sea—were mined for defense, so a Romanian vessel escorted the *Struma* out to sea. On December 15 the ship arrived in Istanbul, Turkey, but not before its diesel engine failed numerous times while in transit. The ship then remained there, at anchor, while British diplomats and Turkish officials discussed the fate of the Jewish passengers on board. The British implored the Turkish government to prevent the *Struma* from continuing her voyage, while the Turks refused to allow any of the passengers to come ashore. Consequently, while the diplomats haggled, the *Struma* ran short of supplies.

After weeks of intense discussion, the British decided to allow a few of the *Struma*'s passengers to continue their journey to Palestine by land. On February 12, 1942, British officials approved that children on the *Struma* aged between eleven and sixteen would be given visas for Palestine, though the Turks objected to transporting them at Turkish expense. The British, in turn, refused to send another ship to rescue the children, while Turkey denied them permission to travel overland.

On February 23, 1942, with her engine still unworkable and her desperate refugee passengers still aboard, Turkish authorities boarded the *Struma* and cast it out into the Black Sea. The next morning there was an enormous explosion, and the *Struma* sank. It was later determined that it had been torpedoed by a Soviet submarine, which classified the ship as an "enemy target." Some passengers survived briefly by hugging pieces of debris, but for hours no rescue came. The torpedo and subsequent sinking of the *Struma* killed all ten crew members and all but one of the 780 Jewish refugees aboard. Only one young man, nineteen-year-old David Stoliar, survived, by hanging onto a floating piece of what remained of the ship's deck.

The events of December 7, 1941, saw, indeed, a "Day of Infamy"; but that awful month saw more than just that one day.

Discussion Questions

1. Do you see any pattern in the events of December 1941, or simply a set of random occurrences?
2. Why do you think the Turkish and British authorities refused to assist the passengers on board the *Struma* in December 1941?

Further Reading

Frantz, Douglas, and Catherine Collins, *Death on the Black Sea: The Untold Story of the Struma and World War II's Holocaust at Sea*, New York: HarperCollins, 2003.

Sarantakes, Nicholas Evan, *Allies against the Rising Sun: The United States, the British Nations, and the Defeat of Imperial Japan*, Lawrence: University of Kansas Press, 2009.

Schmider, Klaus H., *Hitler's Fatal Miscalculation: Why Germany Declared War on the United States*, Cambridge: Cambridge University Press, 2021.

Simms, Brendan, and Charlie Laderman, *Hitler's American Gamble: Pearl Harbor and Germany's March to Global War*, New York: Basic Books, 2021.

Part 10

1942

JANUARY 1942

10.1 The Wannsee Conference

One of the most frequently discussed—and misunderstood—events of the Holocaust took place on January 20, 1942, in a home confiscated from a Jewish family at 56–58 Am Grossen Wannsee, Berlin. Here, a group of high-ranking Nazi officials held a short conference in which they discussed the coordination and implementation of the "Final Solution of the Jewish Problem"—the coded phrase for the extermination of all of Europe's eleven million Jews.

The meeting was convened by Reinhard Heydrich, head of the Reich Security Main Office, or RSHA. Those attending were Heydrich (presiding); Adolf Eichmann (RSHA, Unit IV B4), in attendance; Alfred Mayer and Georg Leibbrandt (Ministry for the Occupied Eastern Territories); Wilhelm Stuckart (Interior); Erich Neumann (Office of the Four Year Plan); Roland Freisler (Justice); Josef Bühler (Director General of the *Generalgouvernement*); Martin Luther (Foreign Office); Gerhard Klopfer and Friedrich Wilhelm Kritzinger (Reich Chancellery); Otto Hofmann (Race and Settlement Main Office); Heinrich Müller (RSHA); Karl Eberhard Schöngarth (Commander SD/SiPO Kraków); and Rudolf Lange (Commander SD Latvia). Within this group of fifteen men were nine lawyers; eight of those attending had earned doctoral degrees.

The German invasion and occupation of Eastern Europe presented a demographic challenge for the Nazis because of the large Jewish populations in those areas. By the end of 1941 the head of the SS, Heinrich Himmler, recognized that deportation and emigration were no longer adequate for the task of eliminating the Jews; he thus authorized Heydrich to create the bureaucracy and arrangements for the Final Solution, and it was the conference at Wannsee that dealt with these matters. Henceforth, Jews from across Europe were to be "evacuated to the East." Those slated to be murdered included the Jews of Britain, Ireland, Sweden, Switzerland, Turkey, and other places, both neutral and yet-to-be-occupied.

The decision to annihilate all of Europe's Jews had already been made during the late spring or early summer of 1941—no one can determine this with precision, but the decision had nothing to do with the meeting at Wannsee several months later. The purpose of the meeting was to further discuss and resolve questions regarding the execution of decisions already made.

Therefore, the conference was intended to move the process of death forward, beyond the work already being accomplished in Russia by the *Einsatzgruppen*. Accordingly, the delegates discussed whether there was a more efficient way to achieve the core aim of mass murder, meeting the organizational challenges of identifying, transporting, housing, and eventually eliminating the European Jews. Among the discussion items stemming from this was the use of mobile gas vans and large-scale stationary gas chambers.

The conference also established policies for the treatment of Jews who were of "mixed blood" (*Mischlinge*), or in mixed marriages, using the Nazi racial laws set down at Nuremberg. Criteria were established for dealing with the *Mischlinge*, who were divided into a complex classification system based on "degrees" of "mixed blood."

Heydrich closed the meeting with a call for cooperation among all ministries present, after which food and drink were provided. Several of the participants remained after the meeting broke up, to socialize and enjoy good fellowship. Eichmann later related that the attendees were quite jovial, the liquor flowed freely and that the cakes were delicious. Heydrich toasted the successful outcome of the meeting with a glass of cognac.

Eichmann was tasked with drawing up the minutes of the meeting, and Heydrich ordered that they were to be carefully drafted using coded language and euphemisms. The result was a short summary document in which the purposes of the meeting were outlined, together with conclusions as to next steps. The resultant document was then edited by Heydrich himself.

Thirty copies were made, and those who had been present were ordered to read over their copy and then destroy it. One, however, remained; in 1947 Martin Luther's copy was located, enabling the story of the conference at Wannsee to be reconstructed. Then, at the trial of Adolf Eichmann in Jerusalem in 1961, many of the tentative conclusions reached by earlier researchers were confirmed by Eichmann's testimony. Soon after the conference, plans for what would eventually become the system of death camps went forward in earnest, and the deadliest phase of the Holocaust began.

It must be emphasized that the purpose of the meeting was *not* to discuss whether to implement the Final Solution but rather to discuss the various and best ways of achieving the objectives of a Europe to be *Judenrein* ("Jew-free"). All too many people, beholding the horror of the meeting in which the fate of eleven million Jews was discussed, conclude automatically that it was here that the decision was taken for the Final Solution. It is, perhaps, a natural conclusion to draw, but it belies the fact that by the time the meeting took place over half a million Jews had already been murdered. All the Wannsee Conference did was to confirm and coordinate—in reality, to make more efficient—a situation of mass annihilation that was already well in train by January 1942. The bureaucracy of death, thus activated, became an unstoppable force that only the defeat of the Nazis in 1945 could halt.

Today, the villa at Wannsee is a Holocaust memorial and museum, visited by hundreds of people every day. It was opened on January 20, 1992, the fiftieth anniversary of the conference.

Discussion Questions

1. If the decision to annihilate the Jews of Europe had already been made earlier, in 1941, what was the purpose of the Wannsee Conference in January 1942 and what was the relationship between the two events?

2. Looking at the list of those present at the meeting, why do you think those particular ministries were represented?

Further Reading

Browning, Christopher, *The Origins of the Final Solution: The Evolution of Nazi Jewish Policy, September 1939-March 1942*, Lincoln: University of Nebraska Press, 2004.

Jasch, Hans-Christian, and Christoph Kreutzmüller (eds.), *The Participants: The Men of the Wannsee Conference*, New York: Berghahn, 2017.

Roseman, Mark, *The Villa, the Lake, the Meeting: Wannsee and the Final Solution*, London: Allen Lane, 2002.

FEBRUARY 1942 (1)

10.2 An Unlikely Holocaust Hero

On February 25, 1942, an Austrian soldier serving in the Wehrmacht, Sergeant Anton Schmid, was summarily court-martialed for high treason. Soon after that, on April 13, 1942, he was executed by firing squad.

He was born in Vienna in 1900, married his wife Stefi, and had a daughter. An electrician by trade, by the time he reached early middle age he owned a radio shop and lived a comfortable life in Vienna. Drafted into the German army after the *Anschluss* with Austria, he was mobilized upon the outbreak of war in September 1939, sent to Poland, and then, after the Nazi invasion of the Soviet Union in June 1941, transferred to Nazi-occupied Lithuania. By the autumn of 1941 Sergeant Schmid was stationed near Vilna (Vilnius).

Witnessing the creation of the Vilna ghetto in September 1941, Schmid soon learned what the fate of the Jews was to be. Mass killings had already been taking place since July 1941 and continued throughout the summer and fall. By the end of the year, about 21,700 Jews had been murdered by *Einsatzgruppen* units and their Lithuanian allies in the Ponary Forest near Vilna. Schmid was appalled, particularly as he saw children being beaten in front of him. From his perspective, it was unthinkable not to try to find a way to go to the Jews' aid.

Based at the Vilna train station, Schmid commanded a unit responsible for reassigning soldiers who had been separated from their detachments. From here, he saw a great deal of malicious treatment meted out to Jews and lost no opportunity to use his position to ease their situation. He would take them off the trains and employ them as workers, arranged for some to be released from prison, organized new papers for others, and even—at immense personal risk—sheltered Jews in his office and personal quarters.

Among those he hid were Herman Adler and his wife Anita, both members of Vilna's prewar Zionist movement. Through this link, Schmid was placed in contact with one of the leaders of the nascent Jewish resistance movement in the ghetto, Mordechaj Tenenbaum. The result saw Schmid developing a relationship with the resistance in which he started smuggling Jews away from Vilna to other Jewish cities such as Białystok—places where it was thought the Jews could have a better chance of survival. The association with Schmid also enabled the various resistance groups to establish contact with each other.

Ultimately, Schmid's actions in hiding Jews, supplying them with false papers and arranging their escape, saved the lives of up to 250 Jewish men, women, and children. Within resistance circles, news of his activities on behalf of Jews spread; inevitably, owing to informers, he began to be watched by the SS. It was obvious that he knew this, but the knowledge that he could be found out only emboldened him to work on behalf of Jews with greater determination and audacity.

Inevitably given the environment in which he was operating, Schmid was found out. In the second half of January 1942 he was arrested, and summarily court-martialed for high treason on February 25. The death penalty was the only possible outcome, and on April 13, 1942, he was executed by firing squad.

Anton Schmid was an extremely brave human being. He clearly knew that he was placing himself in danger through his actions, and that, if caught, his fate could have only one possible outcome. For all that, however, he did not see anything particularly special in what he did. In his last letter to his wife Stefi, written from his prison cell prior to his execution, he wrote "I only acted as a human being and did not want to hurt anyone." Sadly, his actions had an unfortunate outcome for Stefi, besides depriving her of her husband, his income, pension, and a war hero's death. When word got back to Vienna, her neighbors shunned her, referring to her husband as a traitor, and socially ostracized her. At one point, her windows were smashed.

The life-saving deeds of Anton Schmid had another outcome, however, when, on May 16, 1967, Yad Vashem in Jerusalem recognized his actions through naming him one of the Righteous among the Nations. Stefi Schmid received the award personally, having been flown to Jerusalem for the occasion. Then, on May 8, 2000, the German government named a military barracks in Schmid's honor in Rendsburg, northern Germany, as the "Feldwebel-Schmid-Kaserne." At the naming ceremony, Germany's defense minister, Rudolf Scharping, said: "We are not free to choose our history, but we can choose the examples we take from that history. Too many bowed to the threats and temptations of the dictator, and too few found the strength to resist. But Sergeant Anton Schmid did resist."

Discussion Questions

1. Discuss briefly how Anton Schmid was able to protect the lives of some 250 Jewish men, women, and children.

2. Do you think the Nazi government had any other alternative available when it learned of Anton Schmid's actions on behalf of the Jews? If so, what was it?

Further Reading

Silver, Eric, *The Book of the Just: The Unsung Heroes Who Rescued Jews from Hitler*, New York: Grove Press, 1992.

Wette, Wolfram, *The Wehrmacht: History, Myth, Reality*, Cambridge, MA: Harvard University Press, 2007.

FEBRUARY 1942 (2)

10.3 A Young Martyr in the Service of Goodness

On February 5, 1942, a German youth was arrested by the Gestapo. He wasn't Jewish, nor had he been captured for rescuing Jews. He was not an armed resister. Moreover, he had only just turned seventeen years of age. Later that same year, this young man was executed—one of the youngest opponents of the Third Reich to be judicially sentenced to death and executed as a result. His name was Helmuth Hübener.

Born on January 8, 1925, Hübener came from a religious family in Hamburg and was a member of the Church of Jesus Christ of Latter-day

Saints (LDS, or Mormons). As a boy he had belonged to the Boy Scouts, but at the age of ten, after the Nazis banned the scouting movement, he joined the Hitler Youth. Three years later, when *Kristallnacht* occurred in November 1938, he broke with the Hitler Youth on the ground that its violence against Jews was unacceptable.

Hübener's stance went against LDS policy. Earlier, in 1937, the World LDS president from the United States, Heber Grant, visited Germany and counseled members not to oppose the Nazi regime. In the aftermath of *Kristallnacht*, Grant arranged for all non-German Mormon missionaries to be evacuated from the Third Reich, leaving dissidents like Helmuth Hübener dangerously exposed. The local president, Arthur Zander, was an enthusiastic Nazi who, in 1938, posted notices on LDS churches stating, "Jews not welcome." In Hübener's own congregation, Jews were banned from attending services. Some LDS members began seeing Hübener as a young troublemaker.

In 1941 Hübener finished middle school. As he learned more about the outside world he was exposed to the BBC through a radio in a friend's home. That summer he learned that his older brother Gerhard, at that time serving in the German army, had a shortwave radio at home, which enabled further listening sessions. Listening to the BBC, of course, was a crime; and Hübener, armed with information picked up from London, began to write leaflets opposing the government. He drew attention to the regime's criminal activities regarding human rights, particularly concerning the Jews. He wrote about how the war was destroying Germany and that defeat was inevitable, distributing copies in his local vicinity.

As 1941 unfolded, Hübener drew two of his fellow LDS members—Karl-Heinz Schnibbe and Rudi Wobbe—into his project, together with Gerhard Düwer, who he had met at work. The more they learned, the more horrified they became, particularly concerning the situation facing the Jews. Together, they listened to BBC radio and worked on the leaflets. Hübener, Schnibbe, and Wobbe then began distributing the sixty or so pieces Hübener had written.

On February 5, 1942, less than a month after turning seventeen, the Gestapo arrested Helmuth Hübener. Heinrich Mohn, a Nazi with whom he worked, saw him trying to translate his pamphlets into French and denounced him. Then, on February 15, 1942, acting on orders from the Gestapo, the LDS excommunicated him. Over the next few months, he was brutally interrogated and tortured in Gestapo prisons in Hamburg and Berlin, before finally being brought before Judge Otto Georg Thierack of the People's Court (*Volksgerichtshof*) in Berlin on August 11, 1942.

Hübener's performance during the trial would have been remarkable for anyone standing in such a situation; for a seventeen-year-old, it was phenomenal. Tried as an adult despite his age, and having been deprived of his civil rights, he was found guilty of conspiracy to commit high treason and advancing the cause of the enemy. His friends, Schnibbe and Wobbe, were also found guilty and given sentences of five and ten years at hard labor, respectively. Hübener, as the ringleader of the group, received the death penalty. Witnesses said that after the sentence was read, he turned to Judge Thierack and shouted "You have sentenced me to death for telling the truth. My time is now—but your time will come!"

Appeals for clemency proved fruitless, and it was to take only two months from the time of sentencing to execution. When his death appeared imminent, he wrote farewell letters to family and friends. In one of them he wrote: "My Father in Heaven knows that I have done nothing wrong." On another, penned the day of his execution, he stated that: "I know that God lives and He will be the Just Judge in this matter."

On October 27, 1942, the Nazi Ministry of Justice upheld the verdict and sentence. Hübener was told of the ministry's decision at 1:05 p.m. on the scheduled day of execution, and at 8:13 p.m., in Berlin's Plötzensee prison, he was beheaded by guillotine. At the age of seventeen he was the youngest person ever to be sentenced by the People's Court and executed for conspiracy to commit treason against the Nazi regime.

In 1946 Hübener was posthumously reinstated in the LDS Church, ordained an elder, and, on January 7, 1948, rebaptized. Since then, he has been honored many times as a hero of the resistance against Hitler, and an exhibit focusing on his resistance, trial, and execution is in the former guillotine chamber at Plötzensee.

Some have since argued that Helmuth Hübener was a naïve youth who was way out of his league in taking on the Nazi state. Perhaps this was so; but he nonetheless saw a need to try to do *something* to stop what he saw as a senseless war and brutal destruction—and for this, and for the sacrifice he made in its service, he is worth remembering with respect and reverence.

Discussion Questions

1. Given the power of the Third Reich, do you think Helmuth Hübener's actions were naïve?

2. Why do you think Hübener acted on behalf of Jews, at the risk of his life and, possibly, those of his friends? Is he a role model for us to follow? Give reasons for your answer.

Further Reading

Nelson, David Conley, *Moroni and the Swastika: Mormons in Nazi Germany*, Norman: University of Oklahoma Press, 2015.

MARCH 1942

10.4 Bełżec: The Heart of Darkness

Located in southeastern Poland, the Nazi death camp at Bełżec began operating on March 17, 1942. While Auschwitz is without doubt the best-known Nazi killing site, with Treblinka perhaps running second in people's minds, the death camp at Bełżec saw the murder of upward of 600,000 people. The vast majority of those sent to Bełżec were Jews, though Roma and Poles were also victims. Bełżec was the Nazis' first dedicated extermination facility, and overall, so far as can be ascertained, only two Jews are known to have survived their ordeal there.

In early 1940, German officials built several forced labor camps along the Bug River, in occupied Poland. Just outside the village of Bełżec, in Poland's southeast, they erected one such camp that was also intended to serve as a central headquarters for the others in the region.

Administered by the SS, the camp at Bełżec began by interning Jews from the Lublin district, where they were compelled to build various military facilities. By the end of 1940 the labor camp was deactivated. Those who had worked to build it were either shot or deported elsewhere. On November 1, 1941, German SS and local police officials began erecting an extermination camp at the site of the old labor camp. Situated less than a quarter of a mile from a major rail line, it was ideally suited for the location of an extermination camp.

Established as part of the "Operation Reinhard" scheme—the Nazi plan for the eradication of all Jews within the *Generalgouvernment* (General Government) of Poland under the administration of Hans Frank—Bełżec was one of the earliest locations for testing mass extermination processes. As such, it commenced operations on March 17, 1942, when Jews deported from Lublin, Lvov, and Kraków began arriving by train.

The camp was divided into three separate areas: administration, a storage area for plundered goods, and the extermination site, which initially contained three gas chambers that grew to six over time. Measuring around 270 meters per side, the camp was supervised by up to thirty SS and police officers, depending on workload and camp needs. These were supplemented by an auxiliary police unit of some 100 men comprising Ukrainians and Poles, together with former Soviet prisoners of war who had defected to the Nazis.

The Germans had carefully evolved the deportations and killing process: trains of 40 to 60 boxcars, with 80 to 100 people crammed into each car, arrived at the Bełżec station. The prisoners were then force marched to the camp, where they were stripped of their possessions prior to being separated by gender. They were then made to remove their clothes and ordered to walk through a pathway known as the "tube," a narrow alleyway concealed by intertwined branches leading to the gas chambers. The unsuspecting prisoners were told they were going to communal showers.

Once the "bathhouse" was full, the doors were sealed, and carbon monoxide gas was pumped in from a large machine outside. This process was repeated until all the victims brought in on the train had been murdered. The policy of concealment did not end with the prisoners at their death, however, as the Nazis went to considerable trouble to conceal their activities inside the camp to keep the local population ignorant as to what was happening there.

The lives of a few—a very few—prisoners were spared at the time of their arrival in the camp. Spared temporarily to work as slave laborers, these prisoners were compelled to work in the killing areas, separating newly arrived prisoners' possessions, removing bodies from the gas chambers, and burying them in mass graves adjacent to the killing ground. The speed of the killing process at Bełżec was extreme. Between March and December 1942 alone, for example, at least 435,500 Jews, Poles, and Roma, most of who had come from southern Poland (though with others from Austria, Germany, and Czechoslovakia), were murdered at the site.

The first commandant of Bełżec was SS Major Christian Wirth, who ruled over the location from March through June of 1942. He was replaced by the camp's second commandant, SS First Lieutenant Gottlieb Hering, who remained at the site until June 1943 and oversaw its dismantling and closure.

In October 1942, fearful that the Nazis' activities might be discovered, SS chief Heinrich Himmler ordered that the mass graves should be exhumed and the remains incinerated in open-air furnaces. The residual bone fragments from the incinerated bodies were then to be pulverized and shipped back to Germany's farmers for fertilizer. By June 1943, slave laborers had completed their task, only to be subsequently shot or deported to other camps.

The camp was then dismantled. Germans and local collaborators bulldozed the entire site, transformed it into a farm for a Ukrainian family, planted crops and trees, and constructed a large homestead there. The intention was that there would be no traces left of what had taken place at Bełżec, and indeed, this could have been the case were not the entire region overrun and occupied by Soviet troops in July 1944.

Discussion Questions

1. Why do you think the Nazis were so secretive about the functioning of Bełżec while it was operating?

2. Describe in your own words the killing process adopted by the Nazis at Bełżec.

Further Reading

Arad, Yitzhak, *Belzec, Sobibor, Treblinka: The Operation Reinhard Death Camps*, Bloomington: Indiana University Press, 1987.
Bauer, Yehuda, *A History of the Holocaust*, New York: Franklin Watts, 2001.

APRIL 1942

10.5 Third Reich Justice

While it is too much to say that an entire judicial system can rest on the initiative of one person, in April 1942 it appeared as though this was the case in Nazi Germany, when judge Curt Rothenberger wrote to Adolf Hitler a series of reform proposals that would have serious ramifications for the Nazi system for what passed for justice.

Rothenberger was born on June 30, 1896. From 1905 he attended the Wilhelm-Gymnasium, a school well attended by Jewish boys. Completing his secondary schooling in August 1914, he was too young to volunteer for service in the First World War but received his compulsory call-up papers in April 1915. He served until 1918 as a field gunner on the Western Front, rising to the rank of lieutenant.

After the war, Rothenberger enrolled in a specially designed course for war veterans at the University of Hamburg. He passed his first state examination in March 1920 after only five semesters, served a shortened legal clerkship, obtained his doctoral thesis, and passed the second state law examination. In June 1922 he was appointed an auxiliary district court judge before becoming an investigating judge in 1927. In 1928 he was promoted to the Government Council in the State Justice Administration before moving into health administration in mid-1929, working as a senior government counsel.

At the end of 1931, Rothenberger was Hamburg candidate for a position as assistant judge in Leipzig, but he was not appointed: at just thirty-dive years, he was considered too young for such a senior position. His career aspirations now overcame any morals or ethics. While he had been mentored by at least two Jewish professors, he now tied his career to the Nazi Party's success and became a backroom adviser assisting the Nazis.

On March 8, 1933, Rothenberger was elected as Justice Senator. Once in place, he fired two Jewish prosecutors even before the Law for the Restoration of the Professional Civil Service of April 7, 1933 was passed. As he was not publicly aligned to the Nazi Party, the radical changes he made to the judiciary were not immediately evident, but by the time he was done he had sacked thirty-one Jewish judges and prosecutors. In purging Hamburg's judicial system, some 30 percent of Hamburg's lawyers lost their positions.

From May 16, 1935, Rothenberger served as president of the Hamburg Higher Administrative Court, in which he initiated a new system for all courts. Weekly pre-case discussions were held, in which each judge presented the most important cases coming up in the forthcoming week. Rothenberger stated how each case should proceed and at the same time criticized "unacceptable" judgments from the previous week. Over time, he decided almost every case personally. On some occasions he intervened in the cases of other judges. He always blocked any charges brought against Nazis.

After war broke out in 1939, justice was even more controlled. With the appointment in January 1941 of Franz Schlegelberger as justice minister, Rothenberger identified a new career for himself, writing successfully in April 1942 to Adolf Hitler a series of reform proposals for the judicial system. On August 20, 1942, Rothenberger was appointed as state secretary in charge of judicial reform.

One of his first acts was to make a deal with a leading SS officer, Bruno Streckenbach, whereby prisoners deemed as "antisocial" would be removed from jails and handed over to the SS to be worked to death in concentration camps. SS chief Heinrich Himmler decreed that Jews and Roma would join repeat offenders and those with lengthy sentences in this "antisocial" category.

Rothenberger soon returned to his original reform plans and sought to give the Nazi Party a closer role in the training of judges, arguing that justice at the highest level should remain with a fully trained judiciary. By December 1942, however, new justice minister Otto Thierack sought to dismiss Rothenberger, whose reforms were causing friction between the Party and the judiciary just as the war was beginning to turn against Germany and stability was necessary. Eventually fired in late 1943, he returned to Hamburg, where he commenced practice as a public notary.

In May 1945 Rothenberger was arrested by the Allies. He became one of the defendants at the Judges' Trial, which commenced at Nuremberg on January 4, 1947, and on December 4, 1947, he was sentenced to seven years' imprisonment. The tribunal found that Rothenberger had furthered the program of racial persecution and contributed significantly to the degradation of the Ministry of Justice and the courts in submitting to the will of Hitler, the Nazi Party, and the police.

In August 1950 he was released early from Landsberg Prison and settled in Schleswig-Holstein, before returning to Hamburg in 1954. In 1959 a report was published on Rothenberger's activities during the Nazi era. Humiliated, his career in tatters, he committed suicide on September 1, 1959.

Discussion Questions

1. How would you describe Curt Rothenberger: an opportunist, a committed Nazi, or something else? Why?
2. To what extent did the justice system undergo change after Rothenberger's proposals of April 1942 were accepted?

Further Reading

Koch, H. W., *In the Name of the Volk: Political Justice in Hitler's Germany*,
    London: I.B. Tauris, 1997.
Miller, Richard M., *Nazi Justiz: Law of the Holocaust*, Westport: Praeger, 1995.
Muller, Ingo, *Hitler's Justice: The Courts of the Third Reich*, Cambridge,
    MA: Harvard University Press, 1991.

MAY 1942 (1)

10.6 A Courageous Swedish Smuggler

Sven Norrman was the head of the Warsaw office of the Swedish
engineering company ASEA during the German invasion in 1939. Born
in 1891, he enjoyed the life of a business executive in a foreign mission
prior to war breaking out. A fluent Polish speaker, he collected Polish art,
was well liked by his staff, and loved hunting. With the German invasion
in September 1939, he was based in Stockholm, though he visited Poland
every two to three months. The Nazi occupation saw Norrman and other
Swedes in a similar position living relatively comfortable lives. It was in
Germany's interest to ensure good relations with Sweden, which provided
such goods and services as matches, ball bearings, and technical equipment
to which Germany did not have ready access. At first, as the bombs rained
down on Warsaw, the so-called Warsaw Swedes lived much of their time in
a bunker at the Swedish embassy, but over time life resumed to as normal
a condition as was possible under the circumstances. Norrman even fell in
love with his secretary, a young Polish Jew named Gizela "Iza" Zbyszynska.

From their elevated standing, the Warsaw Swedes were able to witness
the unravelling Holocaust before their very eyes. It began with antisemitic
violence, in which Jews, singled out through the compulsory wearing of a
Star of David, were beaten in the streets and otherwise humiliated. Norrman
photographed examples of oppression in October 1939 in Włocławek, in
northern Poland, which became the first town in Europe in which Jews were
required to wear a star. He was also witness to Jews being banned from
using the sidewalks. In Warsaw, Norrman entered the ghetto itself, where he
secretly took thousands of photographs.

All this, however, was but a prelude to other, more vital, acts
of opposition. Norrman noticed that Jewish acquaintances were
disappearing in increasing numbers—whether through death in the ghetto,
deportation, or imprisonment—and became more and more anxious as
to where developments were heading. Swedes such as Norrman could
move around Warsaw as well as to and from Sweden, and he saw that
an opportunity existed for him to make the horrors of Poland known

more widely. Eventually, he and other Warsaw Swedes began smuggling documents and photographs back to Stockholm; not only that, but he brought money back into Warsaw, with which the resistance movement could buy arms.

Both the Polish government-in-exile in London and the *Armia Krajowa* (Home Army) in Warsaw saw the use that could be made of the Swedes' willingness to help. On May 16, 1942, the Home Army's commander-in-chief, General Stefan Rowecki, observed that the Swedes were a valuable resource that needed to be protected; a few days later, on May 21, Norrman took one of the most important consignments of documents to Stockholm thus far, with full particulars of the annihilation of 700,000 Polish Jews. His secret package included thousands of negatives of Nazi crimes in Poland.

Within a few weeks, all this information had been passed on to London, and on June 9, 1942, Poland's exiled premier, Władysław Sikorski, made a broadcast over the BBC revealing the details Norrman had smuggled out. This was the first time that the world heard news of the Nazi crimes in any detail. Some news had previously been revealed but never on such a scale.

In response, the Gestapo began rounding up the Warsaw Swedes, instinctively aware that the only way the information could have been smuggled out would have been through them. On the direct order of SS chief Heinrich Himmler, seven Swedes were arrested by the Gestapo: Nils Berglind, Carl Herslow, Sigfrid Häggberg, Tore Widén, Einar Gerge, Stig Lagerberg, and Reinhold Grönberg. By a quirk of fate, Sven Norrman was in Stockholm at the time of the arrests as his mistress, Iza Zbyszynska, had managed to get a message to him just before he was due to return. Four of the men, Berglind, Herslow, Häggberg, and Widén, were sentenced to death in July 1943, though all seven were eventually released in the fall of 1944 and returned safely to Sweden. It is likely that intercession by King Gustav V led to the releases after he had written to Adolf Hitler seeking an amnesty.

For her part, Iza was found and taken into custody. Although she had lived as a Christian on the Aryan side in Warsaw, the Gestapo became aware of her Jewish identity once she had been captured, and she was sent to the Moabit prison in Berlin, where she survived until the end of the war. Upon her liberation, she and Norrman were reunited in Warsaw; Norrman then divorced his wife in Sweden and married Iza. In 1974 the Polish government awarded him the *Armia Krajowa Cross* in recognition of his services for the Polish people.

Sven Norrman explained his motivation in an interview several years after the war in words that left little room for doubt as to why he acted as he did: "During my entire life I was a businessman. I liked my job and I was good in my field. I joined the struggle because I wanted to do something that was not for profit for once in my life." Sven Norrman died on February 8, 1979, in Stockholm.

Discussion Questions

1. Do you think the Warsaw Swedes betrayed their neutrality by helping the Jews and engaging in smuggling activities during the war? If so, how?

2. Do you think that Sven Norrman's explanation for his actions at the end of the article is convincing? Or were there perhaps additional reasons in his personal life that contributed?

Further Reading

Malm, Sarah, "The Swedes Who Told the World about the Holocaust: Forgotten Heroes of WWII Who Were Sentenced to Death for Smuggling Proof of Nazi Murders Out of Poland," *Daily Mail Online*, January 12, 2015, http://www.dailymail.co.uk/news/article-2877647/The-Swedes-told-world-Holocaust-Forgotten-heroes-WWII-sentenced-death-smuggling-proof-Nazi-murders-Poland.html (accessed on February 9, 2024).

MAY 1942 (2)

10.7 Jewish Heroes in the Heart of the Reich

In mid-1937 Herbert Baum and his wife Marianne had founded an anti-Nazi resistance group in Germany. By May 1942 they were responsible for organizing a dramatic protest against Nazism in Berlin, in the heartland of Reich propaganda minister Joseph Goebbels.

Born on February 10, 1912, in Moschin, eastern Germany, by 1926 Herbert Baum was an active member of various left-wing Jewish youth movements. In 1931 he joined Germany's Young Communist League. After Baum and his childhood sweetheart Marianne Cohn were married in 1934, they were directed by the Communist Party to contact a number of Jewish organizations with which Baum had worked in earlier times. A small circle of friends and acquaintances formed and then grew. Most of them were Jewish, and they met frequently to discuss ways to circumvent Nazi antisemitism. Almost immediately they nominated Baum as their chairman.

By the time of *Kristallnacht* in November 1938, the little group numbered nearly 100, who would attend meetings at various times to discuss their options. After Jewish organizations were banned in 1939 the group grew larger—and, of necessity, more secretive.

In 1940 Baum was drafted into a forced labor unit at the Siemens-Schuckertwerke, an electrical engineering company in Berlin. While here, he engaged in clandestine propaganda, leading to many more recruits from among those at the plant. For some who were communist but not Jewish, the idea of resistance proved to be a problem on account of the alliance signed between the Soviet Union and Nazi Germany in August 1939. For the Jews, there was little option; they could not afford any political dilemmas.

From 1941 onward, members of Baum's network at Siemens saw that if they were to escape deportation to concentration camps, they would have to mount some sort of underground resistance while at the same time making it appear as though they were vital to the war effort. Their activities at this time focused on the preparation and distribution of anti-Nazi propaganda leaflets, rather than physical confrontation.

At the beginning of May 1942 propaganda minister Joseph Goebbels, who was also the Nazi district chief (Gauleiter) of Berlin, organized an enormous exhibition at the Lustgarten, right in the heart of the city. This exhibition, entitled "The Soviet Paradise," was intended to dehumanize the Russian enemy and reinforce an anti-Soviet (and, through this, an anti-Jewish) mindset among the population, thereby justifying the war against the Soviet Union. Well over a million people visited while the exhibition was running. Baum and his circle, recognizing that their actions could always be only symbolic—they knew that they could not by themselves topple the Nazi regime—decided to let symbolism confront symbolism. On May 18, 1942, a group of seven Baum members—Herbert and Marianne Baum, Hans Joachim, Gerd Meyer, Sala Kochmann, Suzanne Wesse, and Irene Walther— set fires around the exhibition that were timed to ignite simultaneously.

The fires were extinguished quickly, however, and within days hundreds of Jewish Berliners, including all seven participants and most of the other members of the Baum group, were arrested by the Gestapo. Herbert Baum was taken to the Siemens plant and ordered to identify fellow workers who were part of the conspiracy; refusing to reveal anything, he was tortured mercilessly in Berlin's Moabit prison and died on June 11, 1942. The Gestapo reported his death as suicide. Marianne was executed in Plötzensee prison on August 18, 1942, along with group members Joachim Franke, Hildegard Jadamowitz, Heinz Joachim, Sala Kochmann, Hans-Georg Mannaberg, Gerhard Meyer, Werner Steinbrink, and Irene Walther.

Other resisters in the Baum group were caught and tried in succeeding months. Most were executed at Plötzensee on March 4, 1943: Heinz Rotholz, Heinz Birnbaum, Hella Hirsch, Hanni Meyer, Marianne Joachim, Lothar Salinger, Helmut Neumann, Hildegard Löwy, and Siegbert Rotholz. Overall, the deaths of the Baum group members represent a tragic roll call of lost youth and dashed hopes. The average age of those in the group's inner circle was twenty-two; Charlotte Päch, aged thirty-two, was the oldest in the group and was nicknamed "Grandma" by the others. Moreover, not all were Jewish; Franke, Jadamowitz, Mannaberg, and Steinbrink were all non-Jewish communists. Ultimately, of the thirty-two members of the group who lost their lives, twenty-two were executed by decapitation, nine died in death camps, and one—Herbert Baum himself—through torture. Only five members of the Baum group survived the war.

As an act of resistance to the Holocaust, the question must be asked: was it worth it? The press was forbidden to report on the fire, and no official news was released regarding the Baum group or the fate of its members. Yet the partial destruction of the exhibit on the Lustgarten must have presented something of a shock to Goebbels and the Berlin Nazis. A small but well-organized resistance circle of Jewish communists had challenged a major Nazi propaganda enterprise, in the heart of the German capital, more than nine years after the Nazis had come to power. Little wonder that the punishments were so overwhelming and devastating. The Baum group, quite simply, rocked the Nazi establishment as few other German resistance movements had at that time.

Discussion Questions

1. In what way(s) was the Baum group effective in protesting against the Nazis?

2. In your view, was there anything significant in the fact that the members of the Baum group were all young people?

Further Reading

Brothers, Eric, *Berlin Ghetto: Herbert Baum and the Anti-Fascist Resistance*, Stroud: Spellmount, 2012.
Suhl, Yuri (ed.), *They Fought Back: The Story of the Jewish Resistance in Nazi Europe*, New York: Crown, 1967.

JUNE 1942

10.8 Butchery at Lidice

Reinhard Heydrich was a key SS leader who commanded the *Reichssicherheitshauptamt*, or Reich Main Security Office, with responsibility for carrying out Hitler's extermination of the Jews. He established the *Einsatzgruppen* murder squads, charged with executing Jews and others, first in German-controlled Poland and later in the Soviet Union. Heydrich also convened and chaired the Wannsee Conference on January 20, 1942, when leading Nazi bureaucrats discussed the best ways to carry out the extermination of European Jewry.

In late 1941, in addition to his other duties, Heydrich was appointed the Reich Protector of Bohemia and Moravia, the name given by the Nazis to the Czech-speaking regions of the former Czechoslovakia. On May 27, 1942, a planned assassination operation (code named Anthropoid) took place against Heydrich. It was carried out by Czech operatives trained and parachuted by the British Special Operations Executive to a location just outside of Prague. Although approved by the Czechoslovak government-in-exile in London, local resistance leaders in Prague pleaded for it not to go ahead, terrified of the reprisals that might follow. They were to be proven correct, with gruesome consequences.

When the commandos ambushed Heydrich on May 27, he was seriously wounded by a grenade thrown into his open car. Bomb fragments from the explosion embedded shrapnel and fibers from the upholstery into Heydrich's back and side; the wounds became infected, and he died of his injuries on June 4, 1942.

In Berlin, a furious Adolf Hitler immediately called for a reprisal killing of 10,000 Czechs. Although he was talked out of this by SS chief Heinrich Himmler, nevertheless over 13,000 were arrested, with many sent to concentration camps where they died subsequently. Far worse, however, was to come.

The town of Lidice was selected as the target of a wholesale symbolic reprisal against the Czech people. Located a little over fifteen kilometers from Prague, the town was, ironically, chosen due to a case of mistaken identity: one of the partisans responsible for the attack had connections to another village named Lidice, and the Nazis chose the one closest to Prague to exact their revenge attack.

On June 10, 1942, the Nazis entered Lidice. The next day, all 110 men and 82 boys of the village were summarily shot, together with 71 women. The remaining 198 women and 98 children were sent to concentration camps, most notably Ravensbrück, where many died. Children deemed to be of "Aryan stock" were sent to Germany, where they were forcibly integrated into German society through "re-education" in Nazi orphanages and foster homes. The village itself was then systematically destroyed, with all references to the town expunged from German maps and any Czech records still existing from before the war. The name of Lidice was removed as though it had never existed.

Several days later, a radio transmitter was found in the nearby village of Ležáky, leading to some 500 SS troops and police surrounding the village on June 24. Again, all the adult inhabitants (thirty three men and women) were shot, and the village destroyed. Thirteen children were spared. Of these, two sisters were removed to Germany; both survived and returned to their families after the war. The remaining eleven children were sent to the extermination camp at Chełmno, where they, together with a girl from Lidice, were gassed.

Only 16 of the children of Lidice not sent away are known to have survived the war, along with 143 of the women. In October 1942, however, relatives and friends of those killed at Lidice were hunted down by Nazi special police. Given their connection to Lidice, they, too, were murdered, this time at Mauthausen concentration camp in Austria.

Reinhard Heydrich's funeral in Berlin on June 9, 1942—the day before German troops moved into Lidice—was remembered as the largest of its kind in Nazi Germany. An even more dramatic and deadly tribute to Heydrich came later in the year, in the form of an operation code named *Aktion Reinhard*, given to the Nazi implementation of the deadliest phase of the Holocaust. This was what became termed the Final Solution of the Jewish Question (*Endlösung der Judenfrage*), lasting from 1942 and into 1943. The name was conferred as a memorial to Heydrich after his assassination.

Initially, the plan was to inaugurate measures that would lead to the eradication of the Jewish population in occupied Poland, but its scope broadened to include Jews transferred to Poland from throughout Nazi-occupied Europe. *Aktion Reinhard* was thus an undertaking embracing the deportation and mass murder of millions of Jews, accompanied by the plunder and transmission of Jewish property back to the Reich.

The operation eventually saw the establishment of three purpose-built extermination camps in eastern Poland: Sobibór, Bełzec, and Treblinka. These were established solely for the purpose of realizing the Nazis' murderous aims and were subsequently known as the *Aktion Reinhard* camps.

The martyrdom of Lidice became a byword for Nazi savagery (even during the most savage war in history), its fate known around the world within a relatively short period. In 1949 the village was rebuilt, together with a memorial to the victims of the massacre. Unlike Lidice, however, Ležáky was not rebuilt, and only memorials remain today.

It is, perhaps, worth pausing for a moment when we think of the horrors of the Holocaust and remember that small towns and villages throughout Nazi Europe suffered their own versions of Nazi brutality. At Lidice and Ležáky, at Kalavryta in Greece in 1943, in Oradour in France in 1944, and in many, many other locations, the statements Nazism made about itself became manifest in the blood and flesh of countless innocents.

The martyrdom of Lidice in the wake of Heydrich's assassination was but a prelude of much worse things to come. Not only did the Holocaust enter its most deadly phase, more and more localized massacres and the destruction of villages and towns followed, in places far removed from each other across Europe.

Discussion Questions

1. What was the relationship between what happened at Lidice and Ležáky and the Holocaust?

2. What does the martyrdom of Lidice tell you about the nature of German National Socialism during the war?

Further Reading

Bradley, J. F. N., *Lidice: Sacrificial Village*, New York: Ballantine Books, 1972.

Brendel, Toni, *Lidice: Remembered Around the World*, Iowa City: Penfield Books, 2015.

Gerrard, Alan James, *The Path to Lidice: And the Legacy of the Lidice Shall Live Campaign*, London: Independent Publishing Network, 2022.

JULY 1942 (1)

10.9 The Roundup at the Vel' d'Hiv

The capture of the Jews of Paris that became known as the Vel' d'Hiv Roundup was organized and carried out on July 16–17, 1942. It was effectively undertaken by French police under the direction of German occupation authorities. Code named Operation Spring Wind (*Opération Vent printanier*), the object of the raid was to round up the Jews of Paris, confine them, and then transport them to their death in Eastern Europe. As they were captured, the captives were taken to the cycling and sports stadium known as the *Vélodrome d'Hiver* (Winter Velodrome) in the fifteenth Arrondissement of Paris, near the Eiffel Tower.

In the months leading up to the roundup, SS leader Reinhard Heydrich, together with Fritz Sauckel, the organizer of forced labor for German armament factories, and Adolf Eichmann, the SS official in charge of Jewish policy, made several trips to Paris. As they familiarized themselves with the French situation, German administrators replaced French officials in charge of the Jewish Question, in a process intended to accelerate anti-Jewish policies.

The result saw a raid that began at 4:00 a.m. on the morning of July 16, 1942. Approximately 4,500 French police began arresting Jews throughout Paris. Over 11,000 were arrested that same day and confined in the Vel'd'Hiv. The arrests were made quickly and without discussion.

Ultimately, 13,152 Jews were taken, of which 5,802 were women and 4,051 were children. This was not the first time that French police had arrested Jews in Paris, but it was the first occasion in which women, children, and the elderly were specifically targeted. Included among those arrested were children aged between two and sixteen, together with their parents. Many of the Jews arrested were already refugees from Germany, Austria, Poland, Czechoslovakia, and Russia.

Conditions in the stadium deteriorated dramatically and very rapidly. The detainees were kept in extremely crowded surroundings, with water, food, and sanitary facilities practically nonexistent. The stadium's dark glass roof was painted blue to avoid bombings, and heat levels rose unbearably in the already hot summer month of July. Moreover, all the windows were sealed shut for security. Of the ten restrooms available, five had been locked to avoid escape through the windows. The only food or water available was brought in by several doctors and members of the Red Cross, who were allowed to enter. Any Jew who tried to escape was shot on the spot; in some cases, desperate individuals took their own lives.

No photographs exist of the events of July 16–17, 1942, other than one showing a row of buses outside the stadium. Over time, the arrested Jews were placed onto these buses, which transported the adults to the transit camp at Drancy, in the Paris suburbs.

In the week following the arrests, Jews were also deported to other transit camps—at Beaune-la-Rolande and Pithiviers in the Loiret region south of Paris as well as to Drancy. At the end of July and the beginning of August, the detainees were separated from their children and deported in freight cars to Auschwitz, where they were murdered. More than 3,000 babies and children were left alone in Beaune-la-Rolande and Pithiviers.

Of the 13,152 Jews arrested during the roundup, fewer than 100 survived. Of the 4,000 children deported to Auschwitz, none survived. In the two months following the arrests, approximately 1,000 Jews were deported to Auschwitz every two or three days. Overall, by the end of September 1942 France had deported almost 38,000 Jews, of whom only some 780 survived to see the liberation in 1945.

There were varied French reactions to the arrests and deportations, ranging from active collaboration with the Germans, indifference, empathy, and rescue efforts. Certain elements of French society, such as the press and some in the churches, voiced repulsion at the treatment of the Jews and publicly protested the events. The sight of Jewish mothers holding their babies, and children being placed under arrest, was a turning point for many, leading to the French public's condemnation of the treatment of the Jews during the German occupation.

For decades the French government declined to apologize for France's role in the roundup. It was not until fifty-three years later, on July 16, 1995, that France publicly acknowledged its role in an historic speech given by President Jacques Chirac. Here, he stated that the roundup was a crime committed "in France, by France." In 2012, on the seventieth anniversary, President François Hollande reaffirmed the message in another address at a monument to the roundup.

On April 10, 2017, however, in an ugly footnote, French presidential candidate Marine Le Pen argued that France bore no responsibility for the Vel' d'Hiv Roundup, questioning the French state's role in the Holocaust and suggesting that France was not responsible for the roundup of Jews. Her remarks were met with widespread condemnation across France.

Discussion Questions

1. Why do you think the roundup at the Vel' d'Hiv and its aftermath was undertaken by French authorities?

2. In view of the roundup at the Vel' d'Hiv, could it be said that France was also a perpetrator of the Holocaust—or was it a victim of doing Germany's bidding?

Further Reading

Dank, Milton, *The French against the French: Collaboration and Resistance*, Philadelphia: Lippincott, 1974.

Lévy, Claude, and Paul Tillard, *Betrayal at the Vel d'Hiv*, New York: Hill and Wang, 1969.

Zuccotti, Susan, *The Holocaust, the French, and the Jews*, Lincoln: University of Nebraska Press, 1999.

MAY 1942 (2)

10.10 The Jews of the Netherlands

A country with a 1939 population of approximately nine million people, the prewar Jewish population of the Netherlands was about 160,000, of whom some 19,500 were children of mixed marriages. These figures included nearly 25,000 Jews who had arrived in the Netherlands from Germany between 1935 and 1939.

Various Netherlands governments had for a long period seen to it that the country remained neutral in European conflicts, and when war commenced in September 1939, Queen Wilhelmina reaffirmed the standard position. For his part, German dictator Adolf Hitler gave a personal guarantee to the Queen that Germany would honor Dutch neutrality.

All previous activities, however, showed that in the cold light of day the Führer's guarantees guaranteed nothing. On May 10, 1940, he reneged on his promise, and German troops invaded the Netherlands at the same time invading Luxembourg, Belgium, and France. Dutch military resistance was immediate, but within a week (at most) the Germans had secured most of the country and Queen Wilhelmina had been evacuated, with her government, to London, where she oversaw a government-in-exile.

German occupation officials, who considered non-Jewish Dutch as fellow Aryans, hoped to incorporate the Netherlands into the Third Reich and set about instituting German-inspired legal systems and establishing a one-party political system. Soon, virtually, every aspect of Dutch life, including education, was suffused with Nazi ideology.

Resistance to the German occupation among the Dutch people remained somewhat limited when compared to some other countries between mid-1940 and late 1942; however, over time resistance became more pronounced and widespread. Unacceptably harsh occupation policies from the Germans played a large part in this, but the deteriorating economic situation under Nazism also played an important role as the occupation authorities shamelessly exploited Dutch industry, agriculture, raw materials, and workers.

Unarguably, however, no single group in the Netherlands suffered more than the Jews. In the fall of 1940, German officials promulgated a repressive set of anti-Jewish ordinances that essentially deprived many Jews of their livelihood, relegating them to third-class citizenship at best. In February 1941 several hundred Jewish men were deported to concentration camps: in protest, Dutch workers called a general strike to support their Jewish fellow citizens. The response saw German occupation authorities tightening restrictions against the Dutch Jews even further.

By early 1942 most Jews had been forced into localized neighborhoods serving the purpose of ghettos, and as many as 15,000 were rounded up and sent to forced labor camps. Soon after, most of the remaining Jews were concentrated in one large ghetto in Amsterdam. Jews who had been refugees from other countries were deported to a transit camp in the north.

Then the hammer blow came. On July 14, 1942, the German authorities, working with Dutch collaborators, began deporting Jews from Amsterdam. This precipitated a process of destruction during which some 110,000 Jews were sent to the euphemistically named "East," where most perished. A very large number arrived at the Sobibór extermination camp, where they were driven to an immediate death. Of the 110,000 who had been sent away, it is estimated that just 5,000 survived the war and returned to the Netherlands.

Meanwhile, between 25,000 and 30,000 Jews remained hidden in the Netherlands, often aided by the Dutch resistance and Dutch civilians. Most of those hidden managed to survive the war, though there were tragic exceptions. The best known of these saw Anne Frank and her family hidden in the famous attic in Amsterdam until they, too, became victims of Nazi brutality after they were denounced and deported.

In the end, at least 75 percent of Jews living in the Netherlands when the war broke out—both native Dutch Jews and those who had arrived as refugees—were murdered between 1940 and 1945. Jewish losses, on a percentage basis, were higher in the Netherlands than any other state in Western Europe. It has been suggested that this development came about, in large part, because of strong collaborationist elements in the country.

The Netherlands, which suffered grievously during the last months of the war, was not liberated until the spring of 1945. In the meantime, at least 20,000 Dutch civilians died of starvation and disease during the brutal "Hunger Winter" of 1944–5, when German authorities sealed off the country from the outside world in a desperate attempt to retain their hold.

After the war ended, the shattered Dutch temporarily reinstated the death penalty, tried collaborators, and executed them. Women known to have collaborated were punished with ritual humiliation, frequently through having their head shaved and paraded in public. The leader of the Dutch Nazi movement, Anton Adriaan Mussert, was tried for treason and executed by a firing squad on May 7, 1946, at The Hague. The German occupation chief in the Netherlands, Arthur Seyss-Inquart, was tried at Nuremberg for war crimes and brutal repression; he too was found guilty and executed.

Discussion Questions

1. Describe briefly how the Holocaust in the Netherlands too place.
2. Why do you think it took until July 1942 for Jews to be deported to their death in "the East."

Further Reading

Fuykschot, Cornelia, *Hunger in Holland: Life during the Nazi Occupation*, Amherst, NY: Prometheus Books, 1995.
Hirschfeld, Gerhard, *Nazi Rule and Dutch Collaboration: The Netherlands under German Occupation 1940–1945*, New York: Berg, 1988.
Presser, Jacob, *The Destruction of the Dutch Jews*, Boston: E.P Dutton, 1969.
Warmbrunn, Werner, *The Dutch under German Occupation, 1940–1945*, Stanford: Stanford University Press, 1963.

AUGUST 1942 (1)

10.11 A Tormented Nazi Meets a Swedish Diplomat

In August 1942, a quite remarkable event took place on a train traveling from Warsaw to Berlin. Kurt Gerstein, a senior SS officer intimately connected to the Nazi mass murder of the Jews at Auschwitz and other death camps was returning from an inspection tour of two of the camps located in Poland, Bełżec and Treblinka. What he had witnessed there defied belief.

On August 17, 1942, at Bełżec, he was present at the gassing of some 3,000 Jews. The next day he went to Treblinka, where he saw a repetition of the killing process. He was then given responsibility for ordering vast quantities of Zyklon-B gas for use in the mass murder of Jews at Auschwitz. Returning to Germany on the night of August 20–1, 1942, and deeply disturbed by what he had seen, Gerstein was desperate to unburden himself.

Fate intervened in the person of the secretary to the Swedish legation in Berlin, Baron Göran von Otter, who was on the same train.

Engaging von Otter in conversation, Gerstein exclaimed: "Yesterday I saw something appalling." "Is it to do with the Jews?" von Otter asked, and the conversation—more like a monologue—began. In a feverish conversation lasting ten hours, Gerstein poured out the whole story, crying and smoking incessantly. While relating all he had seen, he begged von Otter to inform the Swedish government. Von Otter later recalled that Gerstein gave him details, names, and how he had come to be involved; his experience now saw him determined to act as a witness to the Nazi atrocities. He pleaded with von Otter to inform the Allies and the outside world of what he had seen, so that Allied air forces, acting on Swedish information, would drop millions of leaflets over Germany. The German people, horrified, would then rebel against Hitler.

This was not the only occasion on which Gerstein sought to draw attention to what he had witnessed. He attended upon the papal nuncio in Berlin, Archbishop Cesare Orsenigo, but was turned away; he also saw numerous members of the Confessing and Lutheran churches and opponents of the Nazi regime. In his eagerness to get the message out he spoke to anyone who would listen—often, to those he did not even know.

Apart from the Swedish authorities, the Allies, and the Vatican, in February 1943 Gerstein also tried to convey his message about the gas chambers to the Dutch underground. Skeptical, the underground leaders decided not to forward the report or circulate it publicly. Another Gerstein attempt to let the world know had failed.

While attempting to raise consciousness, he also took practical steps to see to it that the devastating effects of his office could be negated, or at least minimized. As the war progressed, a despairing Gerstein ordered that Zyklon-B gas canister shipments be buried on the pretext that they had been spoiled in transit and posed a risk to German soldiers and civilians. He tried, unsuccessfully, to have a chemical that caused severe irritation removed from the gas compound, so that death would be less painful for the victims. He fought with his superiors who demanded that larger consignments of Zyklon-B should be dispatched, arguing that storing large amounts was extremely hazardous; if hit by Allied air raids, the result would see a catastrophic loss of life throughout the region where the gas was stored. His efforts saw only small returns, despite an inner turmoil that aged him prematurely; brought on clinical depression; and saw him attempt suicide on one occasion and discuss it on many others.

Finally, on April 22, 1945, he defected to the Allies, making his way to French lines in the town of Reutlingen. He was given the opportunity to write a full report of what he had done and seen. The report became perhaps the most horrifying eyewitness account of the Holocaust. After he had witnessed the gassing as Bełżec he was told by the commandant, SS Major Christian Wirth: "There are not ten people alive who have seen or will see as much as you." Gerstein worked to ensure that as many people as possible "saw" what he had seen.

On July 25, 1945, while still in French custody, he was found hanged in his cell, an alleged suicide. Later, on August 17, 1950, a denazification court in Tübingen concluded that Gerstein was a Nazi offender for his assistance in the production and delivery of Zyklon-B. Baron von Otter took up his case, working to rehabilitate him. It wasn't until January 1965, however, after a long battle, that Gerstein's reputation was restored, and he received a posthumous pardon.

Gerstein's self-appointed mission was to expose the horrors of Nazism to the world and mitigate the suffering around him. His is the story of a remarkable and highly complex man who refused to surrender his conscience in the face of mass murder. He realized that he was continuing to commit the very acts he repudiated, albeit legally enforceable orders in accordance with the law of the land as it stood at that time. To disobey those orders would have put him totally beyond the pale and into a concentration camp—and, thus, completely unable to achieve the results he sought.

Kurt Gerstein found himself, therefore, in a situation where the conflict between legality and morality could probably not have been resolved, and that, perhaps, is the essence of his tragedy.

Discussion Questions

1. Was Kurt Gerstein a Holocaust perpetrator or a Holocaust resister? Give reasons for your answer.

2. Did Gerstein betray his duty as a German officer by speaking with Göran von Otter and others about what he had seen?

Further Reading

Friedländer, Saul, *Kurt Gerstein, the Ambiguity of Good*, New York: Knopf, 1969.
Joffroy, Pierre, *A Spy for God: The Ordeal of Kurt Gerstein*, New York: Harcourt Brace Jovanovich, 1971.

AUGUST 1942 (2)

10.12 The Riegner Telegram

In August 1942 a telegram was sent by Gerhart Riegner, the representative of the World Jewish Congress in Geneva, to contacts in the governments of the United States and Britain. It contained important information regarding the planned imminent extermination of the Jews under Nazi control. It is as important for the way the telegram was handled as for what it said.

Gerhart Moritz Riegner was born on September 11, 1911, in Berlin. Having fled to Switzerland to escape antisemitism in the early years of the Nazi regime, he became director of the Geneva office of the World Jewish Congress. It was in that capacity that he found himself in receipt of information regarding the Nazi plan to exterminate the Jews of Europe. The information came from a successful German industrialist, Eduard Schulte, and Riegner considered it to be reliable.

On August 8, 1942, Riegner visited the US embassy and the British consulate in Geneva. In the former he asked a vice-consul to send a telegram containing his information to the State Department in Washington and to Rabbi Stephen S. Wise, president of the World Jewish Congress; in the latter, he asked that the information be sent to Samuel Sidney Silverman, a member of parliament, and chairman of the British section of the World Jewish Congress. The telegram stated:

> Received alarming report stating that, in the Fuehrer's Headquarters, a plan has been discussed, and is under consideration, according to which all Jews in countries occupied or controlled by Germany numbering 3½ to 4 millions [*sic*] should, after deportation and concentration in the East, be at one blow exterminated, in order to resolve, once and for all the Jewish question in Europe. Action is reported to be planned for the autumn. Ways of execution are still being discussed including the use of prussic acid. We transmit this information with all the necessary reservation, as exactitude cannot be confirmed by us. Our informant is reported to have close connexions with the highest German authorities, and his reports are generally reliable.

Although it later proved to be inaccurate in parts, at the time Riegner brought the telegram to the attention of the US State Department and the British Foreign Office it was believed that the death of millions of Jews was to start within a month, and the extermination was to be done "at one blow." This made a response to the information urgent.

The British Foreign Office delayed for several weeks but did send the information to Silverman. He, in turn, forwarded the telegram to Wise, who received it on August 28, 1942. The State Department, however, did not send the telegram to Wise, despite Riegner's urgent request. Wise learned of Riegner's telegram only because Silverman sent it to him separately. Upon receipt of the information from Silverman, Wise contacted undersecretary of state Sumner Welles, who asked Wise not to make the information public until it could be confirmed by additional sources. That did not happen until November 24, 1942, by which time the State Department had received numerous corroborating reports of what was happening in Germany and across Europe. At that time Wise was free to make the Riegner Telegram public.

On December 17, 1942, the Allied governments of the United States, the United Kingdom, and the Soviet Union simultaneously issued a statement acknowledging and condemning Germany's extermination of the Jews. That announcement was issued less than a month from the date on which the existence and information of the Riegner Telegram was made public. However, from the time Riegner first informed the US and British governments of the information he had received from Schulte to when it was allowed to be publicized—a full three and a half months—represented a delay during which tens or hundreds of thousands of Jews were killed and in which three and a half to four million were expected to be killed.

The Riegner Telegram was not the first report the Allies had received of mass murder of the Jews, but it was of great significance nonetheless because the information came from a German source. The treatment of the information has been cited as one of many pieces of evidence that the US State Department was unconscionably slow in its response to the crisis of the extermination of the Jews of Europe.

Discussion Questions

1. What was significant about the content of the Riegner Telegram?
2. Why do you think the US State Department was so slow in acting upon Riegner's telegram? Do you think it was deliberate? If so, why?

Further Reading

Gilbert, Martin, *Auschwitz and the Allies*, London: Michael Joseph/Rainbird, 1981.
Riegner, Gerhart M., *Never Despair: Sixty Years in the Service of the Jewish People and the Cause of Human Rights*, Chicago: Ivan R. Dee, 2006.
Wallace, Gregory J., *America's Soul in the Balance: The Holocaust, FDR's State Department, and the Moral Disgrace of an American Aristocracy*, Austin: Greenleaf Book Group Press, 2012.

SEPTEMBER 1942

10.13 The Jews of Belgium Fight Back

In September 1942 two Jewish communists in Belgium, Hertz Jospa and his wife Yvonne, were instrumental in founding the *Comité de Défense des Juifs* (Jewish Defense Committee, or CDJ), which was to become a leading Belgian resistance organization during the Second World War.

The Jospas, who were members of the Jewish revolutionary organization *Solidarité juive*, were a remarkable couple. Yvonne was born in Romania in 1910 with the name Have (Chava) Groisman. The third of four girls, she came from an observant middle-class background. Her father was one of three judges in their hometown, and her mother was actively involved in the work of the local Jewish school. Yvonne attended school in Kishinev (Chişinău) before moving to Belgium to study social work at the University of Liège.

In 1933 she married Hertz, a pharmaceutical chemist. Straight after their wedding, Yvonne and Hertz joined the Communist Party of Belgium and in 1934 became Belgian citizens. Prior to the outbreak of the war, they worked with child refugees from the Spanish Civil War and organized the passage through Belgium of Romanian antifascist volunteers going to Spain to fight with the International Brigades.

During 1935 and 1936 Yvonne also took care of Jewish refugees from Germany and Austria. After *Kristallnacht* in November 1938, her work intensified dramatically. She often shielded illegal immigrants in her house, prior to smuggling them out of Belgium and to a safe third country.

With the Nazi invasion of Belgium and the country's capitulation on May 28, 1940, Yvonne began to devote herself fully to social and relief matters. She and Hertz moved around constantly with false names and papers. Their multiple identities as Jews, communists, and anti-Nazis placed them in a state of constant peril.

An extensive Nazi nighttime raid on the Jewish quarter of Brussels in September 1942 was the spur for many Belgian Jews to join rescue and armed resistance groups. Hertz and Yvonne, along with Zionist associations and the *Front de l'Indépendance*, established the *Comité de Défense des Juifs*, which came to be recognized by the Belgian government-in-exile in London as the representative body of the Belgian Jewish community. Yvonne headed a section working to rescue Jewish children, and through her efforts over 3,000 were saved from deportation through placement with sympathetic non-Jewish families.

The CDJ's activities were many. They hid Jewish children, published anti-Nazi works, functioned as a national social service organization, and created false identification papers for Jews in hiding. There were approximately thirty members in the children's section alone, and it developed a vast network for hiding Jews. The department for forged documents not only provided Jews with false papers but also supplied the broader resistance movement throughout Belgium. The section *Kinderen* was responsible for the hiding and support of individuals who had gone underground.

The most important act of resistance by the CDJ took place on the evening of April 19–20, 1943, when agents derailed a train leaving the Mechelen/ Malines transit camp headed for Auschwitz. The CDJ had learned of the exact date and time of the deportation from Mechelen and smuggled tools from the camp's workshop onto the train cars to enable prisoners to pry open the carriage doors and floorboards. Three members of the CDJ unit

Group G, under the direction of Georges Livchitz, forced the train to a halt by signaling it with a red lantern. While Livchitz held the engineer at gunpoint with his revolver, the other two members, Robert Maistriau and Jean Franklemon, aided in the escape of several prisoners within the cars. The three CDJ agents were able to escape under gunfire, with the operation saving 231 Jews out of the 1,631 heading for Auschwitz. This is the only known instance of an armed assault anywhere in Europe staged to halt a train transporting Jews en route to their deaths. Georges Livchitz was arrested and executed in February 1944 by a German firing squad.

Overall, the creation of the CDJ was the most important achievement of organized Belgian Jewry during the German occupation. It played a critical role in rescue and resistance between September 1942 and Belgium's liberation in February 1945.

In June 1943 Hertz Jospa was arrested, caught while meeting with a Jewish courier. He was deported as a political resister, not as a Jew, which saved him from being sent to Auschwitz. After a period of detention in Belgium, in May 1944 he was deported to Buchenwald. Yvonne lost contact with him and thought he had died, but he returned on May 8, 1945, after the camp was liberated. When he returned, he was but a shadow of what he had been prior to his arrest, emotionally and physically exhausted, and very sick. It took a long period of convalescence for him to return to health.

All the members of Yvonne's family who remained in Romania were murdered during the Holocaust, but a sister, who was with her in Belgium, survived. No one, however, other than those with whom she had the closest contact during the war, knew of her accomplishments on behalf of Jewish children. In 1964, to keep together the community of resisters she had played such an important part in facilitating, she cofounded the *Union des Anciens Résistants Juifs de Belgique* (Union of Former Belgium Jewish Resistance Members). She remained honorary chairperson of this organization until her death, in Brussels, in 2000.

Discussion Questions

1. Do you think the CDJ was an effective resistance and rescue organization during the Holocaust? Why/why not?
2. In your view, why did Hertz and Yvonne, as Jews, undertake the rescue of other Jews instead of trying to save their own lives?

Further Reading

Fraser, David, *The Fragility of Law: Constitutional Patriotism and the Jews of Belgium, 1940–1945*, New York: Routledge, 2009.

Michman, Dan (ed.), *Belgium and the Holocaust: Jews, Belgians, Germans*, Jerusalem: Yad Vashem, 1998.
Schreiber, Marion, *The Twentieth Train: The True Story of the Ambush of the Death Train to Auschwitz*, New York: Grove: 2004.
Veranneman de Watervliet, Jean-Michel, *Belgium in the Second World War*, Barnsley: Pen & Sword Military, 2014.

OCTOBER 1942

10.14 The Anguish of Norway's Jews

The deportation of the tiny Jewish community of Norway began on October 25, 1942. It was the culmination of two years of increasing oppression against a vulnerable community that had previously considered itself to be relatively safe from persecution. At the outset of the Second World War, Norway had a population of approximately 2.9 million people. The Jewish community had grown very slowly but received some refugees from Germany and peaked at around 2,100 by 1939.

In April 1940, in violation of Norway's declared neutrality, Germany invaded as part of its push into Scandinavia. The Nazi plan was to establish naval bases in Norway to counter British control over the North Sea as well as secure important raw materials. With British and French assistance, the Royal Norwegian Navy and the other arms of the military mounted a spirited defense, though ultimately, by late May, the Germans had achieved victory. On June 7 King Haakon VII, along with many members of the Norwegian government, fled and established a government-in-exile in London.

The Nazis then turned to a local fascist, Vidkun Quisling, to govern the country. Born in 1887, Quisling had been Norwegian military attaché in Petrograd, Russia, and after holding several administrative posts he became minister of defense in 1931. Known as a capable army officer and government official, he courted controversy through his support of Germany's Nazis, and in 1933 he helped found the *Nasjonal Samling* (NS) party, a Norwegian fascist organization.

The NS was unpopular with the Norwegian people, however, and did not attract much in the way of electoral success. In 1939 Quisling met with German dictator Adolf Hitler and discussed options for a possible German occupation of Norway, with the object of placing the NS in power. It took the German invasion of April 1940 to achieve this, and Quisling established a government in which he was named as Minister-President. It lasted only one week, the Nazis realizing that Quisling had next to no support from the Norwegian people—most of whom detested Nazism.

A new ruling body was thereby created, in which a German Nazi, Josef Terboven, was made Reich Commissioner. On February 1, 1942, Quisling was given greater political power as Norway's Minister-President in a new NS government supported directly by the Nazis. He subsequently embarked on a program of Nazification for Norway. His policies, which included efforts to convert churches and schools to the principles of National Socialism, still met with opposition from many Norwegians.

Between June 1940 and June 1941, when the Germans launched Operation Barbarossa, there were comparatively few restrictions placed on Norway's Jews. However, that attack prompted German occupation officials to arrest and detain Jews in northern Norway during the summer of 1941. Beginning in October, German officials, working with Norwegian collaborators, began making more arrests, including 260 male Jews living in Oslo. Additional arrests in Oslo took place on November 25–6, 1941. They were sent first to Germany by sea, and from there by train to Auschwitz, where most perished.

The effectiveness of Quisling's government to carve out an autonomous Norwegian fascist identity was impeded by interference from Berlin and by Norwegian partisans. A resistance movement had emerged almost immediately after the German invasion and included both armed and unarmed factions. Much activity involved nonviolent civil disobedience; for example, when Quisling tried to introduce Nazi ideology into school curricula, teachers refused to acquiesce, even after many were arrested and detained.

On the evening of October 25, 1942, members of the Norwegian resistance learned that all remaining Jews in the country were about to be arrested and deported the next day. With only a few hours' notice, as many Jews as possible were warned to go into hiding, and over the next few days attempts were made to smuggle them across the border to neutral Sweden. The process was extremely difficult; there were no plans for taking care of hundreds of people in such a short time, and as a result arrangements had to be improvised. Yet many Jews were saved, with most making the crossing in small groups.

Upon learning that these attempts at saving Jews were taking place, Terboven imposed the death penalty on anyone caught aiding the refugees, and both the German occupiers and local Norwegian police were especially vigilant in their efforts to capture as many Jews as possible.

As a result, rescue efforts were mixed. Perhaps as many as 900 Jewish refugees made their way across the border to Sweden, with others crossing the North Sea to Britain. But 758 Norwegian Jews were murdered by the Nazis (mostly in Auschwitz), while at least another 775 Jews were arrested and detained in local concentration camps and prisons in Norway. Of those deported, only a small number managed to return after Norway's liberation in May 1945, while a few managed to survive in hiding. The German occupation was an almost complete disaster for Norway's Jews, from which few were left untouched.

Discussion Questions

1. With such a small Jewish population, why was Norway such a dangerous place for Jews under the Nazis?
2. Do you think Vidkun Quisling was complicit in the destruction of Norway's Jewish population? Why/why not?

Further Reading

Abrahamsen, Samuel, *Norway's Response to the Holocaust: A Historical Perspective*, New York: Holocaust Library, 1991.
Berman, Irene Levin, *"We Are Going to Pick Potatoes": Norway and the Holocaust, the Untold Story*, Lanham, MD: Hamilton Books, 2010.
Nissen, Henrik S. (ed.), *Scandinavia during the Second World War*, Minneapolis: University of Minnesota Press, 1983.
Riste, Olav, Magne Skodvin, and Johan Andenaes, *Norway and the Second World War*, Oslo: Johan Grundt Tanum Forlag, 1966.

NOVEMBER 1942

10.15 *Casablanca*'s Story without an Ending

On the night of November 26, 1942—Thanksgiving Night in the United States—the movie *Casablanca*, directed by Jewish refugee Michael Curtiz, premiered in New York. In decades since then it has become, arguably, one of the (if not *the*) best loved of all Hollywood films. For some, it is a war story; for many, a love story par excellence; for others, the most quotable movie ever made, with lines such as "Play it Sam," "Here's looking at you, kid!," "We'll always have Paris," "Round up the usual suspects," "Shocked, *shocked!*," "All the gin joints in all the towns in all the world, and she walks into mine," "Louis, I think this is the beginning of a beautiful friendship," "The problems of a three little people don't amount to a hill of beans in this crazy world," and so on. Its characters, together with its memorable lines and a theme song now known to generations (*As Time Goes By*), have all become iconic.

What is often overlooked is just how far this is a quintessentially *Jewish* movie, indeed, a Jewish *refugee* movie. Linked inextricably to the war against the Nazis, it was a major contribution by Jewish exiles in Hollywood to that war. Given the war situation at the time of its release, this was no small contribution.

By Thanksgiving of 1942 war news was everywhere. Operation Torch, the Allied invasion of Vichy-controlled Morocco and Algeria, began on November 8, and units of the US 1st Armored Division landed near

Oran—not far from Casablanca itself. Two days later, Germany invaded Vichy France, while on November 13 the British Eighth Army recaptured Tobruk. On the Eastern Front the Battle of Stalingrad began, and in the Pacific War, the Americans were deeply involved at Guadalcanal.

In this context, *Casablanca* was a work with multiple layers of meaning appealing to a wide audience. On one level it was a simple romantic drama, focusing on an American expatriate (Rick Blaine) who must choose between his love for a woman (Ilse Lund) and helping her husband, a leading Resistance leader (Victor Laszlo), escape Casablanca to continue his fight against the Nazis.

Another reading of the film, however, shows a reinforcement of the American image (whether borne out or not) as a haven for those persecuted by the Nazis. Set in 1941, refugees from Nazism all came to Rick's *Café Américain*, desperate to reach the still-neutral United States. Rick, who claimed no nationality other than "drunkard," was already opposed to Nazi and Fascist totalitarianism, having run guns to Ethiopia against the Italians and fought for the Republicans against Franco's Nationalists in Spain.

The movie's plot line can be found easily for those who have not seen it. Discussing the movie, however, leads us to examine the extraordinary dimension of Jewish—and Jewish refugee—involvement in its making.

Michael Curtiz had arrived in the United States from Hungary in 1926. In 1933 he became a naturalized US citizen, but several members of his family remained in Europe and were murdered by the Nazis at Auschwitz. Before and during the war, Curtiz contributed substantially to the European Film Fund, a benevolent association that collected and distributed money to assist European refugees in the United States involved in the film business. It should also be noted that the script of *Casablanca* was written in stages by other Jews: the twins Julius and Philip Epstein and Howard Koch, who would later go on to be blacklisted during the McCarthy period in the 1950s.

But it was the crucial role of the war and the refugees from Nazi Europe who gave the movie so much of its flavor. Only three of the credited actors were born in the United States: Humphrey Bogart as anti-hero Rick Blaine; Dooley Wilson as the café's resident musician, Sam; and Joy Page as a Bulgarian refugee, Annina Brandel. Beyond these three, the cast was truly international: Claude Rains and Sydney Greenstreet were British, Paul Henreid was Austrian, and Ingrid Bergman was Swedish. After these principal actors, Conrad Veidt was a refugee from Nazi Germany, as were Peter Lorre, Curt Bois, S. Z. Sakall, and Helmut Dantine. Madeleine LeBeau, a French actress married to another Jewish refugee-actor in *Casablanca*, Marcel Dalio, had escaped from the advancing Nazis in France in 1940. (LeBeau would be the last surviving cast member at her death on May 1, 2016.) Indeed, arguably perhaps up to half the film's small and medium roles were played by refugees from the Nazis. Other actors of Jewish background, such as the Russian-born Leonid Kinskey, also featured.

Casablanca resonated with American audiences. It won three Academy Awards, for Best Picture, Best Director (Curtiz), and Best Adapted Screenplay (the Epsteins and Koch) and received nominations in three other categories. It had—and still has—enormous emotional impact, much of which can be attributed to cinematic presence shown by the European exiles and refugees involved. In the words of one commentator, they "brought to a dozen small roles in *Casablanca* an understanding and a desperation that could never have come from Central Casting."

In one highly charged scene, for instance, when Nazi officers in the café sing a German patriotic song, Victor Laszlo orders the house band to drown them out by playing the *Marseillaise*, the French national anthem. During the filming of this scene, many of the actors were crying; Madeleine LeBeau, in an unscripted moment at the end, cried out "*Vive la France! Vive la Démocratie!*" Curtiz decided to retain this in the film, and it is a poignant high point of the movie.

Casablanca regularly features today in movie lists of the greatest films of all time. From a modern vantage point, it is still, to quote another of its memorable lines, "a story without an ending."

Discussion Questions

1. Some people refer to *Casablanca* as one of the greatest films of all time. Are there any clues in the article as to why this might be so?

2. Can a movie be classified as an act of resistance? Explain your answer by reference to the article.

Further Reading

Harmetz, Aljean, *The Making of Casablanca: Bogart, Bergman, and World War II*, Boston: Little, Brown, 2002.

Isenberg, Noah, *We'll Always Have Casablanca: The Life, Legend, and Afterlife of Hollywood's Most Beloved Movie*, New York: Norton, 2017.

DECEMBER 1942

10.16 Żegota: When Help Was Needed

The worst expressions of the Holocaust took place across the years 1942–3. In December 1942, two Polish women, Zofia Kossak-Szczucka (a writer) and Wanda Krahelska-Filipowicz (a socialite known by her nom de guerre, "Alinka"), established an organization named Żegota, a secret group based in Warsaw and run by Christians and Jews. Its goal was singular in nature; to save Jews from being murdered by the Nazis.

The *Rada Pomocy Zydom*, or Council for Aid to the Jews, originated as the Provisional Committee for Aid to Jews (*Tymczasowy Komitet Pomocy Żydom*), which the two women established on September 27, 1942. Unlike many such organizations during the war, it did not abbreviate its formal title into an acronym. From the beginning, it was essentially an independent Catholic body. When it was transformed more formally into Żegota, on December 4, 1942, it became a broad-based joint organization of Jews and non-Jews from different political orientations.

Żegota was the brainchild of Henryk Woliński, a member of the secret Polish Home Army. Once formed, its general secretary was from Poland's Socialist Party; its treasurer was a member of the Democratic Party. Both, of course, had been driven underground by the Nazi invasion and occupation. The fundamental aim of the organization was the common cause of saving Jews in danger from the Nazis, and in this Poland was the only country in Nazi-occupied Europe where such an organization existed. Ultimately, the council operated from its foundation in December 1942 until the liberation of Poland in 1945.

The organization was recognized and received assistance from outside. By the late spring of 1944 much of the funding it received was coming from the Polish government-in-exile in London, though owing to the war this often only arrived after a circuitous, dangerous, and time-consuming route. The financial resources needed to save even one Jewish life ranged from 6,000 to 15,000 zlotys; depending on the situation, Żegota's monthly budget ranged anywhere from 500,000 to two million zlotys, which, though seemingly large, did not meet the needs of saving as many Jewish lives as the organization would like. As a result, and wherever possible, Żegota operatives sought to prop up their resources in alternate ways (including, it has been alleged, robberies).

Żegota's needs were many, but it was found to be much easier to assist Jews if they were outside ghettos and on the Aryan side. Medical attention was provided for Jews in hiding, along with food and false identity documents. Żegota attempted (and often succeeded) in providing help for Jews in forced labor camps, while financial aid was provided whenever possible. Sometimes Żegota even managed to assist in escapes, though all too often such activities could often not be planned; it was more likely that advantage had to be taken of local circumstances as and when they presented themselves.

One of Żegota's major tasks related to the forging of documents, such that on average the organization was said to have been producing up to a hundred sets of forged papers at any one time. Żegota also played an important role in saving Jewish children by placing them with foster families or relocating them to orphanages and convents. In Warsaw the head of Żegota's children section, a Polish social worker named Irena Sendler, assumed near-legendary status through personally taking care of over 2,500 Jewish children. Sendler, who was one of many members of Żegota recognized by Israel's Yad Vashem as Righteous among the Nations, was nominated for a Nobel Prize before her death in 2008.

By the time the council was established, most Polish Jews had already been killed, but the organization's activists, at enormous personal risk, still managed to help several thousand of those remaining. Indeed, it has been estimated that about half of the Jews who survived the Holocaust in Poland—a figure representing over 50,000 people—were helped by Żegota in one way or another.

To as great an extent as possible, Żegota operated as a professional organization. Although extensive in its spread, it operated through small cells, with up to a hundred of these in Warsaw alone. Elsewhere, it operated in Kraków, Vilna (Vilnius), and Lvov (Lviv), with specific "departments" covering such areas as legal, housing, clothing, children's welfare, medical care, and finances, among others. It has been estimated that during the war perhaps as many as 20,000 members of Żegota were captured and executed by the Germans, with thousands of others imprisoned and sent to concentration camps. It was remarkable that the location of Żegota's head office in Warsaw, at 24 Zurawia Street, was well known to Poles but was never raided by the Germans.

Żegota was a truly unique phenomenon within the horror of the Holocaust, which bought the lives of tens of thousands of Jews at the cost of tens of thousands of Poles. In an environment in which the history of Polish relations with Jews has frequently been soured by frequent expressions of antisemitism, this stands as a shining example of what could have been done throughout the rest of Europe if more people of goodwill had decided that it was necessary to take a stand.

Discussion Questions

1. What do you think motivated the members of Żegota, such as Irena Sendler, to save Jews during the Holocaust?

2. In your view, what was needed to ensure that Żegota's activities were successful? Was secrecy alone responsible?

Further Reading

Tec, Nechama, *When Light Pierced the Darkness: Christian Rescue of Jews in Nazi-Occupied Poland*, Oxford: Oxford University Press, 1986.

Tomaszewski, Irene, and Tecia Werbowski, *Code Name: Zegota: Rescuing Jews in Occupied Poland, 1942–1945: The Most Dangerous Conspiracy in Wartime Europe*, Santa Barbara: Praeger, 2010.

Part 11

1943

JANUARY 1943

11.1 Resistance in the Warsaw Ghetto

In January 1943, the Jews of the Warsaw ghetto embarked upon a course of action that Nazi Germany considered impossible: they took up arms and, for the first time, fought back to stop the Nazis from achieving their murderous aims.

Through the summer of 1942, the Germans deported or executed more than 300,000 Jews from the Warsaw ghetto. During a two-and-a-half-month wave of deportations to Treblinka, from July 22, 1942, to September 12, 1942—a period known to the Germans as *Gross-Aktion Warschau* (General Action Warsaw)—it was intended that this would end the Jewish presence completely. On average, more than 5,000 Jews were deported each day, leaving alive only somewhere between 55,000 and 60,000 by the time the operation ended.

While those in the ghetto did not know the precise destination or fate of those who had been deported, vague reports of mass murder at Treblinka did manage to leak back. In response, members of Jewish youth groups, in the forefront of which was *Hashomer Hatzair*, formed the *Żydowska Organizacja Bojowa* (ŻOB), or Jewish Fighting Organization, on July 28, 1942. They issued a proclamation calling on the ghetto residents not to go to the trains when ordered to do so.

While the deportations were taking place, one member of *Hashomer Hatzair*, 23-year-old Mordecai Anielewicz, had escaped to southwest Poland on an underground mission to organize other branches of his movement, but upon returning to Warsaw he found the ghetto devastated. He and others, knowing from the outset that they could not defeat the Nazi war machine, now decided to resist any further deportations. In November 1942 members of the ŻOB elected Anielewicz as their leader, and preparations started for a defense of the ghetto whenever the next wave of deportations began.

Most of the more senior members of the Jewish community leadership in the ghetto disapproved of armed resistance for fear of provoking a devastating German retaliation. However, Anielewicz and another young Zionist leader, Yitzhak Zuckerman, began looking for support outside the ghetto. Contacting the Polish government-in-exile in London, they managed, with difficulty, to obtain a few rifles and pistols. The ŻOB then officially became part of the High Command of the Polish Home Army (*Armia Krajowa*, or AK), which began providing additional weapons and training.

In the meantime, the ŻOB prepared for the next onslaught by the Germans. On December 22, 1942, Zuckerman, Miriem (Gole) Mire, and Adolf Liebeskind were sent by the ŻOB to Kraków to meet with resistance fighters there. While in the city, they took part in an attack on a café that was frequented by the SS and the Gestapo. Liebskind was killed. There is debate regarding Gole's fate. Some say she was killed soon afterward; others assert she played a part in the Warsaw Ghetto Uprising in the spring of 1943. Zuckerman, although shot in the leg, managed to escape and return to Warsaw.

Once back, he then became the unofficial armorer of the ŻOB. He negotiated through contacts he had made with external resistance groups, attempting to procure rifles, pistols, ammunition, and grenades. These were smuggled into the ghetto *via* Warsaw's sewers, and his ongoing negotiations meant that he had a good idea of how he might navigate the labyrinth in the future.

In early January 1943, *Reichsführer-SS* Heinrich Himmler visited the Warsaw ghetto and ordered one final deportation of all the remaining Jews. This began, unannounced, on January 18. In response, although lightly armed and poorly trained for combat, the ŻOB saw its first action. Mordecai Anielewicz developed a plan in which his fighters obeyed the deportation orders until they reached a certain part of town, where they received a signal to attack. Despite the death of most of the early *Hashomer Hatzair* fighters, many Jews escaped at this time. Surprised by the opposition and suffering several casualties, the Germans withdrew to regroup their forces and evaluate the situation. Four days later, they stopped the deportations altogether—at least for the time being.

One of the Jewish leaders in this first expression of armed ghetto resistance was a young woman, Tova (Tosia) Altman. Directly involved in the fighting, she, along with several others, was captured and taken to the *Umschlagplatz* (collection point for deportation). She managed to escape with the aid of a Jewish ghetto policeman acting on behalf of *Hashomer Hatzair*. Placed in charge of maintaining contact with ŻOB members outside the ghetto, she then spent a large part of her time on the Aryan side but returned whenever she heard of an impending roundup.

Shocked that the Jews would arm themselves and fight another round of deportations, the Germans returned in force in April to liquidate the ghetto completely. The resultant Warsaw Ghetto Uprising, the starting date of which Jews employ to commemorate Yom Hashoah each year, saw the first and most extensive expression of urban guerrilla resistance against the Nazis by any population during the Second World War.

Discussion Questions

1. What do you think the fighters of the ŻOB were trying to achieve in January 1943?

2. In your opinion, why do you think the older members of the organized Jewish community in Warsaw disapproved of the younger generation who decided to resist?

Further Reading

Bartoszewski, Wladyslaw, and Anthony Polonsky, *The Jews in Warsaw: A History*, Oxford: Blackwell, 1991.

Engelking, Barbara, and Jacek Leociak, *The Warsaw Ghetto: A Guide to the Perished City*, New Haven: Yale University Press, 2009.

Friedman, Philip, *Martyrs and Fighters: The Epic of the Warsaw Ghetto*, New York: Praeger, 1954.

Gutman, Israel, *The Jews of Warsaw, 1939–1943: Ghetto, Underground, Revolt*, Bloomington: Indiana University Press, 1982.

Ringelblum, Emanuel, *Notes from the Warsaw Ghetto*, New York: McGraw-Hill, 1958.

FEBRUARY 1943

11.2 The Sacrifice of the White Rose

Calling themselves "The White Rose" (*Die Weisse Rose*), a group of anti-Nazi students at Munich University organized themselves to protest at the Nazi regime in late 1942 and early 1943. Its leading members included Hans Scholl and his sister Sophie, Willi Graf, Alexander Schmorell, Christoph Probst, and their professor Dr. Kurt Huber.

Hans and Sophie joined their friends and Professor Huber to publish and distribute a series of numbered leaflets campaigning for the overthrow of Nazism and the revival of a new Germany dedicated to the pursuit of goodness and founded on the purest Christian values. Several of the male students involved in the movement had already undergone military service in the Soviet Union and were thoroughly apprised of the antihuman brutality and massive destruction they had seen while there.

The leaflets they wrote and distributed appealed to educated Germans, the White Rose members believing that such people should be intrinsically opposed to Nazism. Leaflet No. 1 asked the question, "Isn't it true that every honest German is ashamed of his government these days? Who among us has any conception of the dimensions of shame that will befall us and our children when one day the veil has fallen from our eyes and the most horrible of crimes—crimes that infinitely outdistance every human measure—reach the light of day?"

Building on this general statement, Leaflet No. 2 was more explicit regarding the unfolding Holocaust:

> Since the conquest of Poland three hundred thousand Jews have been murdered in this country in the most bestial way ... The German people slumber on in their dull, stupid sleep and encourage these fascist criminals ... Each man wants to be exonerated of a guilt of this kind, each one continues on his way with the most placid, the calmest conscience. But he cannot be exonerated; he is guilty, guilty, guilty!

At first, the leaflets were sent out by post to randomly selected addresses rather than hand delivered, no mean feat for a group possessing little in the way of money, a printing press, or paper. By January 1943, however, the White Rose produced several thousand copies of Leaflet No. 5 using a hand-cranked duplicating machine. Through couriers and trusted runners, copies began to appear in cities all over Germany and Austria. These leaflets warned that Hitler was leading Germany toward ruin and that defeat was highly likely. Readers were urged to "support the resistance movement!" in the struggle for "freedom of speech, freedom of religion, and protection of the individual citizen from the arbitrary action of criminal dictator-states."

In mid-February 1943, the White Rose arranged a small anti-Nazi demonstration, their ideals inspiring them to more and more acts of daring. Their final act saw Hans and Sophie running through the University of Munich, scattering leaflets in the hallways and throwing them from the second- and third-floor balconies.

On February 18, 1943, Hans and Sophie were reported to the Gestapo by a building superintendent. Arrested along with Christoph Probst and the others, they were brought before the People's Court (*Volksgericht*), and on February 22, 1943, Hans, Sophie, and Christoph were found guilty of treason, sentenced to death, and executed by beheading the same day. After a later trial, Dr. Huber, Willi Graf, and Alexander Schmorell met the same fate, while other White Rose members were sentenced to various terms of imprisonment.

After the defeat of the Nazis, the story of the White Rose spread, and in death they became an inspiration to free-thinking peoples everywhere. They also offered rehabilitation—of sorts—for the German nation's inaction to offer any kind of worthwhile opposition to the excesses of the Nazi regime. It is worth reflecting that when confronted by tyranny of a most horrible and obnoxious kind, a teacher and a group of his students, barely in their twenties, took on the most powerful presence in Europe.

Discussion Questions

1. What do you think is the relevance, if anything, of the White Rose for us today?
2. Were the actions of Hans and Sophie in the halls of Munich University, on that last day, foolhardy? Give reasons for your answer.

Further Reading

Dumbach, Annette, and Jud Newborn, *Sophie Scholl and the White Rose*, Oxford: Oneworld, 2007.
Hanser, Richard, *A Noble Treason: The Revolt of the Munich Students against Hitler*, San Francisco: Ignatius Press, 2012.
Vinke, Hermann, *The Short Life of Sophie Scholl*, New York: Harper and Row, 1984.

MARCH 1943

11.3 Rescuing the Jews of Bulgaria

In March 1943, the worst fears and brightest hopes of the 48,000 Jews of Bulgaria were realized. They were saved largely through the effort of one remarkable politician. Dimitar Peshev was a leading Bulgarian lawmaker in the 1930s and 1940s and a major actor in resisting the pro-Nazi government of Premier Bogdan Filov. Through this opposition he prevented the deportation of Bulgaria's Jews to the death camps of Nazi Germany.

Bulgaria had resisted pressure to join the Axis until circumstances beyond its control forced the government to take sides. To spare his country the devastation of possible German occupation Tsar Boris III reluctantly agreed to join the Tripartite Pact on March 1, 1941. This alliance allowed Bulgaria to recapture Macedonia from Yugoslavia and Thrace from Greece, territories which the country lost after the First World War.

Under German pressure Bulgaria enacted antisemitic laws even before becoming an Axis ally. On January 23, 1941, the Law for Protection of the Nation, which copied Nazi Germany's Nuremberg Laws, came into effect, and in 1942 the government set up a special Commissariat for Jewish Affairs.

On January 21, 1943, SS officer Theodor Dannecker, acting on behalf of Adolf Eichmann, arrived in Sofia to force Bulgaria to deport its Jewish population. Soon after, he reached a secret agreement with the head of the Bulgarian Commissariat for Jewish Affairs, Alexander Belev, for the deportation of Jews from the newly acquired Bulgarian territories in Thrace and Macedonia to German-occupied areas, by April 15. The Jews in these territories numbered around 13,000, but in addition the Germans were hoping also to deport some 8,000 Bulgarian citizens of Jewish ancestry living in "old" Bulgaria.

In the spring of 1943, the Bulgarian government ordered that all of Bulgaria's Jews would be deported through Kyustendil on March 10, 1943, and sent to Nazi extermination camps in Poland. Jews in Thrace and Macedonia would also be deported. When the Jews of Kyustendil learned of their imminent deportation, they attempted to have the order overturned through the intercession of one they knew as a friend: Dimitar Peshev, the minister for justice and deputy speaker of the *Sobranie* (Parliament).

On March 8, 1943, a local Jewish delegation, including Jakob Baruch, a personal friend of Peshev's, spoke with him about the government's deportation plan. Peshev had not previously known of it. Upon confirmation of the story, he decided that the deportations had to be stopped. He traveled to Kyustendil and met with the assistant chief of police, who described to him how they were to take place. Peshev now saw all too clearly the consequences of Bulgaria's alliance with Hitler and decided he had to act.

Together with a close friend and colleague from Kyustendil, Petar Mihalev, he went to Parliament and burst into the office of Interior Minister Petar Gabrovski, insisting that he cancel the deportations. Explaining the gravity of the situation, and after a fierce argument, Gabrovski called the governor of Kyustendil and instructed him to stop the deportations. By 5:30 p.m. on March 9—just one day after Peshev had learned about the planned action against the Jews—the deportations had been canceled.

Despite Gabrovski's assurance, however, Peshev needed further guarantees—especially after he learned that the Jews in the occupied territories of Thrace and Macedonia were already being deported. On March 18–19, 1943, Jews in Thrace were taken to Lom, in Bulgaria; from there they were shipped to Vienna and then transferred to trains going to Auschwitz and Katowice. All Macedonian Jews were interned by March 11. On March 22 and 25, some were deported by train to Auschwitz; on March 29, the rest were deported to Treblinka.

Peshev had already decided to raise the matter in Parliament. On March 17, 1943, he wrote a letter of protest and had forty-two members sign it. Disregarding Prime Minister Filov's instruction not to subject the letter to a vote in the House, it was discussed in caucus on March 23, 1943. Refusing to have his authority undermined, Filov demanded that each of the signatories stand and verbally announce their support of Peshev's letter. Shamefully, only thirty of the original forty-two affirmed their position, and when a final vote was taken, it was decided to censure Peshev. The next day he was forced to step down as Deputy Speaker.

The years that followed were not kind to Peshev. Under communist rule, he was arrested as a member of the former Bulgarian collaborationist government but while facing the death penalty, members of the Jewish community from Kyustendil testified on his behalf. He was sentenced to fifteen years in prison at forced labor, but after eighteen months the court reviewed his case and he was released owing to his key role in saving Bulgaria's Jews. He was, however, forced to live in isolation, without a job or a means of sustenance.

In January 1973, Yad Vashem recognized Dimitar Peshev as one of the Righteous among the Nations for his role in saving Bulgaria's Jews. A few weeks later, on February 20, 1973, he died—a Holocaust resister acknowledged, sadly, much too late.

Discussion Questions

1. Why were the Jews of Bulgaria threatened in March 1943?

2. Why do you think Dimitar Peshev stepped in to ensure that the Jews would not be deported through the town of Kyustendil? How successful was he?

Further Reading

Bar-Zohar, Michael, *Beyond Hitler's Grasp: The Heroic Rescue of Bulgaria's Jews*, Holbrook, MA: Adams Media, 1998.
Groueff, Stéphane, *Crown of Thorns*, Lanham, MD: Madison Books, 1987.
Todorov, Tzvetan, *The Fragility of Goodness: Why Bulgaria's Jews Survived the Holocaust: A Collection of Texts with Commentary*, Princeton: Princeton University Press, 2001.

APRIL 1943 (1)

11.4 The Bermuda Conference

On April 19, 1943, two events began which were to have an important impact on the fate of the Jews still left in Europe. In one of history's coincidences, the Jews of the Warsaw ghetto rose in rebellion against the Nazis, and on the same day, American and British representatives met on the island of Bermuda ostensibly to discuss ways of rescuing Jews in Nazi Europe.

Both events, as we now know, were failures: the first a military one, the second diplomatic. The Jews of Warsaw did not liberate themselves (indeed, this was never their intention), nor did the uprising inspire Warsaw's Poles to come to their aid. In Bermuda, the American State Department and the British Foreign Office did not accomplish any effective means to rescue Europe's Jews, their publicized aim in getting together.

The conference, held across April 19–30, 1943, was convened allegedly to discuss the plight of European Jewry. By the latter half of 1942, news of the Nazis' plan to exterminate the Jews had been made public, and while the American press tended to downplay these reports, the British press paid more attention to them. Before long, leaders of the Anglican Church and some British political leaders began lobbying the government of Prime Minister Winston Churchill to do something to alleviate the mounting humanitarian catastrophe. On March 23, 1943, William Temple, the Archbishop of Canterbury, gave an impassioned speech in the House of Lords imploring the British government to address the as-yet unnamed Holocaust—a catastrophe which Churchill had, on August 21, 1941, referred to as "a crime without a name." The archbishop's remarks received wide press coverage and prompted the Foreign Office to propose an Anglo-American conference to address the issue.

From the start, however, the Foreign Office warned others in the British government, as well as the US State Department, that if a comprehensive plan to rescue European Jews did come to fruition, it might force the Germans and their satellite collaborators to abandon their policy of extermination in favor of mass deportation—a move which could well create an unwelcome flood of millions Jews into Allied-controlled areas. The impact would be a disaster for the war effort, in that it would quickly overwhelm Allied logistics, destabilize governments, and possibly further imperil Jewish refugees.

The Americans took several weeks to respond to the British proposal, and the Bermuda Conference did not begin until April 19. The US delegation was led by Harold W. Dodds, president of Princeton University, and the British by Richard Law, son of former prime minister Andrew Bonar Law, and at that time a parliamentary under-secretary of state at the Foreign Office.

Perhaps with an eye to the last international gathering on Jewish refugees, at Evian in July 1938, both governments worked to lower expectations of the meeting, and tried to keep its deliberations secret. Indeed, Bermuda was chosen as the venue largely because of its isolation and the lack of a large media presence. Moreover, the conference was limited strictly to government officials, and no reporters were permitted to attend the sessions. Several Jewish organizations asked to participate but were denied access, and Jews, by name, were not mentioned before or during the meeting. The preferred term was "political refugees."

A major topic for discussion related to the question of refugees who had been liberated by Allied forces and those still suffering under the Nazis. No solutions were forthcoming. In line with the consensus view that victory against Hitler must be the number one priority above all others, refugee rescue (with a hidden agenda that applied to Jews even more) was somewhat lower in the order of affairs.

Beyond that, when it came to substantive issues the Americans did not offer to raise their immigration quotas, while the British made it clear that the prohibition on Jewish refugees seeking refuge in the British Mandate of Palestine would continue. The delegates rejected any recommendations that could not be accomplished under wartime conditions and did not even discuss sending food or other supplies to Jews interned in concentration camps.

British and American Jews, together with others, saw the Bermuda Conference as nothing but a major disappointment. Rabbi Stephen Wise, in New York, considered the meeting to have been "a cynical exercise in futility," in which the Allies could be seen to be doing something worthwhile but in which the Jews themselves got nothing. These days, the term would be "virtue signalling."

And while the delegates talked, no one even thought to mention or acknowledge the Warsaw Ghetto Uprising which had commenced the same day as the conference, continued throughout it, and of which the delegates were fully apprised in daily updates. Eight months later, on December 10, 1943, the conference report was published. Its only positive decision was to revive the refugee committee established at the Evian Conference back in 1938. For most of the Jews murdered under the Nazis, it came too late. The Bermuda Conference accomplished nothing and did not save a single Jew from the Holocaust.

Discussion Questions

1. Why were the United States and Britain reluctant to accept Jewish refugees from a military standpoint?

2. Considering the final sentence in the article, do you think the Bermuda Conference intended to save Jews from the Holocaust? If not, then why do you think it took place?

Further Reading

Penkower, Monty Noam, *The Jews Were Expendable: Free World Diplomacy and the Holocaust*, Champaign: University of Illinois Press, 1983.
Wyman, David S., *The Abandonment of the Jews: America and the Holocaust, 1941–1945*, New York: Pantheon, 1984.

APRIL 1943 (2)

11.5 The Warsaw Ghetto Uprising

The Warsaw Ghetto Uprising was an armed Jewish revolt that took place between April 19 and May 16, 1943. Its intention was to prevent further deportations of the last remaining residents to Nazi death camps. The revolt inspired other uprisings in extermination camps and ghettos throughout German-occupied Eastern Europe.

Soon after Germany invaded Poland in September 1939, over 400,000 Jews in Warsaw were detained in a one-square-mile area of the city. In November 1940, the ghetto was sealed behind brick walls, barbed wire, and armed guards; anyone caught leaving was shot on sight. The Nazis limited the quantity of food brought into the ghetto. Residents were compelled to provide forced labor. Disease and starvation killed thousands each month, and approximately 100,000 ghetto inmates had died by the end of 1941.

On January 20, 1942, during the Wannsee Conference, the Final Solution was confirmed. Pursuant to this, under *Gross-Aktion Warschau*, the Jews of Warsaw were to be rounded up, street by street, under the guise of "resettlement," and marched to the *Umschlagplatz* holding area. From there, they were sent by train to the Treblinka extermination camp, built in a forest 80 kilometers northeast of Warsaw. Mass deportations to the euphemistically named "East" started in the summer of 1942. Throughout the period following, the Germans deported and murdered more than 300,000 Jews from the Warsaw ghetto, leaving between 55,000 to 60,000 remaining.

With reports filtering back of mass killings taking place of those who had been deported, younger inhabitants of the ghetto formed the Jewish Fighting (sometimes rendered as Combat) Organization (*Żydowska Organizacja Bojowa*, or ŻOB) with the intention of preventing any further deportations.

After nearly four months without deportations, on January 18, 1943, the Germans unexpectedly entered the Warsaw ghetto to carry out additional roundups. In short order, around 600 Jews were shot, and 5,000 others were taken from their homes. The Germans expected no resistance, but their actions were halted by ŻOB resisters armed with handguns and Molotov cocktails. This was the first act of resistance in the ghetto; stunned at the Jews' daring, and uncertain of the fighters' strength, the Germans withdrew to regroup their forces and assess the situation.

On the evening of April 19, 1943, the first night of Passover, Himmler sent SS forces, tanks, and heavy artillery back into the ghetto under the command of General Jürgen Stroop. It had but one task: to defeat the uprising and destroy the ghetto. Much to the Germans' surprise, however, the ŻOB, comprised largely Zionist young people and headed by Mordecai Anielewicz, met the aggressors. These guerrilla fighters—consisting of some 500 inexperienced fighters, and another 250 fighters attached to a separate group, the *Żydowski Związek Wojskowy* (Jewish Military Union, or ŻZW)—started the revolt.

The battle became an intense four-week period of desperate hand-to-hand fighting. During that time, given that the Germans were largely unsuccessful in killing the resisters in open combat, they systematically razed the ghetto building by building, block by block, destroying the bunkers where many residents had been hiding. In the process, the Germans killed or captured thousands of Jews. The fighting lasted until May 16, 1943, when the ŻOB command bunker at Miła 18 was finally destroyed and the leadership, including Anielewicz, were all dead. As a symbolic act, that day the Germans blew up Warsaw's Great Synagogue.

An estimated 7,000 Jews perished during the fighting in the Warsaw Ghetto Uprising, while nearly 50,000 others who survived were sent to extermination or labor camps. It is believed that the Germans lost several hundred men in the uprising, though their own figures numbered minimal losses.

By May 16, Stroop was able to report to his military commanders that "the Jewish Quarter of Warsaw is no more! More than 56,000 Jewish bandits have been captured." He created a detailed seventy-five-page report, covering the period April 24 to May 24, 1943, accompanied by sixty-nine pictures and communiqués relevant to the suppression of the uprising. Bound in black leather and entitled *The Jewish Quarter of Warsaw is no More!*, the report was intended as a souvenir album for *Reichsführer-SS* Heinrich Himmler and Stroop's immediate superior, Friedrich Jeckeln. While not materially affecting the outcome of the war itself or the Final Solution, the Warsaw Ghetto Uprising remains the symbol of Jewish resistance to Nazi tyranny.

Discussion Questions

1. What were the aims of the fighters in the Warsaw ghetto, and were they successful in achieving them?
2. Why do you think the Warsaw Ghetto Uprising is such a symbol of Jewish resistance?

Further Reading

Gutman, Israel, *Resistance: The Warsaw Ghetto Uprising*, Boston: Houghton Mifflin, 1994.
Kurzman, Dan, *The Bravest Battle: The Twenty-Eight Days of the Warsaw Ghetto Uprising*, New York: Putnam, 1976.

Stroop, Jürgen, *The Stroop Report: The Jewish Quarter Is No More!*,
    New York: Pantheon, 1979.
Zuckerman, Yitzhak, *A Surplus of Memory: Chronicle of the Warsaw Ghetto
    Uprising*, Berkeley: University of California Press, 1993.

JUNE 1943

11.6 Heinrich Himmler and the End of the Ghettos

Heinrich Himmler was born in Munich in 1900. Originally destined for the
Jesuit priesthood, he studied agriculture and economics and worked as a
salesman and chicken farmer, joining the Nazi Party in the early 1920s. In
1929 he took over leadership of the SS, the feared *Schutzstaffel*, or "Protection
Squad," first created in 1923 to serve as Hitler's personal bodyguard.

Himmler then expanded its size and strength, creating such departments
as the *Sicherheitsdienst* (Security Service) or SD, the intelligence agency of
the SS and the Nazi Party; the *Geheime Staatspolizei* or Gestapo (Secret
State Police), the official secret police of Nazi Germany; and the *Rasse- und
Siedlungshauptamt-SS* (SS Race and Settlement Main Office) or RuSHA, the
organization responsible for "safeguarding the racial purity of the SS."

It was Himmler who authorized the first concentration camp at Dachau
in 1933 and was the primary architect of the *Kristallnacht* pogrom in
November 1938. His racist views, his commitment to "racial purity," and his
belief in occult forces enabled him to become the principal instigator of the
extermination of the Jews, with overall responsibility and implementation
for the concentration and extermination camp system and the criminal
medical experiments undertaken within them.

As a young man, Himmler—a devout Catholic—displayed evidence of
being antisemitic, though not necessarily an extremist. In the early 1920s
he became involved with right-wing paramilitaries in Munich and met
Ernst Röhm, an early member of the Nazi Party and cofounder of the
Sturmabteilung (Storm Detachment, or SA).

In 1922, Himmler became more interested in the "Jewish question," and his
political and antisemitic views became more and more radical. In August 1923
Himmler joined the Nazi Party as a member of Röhm's SA. From this point
on, he became involved in local, then national, politics. After the unsuccessful
Beer Hall Putsch of November 9, 1923, when Hitler attempted to take power
by force, Himmler lost his job and was forced to move back home with his
parents. He now became increasingly irritable, aggressive, and opinionated.

Over the next several years, Himmler became one of the three or four
most powerful men in Nazi Germany behind Hitler. Certainly, from his
office, he was one of those most directly responsible for the Holocaust.

As *Reichsführer-SS* in overall command of all security agencies in Nazi Germany, on June 21, 1943, he ordered the liquidation of all ghettos within the *Reichskommissariat Ostland* (the Baltic States and Belorussia) and the transfer to concentration camps of the remaining Jewish inhabitants still capable of working. For those who could no longer work, they would be transferred to the extermination camps in German-occupied Poland that had been established since the spring of 1942: here, they would be murdered.

Himmler's order of June 21, 1943, directed that all Jews remaining in ghettos be collected into concentration camps. The order stated that after August 1, 1943, it would be forbidden to release Jews from concentration camps for outside work. From this point on, there would be no hope of escape for the Jews of Europe remaining alive in Nazi Europe.

Already, the Jewish community of Warsaw had been destroyed in the aftermath of the Warsaw Ghetto Uprising, which ended the previous month with the death and deportation of the remaining 50,000 ghetto inhabitants. Throughout the rest of June, and in the months following, the other ghettos in Poland, Lithuania, and Latvia were systematically emptied of their Jewish populations. On June 19, 1943, not to be overlooked, Nazi propaganda minister Josef Goebbels declared Berlin to be *Judenfrei* (cleansed of Jews), and on June 25 a new gas chamber and crematorium complex opened at Auschwitz. With its completion, the four crematoria at Auschwitz could "process" a daily capacity of 4,756 bodies.

The month of June 1943, therefore, is one of central significance in the development of the *Shoah*. If we can say that the Nazi invasion of the Soviet Union in June 1941 saw the birth pangs of the Final Solution and the Wannsee Conference of January 1942 its birth certificate, Himmler's order liquidating the ghettos realized its maturation.

Of interest here is that Bełżec and Chełmno had been closed by this stage, leaving Sobibór, Treblinka, Majdanek, and Auschwitz to carry out the remaining tasks of Himmler's directive. After this, Jews who had so far escaped death were murdered, caught in a trap from which there was no escape and no alternatives.

Himmler himself went on to further promotions, and by the end of the war had established himself as an alternative to Hitler as a German leader with whom the Allies, perhaps, could negotiate. As the war was ending, he realized the likelihood of Germany's eventual defeat and sought a parley with the Allies that they would not recognize.

After Germany's surrender on May 9, 1945, he attempted to go into hiding, but was captured by British troops on May 21, 1945. On May 23, during an interrogation session, he bit into a hidden cyanide pill and was dead within fifteen minutes. He thereby cheated the prospect of a trial before the International Military Tribunal at Nuremberg, which would sit just a few months later.

Discussion Questions

1. In view of his background, why do you think Heinrich Himmler became such a murderous radical antisemite?

2. Describe in your own words the reasons for the final liquidation of the ghettos in June 1943.

Further Reading

Arad, Yitzhak, *Ghetto in Flames: The Struggle and Destruction of the Jews in Vilna in the Holocaust*, New York: Holocaust Library, 1982.

Breitman, Richard, *The Architect of Genocide: Himmler and the Final Solution*, Hanover, NH: University of New England Press, 1991.

Himmler, Katrin, and Michael Wildt (eds.), *The Private Heinrich Himmler: Letters of a Mass Murderer*, New York: St. Martin's Press, 2016.

Longerich, Peter, *Heinrich Himmler*, Oxford: Oxford University Press, 2012.

AUGUST 1943

11.7 Uprising in Treblinka

Treblinka was a German death camp located eighty kilometers northeast of Warsaw on the main Warsaw-Białystok railway line, near the villages of Treblinka and Malkina. In July 1941, the Nazis started work on a forced labor camp not far from Treblinka railway station; work was completed in November 1941. Construction on a second camp—to serve as the extermination facility—began a short distance from the forced labor camp at the end of May 1942 and was completed by July 22, 1942. Treblinka II (as it was named), together with camps at Bełżec and Sobibór, were three death camps established as part of *Aktion Reinhard*, named in memory of the assassinated head of the SD, Reinhard Heydrich. This operation was to carry through the extermination of the Jews of the *Generalgouvernment*.

Treblinka seemed an ideal location for its purpose: it was in a thickly treed but sparsely populated area and was near a rail line with a station stop at Malkinia, which enabled a spur to be constructed to the camp. The prisoners at Treblinka I, the forced labor camp (*Arbeitslager*), were political detainees, consisting of Jews and non-Jewish Poles. While Jews and non-Jews were housed in two different areas of the camp, both units labored hard in an adjacent gravel pit. The commandant of Treblinka I was Theodor van Eupen for the duration of its existence from November 1941 until its closing in July 1944. Of the 20,000 or so who were imprisoned there, fewer than half survived.

Treblinka II was the camp's extermination center. It was completely operational in July 1942, and from that time onward nearly all Jews from each deportation train were sent there after being assessed as not being able to perform the tasks required in Treblinka I. They were gassed within hours of their arrival.

There were three commandants of Treblinka II: Irmfried Eberl from July to August 1942, Franz Stangl (who had previously served as commandant of Sobibór) from August 1942 to August 1943, and Kurt Franz, from August to November 1943. Treblinka II was comprised of three areas. The first was the reception part where the Jews, who had been the human consignment packed into railroad cars, were unloaded from the trains that had brought them. The second area was split into two subsections. One was housing for the German and Ukrainian staff, administrative offices, storerooms, a clinic, and workshops. The staff consisted of twenty to thirty SS men in command and administrative posts; all had received their preparation for this role through their involvement in the *Aktion T-4* ("euthanasia") operation. Ninety to 120 Soviet prisoners of war, as well as Ukrainian and Polish civilians, served as auxiliary guards. This second subsection of Treblinka II also contained barracks for the Jews who temporarily worked in the camp's workshops. The third area in Treblinka II was the extermination site. The entire camp was surrounded by two fences of barbed wire and numerous watchtowers. Sometimes this third section was referred to as the "upper camp" and was described to its arriving victims as a transit camp. The extermination process was carried out in its own fully fenced area, with a large earthen mound and branches intertwined in the fence so that no outsiders could see what was occurring there. Initially it encompassed three gas chambers, which over time were supplemented by a further ten chambers as more trainloads of victims kept coming.

On arrival at the reception area, the doors were thrown open. A special work unit of Jewish prisoners (*Sonderkommando*) entered each car; took away the bodies of the dead; collected all food, clothing, and valuables left behind; and cleaned the train so that it could be used again.

Jews unable to walk were taken to an "infirmary" (*Lazarett*). They would pass through the building and exit on the other side, where they were shot and thrown into huge pits that had already been dug. Jews able to walk were immediately divided by gender, children remaining with the women. Only a very few men and women—the strongest among them—were selected to go to the forced labor camp. All the rest entered two barracks—men in one, women and children in the other—where they were ordered to remove all their clothing to prepare for a "shower" before they would be allowed into the camp. They were then forced to run down a fenced-in path, covered with branches to hide what was happening, from the barracks to the third sector building with gas chambers. This path was called the "tube."

The gas chambers at Treblinka used carbon monoxide as the killing agent. It was generated from a large diesel engine in a shed (although some reports refer to other sources for the carbon monoxide) and then piped through to the "shower heads" in the gas chamber. The unsuspecting victims took up to thirty minutes to die.

In April 1942, a Jewish resistance group at Treblinka began planning for an uprising, which took place on August 2, 1943. Their plan was to take weapons from the camp armory, but before this was completed the Germans were alerted, so the prisoners were not armed sufficiently to take control of the camp, as they had planned. Instead, the resisters set fire to buildings (but not the gas chambers, which remained intact), and hundreds of prisoners stormed the fence surrounding the camp. Fewer than 100 were able to escape and survive until the war was over. The camp was dismantled by the Nazis throughout the fall and winter of 1943, with the gas chambers destroyed and a farmhouse built in its place. Soviet forces entered the camp on August 16, 1944.

The Treblinka I and Treblinka II camps killed a vast number of victims. Almost all the victims were Jews from Poland. There were other groups killed there, such as 2,000 Roma, but in the fifteen months from July 1942, when Treblinka II killing operations first began, until the autumn of 1943, when operations ceased, it is estimated that more than 870,000 Jews were murdered, including 254,000 from the city of Warsaw and 112,000 from its surrounding district; 337,000 Jews from Radom; 35,000 from Lublin; more than 107,000 from Białystok; and approximately 29,000 Jews from other countries, including Greece, Macedonia, Slovakia, and Salonika.

Two postwar trials of the perpetrators of these mass killings were held in Düsseldorf. The first—from October 12, 1964, until August 24, 1965—tried and convicted ten defendants, including commandant Kurt Franz. At the second trial—from May 13 to December 22, 1970—the only defendant was commandant Franz Stangl. He was sentenced to life in prison.

Discussion Questions

1. What indications are there that the operations at Treblinka resembled a factory (in this case, a factory for killing people)?

2. Put together an argument that the uprising at Treblinka was *either* successful *or* unsuccessful.

Further Reading

Arad, Yitzhak, *Belzec, Sobibor, Treblinka: The Operation Reinhard Death Camps*, Bloomington: Indiana University Press, 1987.

Rajchman, Chil, *The Last Jew of Treblinka: A Survivor's Memory, 1942–1943*, New York: Pegasus Books, 2009.

Steiner, Jean-Francois, *Treblinka*, New York: Simon and Schuster, 1967.

SEPTEMBER 1943

11.8 *Brundibár* Opens at Theresienstadt

Brundibár—the colloquial name in Czech for a bumblebee—is a children's opera by the Czech composer Hans Krása, usually considered to be an allegory of the triumph of good over evil. It tells the story of a brother and sister, Pepiček (Joey) and Aninka (Annette), who manage—with the help of three animals and many other children—to defeat *Brundibár* (a metaphor for Adolf Hitler), an evil organ grinder, who will not let them sing in the marketplace to raise money to buy milk for their sick mother. With *Brundibár* defeated, the children can finally sing, and because of their singing they earn enough money to buy the milk. As an allegory of good defeating evil, it relates a lesson that this can happen not through violence but rather through solidarity and perseverance. The opera is divided into two short acts and can be staged in less than forty minutes.

The opera was composed in 1938 and first staged in Prague, but where it was most successful was at Theresienstadt (Terezín) ghetto camp, which became operational on November 24, 1941. That same month, *Brundibár* was staged in secret at a Jewish orphanage in Prague. In 1942, the Nazis sent some of that orphanage's directors and children to Terezín. Hans Krása was also arrested and deported at that time.

In 1943 *Brundibár* arrived at Terezín when a well-known Czech pianist, Rudolf Freudenfeld-Franěk, was deported and managed to smuggle a piano arrangement in with him. Hans Krása then orchestrated the opera for the instruments available in the camp, and rehearsals began in secret in the attic of the Dresden Barracks. Theatre director František Zelenka built the scenery with stolen timber, Kamila Rosenbaum, a famous dancer from Vienna, choreographed it, and on September 23, 1943, *Brundibár* opened. It went on to become the camp's greatest musical success, completing fifty-five performances before the last transports left Terezín in the autumn of 1944. It bore witness to the day-to-day life of the prisoners, and, amid suffering, violence, and death, provided some hope and encouragement, particularly for the children who were watching and those performing in it.

Brundibár became Terezín's foremost cultural attraction. Although admission was free, people could only see it through possession of a ticket—and demand for these remained high right through to the last performance. Not only was the music easily accessible and enjoyable for those listening, the story was one that advanced a positive attitude even within a subtext that was clearly political in tone. While the villainous character of *Brundibár* was the personification of Evil, the children's victory chorus that ends the opera told the audience that:

We won a victory
Over the tyrant mean.
Sound trumpets, beat your drums,
And show us your esteem!
We won a victory,
Since we were not fearful,
Since we were not tearful,
Because we marched along
Singing our happy song,
Bright, joyful, and cheerful.

This left no room for doubt: the children were singing loudly and clearly about the eventual defeat of Hitler and the Third Reich.

Jews had earlier been forbidden to attend concerts, but at Theresienstadt the Nazis relaxed this sufficiently to be able to show off the camp to the outside world as a place in which Jews were looked after. Accordingly, musicians, actors, artists, poets, and writers—among whom was Hans Krása—staged a variety of performances. This, of course, played into the hands of the Nazis in their exploitation of the camp as a model location of humanity and good will. Red Cross commissions passed through the area and the reports they made were based on Terezín. It was also here that the Nazi propaganda film *Der Führer schenkt den Juden eine Stadt* ("The Führer Gives the Jews a City") was filmed, using *Brundibár* as an illustration of its children's activities.

Between January and October 1942, the number of prisoners at Theresienstadt increased almost tenfold. As well as the Jews coming in from the Czech lands, increasing numbers were arriving from Austria, Germany, Hungary, and elsewhere. The camp's population grew to 140,000, including no fewer than 11,000 children. They made the best of their situation, with an extraordinary flourishing of artistic and creative activity taking place. All this creative artistry—musical productions, paintings by the children (of which over 4,000 were recovered after the war), comic books, poetry, diaries, and journals—worked to transcend the reality of what was being experienced daily. In the final months of 1944, however, almost all the Jewish artists and intellectuals were transferred to extermination camps like Auschwitz. Among the 87,000 Terezín prisoners sent to their death, more than 83,000 were murdered. These included Hans Krása, the composer of *Brundibár*.

For many theatre directors since the end of the Second World War, it is impossible to divorce *Brundibár* from its context and present it as a purely aesthetic experience, even though it has been performed countless times and on all continents. For best effect, many consider that it is necessary to go beyond merely staging the opera; it is usually held that it is best also to give audiences a wider understanding of its history, the Holocaust context in which it was written and performed, and through this to reinforce Krása's original intention.

Discussion Questions

1. What was the original purpose of *Brundibár*, and why was it staged at Theresienstadt?
2. What do you think was the fate of the children who acted and sang in the play? Should knowledge of this diminish its meaning?

Further Reading

Karas, Joža, *Music in Terezín*, New York: Beaufort Books, 1985.

OCTOBER 1943 (1)

11.9 Denmark and the Rescue of the Jews

In October 1943 almost the entire Jewish community of the tiny kingdom of Denmark was saved as the result of what has become recognized as a national project. Earlier, Denmark had been invaded by Nazi Germany on the morning of April 9, 1940; by midday, completely overwhelmed, the country had surrendered. The Germans maintained that their occupation would be comparatively gentle, and, in turn, the Danish government offered a measure of acquiescence. As a result, most Danish institutions proceeded with a "business-as-usual" approach until 1943. King Christian X and his government stayed in the country, unlike many other occupied regimes that relocated to Britain for the duration of the war.

After a period of relative calm, during which Danish officials played down any possibility of Denmark having a "Jewish Question," it was finally decided in Berlin that the "Final Solution" would have to be applied in Denmark if all of Europe was to be made truly *Judenrein*. This came after a period of intensifying anti-Nazi sabotage by the Danish resistance movement and Nazi patience for the Danish Jews had begun to wear thin.

Orders from Berlin, however, were met with opposition in Copenhagen, and not only from Danes. Germans stationed in Denmark, such as the Nazi-imposed administrator Werner Best, followed a strategy of deferring any discussion relating to the Jews. Best even worked on ways to avoid such discussion altogether. Nonetheless, the roundup and arrest of Denmark's 7,800 Jews was ordered for 10:00 p.m. on October 1, 1943—which was, as it turned out, the second day of Rosh Hashanah. It was expected that all Jews would be at home.

However, on September 28, 1943, a German diplomat, Georg Ferdinand Duckwitz (who was later recognized by Yad Vashem as a Righteous Gentile), had been instrumental in leaking news of the planned operation to influential Danes, who, in turn, informed the leadership of the Danish Jewish community. On September 29, Jews were warned by Rabbi Marcus Melchior, the chief rabbi of Denmark, of the forthcoming German action. They were counseled to go into hiding immediately and to spread the word to all their Jewish friends and relatives. While this was happening, many members of the non-Jewish population were also springing into action to save "their" Jews.

Phone calls were placed, homes were opened as safe houses, and arrangements were made to spirit Jews to the countryside. Then, where possible, a safe passage was arranged to Sweden. This took place across the Sound, the short stretch of water separating the two countries. While some Jews were transported in large fishing boats, many others—individuals or small families—were ferried to freedom in much smaller vessels, even rowboats.

In what became a national underground project, both the organized Danish resistance movement and everyday citizens worked to evacuate as many members of the Jewish community as could be located. King Christian had already become a symbol of Danish resistance when he had earlier refused to implement the Nazis' anti-Jewish legislation. Many believe it was he who served as the inspiration for his people in their heroic rescue of the Jewish population.

Despite these efforts, not all Jews were reached in time. Some 450 were captured by the Nazis or Danish collaborators. The majority of these were sent to the concentration camp at Terezín (Theresienstadt), where it is recorded that fifty-one died of disease before the war ended. Yet even here, Danes worked to assist members of their Jewish population. Food packages were sent from Denmark to Terezín, earmarked specifically for the Danish Jews, while the Danish government was successful in convincing the Nazis not to deport the Jews to Auschwitz—the most frequent destination for deportees from Terezín. By the end of the war, in April 1945, the surviving Danish Jews were allowed by the Nazis to be repatriated to Sweden through the Swedish Red Cross, under the supervision of Count Folke Bernadotte.

Further, some of those who were not captured immediately during the roundup action lost their lives subsequently. A small number committed suicide, unable to bear the pressure or the trauma of the events swirling around them. Some were captured by the Nazis while in the countryside or on the coast. It has been recorded that 23 were lost at sea during the transfer to Sweden. Overall, it has been calculated that 102 Danish Jews were victims of the Nazis during the Holocaust, representing one of the lowest casualty rates of all the countries occupied by the Nazis.

How did most of Denmark's Jews manage to escape? There was more to it than just the tip-off by Duckwitz and Chief Rabbi Melchior. There was more to it, also, than the collective efforts of the Danish Resistance and the ordinary Danes who sought to "do the right thing" by their Jewish fellow citizens. Danish police officers were known to cooperate with the resistance, and coastal vessels of the German navy were only half-hearted in their attempts at intercepting the little boats crossing the Sound with their precious cargo. Many Germans saw the action as beneath their station as combat soldiers and refused to follow their orders with any enthusiasm.

The action of the Danish people in rescuing their Jewish population is considered one of the most effective actions of collective resistance to Nazi repression. The mass rescue and transfer to Sweden, along with the intervention on behalf of the Jews in Terezín, led to over 99 percent of Denmark's Jewish population surviving the *Shoah*. And the heroism did not end there. With the rescue effort viewed as a national project, all proposals to have individual Danes nominated as Righteous Gentiles were later spurned from Copenhagen. The Danish nation, it is held, was responsible for saving the country's Jews, and no individual should be singled out for special recognition.

Discussion Questions

1. Do you think Georg Ferdinand Duckwitz should have been recognized as one of the Righteous among the Nations for tipping off the Jews before their planned deportation? Why/why not?

2. Why do you think the people of Denmark rallied to help rescue the country's Jews, and how does their response differ from that of other countries you have studied?

Further Reading

Haestrup, Jorgen, *Secret Alliance: A Study of the Danish Resistance Movement, 1940–45* (3 vols.), Odense: Odense University Press, 1976–7.
Lidegaard, Bo, *Countrymen*, New York: Knopf, 2013.
Thomas, John Oram, *The Giant Killers: The Story of the Danish Resistance Movement, 1940–1945*, New York: Taplinger, 1976.
Werner, Emmy E., *A Conspiracy of Decency: The Rescue of the Danish Jews during World War II*, Boulder: Westview Press, 2002.

OCTOBER 1943 (2)

11.10 Black Sabbath in Rome

On October 16, 1943, a roundup of the Jews of Rome began. Early on that Saturday morning Rome's ghetto was surrounded by German forces, prior to a thorough door-to-door search for Jews. The Germans were carrying prepared lists of names and addresses and knew exactly who to target. With only a few minutes to prepare themselves, the Jews who had been taken were conveyed to the *Collegio Militaire* (Military College), there to await their fate.

At the outset of the Second World War, Italy had a population of over forty-four million, of whom some 52,000 were Jewish. A Jewish presence dated back well over 2,000 years, and with such longevity the community was completely integrated within Italian society and culture. Italians in general did not exhibit open antisemitism, and unlike National Socialism in Germany, Italian Fascism was not predicated on antisemitism. Indeed, until the Italian National Assembly passed a series of antisemitic laws in 1938, Jews were even permitted membership in the Fascist Party.

As Italy's dictator Benito Mussolini tied his nation closer to Germany, however, he came under increased pressure to crack down on Italian Jews. The anti-Jewish laws of 1938, when they were introduced, were watered-down versions of Germany's Nuremberg Laws: they excluded Jews from serving in the military and from certain professions, Jews were not permitted to hold government positions or to work in radio and journalism, marriage between Jews and non-Jews was prohibited, and resident alien Jews were placed in internment camps. Often, however, local authorities only half-heartedly enforced these measures, and in some instances simply ignored them. This does not mean, however, that Italian Jews in general did not suffer after these laws were passed, and many left Italy for the Americas or elsewhere.

Italy entered the war in June 1940, firmly allied with Germany. In pursuit of Mussolini's grand visions of a new Roman Empire, Italy would eventually establish military occupations in southern France, Albania, Greece, and Yugoslavia. German officials expected the Italians to round up and deport Jews in those areas, but most Italian officials wanted nothing to do with mass murder or deportations. As a result, during 1941–3, thousands of Jews fled German-occupied areas for the relative safety of Italian territory.

Rome was bombed for the first time on May 16, 1943; on July 25, 1943, Benito Mussolini was deposed as prime minister by the Fascist Grand Council and arrested on order of King Victor Emmanuel II. Mussolini's successor, Marshal Pietro Badoglio, then began secret negotiations for Italy's surrender. On September 3 the Allies invaded the Italian mainland from Sicily; the same day, General Giuseppe Castellano signed an armistice agreement in Cassibile. The agreement was made public on September 8, and the Germans, increasingly desperate to ensure that Europe's southern flank be safeguarded—as well as to be done with vacillation regarding the implementation of the Final Solution—hastened to fill the vacuum this created with a full-scale invasion of Italy. There is little doubt that the Germans felt frustrated over the fact that the Final Solution had, as they saw it, been endangered by Italian actions. Italy was, after all, Germany's closest ally in Europe, and it was in Europe that the war against the Jews was being played out.

The consequence was that the Germans now imposed a grinding occupation on the Italians overall—and Italian Jews suffered accordingly. With the raid on the Rome ghetto on October 16, Jews were taken in regardless of age, sex, or health. Some managed to escape. In the days leading up to the *razzia* (raid), officials in the Vatican learned of the possibility of such an action and managed to persuade Pope Pius XII to order the opening of Rome's monasteries and convents as sanctuaries. Several thousand Jews were sheltered this way, which only served to anger the Germans even more. On October 16, however, well over a thousand Jews were caught, with others in succeeding weeks.

Building on this start, throughout October and November 1943 German occupation authorities commenced a roundup of Jews in all of Italy's large cities. The plan was to concentrate them at several points and then transport them to the death camps in Poland, but in many cases Italian civilians and officials warned Jews of the operation in advance. Sometimes, they went so far as to hide Jews they knew or give shelter to those seeking help.

On the other hand, the majority of those arrested were deported to Auschwitz, where most died. Overall, it has been estimated that over 7,000 Italian Jews became victims of the Holocaust. The "Black Sabbath," as identified by author Robert Katz in a book of that title published in 1969, saw the start of the great ordeal for the Jews of Rome, and then all Italy.

Discussion Questions

1. Why did the Holocaust come relatively late for the Jews of Rome, compared to other places in Europe?

2. Do you think the Jews of Italy were safer under Fascism than under the German occupation? Why/why not?

Further Reading

Michaelis, Meir, *Mussolini and the Jews: German-Italian Relations and the Jewish Question in Italy, 1922–1945*, Oxford: Clarendon Press, 1978.

Sarfatti, Michele, *The Jews in Mussolini's Italy: From Equality to Persecution*, Madison: University of Wisconsin Press, 2006.

Stille, Alexander, *Benevolence and Betrayal: Five Italian Jewish Families under Fascism*, New York: Summit Books, 1991.

Zimmerman, Joshua, *The Jews in Italy under Fascist and Nazi Rule, 1922–1945*, Cambridge: Cambridge University Press, 2005.

Zuccotti, Susan, *The Italians and the Holocaust: Persecution, Rescue, Survival*, New York: Basic Books, 1987.

NOVEMBER 1943

11.11 Father Bernhard Lichtenberg, Catholic Martyr

Bernhard Lichtenberg was a German Catholic priest who resisted Nazi antisemitic and racial doctrines by preaching against them from the pulpit, before being arrested and dying while in transit to Dachau concentration camp.

The second oldest of five siblings, he was born on December 3, 1875, at Ohlau (Oława), some thirty kilometers southeast of Breslau (Wrocław) in what was then the Prussian province of Lower Silesia. The merchant family from which he came was part of a Catholic minority in what was, at the time, a predominantly Protestant city.

Lichtenberg obtained his *Abiturium* (school-leaving examination) at the local high school and decided to become a priest. He studied theology in Breslau and Innsbruck and was ordained in 1899. In 1900 he began his ministry in Berlin as pastor of the Heart of Jesus community, Charlottenburg, where he remained for over a decade. The remainder of his career would be focused in and around Berlin.

With an interest in Catholic politics, Lichtenberg served from 1913 until 1920 as a representative of the Center Party in the District Assembly in Charlottenburg, and between 1920 and 1930 was a member of the regional assembly of the Berlin district of Wedding. During the First World War he served as a military chaplain, after which he became a member of the Peace Association of German Catholics (*Friedensbund Deutscher Katholiken*). In 1929 he was elected to the board of the Inter-Denominational Working Group for Peace (*Arbeitsgemeinschaft der Konfessionen für den Frieden*).

In 1931 he was appointed as rector of St. Hedwig's Cathedral, Berlin. Even by this stage, before the Nazis had attained power, he had shown himself to be opposed to their ways of thinking. In 1931 he underwrote an invitation to Catholics to watch a performance of the American anti-war film *All Quiet on the Western Front* (dir. Lewis Milestone, 1930), which led to a personal attack on him by the Nazi newspaper *Der Angriff*.

Then, on March 31, 1933, two months after the Nazi takeover, Lichtenberg arranged for the Jewish banker Oskar Wassermann to meet with Adolf Cardinal Bertram, archbishop of Breslau and president of the German Episcopal Conference, in an attempt to convince him to intervene in the antisemitic boycott of Jewish businesses planned by the government for the next day. Cardinal Bertram, however, held that the matter lay outside the church's sphere of activity, and no action was taken. With this, Lichtenberg had marked himself out as an opponent of Nazism who needed to be watched in the future.

In 1937 Lichtenberg was elected cathedral provost, a role which saw him thrust deeper into helping Berlin's Jewish community. This was followed, in August 1938, by appointment to head the Relief Office of the Berlin episcopate, assisting Catholics of Jewish descent who wished to leave Germany. When the *Kristallnacht* pogrom took place in November 1938, Lichtenberg spoke out against Nazi brutality and prayed publicly for the Jews during services—one of only a few who did so.

After the outbreak of war in September 1939, Lichtenberg continued his protests in another area, this time writing to the air raid authorities remonstrating against an order dated December 14, 1939, decreeing racial segregation in Berlin's air raid shelters.

While the Nazi authorities initially dismissed Lichtenberg as a nuisance, he was nonetheless warned that he should be careful lest he be arrested. However, he continued with his protests, condemning the Nazi euthanasia program, and even organizing demonstrations outside concentration camps. He was finally denounced by two female students who had heard him pray publicly for Jews and concentration camp inmates and was arrested on October 23, 1941, by the Gestapo. In their search of his home and possessions they found incriminating evidence: a pulpit proclamation in favor of Jews to be read in the cathedral that Sunday, in direct defiance of a police order. He refused to retract his words during his interrogation, even going so far as to condemn Hitler's *Mein Kampf* as opposed to Christianity. In May 1942 he was duly sentenced to two years' imprisonment; when asked if he had anything to say upon sentencing, he asked that no harm should come to citizens who pray for the Jews.

Toward the end of his prison term, he was given the opportunity to remain free provided he undertook to refrain from preaching for the duration of the war. The offer was conveyed to him by Berlin's Bishop Konrad von Preysing on behalf of the Gestapo. In response, Lichtenberg requested instead that he be allowed to accompany the deported Jews and Jewish Christians to the Łódź ghetto, where he would serve as a priest. With little other alternative, the Nazi authorities ordered that he be sent to Dachau, where all anti-Nazi priests were imprisoned. On November 5, 1943, while in transit and awaiting his final transport to the camp, he collapsed and died.

Father Bernhard Lichtenberg was beatified as a Blessed Martyr by Pope John Paul II on June 23, 1996. The beatification ceremony took place in Berlin during a Mass celebrated at the city's Olympic Stadium. Lichtenberg's tomb is situated in the crypt of St. Hedwig's Cathedral in Berlin. On July 7, 2004, Jerusalem's Yad Vashem recognized Bernhard Lichtenberg as one of the Righteous among the Nations.

Father Lichtenberg was one who "lived" his faith and the teachings it espoused. He listened and responded to the voice of his conscience as he witnessed the growing power of Nazism and its anti-Jewish ideology. Driven by his faith, he was a courageous resister who lost his life in the cause of stopping an evil he identified as detrimental to all humanity.

Discussion Questions

1. In your view, was Father Bernard Lichtenberg too trusting that he would be safe, despite his many actions and statements opposed to the Nazi government?
2. If you were able to ask Father Lichtenberg one question, what would it be?

Further Reading

Kidder, Annemarie S., *Ultimate Price: Testimonies of Christians Who Resisted the Third Reich*, Maryknoll, NY: Orbis Books, 2012.
Kock. Erich, *Er Widerstand: Bernhard Lichtenberg, Domprobst bei St. Hedwig*, Berlin: Morus Verlag, 1996.
Riebling, Mark, *Church of Spies: The Pope's Secret War against Hitler*, New York: Basic Books, 2015.

DECEMBER 1943

11.12 Charles Coward, the Count of Auschwitz

Charles Joseph Coward was a British prisoner of war who became known as the "Count of Auschwitz" after he helped save the lives of at least 400 Jews working in slave labor camps. Born in England in 1905, he enlisted in the British army in June 1937 and rose to become Quartermaster Battery Sergeant Major. On May 25, 1940, he was captured by the Germans at Calais and made two escape attempts before reaching a prisoner-of-war camp. While at the camp he made numerous further escapes. On one occasion, he even received the Iron Cross while posing as a wounded German soldier in an army field hospital. He was recaptured on each occasion.

In December 1943 he was sent to Auschwitz III (Monowitz). Here he was placed in the E715 labor detachment camp, with other British POWs. Upon discovering that a fellow British prisoner was confined in the Jewish labor section of the camp, he smuggled himself in for one night to meet with this man and witness the conditions under which he was imprisoned. He could not locate the British POW but witnessed the gas chambers, malnutrition, cramped living quarters, and SS treatment of the prisoners and saw it as his humanitarian obligation from then on to resist the brutality confronting the Jews.

Due to his fluency in German, Coward was named the Red Cross liaison officer for the British prisoners. Acting as the go-between for the prisoners and the guards, he used the limited freedom this provided to engage in resistance activities. He and other British prisoners smuggled food and assorted items to the Jewish inmates, and through fictional letters addressed to his deceased father back in England he smuggled reports to the British War Office regarding camp conditions and information that he believed had military value. Coward's wife received these letters; the information they contained was later used as evidence during the Nuremberg Trials. In addition, he witnessed the arrival of trainloads of Jews for extermination.

Coward's greatest achievement at Auschwitz was his liberating of hundreds of Jews. British POWs received packages from the International Red Cross containing Swiss chocolate, and Coward used this to bargain with the SS to obtain the corpses of dead non-Jewish prisoners. He had these placed in ditches along the paths employed for slave laborers on their way to and from work. The Jews would then slowly drop out of the group and hide in the ditches; Coward would swap their clothing and identities with the corpses and give the healthy Jews the documents and clothes he had taken from the corpses. They then adopted these as new identities and were smuggled out of the camp to freedom. It has been estimated that through this scheme Coward saved up to 400 Jewish lives.

After his liberation in January 1945, Coward remained active in his opposition to the Nazis. He acted as a witness during the I.G. Farben Trial at Nuremberg in 1948–9 and attested to the sadistic treatment meted out to Jews. In his court statement, he mentioned that during his imprisonment in the labor camp I.G. Farben workers would openly admit they knew about the gassing and were fully aware what role they were playing in the war.

In 1954 a British author, John Castle, published a biography of Coward, *The Password Is Courage*, which recorded his wartime activities. This book was then made into a movie of the same name in 1962, directed by Andrew L. Stone. Portrayed by Dirk Bogarde, Coward's humanitarian efforts were recognized; however, as the film did not fully illustrate the terror of the Holocaust and the pain and suffering endured by the Jewish prisoners, it did not sufficiently acknowledge the fullness of Coward's feats.

Charles Coward's exploits were a product of his unwavering devotion to human life, rather than his duty as a soldier. In 1963, in recognition of his nonviolent resistance during the war, he was named as one of the Righteous among the Nations by Yad Vashem. Then, after his death in 1976, the Department of the Righteous at Yad Vashem released a further statement commemorating Coward's righteous and brave actions as a humanitarian. He received appreciation and respect from his home country when, in 2010, he was posthumously named a Hero of the Holocaust by the British government.

Discussion Questions

1. How did Charles Coward manage to save Jewish lives at Auschwitz?
2. What was unusual (even remarkable) about the story of Charles Coward?

Further Reading

Castle, John, *The Password Is Courage*, London: Souvenir Press, 1954.
Silver, Eric, *The Book of the Just: The Unsung Heroes Who Rescued Jews from Hitler*, New York: Grove Press, 1992.
Smith, Lyn, *Heroes of the Holocaust: Ordinary Britons Who Risked Their Lives to Make a Difference*, London: Edbury Press, 2012.

Part 12

1944

MARCH 1944 (1)

12.1 The Invasion of Hungary

On March 19, 1944, Germany invaded its ally, Hungary. Seemingly within moments, the country's Jews, who had so far escaped annihilation, now faced the Final Solution. Less than a year later, when the Soviet army captured Budapest on January 17–18, 1945, it was too late to save the lives of the 564,500 Jews who had been murdered by the Nazis and their Hungarian fascist allies. Of all the Jews murdered by the Nazis during the Holocaust, nearly 10 percent were Hungarian Jews, murdered in the space of just a few months.

After Hungary emancipated its Jews in 1867, they were given every opportunity to become wholly Hungarian (on the proviso that they assimilated) in their language, customs, clothing, and, most importantly, their feelings. After 1938, however, they were gradually excluded by a series of internally driven anti-Jewish race laws. With the German invasion in March 1944, the so-called architect of the Final Solution, Adolf Eichmann, moved into Hungary with a hand-picked unit of 200 men. In the spring and early summer of 1944, with the active help of Hungarian clerks, policemen, soldiers, and gendarmes, Eichmann's men then facilitated the deportation of the Jews from Hungary's rural provinces to Auschwitz.

Evidence shows that most of the country's non-Jewish population did little to try to help their persecuted fellow citizens. In many instances, as archival photos documenting the deportation show, it took only a few gendarmes to march the obedient Jews to the railway station, where they joined waiting rail cars ready to take them to what would be their final destination.

The Hungarian regent, Admiral Miklós Horthy, brought the deportations to an end on July 6, 1944, saving the Jews of Budapest. Owing to this and other defiant acts, however, the Nazis soon arranged for Hungarian fascist leader Ferenc Szálasi and his Arrow Cross (Nyilas) Party to come to power. Every day, hundreds of defenseless Jews were then murdered by the Arrow

Cross. Many were tortured horribly before their death, while others were simply shot and thrown into the icy Danube.

There were some from outside who tried to save Jews. The best known is undoubtedly the Swedish diplomat Raoul Wallenberg, whose efforts, along with others, contributed to rescuing up to 200,000 Jews. To his name could be added the Swiss vice-consul to Budapest, Carl Lutz, who used his influence to guarantee the lives of over 62,000 Jews, and a remarkable Italian citizen, Giorgio Perlasca, who posed as a Spanish diplomat in Budapest to save over 5,000 more.

There were also some (though not many) Hungarians who tried to save Jewish lives amidst of the horror; they have gone some tiny way to redeeming Hungary's honor. One such account was uncovered a few years back by an Israeli journalist, Anshel Pfeffer, writing in the newspaper *Haaretz*.

The scene was Budapest in 1944. Information from an informer led an Arrow Cross officer to search for a Jewish man who, it was thought, was hiding in the art studio of painter Lajos Szentivanyi. There was no time to arrange a proper hiding place, and the Jew simply hid himself behind a screen. Fortunately, the room contained a stunning nude painting that Szentivanyi was working on. The officer could not take his eyes off it; he stopped searching, spoke a few words to Szentivanyi, and left.

The incident is one of many that took place at the Open School of Art, founded by Karoly Koffan, which saved hundreds of Jews and other victims of the Nazis. The school did not belong to any organized underground and had neither diplomatic immunity nor access to the resources available to a large organization. They did not have a plan to follow and did not keep orderly records of their activities. They helped people based on personal acquaintanceship, motivated largely by humanitarian feelings.

Koffan's art school enjoyed relative freedom until 1944, but after the Nazi invasion Koffan and Szentivanyi worked to assist people in need. They ran the group's rescue activities, while three students (Andre Meszaros, Laszlo Ridovics, and Sandor Kovacs) carried out the missions.

These students brought Jews forged documents, rescued people from the ghettos and transports, and smuggled them into hiding places. Later, they even began going into the transit camps where Jews were sent before being transported to Auschwitz. At first the group helped anyone who was in danger, but over time the Jews became the main group they assisted. Early in the morning, before classes at the art school, students would take people to nearby hiding places, or hide them in the school itself. Sometimes up to twenty people stayed overnight. Some Jews, who managed to escape on their own, ran to the art school for safety. Koffan's wife hid them in plain sight, gave each one an art book, and when soldiers came in looking for victims it appeared as those present were, indeed, students in an art class.

It says much that in Hungary, where from March 1944 the full force of the Holocaust turned against the Jews like the eruption at Vesuvius, there were some non-Jews who said no in the face of evil. It isn't much, but even tiny acts can have big consequences—and that, of course, is a lesson we can all leave for future generations.

Discussion Questions

1. Why do you think the killing of Jews in Hungary was carried out so rapidly and in such large numbers?
2. Do you think it is possible to speculate why Karoly Koffan, Lajos Szentivanyi, and the art students risked their lives to save Jews? Suggest some possibilities.

Further Reading

Braham, Randolph L. (ed.), *The Nazis' Last Victims: The Holocaust in Hungary*, Detroit: Wayne State University Press, 2002.
Braham, Randolph L., *The Politics of Genocide: The Holocaust in Hungary*, Detroit: Wayne State University Press, 2000.
Cornelius, Deborah S., *Hungary in World War II: Caught in the Cauldron*, New York: Fordham University Press, 2011.
Vági, Zoltán, László Csősz, and Gábor Kádár, *The Holocaust in Hungary: Evolution of a Genocide*, Lanham, MD: Altamira Press, 2013.

MARCH 1944 (2)

12.2 Fredy Hirsch, the Children's Hero

Alfred (Fredy) Hirsch was a Jewish athlete born in Aachen, Germany. In 1935 he fled from Germany to Czechoslovakia, but after the Nazis occupied Prague in 1938, he was sent to Theresienstadt (Terezín). Later, during the war, he was deported to Auschwitz. In both camps he took care of children's education, and the regime he introduced—demanding strict hygiene, exercise, and discipline—lowered their mortality rates.

Fredy Hirsch was born on February 11, 1916, the second son of Heinrich and Olga Hirsch. His older brother Paul was born in 1914. Heinrich Hirsch, a butcher, died when Fredy was ten years old, after which Olga remarried. The boys attended the Aachener Couven-Gymnasium. At fifteen Fredy was already giving lectures, and he left school in March 1931 to lead the Aachen Jewish youth movement. In 1932 he helped found the Aachen branch of the German Jewish Scouting Association (*Jüdischer Pfadfinderbund Deutschland*, or JPD), an organization affiliated with *Maccabee Hatziar*, a Zionist sporting association. In 1933 he moved to Frankfurt, leading a scout group there. Fueled by rumors that he was gay—though not accused of inappropriate behavior or misconduct—he moved to Dresden in 1934 to work as a sports instructor for *Maccabee Hatziar*.

In 1935, the Nuremberg Laws were enacted, and Paragraph 175 of the German Criminal Code outlawing homosexuality was expanded. Now nineteen years old, Fredy fled to Prague, where he was active in *Maccabee Hatzair* and the Zionist *Hechalutz* organization, having convinced the chairman of *Maccabee Hatziar* in Czechoslovakia that his homosexuality did not impact his work. He ran summer camps to prepare young Jews to migrate to Palestine.

From October 1936 to April 1939, Fredy and his partner, Jan Mautner (a medical student from Olomouc), lived together in Brno. Sponsored by the Zionist World Federation, Fredy set up local youth and adult physical education groups. He managed the 1937 Maccabee Games for Czechoslovakia held in Žilina, with 1,600 participants. After the city of Brno refused him a residence permit and threatened to expel him, he returned to Prague. Working at the Zionist Youth Aliyah School run by Egon (Gonda) Redlich, he prepared young Jews seeking to immigrate to Palestine, training them in horticulture, agriculture, and basic military training. Until 1940 he organized an annual Czech camp where youth exercised and learned Hebrew. Fredy Hirsch viewed physical education as essential to promoting well-being and a Zionist consciousness.

After the German occupation of the Czech lands during 1938 and 1939, Fredy continued to prepare young Jews for emigration. In October 1939, eighteen boys he had trained escaped to Denmark, from where they migrated to Palestine in 1940. Fredy drew lots as to who would accompany them; he lost and remained in Prague, where Jan Mautner joined him. After the Nazis banned Czech Jews from public spaces, Fredy organized a playground at Hagibor, Prague, to enable Jewish children to exercise. Fredy and Jan Mautner ran soccer matches, athletic competitions, study groups, and theatrical performances there. As Fredy spoke Czech poorly, he taught the classes in Hebrew.

In late 1941 the Nazis began deporting Czech Jews, first to the Łódź ghetto. Fredy helped those being deported to prepare the fifty kilograms of luggage they were permitted to take with them. On December 4, 1941, Fredy was himself transported to Theresienstadt. Working under Gonda Redlich, he became the deputy leader of the Youth Services Department. Jan Mautner was deported to Theresienstadt in early 1942.

At Theresienstadt, children lived separately from adults. Fredy maintained their self-esteem through discipline, regular exercise, and strict hygiene as a means to maximize their chances of survival. Together with Redlich, he educated the children (despite this being prohibited), teaching Hebrew, English, mathematics, history, and geography. They arranged separate barracks and slightly better conditions for the children. While occasionally they were able to remove children from transports taking them to extermination camps, more than 99 percent of the children at Theresienstadt were eventually deported. Children aged fourteen and older had to work; Fredy got them jobs in the vegetable gardens to improve their health and prepare them for life in Palestine, at the same time negotiating space for a play area inside the camp.

On August 24, 1943, 1,200 children from the Białystok ghetto arrived at Theresienstadt. They were separated from the rest of the camp by a barbed-wire fence and kept strictly segregated from the general population. Fredy, however, jumped the fence; he was arrested, brought to the commandant's office, beaten, and deported to Auschwitz with other Jews on September 8, 1943.

On arrival at Auschwitz, they received privileged treatment. They lived in a separate block (BIIb), known as the Theresienstadt family camp. Tattooed, they avoided selection on arrival, retained their civilian clothes, and did not have their heads shaved. Families could write to relatives at Theresienstadt, and even to friends in neutral countries, to convey the message that "deportation to the East" did not necessarily mean death.

Fredy Hirsch was appointed as Kapo of the family camp because the SS respected his leadership. He refused to use violence against other prisoners and asked to be released from his role so he could manage the children. Replaced by Arno Böhm, a German criminal, Fredy persuaded Böhm to allocate a barracks, Block 31, for children younger than fourteen years of age. Fredy then oversaw Block 31 as the *Blockältester* (block elder). Each morning, counselors would bring those aged between eight and fourteen, who lived with their parents, to the children's block. The children spent the day there, where they were taught German, history, music, and Judaism. There were only twelve books and few supplies, so teachers taught from memory. A children's opera, *Brundibár*, was performed. The walls of Block 31 were decorated with Disney characters and other images by Dina Gottliebová. Block 31 was so orderly that it was shown off to the SS, who visited frequently and helped organize better food for the children.

Fredy also convinced the Germans to hold roll call inside the barracks, so the children were spared the hours-long ordeal of standing outside in all weather. After another transport arrived in December 1943, there were about 700 children in the family camp; Jan Mautner was also on this transport.

Arno Böhm later allocated Hirsch a second barracks for children aged three to eight years of age so that the older children could prepare a performance of Snow White. The play was performed on January 23, 1944, with many SS officers attending.

Fredy's strict hygiene regimen required the children to wash daily even in the frigid winter of 1943–4, and there were regular inspections for lice. Further, his discipline code ensured that there were no acts of violence or theft in the barracks. Under Fredy's management, the mortality rate for the children was nearly zero, compared to the overall rate of about 25 percent of residents in the family camp during the first six months. On February 11, 1944, his twenty-eighth birthday, the children threw him a surprise party, and in the same month a delegation from the Reich Security Main Office and the German Red Cross visited the family camp and reported favorably.

Over time, the Auschwitz resistance movement had drawn the conclusion that most arrivals were murdered with six months of their arrival. For Fredy's transport, this meant around March 8, 1944, and the resistance saw Fredy as a natural leader for an uprising. This was to mark his death knell. According to some accounts, he committed suicide by taking pills on March 8 in order not to have to witness the deaths of "his" children; an alternate view is that he was poisoned by Jewish doctors who would have been killed if an uprising had broken out.

In 1996 a monument was placed on the wall of the former school building at Terezín; Fredy's face is carved in stone alongside the text "In memoriam Fredy Hirsch: Gratefully, Children of Terezín, Birkenau BIIb." On the centenary of his birth in 2016 the gymnasium he attended in Aachen renamed the cafeteria "the Fredy-Hirsch-AG." He was the subject of a documentary in 2016, *Heaven in Auschwitz*, which included accounts from thirteen survivors of Theresienstadt and Auschwitz, and was also featured in the 2017 Israeli documentary *Dear Fredy*, by Rubi Gat.

Discussion Questions

1. What lessons can be learned from the story of Fredy Hirsch about human goodness in the face of the most confronting situations?

2. Based on what you know about the Holocaust, which placed Fredy at greater risk under the Nazis: being gay or being Jewish? Give reasons for your answer.

Further Reading

Adler, H. G., *Theresienstadt 1941–1945: The Face of a Coerced Community*, Cambridge: Cambridge University Press, 1955.
Keren, Nili, "The Family Camp," in Michael Berenbaum and Yisrael Gutman (eds.), *Anatomy of the Auschwitz Death Camp*, pp. 428–40, Bloomington: Indiana University Press, 1998.
Redlich, Egon, *The Terezin Diary of Gonda Redlich*, Lexington: University Press of Kentucky, 1992.

APRIL 1944

12.3 The Vrba-Wetzler Report

On April 7, 1944, a Slovak Jew, Rudolf Vrba, and his comrade Alfred Wetzler, found themselves in the position of possibly being able to save what was left of Europe's Jews when they managed to do the seemingly impossible: they escaped from Auschwitz. On this day, they broke away from the camp, hid between an internal and external perimeter fence for three days, and then, on April 10, escaped the camp completely.

As a teenager, Vrba (born Walter Rosenberg) experienced antisemitism in his hometown of Topol'čany, Czechsoslovakia. This led to an attempt, in 1941, to flee the scene of increasingly hazardous persecution. He was arrested and later, in June 1942, deported to Majdanek. Two weeks later, he was sent to Auschwitz, where he was given the number 44070. He was put to work arranging for the bodies of corpses to be transported to the crematoria before given the task of sorting through the possessions of those who had been selected for the gas chambers or work details.

His escape, when it came, had been carefully worked out in advance and had support from others who remained in the camp. Making their way from Auschwitz to their native Slovakia, Rosenberg and Wetzler crossed the border on April 21 and headed for Zilina. Soon after this, Rosenberg was given his new name, Vrba, by the Slovak Jewish Council as a security measure.

The report the two men then composed divulged all that they had witnessed at Auschwitz. It would provide some of the earliest and most detailed information about the mass murders, including information about the use of gas chambers and crematoria. Before they settled on a final draft, it was written and rewritten several times; ultimately some forty pages long, it was passed on to Jewish officials when Vrba and Wetzler arrived at Bratislava on April 24. It quickly became known—and remains to this day—as the Vrba-Wetzler Report.

Acknowledgement of the report was, however, delayed by several weeks, meaning that the information it contained was slow to be distributed widely enough to gain the attention of governments. The senior members of the Slovak Jewish Council were concerned that if its contents became known among the intended victims it would provoke widespread panic and an even more immediate and deadly response from the Nazis.

While discussions concerning what to do took place over several weeks, more than 400,000 Hungarian Jews, who had been deported to Auschwitz beginning in May, were in the process of being murdered. To the end of his life, Vrba remained bitterly convinced that more could have been done to save them had the Allies, armed with the information in his report, chosen to do so. This controversy would surround him until his death, and, even today, the question of whether the Allies could have done more continues to be debated by Holocaust scholars.

The Vrba-Wetzler Report was copied and given to Rudolf Kasztner, head of the Zionist Aid and Rescue Committee in Bratislava, and from him to a member of the Hungarian Foreign Ministry as well as a representative of the Vatican. Both the British and US governments had copies of the report by June 15, 1944. On that day, BBC Radio broadcast part of it, and a few days later it also received attention in the *New York Times*. Material then appeared in newspapers and radio broadcasts throughout Europe, particularly in Switzerland. Publication of the report had an immediate impact, resulting in spontaneous international denunciations. Protests came from the pope, the US secretary of state (Cordell Hull), the British foreign secretary (Anthony Eden), the International Committee of the Red Cross, and King Gustav V of Sweden.

In Hungary, such condemnation could not go unnoticed. On July 7, 1944, Admiral Miklós Horthy, Hungary's regent, ordered a halt to the deportation of Jews from Hungary, effective two days later. By this action, up to 200,000 Budapest Jews were saved from deportation.

The truth about the Auschwitz-Birkenau extermination camp was the best-kept secret of the Final Solution. The whole complex was guarded by more than 2,000 SS and auxiliary personnel, 200 guard dogs, and two lines of electrified fences. Hundreds of prisoners, including 76 Jews, attempted to escape during the five years of the camp's existence. Of these, only 5 attempts were successful, in that they managed to get away, reveal what was happening at Auschwitz, and survive the war.

Rudolf Vrba would always question whether the report was disseminated and acted upon as rapidly and as forcefully as it should have been. It is one of the greatest of "what if" questions regarding the Holocaust: if more people and governments had known and acted upon the report, and done so in a timely manner, could those who died have been saved, instead?

Discussion Questions

1. Why do you think there was so much delay in releasing the information contained in the Vrba-Wetzler report?
2. What is the most obvious flaw in Vrba's "what if" question?

Further Reading

Braham, Randolph L., and William J. vanden Heuvel (eds.), *The Auschwitz Reports and the Holocaust in Hungary*, New York: East European Monographs/ Columbia University Press, 2011.

Linn, Ruth, *Escaping Auschwitz: A Culture of Forgetting*, New York: Cornell University Press, 2004.

Vrba, Rudolf, *Escape from Auschwitz: I Cannot Forgive*, New York: Grove, 1968.

Wetzler, Alfred, *Escape from Hell: The True Story of the Auschwitz Protocol*, New York: Berghahn, 2007.

MAY 1944

12.4 The Final Solution Hits the Jews of Hungary

On May 15, 1944, a shock of cataclysmic proportions fell upon the Jews of Hungary, the last great center of Jewish population still untouched by the Holocaust.

Between 1920 and 1944 the country was governed by Regent Miklós Horthy, whose principal goal was to regain some or all the land that Hungary had lost due the country's defeat in the First World War. This led him to ally his country with Italy and Germany, resulting in sizable territorial gains for Hungary between 1938 and 1941. In following its goals of territorial reclamation, the Hungarian government joined the Axis powers formally in December 1940; Hungarian forces then fought alongside the Germans in Yugoslavia from April 1941 and in the massive German offensive against the Soviet Union (Operation Barbarossa) beginning in June 1941.

Even before this, however, Hungary's government, which contained strong right-wing and antisemitic elements, sought to marginalize Hungarian Jews, who in 1941 numbered about 825,000. These included Jews who lived in lands that had been annexed by Hungary between 1938 and 1941. In the late 1930s the Hungarian government had implemented racial legislation along similar lines to Germany's Nuremberg Laws. These revoked equal citizenship for Jews, restricted them from working in certain professions, barred them from civil and military service, and prevented them from marrying non-Jews.

Because Jews were forbidden from serving in the military, in 1938 the Hungarian government established a forced labor program for Jewish men. Many of these were compelled to work under impossible conditions, without adequate medical care, food, water, or shelter. It is estimated that between 1940 and 1944 at least 27,000 Jews died under the direction of the Hungarian army, which had put them to work on a variety of defense and infrastructure projects.

Just as Hungarian troops were being deployed eastwards to take part in the invasion of the Soviet Union, the Horthy regime forcibly deported 20,000 Jews to Ukraine, where virtually all were murdered by German killing squads. These Jews were not Hungarian citizens and came from territories recently annexed by Hungary. In early 1942, Hungarian troops killed nearly 3,000 Jews in the portion of Yugoslavia they then controlled, but the government was reluctant to move en masse against Hungarian Jews. Indeed, Horthy's prime minister, Miklós Kállay, refused to deport Hungarian Jews, even under pressure from Berlin to do so.

Defeat at Stalingrad on February 2, 1943, which resulted in catastrophic losses for the Hungarian army, convinced Horthy that the war was lost. Kállay now sought to negotiate an armistice with the Allies, but to prevent this the Germans invaded and occupied most of Hungary in March 1944. Kállay was replaced by Dome Sztójay, who was pro-German and willing to implement fully Berlin's liquidation of the Jews. Almost immediately, Nazi antisemitic measures were imposed over Hungary's Jewish population. Sztójay ordered that all Jews living outside Budapest, numbering nearly half a million, be rounded up and concentrated in hastily established ghettos. There the living conditions were appalling, and Jews were frequently subjected to rape, violence, and extortion by troops and militias guarding the ghetto areas.

In May the mass transfer of Hungarian Jews to Auschwitz began, and in less than two months some 440,000 Jews had been deported, with the killing facilities working nonstop, day and night. This was the fastest killing operation of any of the Nazi campaigns against Jewish populations in occupied Europe. It clogged the murder machinery to such a degree that the crematoria could not keep up, and a vast number of bodies were simply burned in open pits. Mass killing had of course been an ongoing process since 1942 but never did it reach such proportions as in the spring of 1944. The frenzy with which the Nazis undertook their task defied even the demands of winning the war, with both men and transport being diverted from the front lines to assist in the deportations.

In July 1944 Horthy ordered the deportations stopped, mainly because he knew the Germans' military position had deteriorated. He dismissed Sztójay and sounded out the Allied governments regarding the possibility of an armistice. This was too much for the Germans, who, in turn, dismissed him. Horthy was replaced by Ferenc Szálasi, a fascist and leader of the right-wing Arrow Cross (Nyilas) Party.

By this time, only the Jewish community of Budapest remained relatively intact. Szálasi moved immediately against them, and in late 1944 several thousand were force marched toward Austria, with many dying en route. After a brutal and lengthy siege devastated Budapest, Hungary signed a truce with the Soviets, who had already occupied part of the country, in January 1945. By the early spring of 1945, German troops had been expelled from Hungary, replaced by Soviet occupation forces.

In the end, perhaps up to 600,000 Hungarian Jews were murdered following the German occupation in March 1944, and particularly the period between May and December 1944. This figure, with the war so close to ending, represented perhaps 10 percent of all Jews killed in the Holocaust—murdered in just a seven-month period.

Discussion Questions

1. Why did Miklos Horthy order that the mass slaughter of the Jews be stopped, and why was he unsuccessful?

2. To what degree do you think the mass murder of the Hungarian Jews
   was a Hungarian—rather than a German—project?

Further Reading

Ben-Tov, Arieh, *Facing the Holocaust in Budapest: The International Committee of
   the Red Cross and the Jews in Hungary, 1943–1945*, Berlin: Springer-Verlag, 1988.
Braham, Randolph L., *The Politics of Genocide: The Holocaust in Hungary*,
   Detroit: Wayne State University Press, 2000.
Braham, Randolph L., and William J. vanden Heuvel (eds.), *The Auschwitz Reports
   and the Holocaust in Hungary*, New York: East European Monographs/
   Columbia University Press, 2011.
Cornelius, Deborah S., *Hungary in World War II: Caught in the Cauldron*,
   New York: Fordham University Press, 2011.
Fenyo, Mario D., *Hitler, Horthy, and Hungary: German-Hungarian Relations,
   1941–1944*, New Haven: Yale University Press, 1972.

JULY 1944

12.5 The Passion of Marianne Cohn

On the night of July 7–8, 1944, a young Jewish woman in France, Marianne
Cohn, was murdered by the Gestapo. Her life was a remarkable example of
selflessness in the service of life.

Born on September 17, 1922, in Mannheim, Germany, she moved with
her family to Berlin in 1929, and in 1934, after the Nazi seizure of power
the previous year, to Spain. With the onset of the Spanish Civil War in 1936,
they moved again in 1938, this time settling in France.

When the Second World War started, Marianne's parents, as German
nationals, were detained at the Gurs internment camp in southern France.
Marianne and her sister were sent to a farm. After the Fall of France in June
1940, they were subjected to Nazi-imposed antisemitic laws and took refuge
in a home for Jewish children in Moissac, in the so-called Unoccupied Zone
centered on the city of Vichy.

Marianne was taken under the care of the Jewish Scouts (*Éclaireurs Israélites
de France*), and in 1941 joined the Young Zionist Movement (*Mouvement de
la Jeunesse Sioniste*, or MJS). It was through this secret organization that she
was brought into resistance activities. By 1942 she was active in producing
forged passports and, later, smuggling Jewish children out of France.

Volunteers known as "*passeurs*," who escorted the children to Switzerland,
undertook hazardous missions under constant risk of detection by Nazis and
French collaborators. This led inevitably to Marianne's arrest, though after
three months' detention in a Vichy prison in Nice, she was released. It was
during this period of imprisonment that, in early 1943, she wrote a poem

that would become famous in resistance circles, "I Shall Betray Tomorrow" (*"Je trahirai demain"*). It has become an immortal statement of defiance in the face of the Holocaust:

> *Tomorrow I shall betray, but not today*
> *Today, pull out my fingernails,*
> *I shall not betray.*
> *You don't know the limits of my bravery.*
> *I do.*
> *You are five men with knuckledusters.*
> *You are five men with nails in the soles of your boots.*
> *Tomorrow I shall betray, but not today.*
> *Tomorrow.*
> *I need night to come to make up my mind,*
> *Only one night,*
> *To sell out, to give up, to betray.*
> *To sell out my friends,*
> *To give up bread and wine,*
> *To betray my life,*
> *To die.*
> *Tomorrow I shall betray, but not today.*
> *The file is under the window pane.*
> *The file isn't for the bars*
> *The file isn't for the executioner,*
> *The file is for my own wrists.*
> *Today, I have nothing to say.*
> *Tomorrow, I shall betray.*

At the end of the war, the poem was retrieved by one of the children Marianne had saved. It is a testimony of courage and one of the great poems of the resistance.

After her release, and using the false identity of Marie Colin, she undertook nearly a dozen transfers of children, taking groups of about thirty over the border into Switzerland on each occasion. In January 1944 she began working with a Catholic rescuer named Rolande Birgy, with whom she ferried further groups of up to twenty children across the border.

By the start of 1944, Marianne had taken hundreds of children to Switzerland, but on the evening of May 31, 1944, a German patrol arrested her near Annemasse, just 200 meters from the border. She was at this time escorting a group of twenty-eight children ranging in age from four to fifteen and was held at the local Gestapo jail, the Prison de Pax. Jean Deffaugt, the mayor of Annemasse, who sympathized with the Resistance, intervened. The younger children were sent to local orphanages, while Marianne and the older children were paroled to work under guard in Annemasse during the day. This worked for a short time, but the Resistance outside knew that Marianne was in extreme danger—as also was the whole escape operation. A plan was arranged to rescue her, but she refused to leave the children who were in her care.

The underground then sent a message to the Gestapo, threatening to kill its members if the detainees were harmed. Dismissing this threat, the Gestapo then began Marianne's interrogation. On July 3, 1944, a specially selected squad was sent to Annemasse from Lyon with the assignment of removing six Resistance prisoners, including Marianne. In her defiance, she now refused to hide behind her alias and revealed her identity; for her rebelliousness, she was tortured horribly. She did not, however, speak—other than to say that she had no regrets for her actions.

On the night of July 7–8, 1944, only three weeks before the liberation of Annemasse, Marianne and the others were taken to nearby Ville-la-Grand and murdered. The Gestapo, it was said, struck them with shovels and kicked them repeatedly until they were dead. All the children who had been imprisoned with her were saved due to her efforts and released at the time of the liberation in August.

The hastily buried and mutilated bodies of Marianne and the others were discovered in an open grave at La Rape, near Ville-La-Grande. Marianne's funeral took place on September 26, 1944, in Grenoble. A guard of honor mounted by soldiers of the Resistance and members of the MJS accompanied the bodies. Prayers were recited and speeches were made. After the burial, two salutes were fired, and the ceremony ended with the singing of *Hatikvah*. Some members of the MJS, together with children saved by Marianne in the Pax Prison, then conducted an all-night vigil over her grave.

Celebrated as a heroine of the resistance, Marianne Cohn was just twenty-two years old at the time of her death.

Discussion Questions

1. When given the chance of rescue, Marianne refused to leave the children, yet doing so would have enabled her to save even more, later. Do you think she made the right decision?

2. What do you think Marianne means when she writes, "Tomorrow I shall betray, but not today"?

Further Reading

Bartrop, Paul R., and Samantha J. Lakin, *Heroines of Vichy France: Rescuing French Jews during the Holocaust*, Santa Barbara: Praeger, 2019.
Latour, Anny, *The Jewish Resistance in France, 1940–1945*, New York: Holocaust Library, 1981.

Lazare, Lucien, *Rescue as Resistance: How Jewish Organization Fought the Holocaust in France*, New York: Columbia University Press, 1996.
Lefenfeld, Nancy, *The Fate of Others: Rescuing Jewish Children on the French-Swiss Border*, Clarksville, MD: Timbrel Press, 2013.

AUGUST 1944

12.6 Calel Perechodnik and the Jewish Ghetto Police

The Jewish ghetto police (*Jüdischer Ordnungsdienst*) were police units established by the Nazis in the ghettos of German-occupied Eastern Europe during the Second World War. Calel Perechodnik was a Polish Jew who joined one of these ghetto police units, in the Otwock ghetto. His wartime diaries, published posthumously as *Am I a Murderer?*, outlived him; he died, aged twenty-seven, during the Warsaw Revolt of August 1944. His testimony provides a rare and detailed account of his life as a ghetto policeman, highlighting the extent to which, all too often, moral choices were vexed during the fight for survival.

With the German conquest of Poland in 1939, the Nazis set up nominally self-governing Jewish Councils (*Judenräte*) and ordered that they establish policing units for the purpose of maintaining order in the ghettos. The occupiers set strict guidelines (not always followed) regarding recruitment, involving a certain level of physical fitness, military experience, and secondary or higher education. When first established the ghetto police did not have uniforms; often, all they possessed to distinguish themselves from the rest of the population was an armband, a police hat, and a badge. They carried batons to maintain order but were not permitted firearms.

At first, they had a prescribed set of duties, often less in the way of law and order and more along the lines of maintaining a viable form of existence in the ghetto. Thus, their roles included such activities as traffic control, sanitation, garbage collection, organizing for snow clearance, and generally ensuring that life continued in as nondisruptive a manner as possible under the circumstances. In addition, the hope was that the ghetto police would be able to serve as a force to prevent crime—a desperate need in view of the poverty and overcrowding characterizing ghetto life.

From late 1941 onward, the ghetto police were used by the Nazis as a means to assist rounding up and deporting Jews. Unfortunately, this often resulted in an excessive use of violence, and even cruelty, as the policemen attempted to ensure that they would themselves be spared through demonstrating their efficiency and effectiveness in carrying out their duties.

All too often, however, members of the ghetto police and their families were murdered along with other ghetto Jews (particularly during the

Holocaust's most murderous phase in 1942 and 1943) once it was deemed by the Nazis that their effectiveness had come to an end. For many, this was the direct opposite to their reasons for joining the police in the first place, as membership in what was recognized as a protected part of the ghetto administration was seen to provide some measure of immunity from persecution. Such immunity also extended to additional benefits such as more food, money, clothing, and shelter; these were often obtained owing to a notorious level of corruption and intimidation practiced by the more unscrupulous ghetto policemen.

Calel Perechodnik joined to keep his wife and daughter safe, but it was for naught: despite his position, they were deported to Treblinka and murdered in September 1942 while he remained in the ghetto.

In the long run, it rarely mattered whether an officer compromised his values to keep his family safe; indeed, some remained at their posts right up to the last moment, when they were themselves deported. Others left the police service long before, unable to look their neighbors in the eye—even though they had first joined in the belief that by joining they would have an opportunity to serve their community.

One of the characteristics of ghetto life in many places was the existence of a resistance movement—sometimes vigorous, other times weak, and on yet others relatively unformed. Given that the role of a police force should be the maintenance of law and order, the attitude of the Jewish police toward such movements was mixed. Frequently, the relationship between the resistance and the police was strained. While the former saw the ghetto police as traitors to their people who did the Nazis' work for them, the latter saw it as their role to eliminate threats to the smooth running of the ghetto and not bring down the wrath of the occupiers. Sometimes, the police refused to intervene in resistance activities, or gave assistance to those who would become ghetto fighters; indeed, in certain places some were simultaneously members of both groups.

Jewish ghetto police forces varied in strength, but, depending on the ghetto, could be relatively large. Probably the biggest was in the Warsaw ghetto, numbering up to 2,500 officers and men at its maximum. The ghetto at Łódź comprised about 1,200, while that in Lvov (Lviv) numbered some 500, and those in Kovno (Kaunas) and Kraków were 200 and 150, respectively. The size of the Jewish ghetto police force depended on the size of the Jewish community.

It can be difficult to pass judgment on the Jewish ghetto police. To a large degree they fall into a similar "grey zone" as the leaders and members of the *Judenräte* for whom they worked. Each policeman had his own motives for joining the force, behaving in certain ways while in it, and remaining there for as long—or as short—as he did. There are no simple solutions to the complex questions posed by the existence of the ghetto police.

Discussion Questions

1. In your opinion, were the men of the ghetto police naïve to think that by their service they and their families would be spared?

2. What does the experience of Calel Perechodnik tell us about the "grey zone" mentioned in the article?

Further Reading

Anonymous, *The Clandestine History of the Kovno Jewish Ghetto Police*, Bloomington: Indiana University Press, 2014.

Gutman, Yisrael, and Cynthia Haft (eds.), *Patterns of Jewish Leadership in Nazi Europe, 1933–1945*, Jerusalem: Yad Vashem, 1979.

Perechodnik, Calel, *Am I a Murderer? Testament of a Jewish Ghetto Policeman*, Boulder: Westview Press, 1996.

SEPTEMBER 1944

12.7 The Story of Mala Zimetbaum

Mala Zimetbaum was a Jewish woman from Belgium best remembered as the first female prisoner to escape from Auschwitz. She was born on January 26, 1918, in Brzesko, Poland, the fifth daughter in a large family. In 1928 they all emigrated from Poland and settled in Antwerp, Belgium. Mala, an excellent student, became proficient in several languages (Flemish, French, German, English, and Polish) but was forced to leave school because of the family's difficult economic circumstances. She went to work, first as a seamstress for a major fashion house and then in one of Antwerp's many diamond factories.

On or about July 22, 1942, Mala was arrested for the first time by the SS. She was released but arrested a second time during a roundup on September 11–12, 1942; sent to the transit camp at Mechelen/Malines; and then, on September 15, to Auschwitz. Arriving two days later, and having survived the preliminary selection process, she was sent to the women's camp at Birkenau and given the registration number 19880.

Owing to her proficiency in languages, Mala was chosen to serve as a "runner," or courier, and a translator for the SS. This position came with privileges: she could move relatively freely between different parts of the camp and could speak up on behalf of her fellow inmates. She was also able to smuggle tiny items between compounds. She considered that she had been given a gift in which she could help those around her. Her position also provided her with an opportunity to make connections with the camp resistance movement.

Other tasks included working in the camp hospital, where she could warn of forthcoming selections among patients too weak to continue working or who seemed less likely to recover quickly. She tried to ensure that they would leave the hospital as soon as possible if she knew that a selection was imminent. She also had responsibility for assigning to new work details those who had been sick once they had been released from the hospital. This gave her some measure of discretion in allocating less demanding work to women who were physically less able to handle harder forms of labor.

Among the prisoners Mala met was a Pole, Edward (Edek) Galiński. Edek was brought to Auschwitz as an early Polish political prisoner, having arrived on June 14, 1940. Determined to escape, he had made attempts before he met Mala, though nothing had materialized. After he met her, however, things changed. The two fell in love, and Mala said she was prepared to escape with him, her motive being to let the world know about Auschwitz.

On Saturday, June 24, 1944, they made their escape. Edek wore an SS uniform and carried a gun obtained from Edward Lubusch, a member of the SS guard detachment known to assist prisoners. Disguised as a guard, Edek led Mala, as a prisoner on a work detail, out of the camp by showing a fake SS pass. They succeeded in escaping to a nearby town, but on July 6, 1944, were captured by a German patrol. Returned to Auschwitz, they were sent to Block 11, the punishment block, where they underwent a long period of interrogation and torture. The Gestapo was particularly interested in learning who their conspirators were in the escape and who provided them with the SS uniform. They remained true to their promise to Lubusch and did not break under the torture.

On September 15, 1944, Mala and Edek were executed. Orders were received at Birkenau that the executions were to take place separately but at the same time, in the men's and women's camps, respectively.

As he was hanged, Edek shouted defiantly, "Long Live Poland." Mala's death has become shrouded in legend. According to one version, she was brought forward toward the gallows by SS *Unterscharführer* Johan Ruiters, and as her sentence was read out by SS officer Maria Mandl, Mala took a razor blade she had hidden in her hair and slit her wrists. At the same time, as blood poured from the wound, she slapped Ruiters, who attempted to stop her. This resulted in other SS officers closing in on her and beating her as they attempted to take the razor blade away.

It is here that reality becomes mixed with fable. With the blood draining away her life, some accounts assert that she shouted at Ruiters, saying that she was dying a hero while he would die a dog. Others assert that she shouted at the prisoners assembled to witness her execution that they should revolt. Another claimed that she told the prisoners they would soon be liberated. Even the precise circumstances of her death are uncertain. For some, she was taken to the camp hospital and died on the way to the crematorium. One account has it that an SS officer had said an order arrived from Berlin that

Mala was to be burned alive in the crematorium. Other accounts hold that she was poisoned or shot to death at the crematorium entrance, while yet others say that she was thrown into the furnace alive.

Notwithstanding the differences between the various versions of Mala's death, this was unquestionably a remarkable young woman. Her courage in the face of the Nazi terror, her willingness to put herself at risk to ease the lives of those around her (and even to save those lives), her attempt to escape and thereby tell the world the truth about Auschwitz, even the love with Edek she managed to find amidst the horror—all these point to a woman who refused to allow the Nazi evil to prevail. Her resistance was truly inspirational to all those around her and remains so today, making Mala Zimetbaum a genuine heroine of the Holocaust.

Discussion Questions

1. Do you agree that Mala was a heroine? If so, why? If not, why not?
2. Why do you think Mala's tragic death is so shrouded in mystery?

Further Reading

Suhl, Yuri (ed.), *They Fought Back: The Story of the Jewish Resistance in Nazi Europe*, New York: Crown Publishers, 1967.

OCTOBER 1944 (1)

12.8 The *Sonderkommando* Revolt at Auschwitz

On October 7, 1944, a most remarkable event took place at Auschwitz. The prisoners fought back. The XII *Sonderkommando* rose in revolt, blew up Crematorium IV, and killed the guards.

Originally an SS term for units designated special tasks, the word *Sonderkommando* later came to mean Jewish prisoners in the death camps assigned to work as labor in the gas chambers and crematoria. They would help the victims remove their clothing, shave their hair, usher them into the gas chambers, and later, after the victims had been murdered, inspect the bodies for hidden coins and jewels, remove any gold teeth, and then take the corpses from the gas chambers to the crematoria. Their job was also to stoke the crematoria and do the heavy work involved in such operations.

The life of the *Sonderkommando* prisoners themselves was short, as they would be murdered after approximately three months. As witnesses to industrialized mass murder, the Nazis held that there was no other way to ensure secrecy. The knowledge possessed by the *Sonderkommando* men was far too sensitive for anyone in the outside world to know about, so the Nazis would regularly gas the men of a *Sonderkommando* unit and replace them with a new team. The first task of the incoming group would be to dispose of their predecessors' remains.

The imminence of extermination was the trigger that saw Jewish prisoners assigned to the XII *Sonderkommando* in Birkenau decide to stage a rebellion. As they saw it, there was little alternative. Driven by desperation of a kind that had not motivated the eleven *Sonderkommando* groups before them—and faced with an imminence of death to which the previous groups had not been privy—the prisoners knew that they should either sell their lives dearly or that, somehow, the killing would go on regardless of their deaths. When leaders of the Auschwitz underground outside the crematoria sent an urgent warning to the tiny resistance movement in the *Sonderkommando* of a forthcoming SS murder action, they immediately requested that the underground join with them launching an uprising. Such collaboration was for various reasons not forthcoming, so the members of the *Sonderkommando* decided to go ahead on their own.

On October 7, 1944, the men working at Crematorium IV rose in revolt. Setting fire to the crematorium, they attacked the SS guards with hammers, axes, and stones. Upon learning that the revolt had begun, the men working at Crematorium II joined in, killing a Kapo and several SS men. Then the Hungarian prisoners working in Crematorium III also entered what by now had become a full-scale rebellion. The revolt so damaged Crematorium IV that it was never used again. During the revolt, several hundred prisoners escaped from Birkenau, though most were caught and killed by the SS. Later that day, an additional 200 prisoners who took part in the revolt were executed. One month later, on November 7, 1944, the Nazis destroyed the entire gas chamber-crematorium complex and terminated the operation altogether.

The uprising was, however, unexpected, breaking out before a hoped-for general revolt could take place. In the chaos, around 600 *Sonderkommando* men broke through the fences separating the crematorium from the rest of the camp, though ultimately all those who escaped were caught and shot.

The revolt of the XII *Sonderkommando* at Auschwitz was triggered by the imminence of their extermination, but many of those involved were no doubt also motivated by a desperate desire to destroy the machinery of death that had murdered so many innocent people before them. It was, however, an isolated incident in the history of the camp; further, it was restricted in scope and did not involve the entire Auschwitz complex. It was, however, an instance of the most positive form of physical, armed resistance, all too uncommon in the death camps.

Discussion Questions

1. Why did the men of the XII *Sonderkommando* at Auschwitz stage a revolt in October 1944?

2. Reading through the article carefully, could it be said that the *Sonderkommando* revolt at Auschwitz was successful? Give reasons for your answer.

Further Reading

Müller, Filip, *Eyewitness Auschwitz: Three Years in the Gas Chambers*, Chicago: Ivan R. Dee, 1979.

Rees, Laurence, *Auschwitz: The Nazis and the Final Solution*, New York: Random House, 2005.

Venezia, Shlomo, *Inside the Gas Chambers: Eight Months in Sonderkommando at Auschwitz*, Cambridge: Polity, 2011.

OCTOBER 1944 (2)

12.9 Rabbinerin Regina Jonas

In October 1944, a Jewish woman was deported to her death at Auschwitz. By itself, this might not seem all that momentous; after all, tens of thousands of Jews were deported to Auschwitz in October 1944. Yet this was a woman unique in the entire world: Regina Jonas, the world's first (and, to that point, only) female rabbi.

Regina Jonas was born in Berlin on August 3, 1902, the daughter of Wolf and Sara Jonas. She grew up in the Scheunenviertel, a poor, mostly Jewish, Berlin neighborhood. Her father was a merchant; when Regina was eleven, he died of tuberculosis, leaving her mother to take care of herself, her son Abraham, and Regina.

At high school, Regina's passions for Jewish history, Bible, and Hebrew saw her develop an interest in what at the time was unthinkable for a girl: she wanted to become a rabbi. She spoke about it often with her fellow students and studied hard in order to be able to teach. She enrolled in Berlin's *Hochschule für die Wissenschaft des Judentums* and took courses designed for liberal student rabbis.

Several people supported her along the way, leading Orthodox rabbis among them. She was even tutored in a weekly *shiur* (study session) by Rabbi Max Weyl, who was deported during the war to Theresienstadt. In 1924 she graduated as an "Academic Teacher of Religion," along with her fellow women students. She then became the only woman who hoped to go one step further and be ordained as a rabbi.

The thesis that followed would, in the normal run of events, have been required as one of the important steps leading to ordination. Supervised by Professor Eduard Baneth (who was responsible for rabbinic ordination at the College), the thesis was entitled "Can a Woman Be a Rabbi According to Halachic Sources?" Submitted in June 1930, this was the first known attempt to find a basis in Jewish religious law that would allow for female ordination. Her conclusion was that there was no prohibition in law holding women back from being ordained.

The thesis received a grade of "good," which should have paved the way for ordination, but Professor Baneth died shortly afterward and his conservative successor, Rabbi Chanokh Albeck, refused to ordain a woman. The result saw Regina graduate as a teacher of religion—but only that.

After the Nazis came to power in early 1933, there was an increased demand for Jewish religious teachers. Students were forced out of public schools and into Jewish establishments, and "Miss Jonas" worked hard to impart both Jewish knowledge and *Ahavat Yisroel* (a love of the Jewish people). Throughout the years following, she continued to pursue ordination, until finally, in 1935, Rabbi Max Dienemann agreed. On December 27, 1935, she became Rabbinerin Regina Jonas. She began working as a chaplain in various Jewish organizations, though as a woman she was denied a pulpit by congregations across Germany. The spiritual head of German Jewry, Rabbi Leo Baeck, endorsed her ordination after the fact, though he had refused to assist in the process leading her to the rabbinate on the ground that a female rabbi, at that time in German Jewish history, would have caused massive and unnecessary problems within the Jewish community.

From 1935 on, Rabbi Regina threw herself into pastoral work. Although she did not have her own pulpit, she spent long hours visiting the sick in Berlin's Jewish Hospital and cared for elderly Jews whom circumstances— whether through age or finances—had left in a precarious position owing to Nazi antisemitic measures. With the onset of war, she became a roving rabbi, ministering to Jewish communities in towns which no longer had a spiritual leader.

In 1941, she led special services in lieu of regular worship, this no longer being viable in smaller communities from where large-scale emigration had taken place. Her messages were always positive, emphasizing the need to remain true to Judaism and a Jewish identity, despite the horrors taking place outside.

On November 6, 1942, Regina and her mother were deported to Theresienstadt. Two days before, in advance of this, she was forced to fill out a declaration form listing all her property which was then confiscated by the state.

At Theresienstadt she continued working as a rabbi. In this case, as well as counseling older Jews, she also spent a lot of her time and energy preaching to children about the glory of being Jewish and the privilege of doing God's work. She helped the renowned Austrian Jewish psychoanalyst Viktor Frankl establish a department of mental hygiene as at least one way of to preventing suicide attempts.

Working without a break for two years, she lectured, preached, counseled, and gave hope constantly to those around her. Being a "woman rabbi" was never a concern to her; being a rabbi was. She was aware of her unique status but considered that only to be a temporary uniqueness; her hope was that this would be the harbinger of something much bigger to follow.

On October 12, 1944, time ran out. Rabbi Regina and her mother were deported to Auschwitz, and probably killed the same day. Among her papers, found in 1991 by Dr. Katharina von Kellenbach from St. Mary's College of Maryland, was a sermon that could have been her epitaph: "May all our work be a blessing for Israel's future (and the future of humanity) ... Upright 'Jewish men' and 'brave, noble women' were always the sustainers of our people. May we be found worthy by God to be numbered in the circle of these women and men ... The reward of a mitzvah is the recognition of the great deed by God."

Discussion Questions

1. Why do you think women had been denied the chance to become rabbis until Regina Jonas broke through?
2. Describe in your own words how Rabbi Regina gave hope to Jews before and after being sent to Auschwitz.

Further Reading

Klapheck, Elisa, *Fräulien Rabbiner Jonas: The Story of the First Woman Rabbi*, San Francisco: Jossey-Bass, 2004.
Silverman, Emily Leah, *Edith Stein and Regina Jonas: Religious Visionaries in the Time of the Death Camps*, Durham: Acumen, 2013.

DECEMBER 1944

12.10 Rudolf Kasztner and the Satmar Rebbe

On December 7, 1944, a train carrying Rabbi Joel Teitelbaum, founder of the Satmar Hasidic dynasty, departed Bergen-Belsen concentration camp on what became known as the Kasztner Train. The train, carrying 1,370 Jews, traveled to Switzerland—and safety. It was unique among such transports, a "life train," as distinct from the death trains that had been conveying

Jews to their fate in the extermination camps up to that point. The story of the Kasztner Train, by which Rebbe Teitelbaum was rescued in December 1944, is a controversial episode in the history of Jewish rescue during the Holocaust.

Teitelbaum, who grew up in Sighet, Romania, was the son of the local rabbi. As a young man he moved to the town of Satmar, and in 1934 became its chief rabbi. In 1940, Satmar again became part of Hungary. When war came to Satmar in 1944, he attempted to flee Hungary for Romania but was caught by Hungarian police and sent to the Koloszvár (Romanian, Cluj) ghetto.

Rudolf (Rezső) Kasztner was a Hungarian Jew and senior member of the Budapest Jewish community. As a leader of the *Vaada Etzel Vehatzalah* (Jewish Relief and Rescue Committee), he helped Jews try to escape from the Nazis and smuggle them into neutral countries. In this capacity—and given that the committee was never formally part of the Nazi-imposed Jewish Council—Kasztner found himself looked to increasingly as one who would try to orchestrate the saving of Jews. This would take place in direct dealings with the notorious Adolf Eichmann. Such negotiations led to an agreement whereby the Nazis would permit a single trainload of Jews to leave Budapest and go to a neutral country.

Kasztner and his committee arranged for a diverse group of Jews to be assembled for rescue. People of all ages and social classes were included: Zionists and non-Zionists, Orthodox and ultra-Orthodox, 972 females and 712 males. Baron Fülöp von Freudiger, director of the Orthodox congregation in Budapest, selected eighty rabbis and other prominent figures and paid for their inclusion in the passenger list, among them Teitelbaum.

It was, however, because of the 150 seats that were auctioned off to wealthy Jews that caused Kaszter's name to be forever vilified and was to cost him his life several years later. He was criticized not only for charging wealthy Jews but also for rescuing some of his family members at the expense of others.

His success in arranging for the transfer of these Jews to Switzerland between August 18, and December 6, 1944, would come to be viewed later as both self-serving and harsh evidence of collaboration with the Nazis. Later, at his trial in Israel, Eichmann said that Kasztner had "agreed to help keep the Jews from resisting deportation—and even keep order in the collection camps—if I would close my eyes and let a few hundred or a few thousand young Jews emigrate to Palestine. It was a good bargain."

This to one side, on June 10, 1944, Rebbe Teitelbaum, with a small group of family and entourage, arrived in Budapest aboard a special train that carried those from the Kolozsvár (Cluj) ghetto who were included in the list. The Kasztner train left Budapest on June 30, 1944, but instead of heading directly to Switzerland it was diverted to the Bergen-Belsen concentration camp on July 9. Then followed months of delay, during which Kasztner worked to negotiate the Jews' release. They were segregated from the other inmates and given a subsistence diet. Prior to their release in two batches—some in August and others in December—several, unfortunately, died.

Teitelbaum's group finally left Bergen-Belsen on December 4. On the night of December 7–8, 1944, the train arrived in neutral Switzerland. The Rebbe received a visa, and an apartment was organized for him and his wife in Geneva.

Overall, some 1,670 Jews survived owing to Kasztner's negotiations with Adolf Eichmann, which is about 400 more than Oskar Schindler saved through his famous list. The difference between Kasztner and Schindler, however, is that some viewed Kasztner, a Jew, as having sold out vast numbers of other Jews in order to save his own life and that of his family and favorites, whereas Schindler, a Gentile, has been recognized for his unconditional goodwill toward Jews.

As for the Satmar Rebbe, a legend had it that one of Kasztner's relatives had a dream that the Rebbe had to be included on the train to freedom—either this or none of its passengers would survive. He therefore went, and, on theological grounds, became one of the bitterest opponents of Zionism and the establishment of a Jewish state. When he died in 1979 aged ninety-two, followers of Satmar Hasidism were already celebrating Kislev 21, 5705 (December 7, 1944) as the date of their Rebbe's "miracle" rescue.

Kasztner, for his part, was murdered in Tel Aviv on March 4, 1957, by a group of veterans from the prestate right-wing militia Lehi (known also as the Stern Gang), who accused him of selling out the Jewish people for his own convenience. The killers were given life sentences but were released seven years later. To this day, despite the rescue of over 1,600 Jews and the many thousands of descendants they produced, Rudolf Kasztner remains a divisive figure among survivors.

Discussion Questions

1. Rudolf Kasztner is either a hero or a villain but cannot be both. Discuss.

2. Why do you think Adolf Eichmann was prepared to allow an initiative like the Kasztner Train to proceed?

Further Reading

Aronson, Shlomo, *Hitler, the Allies, and the Jews*, Cambridge: Cambridge University Press, 2004.

Braham, Randolph L., and William J. vanden Heuvel (eds.), *The Auschwitz Reports and the Holocaust in Hungary*, New York: East European Monographs/Columbia University Press, 2011.

Porter, Anna, *Kasztner's Train: The True Story of an Unknown Hero of the Holocaust*, New York: Walker Books, 2008.

Zweig, Ronald W., *The Gold Train: The Destruction of the Jews and the Looting of Hungary*, London: Allen Lane, 2002.

Part 13

1945

JANUARY 1945

13.1 Roza Robota and the Heroines of Auschwitz

Roza Robota was one of a group of four women hanged at Auschwitz for their role in the October 7, 1944, revolt of the XII *Sonderkommando*. She was born in 1921 in Ciechanów, Poland, and when young she was a member of the Zionist *Hashomer Hatzair* youth movement. During the Nazi occupation she found herself engaged in underground resistance activities. When the liquidation of the Ciechanów ghetto was carried out in 1942 she was deported with her family to Auschwitz. She was the only member of the family to survive the selection process, the others being sent direct to their deaths upon arrival. At first, she was allocated to the women's camp at Auschwitz I but was transferred to Birkenau later in 1942.

She was assigned to the clothing shed in the *Kanadakommando*, right next to Birkenau's Crematorium III. Here, the belongings of Jews transported to Auschwitz-Birkenau were sorted before being transported back to Germany for the war effort. The name "Kanada" was given by the prisoners to this area rich in all manner of items such as clothing, jewelry, and foodstuffs, as Canada, the country, symbolized wealth and abundance.

In view of her past membership of *Hashomer Hatzair* and given that through this she was known to some of those working in the Auschwitz underground, she was recruited to smuggle a form of gunpowder—*schwartzpulver*—to the men working in the *Sonderkommando* in Crematorium III. She was one of a few such women brought into the resistance movement. Others, such as Estusia Wajcblum, Ala Gertner, and Regina Safirsztajn, had already been smuggling small amounts of gunpowder, at enormous personal risk, from their workplace at the *Weichsel-Union-Metallwerke*, a munitions factory in the Auschwitz complex, to those in the camp proper.

Roza established contact with about twenty women in the Union plant who were willing to cooperate, and over a period of several months they smuggled in the gunpowder. There were risks: prisoners were searched when returning from work on *aussenarbeit* (outside labor beyond the wire), though each day they were able to pass on tiny amounts to the men of the underground in matchbox-size quantities.

It took a year and a half of careful preparations before the revolt took place, but there was, unfortunately, never a large enough quantity of powder to enable the prisoners to stage a fully successful revolt of sufficient strength. When the men of the *Sonderkommando* rose in rebellion on October 7, 1944, however, enough had been accumulated to enable the resisters to blow up Crematorium IV. The unexpected uprising saw around 600 of the *Sonderkommando* workers break through the fences separating the crematorium from the rest of the camp, though ultimately all those who escaped were caught and shot.

The Gestapo was brought in after the revolt had been crushed with the express purpose of tracing the source of the explosives. They were tracked back to the Union plant. In subsequent days, Roza, Ala, Estusia, and Regina were arrested and placed in the notorious Block 11, where the Kapo Yakov Kozalchik managed to sneak in the occasional visitor. Under brutal torture, they were then subjected to weeks of interrogation. They refused to reveal the names of others who had participated in the smuggling operation and were duly hanged on January 5, 1945—Estusia and Regina at the morning roll-call assembly, and Roza and Ala in the evening. The executions, only two weeks before the camp was liberated, were in public, as a warning to the entire camp.

According to some eyewitness accounts, Roza Robota and her comrades shouted "*Nekamah!*" ("Revenge!") to the assembled inmates before they died. Roza's last message was a note in Hebrew, scratched on a piece of paper she managed to smuggle from her cell: "*Chazak V'amatz*" ("Be strong and have courage"). When the Nazis murdered her, Roza Robota was just twenty-three years old.

Discussion Questions

1. Outline briefly how the women of the Union munitions factory helped the men of the XII *Sonderkommando* in the period leading up to the October revolt.

2. Do you think Roza, Ala, Estusia, and Regina can be classed as resistance fighters against the Nazis? Why/why not?

Further Reading

Suhl, Yuri (ed.), *They Fought Back: The Story of the Jewish Resistance in Nazi Europe*, New York: Crown, 1967.

Tec, Nechama, *Resistance: Jews and Christians Who Defied the Nazi Terror*,
    New York: Oxford University Press, 2013.
Venezia, Shlomo, *Inside the Gas Chambers: Eight Months in the Sonderkommando
    of Auschwitz*, London: Polity, 2009.

FEBRUARY 1945

13.2 The Horror that Was Gross-Rosen

In February 1945, Gross-Rosen, a large Nazi concentration camp located
near the village of the same name (now Rogoźnica, Poland) was liberated
by Soviet forces. We tend to think of the Nazi concentration camps being
liberated in April and May of 1945, but after Auschwitz at the end of
January 1945, Gross-Rosen was an early example of the horror that was to
confront Allied forces later.

Located about forty miles southwest of Wrocław in modern-day Poland,
Gross-Rosen was at once a concentration and a forced labor camp. Built
initially in 1940 as a sub-camp of Sachsenhausen, on May 1, 1941, it became
independent. Eventually, it would encompass some ninety-seven sub-camps,
where prisoners were put to work in a nearby granite quarry. Here, large
numbers died.

In many of these sub-camps where prisoners were exploited as slave
labor, conditions were deplorable. Food was meager and poor, sanitation
primitive, and medical care virtually nonexistent. Thousands fell victim to
starvation and disease, with large numbers killed arbitrarily by guards through
beatings and cruel punishments. Jews were not allowed to receive medical care
and forbidden from talking to other prisoners. All those sent into slave labor
were severely overworked, and many simply collapsed where they stood.

Hanna Granek Erlich was one of these slave workers. She was sent to a
factory sub-camp at Peterswaldau, where a weapons manufacturing plant
was located. At night, she recalled, "we slept in a room with over fifty women.
We slept downstairs on bunks covered with straw, and over us, upstairs, the
men used to sleep." Conditions, she remembered, were dreadful. The hall
was filthy, and the prisoners were full of lice. Hanna worked seven days a
week, from morning to night, and "didn't dare make a mistake." These were
met by German guards who, she said, "would beat us or even kill us."

When Gross-Rosen was first opened, most prisoners were political
detainees, resistance fighters, or those deemed "socially unacceptable" such
as gay men or Roma. The number of prisoners in the camp rose steadily,
however, from an initial 1,500 or so in 1941. In late 1943 and early 1944
Jews began arriving in large numbers, until they formed the biggest single
group in the camp complex. It is estimated that at least 125,000 prisoners
passed through Gross-Rosen between 1941 and 1945, and even in late

1944, just before the camp's liberation, Gross-Rosen and its sub-camps held 76,728 prisoners.

A census of the camp population in January 1945 indicated that almost 26,000 women were incarcerated there. This represented one of the largest aggregations of female prisoners in any of the German concentration camps outside of the women's concentration camp at Ravensbrück and the massive Auschwitz complex. The census revealed that most of the Jews at Gross-Rosen had been relocated there from camps in Poland and Hungary. Set to work under the close supervision of sadistic Nazi guards, they suffered under especially cruel working conditions.

As the war progressed and Germany's demands began relying more and more on forced labor, the reach of the Gross-Rosen complex became one of the largest in all of Europe. At the end of 1943, transports of Jews to Gross-Rosen and its sub-camps, located throughout Lower Silesia and the Sudetenland, intensified. Eventually, prisoners worked throughout eastern Germany and western Poland for companies like I.G. Farben, Daimler-Benz, and Krupp. Some of the sub-camps focused on "special" Nazi projects deep underground.

Brünnlitz, one of Gross-Rosen's sub-camps, became famous later after German industrialist Oskar Schindler relocated his factory there. At Brünnlitz, in unique circumstances, he managed to protect some 1,100 Jews working in his factory, at the same time ensuring that they did not suffer from the same tortures inflicted elsewhere. He also made sure that his factory did not produce anything of value for the German war effort.

When Soviet troops began approaching Gross-Rosen at the end of January 1945, camp officials began the process of closing it down. Male prisoners were relocated to the main camp from the external sites, while the women were forced onto cruel death marches where many died. The destination of these marches was, for the most part, other camps deep inside Germany. In total up to 40,000 prisoners underwent this brutal trial, in bitterly cold weather.

The rest of the camp, and most of those in the sub-camps, were evacuated from the beginning of February 1945. Some of the remaining Jews were transported to Bergen-Belsen, while others were sent to Buchenwald, Dachau, Flossenbürg, Mauthausen, and Dora-Mittelbau. The few remaining prisoners still in the sub-camps, by the end of the war, were liberated by Soviet troops on May 8–9, 1945. In sum, it has been estimated that about one-third of all those who passed through Gross-Rosen died because of their experiences between 1940 and February 1945.

Discussion Questions

1. Gross-Rosen is not listed as one of the six Nazi extermination camps, yet vast numbers of people died there. Can you explain why?

2. Could the survivors of Gross-Rosen be described as lucky? Explain
   your answer.

Further Reading

Hilberg, Raul, *The Destruction of the European Jews*, New York: Holmes and
    Meier, 1962.
Kogon, Eugen, *The Theory and Practice of Hell: The German Concentration
    Camps and the System Behind Them*, New York: Farrar, Straus and
    Giroux, 2006.
Wachsmann, Nikolaus, *KL: A History of the Nazi Concentration Camps*,
    New York: Farrar, Straus and Giroux, 2015.

MARCH 1945

13.3 The Sacrifice of Mila Racine

On March 22, 1945, a Jewish resister in France, Mila Racine, was killed
at Mauthausen concentration camp in Austria. Prior to this, as a rescuer
in Vichy France, she had saved the lives of dozens of Jewish children and
others by smuggling them across the border into Switzerland.

Born on September 14, 1921, in Moscow, she was the daughter of
Georges (Hirsch) Racine and his wife Berthe (Bassia). One of three children,
she had a brother, Emmanuel, and a sister, Sacha. Fleeing the Soviet Union
and a climate of pogroms in the aftermath of the Russian Revolution, the
family relocated to France, settling in Paris.

With the German invasion and occupation in 1940, the Racine family
moved out of northern France and into the so-called free zone at Vichy. Mila
joined the Resistance on January 5, 1942. While her parents were in a safe
house in Nice, Mila, Emmanuel, and Sacha worked for *Éducation Physique*
(Physical Education), a code name for a scheme producing false documents
and rescuing Jews under the overall direction of Simon Lévitte in Grenoble.

Mila, operating under the alias of Marie Anne Richemond, came from
a Zionist background and had been an active member of the Women's
International Zionist Organization (WIZO). In the summer of 1943, she
was given command of a unit of the *Mouvement de jeunesse sioniste* (Zionist
Youth Movement, or MJS) in Saint-Gervais-Le Fayet (Haute-Savoie) in the
Italian zone of occupation—but her field of operations ranged much wider
than this, covering a region that included Toulouse, Gurs, Saint-Gervais,
Nice, and Annemasse, under the overall command of Netanel "Tony" Gryn.

Gryn was another young Jewish resister who was entrusted by Simon
Lévitte with the task of organizing a means to enable the smuggling of Jews
from France into Switzerland. The network he created brought together a

team of about a dozen young people who collectively managed to rescue about a hundred children.

After the Italian armistice on September 3, 1943, and the German takeover of southern France, Mila undertook to drive convoys of children and adults to Annemasse, right on the Swiss frontier, and arranged to have them smuggled across. Her activities, particularly around the city of Annecy, saw the creation of links with local people smugglers (*passeurs*), who functioned as an "underground railroad" running Jews across the border. Throughout September 1943 and beyond, she helped hundreds of families and children who fled into her area. From her base in the French Alps, and often working close to German patrols, Mila and the others in her network took in children from French cities often many miles distant. To protect them, they organized the children into small groups and then accompanied them to the border, where they were helped by Christian rescuers.

On October 21, 1943, she was conducting a convoy that included thirty children from Nice, accompanied by another rescuer, Roland Epstein. This was a difficult group. It comprised children, an older couple, a young mother with a baby, and another couple with a small child. Without warning, they were intercepted by Germans with police dogs. Gunshots rang out; one woman was killed and another wounded. Mila, Roland, and the children were taken to Annemasse and incarcerated in the Pax Hotel, the prison at Gestapo headquarters.

Suffering continued Nazi torture as the Gestapo sought information regarding the smuggling operations, Mila divulged nothing. Through the underground movement, the mayor of Annemasse, Jean Deffaugt (later recognized as one of the Righteous among the Nations for his own efforts in saving Jewish children), managed to provide Mila with an escape plan. This was not something she could accept, however, as she had an instinctive feeling that the children would be punished—or worse—if she escaped.

Mila and Roland were transferred to the prison at Fort Montluc in Lyon. From there, Roland was sent to the transit camp at Drancy, from where he was deported to Buchenwald as a member of the Resistance. He lived to see the end of the war and ultimate survival. Mila was deported, *via* the Royallieu transit camp at Compiègne, to the women's camp at Ravensbrück. While there, it was observed, her conduct was exemplary, as she tried to maintain morale among the other prisoners and help them when they were too exhausted to go on.

Her stay at Ravensbrück was not to be permanent. In 1945 a large group of women, including Mila, was transferred from Ravensbrück to Mauthausen, where they were put to work repairing railway tracks destroyed by Allied bombing. On March 22, 1945, on the eve of liberation, a British air raid targeted the camp and Mila, then on *aussenarbeit* (work outside the camp), was killed by shrapnel.

The work of Mila Racine did not end with her arrest, however. After her capture, her brother, Emmanuel Racine (code named Mola) sent another resister, Marianne Cohn, to replace her in the smuggling of Jewish children across the border. When Marianne, in turn, was captured on the evening of May 31, 1944, she was herself replaced by another young rescuer, Charlotte Sorkine. Such importance did the Jewish resistance place on the work of these young women that it determined nothing should stand in the way of their rescue activities, even at the risk of their very lives.

After the war, Mila Racine was posthumously awarded the *Medaille de la Resistance* and the *Croix de Guerre* by the French government. And it is perhaps fitting as a final testament that the recognition she received in Israel, many years later, was for a kindergarten and nursery in Tel Aviv to be named in her memory.

Discussion Questions

1. Describe in your own words the efforts made by Mila's network to rescue Jewish children into Switzerland.

2. Can the rescue activities in which Mila, Marianne, and Charlotte were involved be counted as resistance? Explain your answer by reference to the article.

Further Reading

Bartrop, Paul R., and Samantha J. Lakin, *Heroines of Vichy France: Rescuing French Jews during the Holocaust*, Santa Barbara: Praeger, 2019.
Lefenfeld, Nancy, *The Fate of Others: Rescuing Jewish Children on the French-Swiss Border*, Clarksville, MD: Timbrel Press, 2013.

APRIL 1945

13.4 The Liberation of the Camps

When discussion gets around to the liberation of the camps in April 1945, questions abound. Was the period under discussion one singular event? How did liberation take place? Who brought it about? The answer, as with most momentous events, is far from easy to explain.

In January 1945, Auschwitz was evacuated by the Nazis, and a great many of the prisoners there were sent on hideous death marches. They were evacuated in the face of Soviet progress; indeed, the Russians were so close while the prisoners were marching away that the sounds of battle could be distinguished nearby. They suffered terribly as they moved westward, and countless numbers perished. When they arrived at their new destinations their trials were hardly eased, as they faced massive overcrowding in the camps to which they had been evacuated.

Bergen-Belsen was perhaps the supreme example of the chaos, overcrowding, and general horror that struck all the camps. Belsen, a euphemistically termed *Krankenlager*, or "sick camp," has left just as indelible an image of the Nazi system on the Western mind as Auschwitz has in its. Established during the second half of 1943, the camp is best remembered for the images brought to the world at the time of its liberation by the British on April 15, 1945.

As recalled by one British observer, "The camp area was strewn with corpses; thousands of skeletally emaciated and fatally ill people were crowded into miserable barracks, so spent by hunger and disease that even in the days and weeks following liberation large numbers of them died."

Pictures of this horror were circulated throughout the world. Newsreels were broadcast in local theatres, and citizens were urged to view them as a civic duty. Bergen-Belsen became the first evidence of the inhuman barbarity of the National Socialist concentration camp system.

On April 15, the day of the liberation, the British found approximately 60,985 survivors; there were some 10,000 unburied dead who lay where they had fallen in the compound, and another 15,000 succumbed to disease and starvation after the British arrived. Ironically, Bergen-Belsen had never been given formal concentration camp status. In the final months of the war, however, fierce epidemics devastated the camp, which had grown fourfold in population within two months, and as a result the area looked like a charnel house from ancient times when the British arrived. As they grasped the reality of their first liberated camp, their only impression was that this was a metaphor for horror.

Due to the dislocation of the north German rail network because of constant Allied bombing, food could not be transported to Belsen; medicine, in the form of both doctors and equipment, was completely lacking. Moreover, no attempt had been made by the Nazis to clean the place up. One of the first things the British did, therefore, was to set the captured Nazi guards to work helping gather the dead together prior to their burial. In images that have come to represent what liberation signified for many, most of those who had died were simply piled up in what became mountains of putrescent flesh and then shoved unceremoniously into giant pits dug by British army bulldozers.

Elsewhere, concentration camp prisoners, dropped into places like Belsen to await liberation, had little time to wait in real terms, though each day dragged by unendingly. Painfully slowly, as German units both west and east surrendered, the prisoners were freed. On April 12, 1945, the Dutch transit camp at Westerbork was set free; the next day, Buchenwald's inmates rose against their SS guards and took over the camp, handing it to the arriving Americans. On April 23, the SS transferred Mauthausen to the International Committee of the Red Cross. The next day Dachau, after twelve years and twenty-eight days of unending misery and abuse, was overrun by the US army. Five days later, on April 29, Ravensbrück was liberated.

The liberations continued into the next month, with Theresienstadt handed over to the Red Cross by the Nazis themselves on May 2 and then transferred by the Red Cross to the Russians on May 4. American troops took possession of Mauthausen—the last major camp to be liberated in the west—on May 8.

By this stage, the military side of the war was over. What now remained was to reconstruct new lives and a new Europe from the ashes and ruins of the old, a task that would prove as daunting as it was heartrending. As the present looked as though it was coming under control, thoughts turned uncertainly toward the future, with one question uppermost in the minds of many: what was to be the fate of the survivors? Only the passage of time, over the next few weeks, months, and years, would tell.

Discussion Questions

1. Why was there so much death and devastation at Bergen-Belsen at the end of the war?
2. What do you think liberation meant for survivors of the Holocaust in April 1945?

Further Reading

Abzug, Robert H., *Inside the Vicious Heart: Americans and the Liberation of Nazi Camps*, New York: Oxford University Press, 1985.
Bridgman, Jon, *The End of the Holocaust: The Liberation of the Camps*, Portland: Areopagitica Press, 1990.
Hirsh, Michael, *The Liberators: America's Witness to the Holocaust*, New York: Bantam Books, 2010.
Stone, Dan, *The Liberation of the Camps: The End of the Holocaust and Its Aftermath*, New Haven: Yale University Press, 2015.

MAY 1945

13.5 The Poet of the Jewish People

In May 1945, a poem was published which, for many, is one of the most eloquent testimonials to the Holocaust ever expressed in that literary genre. Written in Yiddish and entitled *Dos Lid funem Oysgehargen Yidishn Folk*, the English title translates to *The Song of the Murdered Jewish People*.

The author was Itzhak Katzenelson, a Hebrew and Yiddish poet and dramatist. Born on July 21, 1886, in Karelichy (Korelichi), a small town in Belarus near Minsk, Katzenelson was a descendant of a long line of sages and scholars dating back to the great Talmudic commentator, Rabbi Yom-Tov Lipmann Heller. He was raised in Łódź, Poland, where his family had moved soon after he was born. Considered a literary prodigy, by the age of twelve he already had written his first play, *Dreyfus un Esterhazy*. Prior to the First World War, he opened a secular Hebrew school and undertook the creation of a network of such schools ranging from kindergarten through high school. He also became known for his Hebrew textbooks and books for children, which were the first of their kind.

In addition, he wrote Yiddish comedies (translated into Hebrew), and in 1912 founded *Habima Halvrit* ("The Hebrew Stage"), a theatre troupe that toured Poland and Lithuania. His first volume of poetry, *Dimdumim* (*Twilight*), appeared in 1910. He also found time to visit Palestine several times across the years. From 1930 onward, Katzenelson belonged to the *Dror Hechalutz* Zionist movement—which, with emigration to Palestine its goal, operated a training commune, Kibbutz Hakhsharah. He considered that Jewish life in Poland was utterly without hope due to an ingrained antisemitism within the national consciousness and that emigration to Palestine was the only solution for the Jewish people.

After Nazi Germany invaded Poland on September 1, 1939, and Łódź was occupied, Katzenelson's school was forced to close. Later, it served as the city's Gestapo headquarters. In late November 1939 he fled to Warsaw, with his wife Hanna and their three children joining him there later. Hanna and their two younger sons, Benjamin and Ben Zion, would be deported to their deaths at Treblinka on August 14, 1942.

In the ghetto, Katzenelson entered his most creative period, writing poems and articles in the underground Zionist press, as well as approximately fifty plays. He wrote poems that reflected the contemporary suffering of the ghetto, though masked through Biblical or historic themes. His descriptions were a response to the wretched conditions in which the Warsaw Jews found themselves. His Yiddish play *Iyov* (*Job*) was published on June 22, 1941, possibly the only Jewish book published in the ghetto during the German occupation.

With the onset of the Warsaw Ghetto Uprising in April 1943, friends smuggled Katzenelson and his surviving son Zvi into the Aryan part of the city. They went to the Polski Hotel, from where they obtained forged passports certifying that they were citizens of Honduras. With these in hand, they were transferred to the French internment camp at Vittel, where the Nazis held Allied citizens and nationals of other neutral countries for possible later prisoner exchange.

It was here, on October 3, 1943, that he wrote *The Song of the Murdered Jewish People*. He completed this epic poem of fifteen chapters on January 18, 1944. Among its lines were included:

And it continued. Ten a day, ten thousand Jews a day.
That did not last very long. Soon they took fifteen thousand.
Warsaw, The City of Jews—the fenced-in, walled-in city,
Dwindled, expired, melted like snow before my eyes.
Warsaw, packed with Jews like a synagogue on Yom Kippur, like a
*   busy market place*
Jews trading and worshiping, both happy and sad
Seeking their bread, praying to their God.
They crowded the walled-in, locked-in city.
You are deserted now, Warsaw, like a gloomy wasteland.
You are a cemetery now, more desolate than a graveyard.
Your streets are empty—not even a corpse can be found there.

The poem ended with the words "Woe to me, everything is over ... there once existed a nation but she is no more."

Katzenenlson made two copies of the poem, one of which was given to Ruth Adler, a German Jew from Dresden who had a British Palestinian passport. In the spring of 1944, she received permission to leave the country in a prisoner exchange and smuggled out her copy. Katzenelson buried the manuscript of the other copy in bottles under a tree at Vittel with the help of a fellow prisoner, French resistance fighter and later historian, Miriam Novitch. After the war, Novitch retrieved the manuscript and arranged for it to be published; this was done in May 1945. Extracts have since been published in numerous languages, and an individual volume has also appeared.

In the early spring of 1944, the Jews interned at Vittel were declared stateless, and on April 18, 1944, those of Polish origin were transported in three railroad cars to the Drancy transit camp near Paris. In late April 1944, Itzhak and Zvi Katzenelson were sent from there to Auschwitz, where they were murdered on May 1, 1944.

In Israel, a lasting monument to Katzenelson was created when the Ghetto Fighters' House (*Beit Lohamei Ha-Getaot*), established in 1949, was named in his honor as the Itzhak Katzenelson Holocaust and Jewish Resistance Heritage Museum. The museum has since made extensive efforts to collect as many of Katzenelson's manuscripts as can be located and to translate his works into English and other languages.

Discussion Questions

1. Do you think that poetry such as that written by Itzhak Katzenelson can be classed as resistance?

2. What, if anything, is significant about Katzenelson's poetry?

Further Reading

Shner, Moshe, *Janusz Korczak and Yitzhak Katzenelson: Two Educators in the Abysses of History*, Berlin: De Gruyter, 2020.
Zuckerman, Yitzhak, *A Surplus of Memory: Chronicle of the Warsaw Ghetto Uprising*, Berkeley: University of California Press, 1993.

OCTOBER 1945

13.6 The International Military Tribunal Opens

Thirteen trials were held in Nuremberg, Germany, between 1945 and 1949 to bring Nazi war criminals to justice. By the end of the Second World War, the Nazi state had systematically murdered some six million European Jews, with an estimated four to six million non-Jews also losing their lives at the hands of the Nazis.

On December 17, 1942, a joint declaration from the United States, Britain and the Soviet Union documented the mass murder of European Jewry. It resolved to act against those responsible, both military and civilian, for crimes against civilian populations. In October 1943 the Moscow Declaration, signed by British, Soviet, and US representatives, stated that war criminals would be brought to trial. This was discussed further at meetings in Tehran (November-December 1943), Yalta (February 1945), and Potsdam (July 1945).

On August 8, 1945, the London Charter of the International Military Tribunal issued detailed court procedures for the trials to take place. The charter identified four categories of crimes: (1) crimes against peace: planning and/or preparing a war of aggression and violating international agreements; (2) crimes against peace: participating in a conspiracy to plan a war of aggression; (3) war crimes: a violation of the customs and laws of war, use of slave labor, killing of hostages; and (4) crimes against humanity. Criminal proceedings would document the crimes charged against the defendants and prevent later accusations that the defendants had been condemned without evidence.

Nuremberg was chosen as the location for the trials because of its symbolic value. It had hosted the annual Nazi Party rallies and where the Third Reich's racial laws were proclaimed, so the postwar trials there symbolized the end of Hitler's Third Reich. The Palace of Justice, with cells which could hold 1,200 detainees, was relatively undamaged by war, allowing all prospective defendants to be held on site.

The Nuremberg proceedings fell into two categories. The Trial of Major War Criminals was held from November 20, 1945, to October 1, 1946. Twenty-two defendants were tried before an International Military Tribunal

(IMT) established by Britain, France, the Soviet Union, and the United States. The tribunal was a panel of judges, rather than a single judge and a jury, and the four Allied powers, France, Great Britain, the Soviet Union, and the United States, each supplied a main judge and an alternate.

On October 6, 1945, prosecutors indicted twenty-four Nazi war criminals and six organizations. Those indicted were Martin Bormann, head of the Reich Chancellery (tried *in absentia*); Karl Doenitz (naval commander, 1943–1945); Hans Frank (governor-general of occupied Poland); Wilhelm Frick (minister for internal affairs); Hans Fritzsche (journalist, broadcaster, and senior official in the ministry of propaganda); Walther Funk (minister of economic affairs); Hermann Göring (Hitler's former deputy and commander of the Luftwaffe); Rudolf Hess (deputy leader of the Nazi Party until May 1941); Alfred Jodl (head of operations of the armed forces); Ernst Kaltenbrunner (head of security forces); Wilhelm Keitel (chief of the armed forces); Gustav Krupp von Bohlen und Halbach (head of Krupp armaments); Robert Ley (head of the Labor Front); Konstantin von Neurath (governor of Bohemia and Moravia); Franz von Papen (former German Chancellor); Erich Raeder (naval commander until 1943); Joachim von Ribbentrop (foreign minister); Alfred Rosenberg, minister for occupied eastern territories); Fritz Saukel (head of forced labour allocation); Hjalmar Schacht (former minister of economics and president of the Reichsbank); Baldur von Shirach (Hitler Youth leader); Arthur Seyss-Inquart (commissioner for the occupied Netherlands); Albert Speer (minister of armaments); and Julius Streicher (publisher of the antisemitic newspaper *Der Stürmer*). These individuals consisted of most of the top surviving Nazi leaders. The six organizations indicted as criminal organizations, and subject to separate trials later, were the Nazi Party, SS, SD, Gestapo, the General Staff, and Hitler's cabinet.

The trial lasted 218 days. After a week, the tribunal was shown German films of concentration camps, some of the defendants becoming noticeably distressed at what they saw. Most revealing were testimonies regarding the brutalities of the death camps. Around 360 witnesses gave either written or oral testimony. The trial was translated simultaneously into four languages using a new IBM translation system. The defense could call its own witnesses but was not allowed to present any evidence against the Allies. An aspect of the trial that caused debate at the time was the legality of trying military officers. Some suggested it was the role of military officers to carry out orders, but the defense of "only following orders" was banned at Nuremberg.

On October 1, 1946, the tribunal announced its verdicts. Three were not present: Martin Bormann was tried *in absentia*, Robert Ley had committed suicide before the trial had begun, and Gustav Krupp von Bohlen und Halbach was too weak to be present. The tribunal delivered the verdicts first and then the sentences. Twelve defendants were sentenced to death by hanging—the counts on which they were found guilty are in parentheses: Hans Frank (3 and 4), Wilhelm Frick (2, 3, and 4), Hermann Göring (all four), Alfred Jodl (all four), Ernst Kaltenbrunner (3 and 4), Wilhelm Keitel (all four), Robert

Ley (all four), Joachim von Ribbentrop (all four), Alfred Rosenberg (all four), Fritz Saukel (3 and 4), Arthur Seyss-Inquart (2, 3, and 4), and Julius Streicher (1 and 4). Göring escaped hanging, having committed suicide with cyanide poison smuggled into the prison just prior to his intended execution. Franz von Papen, Hans Fritzsche, and Hjalmar Schacht were acquitted on all charges, with those against Gustav Krupp von Bohlen und Halbach dropped as he was deemed physically and mentally unable to stand trial.

The remaining defendants received lesser terms: Karl Doenitz, ten years (2 and 3); Walter Funk, life imprisonment (2, 3, and 4); Rudolf Hess, life imprisonment (1 and 2); Konstantin von Neurath, fifteen years (all four); Erich Raeder, life imprisonment (1, 2, and 3); Baldur von Schirach, four to twenty years (1 and 4); and Albert Speer, four to twenty years (3 and 4). Of those sentenced to life imprisonment, both Funk and Raeder were released early due to poor health, Raeder in 1955 and Funk in 1957. Each died in 1960. Hess lived until the age of ninety-three, dying in Berlin's Spandau Prison in 1987.

The trial was the most important of the judicial proceedings held at Nuremberg. Twelve further trials, covering nearly 200 other Nazis, took place at Nuremberg before US tribunals between November 1946 and April 1949. These trials were conducted by American occupying forces, in accordance with Control Council Law No. 10 (December 1945), that empowered Allied forces to conduct trials within their own zones of occupation. Most of the trials grouped defendants accused of similar crimes together. The Doctors Case was a trial of twenty-three doctors accused of conducting medical experiments on inmates in concentration camps. The Justice Case focused on the lawyers and judges who abused the legal process under Nazism; the Pohl Case tried eighteen SS officers for their role in administering the concentration camps and the use of those imprisoned for slave labor. Four defendants were also charged for their role in the Nazi "Euthanasia" (T-4) program. A case was brought against industrialists who profited from slave labor and plundered occupied countries.

The *Einsatzgruppen* Case tried twenty-three SS leaders with being collectively responsible for the murder of more than a million civilians (mostly Jews) in the Nazi-occupied area of the Soviet Union between 1941 and 1943. The trial took place between September 1947 and April 1948. The tribunal rejected the defense of following "superior orders," while defense attorneys claimed the accused could not be convicted for killing civilians, as the Allies had similarly done so through their bombing campaigns. One defendant fell ill at trial; all the remaining twenty-two defendants were found guilty on at least one count, with twenty found guilty on all counts. Of those convicted, fifteen were sentenced to death by hanging, the others to various terms of imprisonment. Later, because of the Cold War, ten of the fifteen death sentences were commuted to terms of imprisonment, which were only a fraction of their sentences; all defendants were released by 1958.

The Nuremberg Trials marked the first prosecutions for crimes against humanity. The legal justifications for the trials and their procedural innovations were controversial at the time, but the trials were a milestone toward the establishment of a permanent international court and a precedent for dealing later with genocide and other crimes against humanity.

Discussion Questions

1. Why do you think the victorious Allies decided to put the leading Nazis on trial, rather than simply executing them once captured (as some had suggested)?
2. Do you think some of the Nazis should have been released early from their sentences? Give reasons for your answer.

Further Reading

Conot, Robert E., *Justice at Nuremberg*, New York: HarperCollins, 1983.
Persico, Joseph E., *Nuremberg: Infamy on Trial*, New York: Viking Penguin, 1994.
Taylor, Telford, *The Anatomy of the Nuremberg Trials: A Personal Memoir*,
   New York: Knopf, 1992.

DOCUMENTS

The documents that follow are intended to assist teachers and students—indeed, all readers—contextualize the Holocaust by identifying what the Nazi leaders did to legitimize their actions: the propaganda they employed and how they viewed the actions taken in the name of Nazism. Most of the documents are extracts from much longer records, reports, or pieces of legislation. The words included are as they appeared in the original. Omissions or deletions are signified by an ellipsis (three dots).

1 Decree for the Protection of the People and the State, February 28, 1933

On February 28, 1933—one day after fire had destroyed the Reichstag, Germany's Parliament building—Germany's recently installed chancellor, Adolf Hitler, on the pretext that revolution was imminent, persuaded President Paul von Hindenburg to sign a Decree for the Protection of the People and the State (which became known as the Reichstag Fire Decree), suspending all basic civil and individual liberties guaranteed under the constitution. It empowered the government to take whatever steps were necessary to ensure that the threat to German society was removed. It did not make any specific references to definite adversaries but contained the menacing portent of later restrictions that might be applied toward other "enemies." Its terms enabled the new regime to begin to entrench itself in office, paving the way for the Nazi dictatorship and dismantling Germany's Weimar Republic.

Pursuant to article 48, paragraph 2 of the German constitution, the following is decreed as a defensive measure against Communist acts of violence endangering the State:

Article 1

Articles 114, 115, 117, 118, 123, 124, and 153 of the constitution of the German Reich are suspended until further notice. Thus, restrictions on personal liberty, on the right of free expression of opinion, including freedom of the press, on the right of assembly and the right of association and interferences with the secrecy of postal, telegraphic, and telephonic communications, and warrants for house searches, orders for confiscations as well as restrictions on property, are also permissible beyond the legal limits otherwise prescribed.

Article 2

If in a state the measures necessary for the restoration of public security and order are not taken, the Reich government may temporarily take over the powers of the highest State authority. ...

Article 4

Whoever disobeys the orders issued by the supreme State authorities or by the authorities subordinate to them for the implementation of this decree, or the orders issued by the Reich government in pursuance of article 2, or whoever solicits or incites others to disobey such orders, will be punished with imprisonment of not less than 1 month or a fine from 150 up to 15,000 Reichsmarks, unless other regulations make his act liable to a more severe punishment.

Whoever, by a violation of paragraph 1, induces a common danger for human life, will be punished with hard labour, or, in case of extenuating circumstances, with imprisonment of not less than 6 months, and, if the violation causes the death of a person, with death, or, in case of extenuating circumstances, with penal servitude of no less than 2 years. In addition, his property may be confiscated.

Whoever solicits or incites to commit a violation under the qualifications of paragraph 2, will be punished with hard labour or, in case of extenuating circumstances, with imprisonment of not less than 3 months.

Article 5

The crimes, which under the penal code are punishable with hard labour for life, are to be punished with death; i.e., in articles 81 (high treason), 229 (poisoning), 307 (arson), 311 (use of explosives), 312 ([intentional] flooding), 315 paragraph 2 (damaging of railroad installations), and 324 (poisoning causing public danger). ...

Article 6

This decree comes into force on the day of its promulgation.

Source: Trials of War Criminals before the Nuremberg
Military Tribunals Under Control Council No. 10
(Washington, DC: U.S. Government Printing Office, 1946),
Green Series, vol. III, pp. 160–163, Doc. NG-715.

2 The Enabling Act: Law to Remove the Distress of People and State, March 24, 1933

Less than one month after the Reichstag Fire Decree, the Law to Remove the Distress of People and State (the Enabling Act) was passed by the Reichstag, vesting in the government the authority to decree laws without requiring laws to be passed by the Reichstag. It also allowed for the creation of new laws that "deviate from the constitution." Thus, the Enabling Act codified in legislation the sole power of the government to control all legal authority at the expense of the safeguards and procedures in the constitution that were intended to prevent that very thing.

The Reichstag has decreed the following law, which is hereby promulgated in agreement with the Reich Council, after it has been duly established that the prerequisites of legislation changing the constitution have been fulfilled.

Article 1
   Laws of the Reich can be decreed, apart from the procedure provided by the constitution of the Reich, also by the government of the Reich. This also applies to the laws mentioned in articles 85, paragraphs 2, and 87 of the constitution of the Reich.
   Article 2
   The laws decreed by the government of the Reich may deviate from the constitution of the Reich as far as they do not concern the institution of the Reichstag and the Reich Council as such. The rights of the Reich President remain untouched. ...

Source: *Trials of War Criminals before the Nuremberg*
Military Tribunals Under Control Council No. 10
(Washington, DC: U.S. Government Printing Office, 1946),
Green Series, vol. III, pp. 163–164, Doc. NG-715.

3 Reich Citizenship Law, September 15, 1935

The Nuremberg Laws consisted of two laws issued by a special session of the Reichstag on September 15, 1935, at the Annual Nazi Party Rally in Nuremberg. Both were designed to exclude Jews from all manner of public life. The first, the Reich Citizenship Law, stated that only Germans or those related by blood could be citizens, thereby excluding Jews from citizenship. This represented the ultimate legal division between Jews and non-Jews in Germany. For the many Jews who had been hoping that earlier anti-Jewish laws would not last or become too draconian, this law represented undeniable proof of the extent to which their presence in German society was not wanted and would not be tolerated.

Article 1
   1. A subject of the State is a person, who belongs to the protective union of the German Reich, and who, therefore, has particular obligations towards the Reich.

2. The status of the subject is acquired in accordance with the provisions of the Reich and State Law of Citizenship.

Article 2

1. A citizen of the Reich is only that subject, who is of German or kindred blood and who, through his conduct, shows that he is both desirous and fit to serve faithfully, the German people and Reich.

2. The right to citizenship is acquired by the granting of Reich citizenship papers.

3. Only the citizen of the Reich enjoys full political rights in accordance with the provision of the laws. ...

Source: Nazi Conspiracy and Aggression,
Office of the United States Chief of Counsel for the
Prosecution of Axis Criminality (Washington, DC: U.S. Government
Printing Office, 1946), Red Series, vol. IV, pp. 7–8, Doc. 1416-PS.

4 Law for the Protection of German Blood and German Honor, September 15, 1935

The second of the Nuremberg Laws, the Law for the Protection of German Blood and German Honor, prohibited Jews from marrying or having extramarital relations with non-Jews. It also prohibited the employment of German female domestic servants under the age of forty-five in Jewish households, as well as prohibiting the raising of the German flag by Jews. Of greater importance, it set forth a definition of the term "Jew" to be used for application of these and subsequent laws. Generally, a Jew was defined as someone with three of four Jewish grandparents. A person with one or two Jewish grandparents would be considered, respectively, a Mischling *of the second class and a* Mischling *of the first class, that is, one of "mixed blood."*

Imbued with the conviction that the purity of the German blood is the prerequisite for the permanence of the German people, and animated by the inflexible will to safeguard the German nation for all future, the Reichstag has unanimously enacted the following law, which is promulgated herewith:

Article 1

1. Marriages between Jews and German nationals of German or related blood are prohibited. Marriages concluded despite of this are void, even if concluded abroad in order to circumvent this law. ...

Article 2

Sexual intercourse (except in marriage) between Jews and German nationals of German or related blood is forbidden.

Article 3

Jews may not employ female German nationals of German or related blood below 45 years of age in their households.

Article 4

1. Jews are forbidden to show the Reich and national flag or the colors of the Reich.

2. They are, however, allowed to show the Jewish colors. The exercise of this right will be protected by the State.

Article 5

1. Whoever violates the prohibition of article 1will be punished with hard labour.

2. Any man violating the prohibition of article 2 will be punished with imprisonment or hard labour.

3. Whoever violates the regulations under articles 3 or 4, will be punished with imprisonment up to 1 year or with a fine, or with both of these penalties. ...

Source: Trials of War Criminals before the Nuremberg
Military Tribunals Under Control Council No. 10
(Washington, DC: U.S. Government Printing Office, 1946),
Green Series, vol. III, pp. 180–181, Doc. NG-715.

5 First Regulation to the Reich Citizenship Law of November 14, 1935

With the passage of the Nuremberg Laws, the need for an unambiguous definition of who was to be classified as a Jew became critical. This regulation sought to provide that definition by looking at the race of the person's grandparents or parents. If three or four of an individual's grandparents were "full Jews," then the individual would be considered a "full Jew." If two of the parents were "full Jews," the individual would be considered a "full Jew" if any one of four additional conditions were met. The regulation, which also refers to an individual "of mixed Jewish blood" but does not define what that means, reflects the difficulty of maintaining the Nazi position that Jews are a race rather than a religion: Jewish status depended, under certain circumstances, on whether a person's parents or grandparents belonged to the Jewish community, or if a person was married to a Jew.

Article 1

1. Until further issue of regulations regarding citizenship papers, all subjects of German or kindred blood, who possessed the right to vote in the Reichstag elections, at the time the Citizenship Law came into effect, shall, for the time being, possess the rights of Reich citizens. The same shall

be true of those whom the Reich Minister of the Interior, in conjunction with the Deputy of the Führer, has given the preliminary citizenship.

2. The Reich Minister of the Interior, in conjunction with the Deputy of the Führer, can withdraw the preliminary citizenship.

Article 2

1. The regulations in Article 1 are also valid for Reich subjects of mixed Jewish blood.

2. An individual of mixed Jewish blood, is one who descended from one or two grandparents who were racially full Jews, insofar as does not count as a Jew according to Article 5, paragraph 2. One grandparent shall be considered as full-blooded if he or she belonged to the Jewish religious community. ...

Article 4

1. A Jew cannot be a citizen of the Reich. He has no right to vote in political affairs, he cannot occupy a public office.

2. Jewish officials will retire as of 31 December 1935. If these officials served at the front in the World War, either for Germany or her allies, they will receive in full, until they reach the age limit, the pension to which they were entitled according to last received wages; they will, however, not advance in seniority. After reaching the age limit, their pension will be calculated anew, according to the last received salary, on the basis of which their pension was computed.

3. The affairs of religious organizations will not be touched upon.

4. The conditions of service of teachers in Jewish public schools remain unchanged, until new regulations of the Jewish school systems are issued.

Article 5

1. A Jew is anyone who descended from at least three grandparents who were racially full Jews. Article 2, paragraph 2, second sentence will apply.

2. A Jew is also one who descended from two full Jewish parents, if: (a) he belonged to the Jewish religious community at the time this law was issued, or who joined the community later; (b) he was married to a Jewish person, at the time the law was issued, or married one subsequently; (c) he is the offspring from a marriage with a Jew, in the sense of Section 1, which was contracted after the Law for the protection of German blood and German honor became effective; ... (d) he is the offspring of an extramarital relationship, with a Jew, according to Section 1, and will be born out of wedlock after July 31, 1936. ...

Article 7

The Führer and Reichs Chancellor can grant exemptions from the regulations laid down in the law.

Source: *Nazi Conspiracy and Aggression,* Office of
the United States Chief of Counsel for the Prosecution
of Axis Criminality (Washington, DC: U.S. Government Printing
Office, 1946), Red Series, vol. IV, pp. 8–10, Doc. 1417-PS.

6 Evian Conference: Decisions on Jewish Refugees, July 14, 1938

In March 1938, President Franklin D. Roosevelt of the United States invited some thirty-two countries from Europe, Latin America, and the British Commonwealth to meet and discuss their respective immigration policies in light of the increase of Jewish refugees from Germany and Austria. Some nations refused; others sent low-level bureaucrats with little or no authority to act. In July 1938, the representatives of these nations met in Evian, France. Almost all of those present went to great lengths to explain why their governments could not assist the refugees. The nine-day meeting produced no resolution to the refugee issue. This affirmed for Hitler and the Nazis the unwillingness of Western democracies to extend themselves on behalf of the Jews. The only outcome of the meeting was setting up an Intergovernmental Committee to meet in London to continue the discussion later.

Having met at Evian, France, from July 6th to July 13th, 1938 ... Recommends:

a. That the persons coming within the scope of the activity of the Intergovernmental Committee shall be 1) persons who have not already left their country of origin (Germany, including Austria), but who must emigrate on account of their political opinion, religious beliefs or racial origin, and 2) persons as defined in 1) who have already left their country of origin and who have not yet established themselves permanently elsewhere;

b. That the Governments participating in the Intergovernmental Committee shall continue to furnish the Committee for its strictly confidential information, with 1) details regarding such immigrants as each Government may be prepared to receive under its existing laws and practices and 2) details of these laws and practices;

c. That in view of the fact that the countries of refuge and settlement are entitled to take into account the economic and social adaptability of immigrants, these should in many cases be required to accept, at least for a time, changed conditions of living in the countries of settlement;

d. That the Governments of the countries of refuge and settlement should not assume any obligations for the financing of involuntary emigration ...

Source: Proceedings of the Intergovernmental Committee, Evian, July 6th to 15th, 1938. Record of the Plenary Meetings of the Committee. Resolutions and Reports, London, July 1938.

7 Hitler's Euthanasia Authorization, 1 September 1939

To protect doctors and other medical professionals, Adolf Hitler signed a secret order in the fall of 1939, authorizing them to kill individuals considered to have "lives not worthy of living." The program—referred to as Aktion T-4 *for the program's headquarters at number 4, Tiergartenstrasse, in Berlin—was the first of Nazi Germany's programs for mass murder. It applied to non-Jews throughout the Reich. Hitler's authorization was dated September 1 to suggest that it was undertaken in response to the outbreak of war. From a Nazi racial perspective, the death of young Germans in the war eliminated the best of the German gene pool, necessitating special measures to keep "inferior" genes—those of the mentally or physically disabled— from contaminating the German race.*

Reichsleiter Bouhler and Dr. Brandt, M.D. are charged with the responsibility of enlarging the authority of certain physicians to be designated by name in such a manner that persons who, according to human judgment, are incurable can, upon a most careful diagnosis of their condition of sickness, be accorded a mercy death.

[signed] A. Hitler

Source: *Nazi Conspiracy and Aggression,* Office of the United States Chief of Counsel for the Prosecution of Axis Criminality (Washington, DC: U.S. Government Printing Office, 1946), Red Series, vol. III, p. 451, Doc. 630-PS.

8 Reinhard Heydrich's Instructions on Jews in Occupied Territories, September 21, 1939

Shortly after Germany's invasion of Poland in September 1939, Reinhard Heydrich, chief of the Security Police, issued instructions to the heads of the Einsatzgruppen, *mobile killing units that followed behind the German army as it moved east. Their primary role was to kill all Jews and communists they encountered. Heydrich's instructions called for the movement of Jews into "concentration centres," each to be administered by a "Council of Jewish Elders" (Judenrat). He instructed that evacuating Jews into the concentration centers must not disrupt critical economic needs, such as the needs of the army. Heydrich also required the "Aryanization" of Jewish factories to be expropriated for the use of the Reich. Each* Einsatzgruppe *leader must provide information, such as a count of the Jews in each concentration center, and a survey of Jewish industries in their territory.*

To The chiefs of all detail groups [Einsatzgruppen] of the Security Police

Concerning: The Jewish problem in the occupied zone.

I refer to the conference held in Berlin today, and again point out that the *planned joint measures* (i.e., the ultimate goal) are to be kept *strictly secret*. ...

I

The first prerequisite for the ultimate goal is first of all, the concentration of the Jews from the country to the larger cities.

This is to be carried out speedily. In doing so distinction must be made:

(1) between the zones of Danzig and West Prussia. Poznan, Eastern Upper Silesia; and

(2) the other occupied zone.

If possible, the zone mentioned under item 1 shall be cleared completely of Jews, or at least the aim should be to form as few concentration centres as possible. ...

On principle, all Jewish communities under 500 heads are to be dissolved and to be transferred to the nearest concentration centre. ...

II

Councils of Jewish Elders

(1) In each Jewish community, a Council of Jewish Elders is to be set up which, as far as possible, is to be composed of the remaining influential personalities and rabbis. The Council is to be composed of 24 male Jews (depending on the size of the Jewish community).

It is to be made *fully responsible* (in the literal sense of the word) for the exact execution according to terms of all instructions released or yet to be released.

(2) In case of sabotage of such instructions, the Councils are to be warned of severest measures. ...

(5) The Councils of Elders of the concentration centres are to be made responsible for the proper housing of the Jews to be brought in from the country. ...

(6) The Council of Elders is also to be made responsible for the adequate maintenance of the Jews on the transport to the cities. ...

(7) Jews who do not comply with the order to move into cities are to be given a short additional period of grace when there is good reason. They are to be warned of strictest penalty if they should not comply by the appointed time.

III

All necessary measures, on principle, are always to be taken up in closest agreement and collaboration with the German civil administration and the competent local authorities.

In the execution of this plan, care must be taken that economic security suffer no harm in the occupied zones.

(1) The needs of the army, should particularly be kept in mind e.g. it will not be possible to avoid leaving behind here and there some Jews

engaged in trade who absolutely must be left behind for the maintenance of the troops, for lack of any other way out. In such cases, the immediate aryanization of these plants is to be planned for and the emigration of the Jews is to be completed later in agreement with the competent local German administrative authorities.

(2) For the preservation of German economic interests in the occupied territories it is self understood that Jewish war and ordinary industries and factories and those important to the 4-Year Plan must be kept going for the time being.

In these cases also, immediate Aryanization must be planned for and the emigration of the Jews must be completed later. …

Source: *Nazi Conspiracy and Aggression*, Office of the United States Chief of Counsel for the Prosecution of Axis Criminality (Washington, DC: U.S. Government Printing Office, 1946), Red Series, vol. VI, pp. 97–101, Doc. 3363-PS.1222.

9 Hitler Threatens the Jews, January 30, 1939

On the sixth anniversary of his accession to power, Adolf Hitler delivered a long speech to the Reichstag. It was primarily concerned with the economic, political, military, and diplomatic recovery of Germany in the aftermath of the devastating Versailles Treaty of 1919 after the First World War, but one passage stood out and is most often noted. It reflects his worldview about the role "international Jewish financiers" play in global affairs and is a warning that if there should be a new world war, it will result in "the annihilation of the Jewish race in Europe."

I believe that this problem will be solved—the sooner the better—for Europe cannot rest again before the Jewish problem has been eliminated. …

Once more I will assume the part of a prophet:

If the international Jewish financiers within and without Europe, succeeded in plunging the nations once more into a world war, then the result will be not the Bolshevization of the world and thereby the victory of Jewry—but the annihilation of the Jewish race in Europe.

Source: *Nazi Conspiracy and Aggression*, Office of the United States Chief of Counsel for the Prosecution of Axis Criminality (Washington, DC: U.S. Government Printing Office, 1946), Red Series, vol. V, p. 367, Doc. 2663-PS.

10 The Madagascar Plan, July 3, 1940

Franz Rademacher had recently been appointed to head the Jewish Department of the Ministry of Foreign Affairs when he wrote a memorandum suggesting that the Jewish question in Europe could be solved by deporting all Jews to the island of Madagascar in the Indian Ocean east of South Africa. Although not a new idea, it became a matter of particular interest for the Nazi regime after the defeat of France in May 1940 made this French colony potentially available to the Germans. The idea was received positively by the highest levels of the Nazi government, including Hans Frank, Reinhard Heydrich, and even Adolf Hitler. Rademacher envisioned the island as a German Mandate, to be administered by the Jews themselves, subject to the authority of a German police governor. The idea was abandoned when Germany lost the Battle of Britain, meaning that the ability to transport millions of Jews over the tremendous distance from Europe to the island could not be assured.

[The Foreign Office] suggests the following for the solution of the Jewish question: The peace treaty with France contains a clause whereby France has to put the isle of Madagascar at our disposal for the solution of the Jewish question, and its approximate 25,000 Frenchmen domiciled there are to be evacuated and compensated. The island will be transferred to Germany as a mandate. The bay of Diego-Suarez, important for reasons of naval strategy, as well as the harbor of Antsirana become German naval bases (there will perhaps also be the possibility for the further extension of these naval bases to the harbors—open landing places—Tamatave, Andevorante, Mananjary, etc., if the Navy so desires. Apart from these naval bases merely parts of the country which are suitable for establishing air bases are cut out from the territory of the Jews. The part of the island that is not required for military reasons is put under the administration of a German Police Governor, who in turn is subordinated to the administration of the Reich Leader SS. Otherwise the Jews will get autonomy in the territory; their own mayors, their own police, their own post and railway administration, etc. The Jews are responsible as joint debtors for the value of the island. The whole European property, owned by them so far, is transferred for this purpose to a European bank which is to be founded. As far as this property is not sufficient for the payment of the real estate values which change into their hands and for the purchase in Europe of goods, necessary for the reconstruction of the island, they will receive at their disposal bank credits from this source.

As Madagascar becomes only a mandate, the Jews settling there do not acquire German citizenship. However, all Jews who are deported to Madagascar are deprived of their citizenship of the individual European countries, effective from the time of deportation. Instead they become members of the Mandate Madagascar. This regulation removes the chance that the Jews establish a Vatican state of their own in Palestine and thus exploit for their own aims the symbolic value which Jerusalem has for the Christian and Mohammedan world. Besides, the Jews remain under German domination as a pawn for the future good conduct of their racial comrades in America. The generosity shown to the Jews by Germany in granting the cultural, economic, administrative, and judicial autonomy, can be exploited from the point of view of propaganda. It can be emphasized in this respect that our German sense of responsibility toward the world forbids to offer immediately the gift of an independent state to a race which knew no national independence for thousands of years; national independence must of necessity stand the trial of history.

Source: *Trials of War Criminals before the Nuremberg
Military Tribunals Under Control Council No. 10*
(Washington, DC: U.S. Government Printing Office,
1946), Green Series, vol. XIII, pp. 154–156, Doc. NG-2586-B.

11 Göring Orders Heydrich to Prepare a General Solution of the Jewish Problem, July 31, 1941

In this letter, Hermann Göring orders the chief of the Security Police, Reinhard Heydrich, to bring about "a complete solution of the Jewish question in the German sphere of influence in Europe." This letter was cited by Heydrich as proof of his authority when later, on January 20, 1942, he convened a conference at Wannsee, a suburb of Berlin, to discuss the implementation of Hitler's order to exterminate the Jews.

Complementing the task that was assigned to you on 24 January 1939, which dealt with arriving at—through furtherance of emigration and evacuation—a solution of the Jewish problem, as advantageously as possible, I hereby charge you with making all necessary preparations in regard to organizational and financial matters for bringing about a complete solution of the Jewish question in the German sphere of influence in Europe.

Whenever other governmental agencies are involved, these are to cooperate with you.

I charge you furthermore to send me, before long, an over-all plan concerning the organizational, factual, and material measures necessary for the accomplishment of the desired solution of the Jewish question.

Source: *Trials of War Criminals before the Nuremberg
Military Tribunals Under Control Council No. 10*
(Washington, DC: U.S. Government Printing Office, 1946),
Green Series, vol. IV, pp. 132–133, Doc. 710-PS.

12 Speech by Hans Frank to His Cabinet, Krakow, December 16, 1941

Hans Frank was the governor-general of the Generalgouvernement, *that portion of German-occupied Poland that was not incorporated into the Reich. Its Jewish population, as Frank observes here, was more than two and a half million. This speech is particularly significant because it represents one of the first times that extermination—not just relocation or ghettoization— of the Jews is discussed in such straightforward language, making it clear that annihilation is now the policy of the Reich. An interesting reference is made by Frank to an forthcoming conference to take place in Berlin to discuss the extermination process. That conference would be the Wannsee Conference, which would be held on January 20, 1942.*

As far as the Jews are concerned, I want to tell you quite frankly that they must be done away with in one way or another. The Führer said once: should united Jewry again succeed in provoking a world war, the blood of not only the nations, which have been forced into the war by them, will be shed, but the Jew will have found his end in Europe. I know that many of the measures carried out against the Jews in the Reich at present are being criticized. It is being tried intentionally, as is obvious from the reports on morale, to talk about cruelty, harshness, etc. Before I continue, I want to beg you to agree with me on the following formula: We will principally have pity on the German people only, and nobody else in the whole world. The others, too, had no pity on us. As an old National Socialist, I must say: This war would only be a partial success if the whole lot of Jewry should survive it, while we would have shed our best blood in order to save Europe. My attitude towards the Jews will, therefore, be based only on the expectation that they must disappear. They must be done away with. I have entered negotiations to have them deported to the East. A great discussion concerning that question will take place in Berlin in January to which I am going to delegate the State-Secretary Dr. Bühler. That discussion is to take place in the Reich Security Main Office with SS-Lt. General Heydrich. A great Jewish migration will begin in any case.

But what should be done with the Jews? Do you think they will be settled down in the "Ostland," in villages? This is what we were told in Berlin: Why all the bother? We can do nothing with them either in the "Ostland" nor in the "Reichkommissariat. So, liquidate them yourself.

Gentlemen, I must ask you to rid yourself of all feeling of pity. We must annihilate the Jews, wherever we find them and wherever it is possible, in order to maintain there the structure of the Reich as a whole. This will, naturally, be achieved by other methods, than those pointed out by Bureau Chief Dr. Hummel. Nor can the judges of the Special Courts be made responsible for it, because of the limitations of the framework of the legal procedure. Such outdated views cannot be applied to such gigantic and unique events. We must find at any rate a way which leads to the goal, and my thoughts are working in that direction.

The Jews represent for us also extraordinarily malignant gluttons. We have now approximately 2,500,000 of them in the General Government, perhaps with the Jewish mixtures and everything that goes with it, 3,500,000 Jews. We cannot shoot or poison those 3,500,000 Jews, but we shall nevertheless be able to take measures which will lead, somehow, to their annihilation, and this in connection with the gigantic measures to be determined in discussions in the Reich. The General Government must become free of Jews, the same as the Reich. Where and how this is to be achieved is a matter for the offices which we must appoint and create here. Their activities will be brought to your attention in due course.

Source: *Nazi Conspiracy and Aggression,* Office of the
United States Chief of Counsel for the Prosecution of
Axis Criminality (Washington, DC: U.S. Government Printing
Office, 1946), Red Series, vol. IV, pp. 891–892, Doc. 2233-D-PS.

13 Regarding Ribbentrop's Instructions on Speeding up Evacuation of Jews from Europe, September 24, 1942

Martin Luther, Undersecretary of the Foreign Ministry, conveys here a decision made by Foreign Minister Joachim von Ribbentrop. The recipient is Ernst von Weizsäcker, secretary of state at the Foreign Office in Berlin. Ribbentrop is demanding that the evacuation of Jews from various occupied countries be expedited. The reason given is that the Jews "stir up" others against the Nazi regime. In fact, the increased evacuations were part of the overall Nazi plan to deport as many Jews as possible to "the East," meaning to their deaths in the extermination camps.

The Reich Foreign Minister has given me instructions today over the telephone to hurry as much as possible the evacuation of Jews from the various countries of Europe, because it is a known fact that the Jews stir up people against us everywhere and that they must be made responsible for attempts of murder and acts of sabotage. Upon a brief report concerning the present stage of evacuation of the Jews from Slovakia, Croatia, Rumania, and the occupied territories, the Reich Foreign Minister has given instructions now to start contacting the governments of Bulgaria,

Hungary, and Denmark with the object of starting the evacuation of the Jews from these countries.

[Signed] LUTHER

Source: *Trials of War Criminals before the Nuremberg Military Tribunals Under Control Council No. 10* (Washington, DC: U.S. Government Printing Office, 1946), Green Series, vol. XIII, pp. 255–256, Doc. NG-1517.

14 The Wannsee Protocol, January 20, 1942

This record of the meeting held at the Wannsee House in January 1942 summarizes events already in place. Convened by chief of the Security Police Reinhard Heydrich, the minute taker was Adolf Eichmann with thirteen high- and medium-level bureaucrats in attendance. Presuming a figure of 11,000,000 Jews were still alive in Europe, discussion focused on "preparations for the final solution of the Jewish question" regarding emigration and evacuation, "the problem of mixed marriages and persons of mixed blood," and sterilization. Discussions of murder were not recorded nor were any references made to extermination or death camps, but there is no doubt that these were also on the minds of the participants. The only existing copy of the thirty copies that were made of this record was found by American troops after the war.

II. At the beginning of the discussion SS-Obergruppenführer HEYDRICH gave information that the Reich Marshal had appointed him delegate for the preparations for the final solution of the Jewish problem in Europe and pointed out that this discussion had been called for the purpose of clarifying fundamental questions. The wish of the Reich Marshal to have a draft sent to him concerning organisatory, factual and material interests in relation to the final solution of the Jewish problem in Europe, makes necessary an initial common action of all central offices immediately concerned with these questions in order to bring their general activities into line.

He said that the Reichsführer-SS and the Chief of the German Police (Chief of the Security Police and the SD) was entrusted with the official central handling of the final solution of the Jewish problem without regard to geographic borders.

The Chief of the Security Police and the SD then gave a short report of the struggle which has been carried on against this enemy, the essential points being the following:

a) the expulsion of the Jews from every sphere of life of the German people,

b) the expulsion of the Jews from the Lebensraum of the German people.

In carrying out these efforts, an increased and planned acceleration of the emigration of Jews from the Reich territory was started, as the only possible present solution.

By order of the Reich Marshal, a Reich Central Office for Jewish Emigration was set up in January 1939 and the Chief of the Security Police and SD was entrusted with [its] management. ... The aim of all this being that of clearing the German Lebensraum of Jews in a legal way. ...

III. *Another possible solution of the problem has now taken the place of emigration, i.e. the evacuation of the Jews to the East, provided the Führer agrees to this plan.* ...

Approx. 11,000,000 Jews will be involved in the final solution of the European problem ...

Under proper guidance the Jews are now to be allocated for labour to the East in the course of the final solution. Able-bodied Jews will be taken in large labour columns to these districts for work on roads, separated according to sexes, in the course of which action a great part will undoubtedly be eliminated by natural causes.

The possible final remnant will, as it must undoubtedly consist of the toughest, have to be treated accordingly, as it is the product of natural selection and would, if liberated, act as a bud cell of a new Jewish reconstruction (see historical experience.)

In the course of the practical execution of this final settlement of the problem, Europe will be cleaned up from West to East. Germany proper, including the protectorate Bohemia and Moravia, will have to be handled first because of reasons of housing and other social-political necessities.

The evacuated Jews will first be sent, group by group, to so-called transit-ghettos from which they will be taken to the East. ...

IV. The implementation of the final solution problem is supposed to a certain extent to be based on the Nuremberg Laws, in which connection also the solution of the problems presented by the mixed-marriages and the persons of mixed blood is seen to be conditional to an absolutely final clarification of the question. ...

Under Secretary of State Dr. BÜHLER stated that it would be welcomed by the General Government if the implementation of the final solution of this question could start in the General Government, because the transportation problem there was of no predominant importance and the progress of this action would not be hampered by considerations connected with the supply of labour. The Jews had to be removed as quickly as possible from the territory of the Government General because especially there the Jews represented an immense danger as a carrier of epidemics, and on the other hand were permanently contributing to the disorganization of the economic system of the country through black market operations. Moreover, out of the two and a half million to be affected, the majority of cases was *unfit for work*.

Source: Trials of War Criminals Before the Nuremberg
Military Tribunals Under Control Council Law No. 10.
Vol. 13, pp. 210–217, Doc. NG-2586.

15 Use of Gas Vans in the Ukraine, May 16, 1942

This report from August Becker to Walter Rauff, both involved in the creation and development of gas vans used for extermination, describes some of the problems that had been encountered. For example, a certain type of gas van could not move in wet weather, and it proved impossible to prevent the civilian populations from recognizing the vans for what they were. Becker observes the difficulty incurred by the men of several commands making use of the gas vans when they unloaded the bodies from the vans after the death of the victims. He shows concern for the psychological impact of the task, as well as physical complaints arising from the men's exposure to any of the carbon monoxide still left after the killings. Finally, Becker recommends that the gas pedal of the van should not be pushed to the floor but should be slowly applied. The former method results in agonizing asphyxiation, while the latter produces a slow and painless death.

The overhauling of vans by groups D and C is finished. While the vans of the first series can also be put into action if the weather is not too bad, the vans of the second series *stop completely in rainy weather*. If it has rained for instance for only one half hour, the van cannot be used because it simply skids away. It can only be used in absolutely dry weather. It is only a question now whether the van can only be used standing at the place of execution. First the van has to be brought to that place, which is possible only in good weather. The place of execution is usually 10–15 km away from the highways and is difficult to access because of its location; in damp or wet weather it is not accessible at all. If the persons to be executed are driven or led to that place, then they realize immediately what is going on and get restless, which is to be avoided as far as possible. There is only one way left; to load them at the collecting point and to drive them to the spot.

I ordered the vans of group D to be camouflaged as house trailers by putting one set of window shutters on each side of the small van and two on each side of the larger vans, such as one often sees on farmhouses in the country. The vans became so well-known, that not only the authorities, but also the civilian population called the van "death van," as soon as one of these vehicles appeared. It is my opinion, the van cannot be kept secret for any length of time, not even camouflaged. ...

The application of gas usually is not undertaken correctly. In order to come to an end as fast as possible, the driver presses the accelerator to the fullest extent. By doing that the persons to be executed suffer death from suffocation and not death by dozing off as was planned. My directions now have proved that by correct adjustment of the levers death comes faster and the prisoners fall asleep peacefully. Distorted faces and excretions, such as could be seen before, are no longer noticed. ...

Source: Nazi Conspiracy and Aggression, Office of the
United States Chief of Counsel for the Prosecution of
Axis Criminality (Washington, DC: U.S. Government
Printing Office, 1946), Red Series, vol. III, pp. 418–419, Doc. 501-PS.

16 "The Warsaw Ghetto Is No More": Report of General Jürgen Stroop, May 16, 1943

SS General Jürgen Stroop had an impressive record of service on behalf of Germany in both World Wars, but it was his role in suppressing the Warsaw Ghetto Uprising and his report on that operation that marked him out as notorious. Resistance began in January 1943 when, for the first time, German troops who entered the Warsaw Ghetto to continue the deportations of Jews were met with small arms fire. They were forced to withdraw, but on April 19, 1943, they returned in force, this time under Stroop's command. It was not until May 16, 1943, that the uprising was suppressed. Stroop's report, which included photographs taken by a Nazi propaganda unit, is the best description of the fighting from the perspective of the Nazis. It also includes an overview of the establishment of the ghetto.

I arrived in Warsaw on 17 April 1943 and took over the command of the action on 19 April 1943, 0800 hours, the action itself having started the same day at 0600 hours. ...

When we invaded the Ghetto for the first time, the Jews and the Polish bandits succeeded in repelling the participating units, including tanks and armored cars, by a well-prepared concentration of fire. When I ordered a second attack, about 0800 hours, I distributed the units, separated from each other by indicated lines, and charged them with combing out the whole of the Ghetto, each unit for a certain part. Although firing commenced again, we now succeeded in combing out the blocks according to plan. The enemy was forced to retire from the roofs and elevated bases to the basements, dug-outs, and sewers. In order to prevent their escaping into the sewers, the sewerage system was dammed up below the Ghetto and filled with water, but the Jews frustrated this plan to a great extent by blowing up the turning off valves. Late the first day we encountered rather heavy resistance, but it was quickly broken by a special raiding party. In the course of further operations we succeeded in expelling the Jews from their prepared resistance bases, sniper holes, and the like, and in occupying during the 20 and 21 April the greater part of the so-called remainder of the Ghetto to such a degree that the resistance continued within these blocks could no longer be called considerable.

The main Jewish battle group, mixed with Polish bandits, had already retired during the first and second day to the so-called Muranowski Square. There, it was reinforced by a considerable number of Polish bandits. Its plan was to hold the Ghetto by every means in order to prevent us from invading it. The Jewish and Polish standards were hoisted at the top of a concrete building as a challenge to us. These two standards, however, were captured on the second day of the action by a special raiding party. SS Untersturmführer Dehmke fell in this skirmish with the bandits; he was holding in his hand a hand-grenade which was hit by the enemy and exploded, injuring him fatally. After only a few days I realized that the original plan had no prospect of success, unless the armament factories and other enterprises of military importance distributed throughout the Ghetto were dissolved. It was therefore necessary to approach these firms and to give them appropriate time for being evacuated and immediately transferred. Thus one of these firms after the other was dealt with, and we very soon deprived the Jews and bandits of their chance to take refuge time and again in these enterprises, which were under the supervision of the Armed Forces. In order to decide how much time was necessary to evacuate these enterprises thorough inspections were necessary. The conditions discovered there are indescribable. I cannot imagine a greater chaos than in the Ghetto of Warsaw. The Jews had control of everything, from the chemical substances used in manufacturing explosives to clothing and equipment for the Armed Forces. The managers knew so little of their own shops that the Jews were in a position to produce inside these shops arms of every kind, especially hand grenades, Molotov cocktails, and the like.

Moreover, the Jews had succeeded in fortifying some of these factories as centers of resistance. Such a center of resistance in an Army accommodation office had to be attacked as early as the second day of the action by an Engineer's Unit equipped with flame throwers and by artillery. The Jews were so firmly established in this shop that it proved to be impossible to induce them to leave it voluntarily; I therefore resolved to destroy this shop the next day by fire. ...

The number of Jews forcibly taken out of the buildings and arrested was relatively small during the first few days. It transpired that the Jews had taken to hiding in the sewers and in specially erected dug-outs. Whereas we had assumed during the first days that there were only scattered dug-outs, we learned in the course of the large-scale action that the whole Ghetto was systematically equipped with cellars, dug-outs, and passages. In every case these passages and dug-outs were connected with the sewer system. Thus, the Jews were able to maintain undisturbed subterranean traffic. They also used this sewer network for escaping subterraneously into the Aryan part of the city of Warsaw. Continuously, we received reports of attempts of Jews to escape through the sewer holes. While pretending to build air-raid shelters they had been erecting dug-outs within the former Ghetto ever since the autumn of 1942. These were intended to conceal every Jew during the new evacuation action, which they had expected for quite a time, and to enable them to resist the invaders in a concerted action. Through posters, handbills, and whisper propaganda, the communistic resistance movement actually brought it about that the Jews entered the dug-outs as soon as the new large-scale operation started. How far their precautions went can be seen from the fact that many of the dug-outs had been skillfully equipped with furnishings sufficient for entire families, washing and bathing facilities, toilets, arms and munition supplies, and food supplies sufficient for several months. There were differently equipped dug-outs for rich and for poor Jews. To discover the individual dug-outs was difficult for the units, as they had been efficiently camouflaged. In many cases, it was possible only through betrayal on the part of the Jews.

When only a few days had passed, it became apparent that the Jews no longer had any intention to resettle voluntarily, but were determined to resist evacuation with all their force and by using all the weapons at their disposal. So-called battle groups had been formed, led by Polish-Bolshevists; they were armed and paid any price asked for available arms.

During the large-scale action we succeeded in catching some Jews who had already been evacuated and resettled in Lublin or Treblinka, but had broken out from there and returned to the Ghetto, equipped with arms and ammunition. Time and again Polish bandits found refuge in the Ghetto and remained there undisturbed, since we had no forces at our disposal to comb out this maze. Whereas it had been possible during the first days to catch considerable numbers of Jews, who are cowards by nature, it became more and more difficult during the second half of the action to capture the bandits and Jews. Over and over again new battle groups consisting of 20 to 30 or more Jewish fellows, 18 to 25 years of age, accompanied by a corresponding number of women kindled new resistance. These battle groups were under orders to put up armed resistance to the last and if necessary to escape arrest by committing suicide. One such battle group succeeded in mounting a truck by ascending from a sewer in the so-called Prosta, and in escaping with it (about 30 to 35 bandits). One bandit who had arrived with this truck exploded 2 hand grenades, which was the agreed signal for the bandits waiting in the sewer to climb out of it. The bandits and Jews—there were

Polish bandits among these gangs armed with carbines, small arms, and in one case a light machine gun, mounted the truck and drove away in an unknown direction. The last member of this gang, who was on guard in the sewer and was detailed to close the lid of the sewer hole, was captured. It was he who gave the above information. The search for the truck was unfortunately without result.

During this armed resistance the women belonging to the battle groups were equipped the same as the men; some were members of the Chaluzim movement. Not infrequently, these women fired pistols with both hands. It happened time and again that these women had pistols or hand grenades (Polish "pineapple" hand grenades) concealed in their bloomers up to the last moment to use against the men of the Waffen SS, Police, or Wehrmacht.

The resistance put up by the Jews and bandits could be broken only by relentlessly using all our force and energy by day and night. *On 23 April 1943 the Reichsführer SS issued through the higher SS and Police Führer East at Cracow his order to complete the combing out of the Warsaw Ghetto with the greatest severity and relentless tenacity.* I therefore decided to destroy the entire Jewish residential area by setting every block on fire, including the blocks of residential buildings near the armament works. One concern after the other was systematically evacuated and subsequently destroyed by fire. The Jews then emerged from their hiding places and dug-outs in almost every case. Not infrequently, the Jews stayed in the burning buildings until, because of the heat and the fear of being burned alive they preferred to jump down from the upper stories after having thrown mattresses and other upholstered articles into the street from the burning buildings. With their bones broken, they still tried to crawl across the street into blocks of buildings which had not yet been set on fire or were only partly in flames. Often Jews changed their hiding places during the night, by moving into the ruins of burnt-out buildings, taking refuge there until they were found by our patrols. Their stay in the sewers also ceased to be pleasant after the first week. Frequently from the street, we could hear loud voices coming through the sewer shafts. Then the men of the Waffen SS, the Police or the Wehrmacht Engineers courageously climbed down the shafts to bring out the Jews and not infrequently they then stumbled over Jews already dead, or were shot at. It was always necessary to use smoke candles to drive out the Jews. Thus one day we opened 183 sewer entrance holes and at a fixed time lowered smoke candles into them, with the result that the bandits fled from what they believed to be gas to the centre of the former Ghetto, where they could then be pulled out of the sewer holes there. A great number of Jews, who could not be counted, were exterminated by blowing up sewers and dugouts. ...

Only through the continuous and untiring work of all involved did we succeed in catching a total of 56,065 Jews whose extermination can be proved. To this should be added the number of Jews who lost their lives in explosions or fires but whose numbers could not be ascertained. …

The large-scale action was terminated on 16 May 1943 with the blowing up of the Warsaw synagogue at 2015 hours.

Now, there are no more factories in the former Ghetto. All the goods, raw materials, and machines there have been moved and stored somewhere else. All buildings etc., have been destroyed. The only exception is the so-called Dzielna Prison of the Security Police, which was exempted from destruction. …

Source: *Nazi Conspiracy and Aggression,* Office of the United States Chief of Counsel for the Prosecution of Axis Criminality (Washington, DC: U.S. Government Printing Office, 1946), Red Series, vol. III, pp. 718–728, Doc. 1061-PS.

17 Report to the Secretary on the Acquiescence of This Government in the Murder of the Jews, January 13, 1944

This extraordinary document was written by US Treasury officials John Pehle, Randolph Paul, and Josiah DuBois and submitted to Treasury secretary Henry Morgenthau Jr. on January 13, 1944. It is a scathing attack on the State Department's efforts to obstruct Jewish immigration to the United States when it was well known that such obstruction allowed for the continuing extermination of Europe's Jews. Of those the report accused, Breckinridge Long, assistant secretary in charge of the Visa Division, was cited most often. The following served as the report's executive summary.

One of the greatest crimes in history, the slaughter of the Jewish people in Europe, is continuing unabated.

This Government has for a long time maintained that its policy is to work out programs to save those Jews of Europe who could be saved.

I am convinced on the basis of the information which is available to me that certain officials in our State Department, which is charged with carrying out this policy, have been guilty not only of gross procrastination and willful failure to act, but even of willful attempts to prevent action from being taken to rescue Jews from Hitler.

I fully recognize the graveness of this statement and I make it only after having most carefully weighed the shocking facts which have come to my attention during the last several months.

Unless remedial steps of a drastic nature are taken, and taken immediately, I am certain that no effective action will be taken by this Government to prevent the complete extermination of the Jews in

German controlled Europe, and that this Government will have to share for all time responsibility for this extermination.

The tragic history of this Government's handling of this matter reveals that certain State Department officials are guilty of the following:

1. They have not only failed to use the *Governmental machinery* at their disposal to rescue Jews from Hitler, but have even gone so far as to use this Government machinery to prevent the rescue of these Jews.
2. They have not only failed to cooperate with *private organizations* in the efforts of those organizations to work out individual programs of their own, but have taken steps designed to prevent these programs from being put into effect.
3. They not only have failed to facilitate the obtaining of information concerning Hitler's plan to exterminate the Jews of Europe but in their official capacity have gone so far as to surreptitiously attempt to stop the obtaining of information concerning the murder of the Jewish population of Europe.
4. They have tried to cover up their guilt by:
   (a) concealment and misrepresentation;
   (b) the giving of false and misleading explanations for their failures to act and their attempts to prevent action; and
   (c) the issuance of false and misleading statements concerning the "action" which they have taken to date.

Although only part of the facts relating to the activities of the State Department in this field are available to us, sufficient facts have come to my attention from various sources during the last several months to fully support the conclusions at which I have arrived.

Source: Franklin D. Roosevelt Presidential Library and Museum. Diaries of Henry Morgenthau Jr., April 27, 1933-July 27, 1945, vol. 693, 11–13 January 1944, pp. 212–229.

18 The Gerstein Report, May 1945

Kurt Gerstein was an SS officer assigned to the Hygiene Institute of the Waffen SS. His duties included assisting with the delivery of large quantities of Zyklon-B gas canisters to Auschwitz and other camps, and he witnessed a carbon monoxide gassing of Jews at the Bełżec death camp. By April 1945, as defeat loomed for the Third Reich, Gerstein surrendered to French authorities at Reutlingen. In his statement, he declared that he had surrendered to make available his knowledge to punish those responsible for the atrocities. Transferred to Paris, he wrote his final account, now known as the Gerstein Report. Here, he made a full disclosure of what he had

*witnessed as an SS officer. The following excerpts form part of his otherwise
lengthy and detailed report.*

... On 8 June 1942, the SS Sturmbannführer GÜNTHER of the RSHA
entered my office. He was in plain clothes and I did not know him. He
ordered me to get a hundred kilograms of prussic acid and to accompany
him to a place which was only known to the driver of the truck. We
left for the potassium factory ... Once the truck was loaded, we left for
Lublin (Poland). We took with us Professor PFANNENSTIEL Md. ...
At Lublin, were received by SS Gruppenführer GLOBOCNIK. He told
us: this is one of the most secret matters there is, even the most secret.
Whoever talks of this shall be shot immediately. Yesterday, two talkative
ones died. Then he explained to us: at the present moment—August 17,
1942—there are three installations:

1. Belcec, on the Lublin-Lemberg road, in the sector of the Russian
   demarcation line. Maximum 15,000 persons a day. (Seen!)
2. Sobibor, I do not know exactly where it is located. Not seen. 20,000
   persons per day.
3. Treblinka, 120 km NNE of Warsaw. 25,000 persons per day. Seen!
4. Maidanek, near Lublin. Seen in the state of preparation.

Globocnik then said: You will have to handle the sterilization of very
huge quantities of clothes, 10 or 20 times the result of the clothes and
textiles collection which is only arranged in order to conceal the source
of those Jewish, Polish, Czech and other clothes. Your other duties will be
to change the method of our gas chambers (which are run on the present
time with the exhaust gases of an old Diesel engine), employing more
poisonous material, having a quicker effect, prussic acid. ...

The next day we left for Belcek. A small special station of two
platforms leans against a hill of yellow sand, immediately to the north
of the road and railway: Lublin-Lemberg. ... GLOBOCNIK introduced
me to SS-Hauptsturmführer OVERMAYER from Pirmasens, who with
great restraint showed me the installations. That day no dead were to
be seen, but the smell of the whole region, even from the large road, was
pestilential. Next to the small station there was a large barrack marked
"Cloakroom" and a door marked "Valuables." Next a chamber with a
hundred "barber" chairs. Then came a corridor, 150 metres long, in the
open air and with barbed wire on both sides. There was a sign-board: "To
the bath and inhalations." Before us we saw a house like a bath house
with concrete troughs to the right and left containing geraniums or
other flowers. After climbing a small staircase, 3 garage-like rooms on
each side, 4 x 5 metres large and 1.90 metres high. At the back, invisible
wooden doors. On the roof a Star of David made out of copper. At the

entrance to the building, the inscription: Foundation Hackenholt. That was all I noticed on that particular afternoon. Next morning, a few minutes before 7, I was informed: In 10 minutes the first train will arrive. And indeed, a few minutes later the first train came in from Lemberg. 45 cars, containing 6,700 persons; 1450 of whom were already dead on their arrival. Behind the little barbed-wire opening, children, yellow, scared half to death, women, men. The train arrives: 200 Ukrainians, forced to do this work, open the doors, and drive all the people out of the coaches with leather whips. Then, through a huge loudspeaker instructions are given: To undress completely, also to give up false teeth and glasses—some in the barracks, others right in the open air—To tie one's shoes together with a little piece of string handed everyone by a small Jewish boy of 4 years of age, hand in all valuables and money at the window marked "Valuables," without bond, without receipt. Then the women and girls go to the hairdresser, who cuts off their hair in one or two strokes, after which it vanished into huge potato bags "to be used for special submarine equipment, door mats, etc.," as the SS-Unterscharführer on duty told me. Then, the march begins: Right and left, barbed wire, behind, two dozen Ukrainians with guns. Led by a young girl of striking beauty they approach. With police-Captain Wirth, I stand right before the death chambers. Completely naked they march by, men women, girls, babies, even one-legged persons, all of them naked. In one corner, a strong SS-man tells the poor devils, in a strong deep voice: Nothing whatever will happen to you. All you have to do is to breathe deeply, it strengthens the lungs; this inhalation is a necessary measure against contagious diseases, it is very good disinfectant!" Asked what was to become of them, he answered: "Well, of course the men will have to work, building streets and houses. But the women do not have to. If they wish to, they can help in house or kitchen." Once more, a little bit of hope for some of these poor people, enough to make them march on without resistance to the death chambers. Most of them, though, know everything, the odour has given them a clear indication of their fate. And then they walk up the little staircase—and see the truth!

Mothers, nurse-maids, with babies at their breasts, naked, lots of children of all ages, naked too; they hesitate, but they enter the gas chambers, most of them without a word, pushed by the others behind them, chased by the whips of the SS men. A Jewess of about 40 years of age, with eyes like torches, calls down the blood of her children on the heads of their murderers. Five lashes into her face, dealt by the whip of Police Captain Wirth himself, chase her into the gas chamber. Many of them say their prayers, others ask: who will give us the water for our death? (Jewish rite?). Within the chamber, the SS press the people closely together, Captain Wirth had ordered: "Fill them up full." Naked men stand of the feet of the others. 7–800 crushed together on 25 square metres, in 45 cubic metres! The doors are closed. Meanwhile the rest of the transport, all naked wait. Somebody says to me: "Naked, in winter! But they can die that way!" The answer was: "Well, that's just what they are here for!" And at that moment I understood why it was called "Foundation Hackenholt." Hackenholt was the man in charge of the Diesel engine, the exhaust gases of which were to kill those poor devils. SS-Unterscharführer Hackenholt tries to set the Diesel engine moving. But it does not start! Captain Wirth comes along. It is plain that he is afraid because I am a witness to this breakdown. Yes, indeed, I see everything and wait. Everything is registered by my stopwatch. 50 minutes 70 minutes—the Diesel engine does not start! The people wait in their gas chambers. In vain. One can hear them cry. "Same as in a synagogue," says SS-Sturmführer Professor Dr. Pfannenstiel, Professor for Public Health at the university of Marburg/Lahn, holding his ear close to the wooden door. Captain Wirth, furious, deals the Ukrainian who is helping Hackenholt 11 or 12 lashes in the face with his whip. After 2 hours and 49 minutes as registered by my stopwatch the Diesel engine starts. Up to that moment the people in the four already filled chambers were alive, 4 times 750 persons in 4 times 45 cubic metres. Another 25 minutes go by, many of the people it is true are dead at that point. One can see this through the little window through which the electric lamp reveals, for a moment, the inside of the chamber. After 28 minutes only a few are living. After 32 minutes, finally all are dead! From the other side, Jewish workers open the wooden doors. In return for their terrible job, they have been promised their freedom and a small percentage of the valuables and the money found. Like stone statues, the dead are still standing, there having been no room to fall or bend over. Though dead, the families can still be recognized; their hands still clasped. It is difficult to separate them in order to clear the chamber for the next load. The bodies are thrown out, blue, wet with sweat and urine, the legs covered with excrement and menstrual blood. Everywhere among the others, the bodies of babies and children. But there is not time! Two dozen workers are engaged in checking the mouths, opening them by means of iron hooks. "Gold to the left without gold to the right!" Others check anus and genitals to look for money, diamonds, gold etc. Dentists with chisels tear out the gold teeth bridges or caps. In the centre of everything, Captain Wirth. He is on familiar ground here. He hands me a large tin full of teeth and says: "Estimate for yourself the weight of gold. This is only from yesterday and the day before yesterday! And you would not believe what we find here every day! Dollars, diamonds, gold! But look for yourself!" ... The bodies were then thrown into large ditches of about 100 x 20 x 12 metres, located near the gas chambers. After a few days the bodies would swell up and the whole contents of the ditch would rise 2–3 metres high because of the gases that developed in the bodies. After a few more days swelling would stop and the bodies would collapse. The next day the ditches were filled again, and covered with 10 centimetres of sand. A little later, I heard, they constructed grills out of rails and burned the bodies on them with Diesel oil and gasoline in order to make them disappear. At Belcek and Treblinka nobody bothered to take anything approaching an exact count of the persons killed. ...

The Police-Captain, Wirth, asked me not to propose any other kind of gas chamber in Berlin, to leave everything the way it was. I lied—as I did in each case all the time—that the prussic acid had already deteriorated in shipping and had become very dangerous, that I was therefore obliged to bury it. This was done right away. The next day, Captain Wirth's car took us to Treblinka, about 75 miles NNE of Warsaw. The installations of this death center differed scarcely from those at Belcek, but they were still larger. There were 8 gas chambers and whole mountains of clothes and underwear about 35–40 metres high. Then, in our "Honor" a banquet was given, attended by all of the employees of the institution. The Obersturmbannführer, Professor Pfannenstiel MD., Professor Hygiene at the University of Marburg/Lahn, made a speech: "Your task is a great duty, a duty so useful and so necessary." To me alone he talked of this institution in terms of "beauty of the task, humane cause," and to all of them: "Looking at the bodies of these Jews one understands the greatness of your good work!" ...We left for Warsaw by car. ...

Kurt GERSTEIN

Source: Trials of War Criminals before the Nuremberg Military Tribunals Under Control Council No. 10 (Washington, D.C.: U.S. Government Printing Office), Green Series, vol. 1, pp. 865–870 (excerpts: Prosecution Exhibit 428), Office of Chief Counsel for War Crimes. Document No. 1553-PS.

GLOSSARY

Aktion	A Nazi-initiated operation against Jews from villages or ghettos, who were then assembled and deported, either as slave labor or murdered in death camps.
Antisemitism	An umbrella term for a variety of negative beliefs or actions held or taken against Jews for the sole reason that they are Jewish.
Aryan	The Nazi term for white people of Northern European racial background but excluding others such as Slavs, Latins, and especially Jews.
Concentration Camp	Camps established from 1933 onward for the extrajudicial imprisonment of those identified by the Nazis as enemies of the Third Reich. These would include all political opponents, Jehovah's Witnesses, Roma, gay men, so-called asocials, and Jews.
Einsatzgruppen	SS mobile killing squads that followed the German military operations, largely in Poland and the Soviet Union after June 1941. Supported by units of German police and local volunteers, they executed over a million Jews and others, mainly through shooting and the use of gas vans.
Eugenics	A pseudo-science focused on breeding "racially pure" human beings while at the same time "breeding out" so-called defective genes.
Euthanasia	In the Third Reich, the adoption of eugenic measures to improve the quality of the German "race" through the murder of those with incurable psychological problems, the permanently disabled, or those with physical and emotional disorders.
Extermination Camp	A purpose-built site to which Jews and others were sent to be murdered. Six of these were in occupied Poland: Auschwitz-Birkenau, Bełżec, Chełmno, Majdanek, Sobibór, and Treblinka.

Final Solution of the Jewish Question The euphemistic cover name for the Nazi plan to exterminate the Jewish population of Europe (*Endlösung der Judenfrage*). Beginning in the late fall of 1941, Jews were rounded up in occupied German territories and sent to death camps to be murdered. To avoid resistance, Jews were told beforehand that they were going to be "resettled" in the east.

Gas Chamber A sealed room or other enclosed space in which victims could be killed together by inhaling poison gas (such as carbon monoxide [CO] or by hydrocyanic acid [HCN], known by its commercial name of Zyklon B).

Genocide Any one of several possible acts committed with intent to destroy, in whole or in part, a national, ethnic, racial or religious group, in accordance with the UN Convention on Genocide 1948.

Gestapo Germany's secret state police force (*Geheime Staatspolizei*) and a branch of the SS, which created a climate of fear and hunted down state enemies throughout occupied Europe.

Ghetto A clearly defined area where Jews from a city and its surrounding areas were forced to reside. The ghetto would be surrounded by barbed wire or walls and was guarded from the outside. Established mostly in Eastern Europe, ghettos were usually sealed so that those imprisoned inside were prevented from leaving (or others from entering).

Holocaust A term (along with *Shoah* and *Churban*) used to describe the destruction of approximately six million Jews by the Nazis and their collaborators in Europe and North Africa between the years 1933 and 1945.

Judenrat	Jewish Council (plural, *Judenräte*), established by the Nazis in ghettos for the purpose of enforcing German directives, especially in Eastern Europe.
Kristallnacht	"Crystal Night" or "Night of Broken Glass" was the Nazi name given to a pogrom that took place on November 9–10, 1938, throughout Germany and Austria, committed by Nazis against Jews and conducted by *Sturmabteilung* forces and civilians. Synagogues were burned; Jewish homes, schools, and businesses were vandalized; 91 Jews were murdered. About 35,000 Jewish men were sent to labor or concentration camps.
Massacre	The intentional, random, and often brutal killing of a significant number of relatively defenseless people by a more powerful group or state force.
Nazi	Member of the National Socialist German Workers' Party, which was founded after the First World War and which Adolf Hitler led from 1921.
Nuremberg Laws	A series of antisemitic and racial laws in Nazi Germany, enacted on September 15, 1935. These laws deprived German Jews of citizenship; removed Jews from German political, social, and economic life; and created definitions of Jewishness based on biological descent.
Nuremberg Trials	The prosecution by the Allies in 1945–6 of the key Nazi leaders for crimes committed during the Second World War.
Persecution	The systematic abuse of a person or group by others, usually based on difference in religion, race, or politics.
Pogrom	A term usually associated with mob attacks against Jewish communities, it is now applied when violence takes place against any persecuted group. Pogroms can involve murder, rape, pillage, physical assault, and wanton or random destruction and can also lead to genocidal massacres.
Prejudice	Prejudgment of another person, community, or group, based on factors unrelated to merit or ability. Prejudicial conduct is based on accepting stereotypical misunderstandings in conjunction with a tendency to single out those who differ from the majority.

Propaganda   Biased information used to manipulate populations and generate an emotional rather than a rational response. Propaganda can be produced by governments, activist groups, companies, religious organizations and the media through paintings, cartoons, posters, pamphlets, films, radio shows, television shows, and websites.

Racism   The prejudicial belief that biological characteristics such as skin pigmentation, facial features, bone structures, and hair quality are the primary determinant of human abilities, and that the human species is unequally divided along superior and inferior lines based on such attributes. Racism can lead to active forms of discrimination in the areas of politics, society, culture, economics, religion, and the military, and can be expressed through laws, socioeconomic exclusion, discrimination, violence, and genocide.

Refugee   A person who has been forced to leave their nation, state, or place of living because of war or general unrest, cannot return home safely, and carries a well-founded fear of persecution should they attempt to do so.

Righteous among the Nations A recognition by Yad Vashem in Jerusalem of the efforts of non-Jews who, at the risk of their own lives, saved Jews from their Nazi persecutors.

Sonderkommando   Work units in Nazi death camps, usually prisoners who were forced to work in the gas chambers, undressing rooms, and crematoria.

Third Reich   When Adolf Hitler became chancellor on January 30, 1933, the Nazi state was declared to be Germany's Third Reich (Empire), intended to last for a thousand years. The First Reich was the medieval Holy Roman Empire (800–1806). The Second Reich (1871–1918) was Imperial Germany united under the rule of the Hohenzollerns.

Wannsee Conference A meeting of senior government Nazi and SS leaders, held in the Berlin suburb of Wannsee on January 20, 1942. The meeting was called to ensure the cooperation of administrative leaders of various government departments in the implementation of the Final Solution.

War A state of organized, armed conflict between different states, or different groups within a state, that is usually open and declared. War is characterized by aggression and violence, is often prolonged, and is usually waged by military forces fighting against each other. Conflict taking place during war is typified by high mortality, economic and social disruption, and physical devastation in the areas where fighting takes place.

Weimar Republic The German democratic republic established in 1919, after the First World War. Adolf Hitler was able to use rampant inflation and unemployment to end the Republic, which occurred when he became chancellor in 1933.

Yellow Star In Germany in 1937, Jewish prisoners in concentration camps had to wear a yellow triangle. By 1941 a yellow star was the standard emblem for all Jews over the age of six years throughout the Greater Reich. If caught outside the ghettos for failing to wear it, Jews were subject to beatings, imprisonment, and sometimes worse. On occasion the star alone was employed, but variations could also see the local word for Jew, such as *Jude, Jood,* or *Juif,* imprinted on it.

CHRONOLOGY OF THE HOLOCAUST

1919

January 5: The German Workers' Party (DAP) is founded by Anton Drexler and Karl Harrer
September 12: Adolf Hitler joins the DAP

1920

February 24: Nazi Party established when the DAP is renamed; it becomes the National Socialist German Workers' Party (NSDAP); Hitler presents a 25-point program, the Nazi Party Platform

1923

November 9: Hitler leads an attempt to overthrow the government of Bavaria; he fails

1924

February 24: Trial of Adolf Hitler for treason begins; he is found guilty and sentenced to five years in prison
December 19: Hitler released from Landsberg having served just eight months of his five-year sentence

1925

February 27: Hitler declares the Nazi Party (NSDAP) to be reestablished, with himself as leader (Führer)

1933

January 30: Adolf Hitler is appointed chancellor of Germany by President Paul von Hindenburg
February 27–8: Reichstag fire; arrests of political opponents of the Nazis begin almost immediately
March 5: Reichstag elections: Nazis gain 44 percent of vote in manipulated elections

March 20: Dachau concentration camp is established
March 27: The Enabling Act is passed
April 1: Jewish businesses are boycotted across Germany
April 26: Hermann Göring establishes the Gestapo
May 10: Books written by Jews and "undesirables" are publicly burned
July 14: The Law for the Prevention of Offspring with Hereditary Defects is passed, forcing many Germans with "undesirable genes" to be sterilized

1934

June 30: *Sturmabteilung* (SA) leadership is purged during what becomes known as the "Night of the Long Knives"
August 2: President Paul von Hindenburg dies; Hitler declares the office of president abolished and names himself Führer of Germany

1935

September 15: The Nuremberg Laws are announced at the annual Party rally

1936

July 1: Hitler Youth membership becomes compulsory for all Aryan boys
August 1: Summer Olympic Games begin in Berlin

1937

March 21: Papal encyclical *Mit Brennender Sorge* issued by Pope Pius XI
July 19: Buchenwald concentration camp is established

1938

March 12: The *Anschluss* (union) of Austria with Germany; all German antisemitic decrees are applied immediately to Austria
July 6–14: International conference on refugees held at Evian, France
August 1: Nazi Office of Jewish Emigration established to speed up the pace of Jewish emigration from Germany
August 8: Mauthausen concentration camp established in Austria
August 17: Nazis require Jewish women to add "Sarah" and men to add "Israel" to their names on all legal documents
August 19: Swiss government refuses entry to Austrian Jews seeking sanctuary
September 27: German Jews banned from practicing law
September 29–30: Munich Conference: Britain and France surrender the Sudetenland regions of Czechoslovakia to Germany by negotiation

October 5: Passports belonging to German Jews are marked with the letter "J" to indicate their identity

November 7: Ernst vom Rath, third secretary in the German Embassy in Paris, is shot and mortally wounded by Herschel Grynszpan; vom Rath dies on November 9, precipitating *Kristallnacht*

November 9–10: *Kristallnacht* pogrom occurs in Germany and Austria. Nazi figures give 91 Jews killed, and up to 10,000 are arrested; 267 synagogues are destroyed; figures are likely much higher

1939

March 15: Germany invades Czechoslovakia

May 15: The first prisoners arrive at Ravensbrück

June 17: The *S.S. St. Louis*, a ship carrying 936 Jewish passengers, returns to Europe after being denied entry into the United States and Cuba

August 23: The Nazi-Soviet Non-Aggression Pact is signed

September 1: Germany invades Poland; a curfew is imposed on German Jews

September 3: France and Britain declare war against Germany

September 17: Soviet Union invades Poland

September 21: Reinhard Heydrich orders *Einsatzgruppen* commanders to establish ghettos in German-occupied Poland

September 27: Warsaw surrenders; Jewish Councils (*Judenräte*) are established in Poland

November 23: Yellow stars required to be worn by Polish Jews over the age of ten years

1940

February 8: Łódź ghetto is established

April 1: Thousands of refugees are permitted into Shanghai, China

April 9: Denmark and southern Norway are invaded and occupied by Germany; Heinrich Himmler issues a directive to establish a concentration camp at Auschwitz

April 30: The Łódź ghetto is sealed off from the outside world

May 7: Nearly 165,000 inhabitants are sealed in the Łódź ghetto

May 10: France, the Netherlands, Belgium, and Luxembourg are invaded by Germany

May 20: Auschwitz concentration camp established for Polish political prisoners

June 4: Neuengamme concentration camp opens

June 22: France surrenders to Germany; Marshal Philippe Pétain leads the pro-Nazi government established in Vichy

July 17: The first anti-Jewish measures are taken in Vichy France

September 7: German forces begin aerial bombings of Britain

October 3: Vichy France passes its own version of the Nuremberg Laws
October 16: Germans officially establish the Warsaw ghetto
November 4: Jewish civil servants in the Netherlands are dismissed
November 16: The Warsaw ghetto, containing nearly 500,000 Jews, is
sealed

1941

January 21–6: Romanian Iron Guard annihilates hundreds of Jews
February 9: Dutch Nazis riot against Amsterdam Jews
March 1: Construction of Birkenau begins
April 21: Natzweiler-Struthof concentration camp opens in France
May 14: Thousands of Jews are rounded up in Paris at the Vel' d'Hiv
June 22: Germany violates its non-aggression pact with the Soviet
Union and invades (Operation Barbarossa)
June 27: Białystok occupied by Nazis; Białystok ghetto established
July 2: Ukrainian nationalists murder thousands in Lvov
July 17: *Einsatzgruppen* ordered to execute captured communists and
Jews during Soviet campaign
July 20: Minsk ghetto established
July 31: Adolf Eichmann appointed to prepare the "Final Solution"
September 1: The German "Euthanasia" program is formally ended,
following the deaths of some 100,000 people
September 6: The Vilna ghetto is established
September 19: Jews in Germany are ordered to wear yellow armbands
bearing the Star of David
September 29: The *Einsatzgruppen* murders some 34,000 Jews at Babi
Yar ravine, outside Kiev
October 7: Birkenau is established as the primary mass murder site of
Auschwitz
October 22–4: Romanian and German forces massacre an estimated
50,000 Jews in Odessa
October 28: Approximately 9,000 Jews are killed outside of Kovno
(Kaunas)
November 8: Plans are made for the creation of a ghetto in Lvov
(Lwów, Lviv)
November 24: Terezín (Theresienstadt) ghetto/concentration camp
established
December 7: Japan attacks Pearl Harbor, drawing the United States into
the Second World War
December 8: Chełmno extermination camp becomes fully operational;
some 320,000 Jews will be murdered here
December 11: Germany and Italy declare war on the United States

1942

January 10: *Armée Juive* (Jewish Army) created in France

January 20: The Wannsee Conference takes place in Berlin

January 16: Deportations from Łódź begin

February 23: Some 768 Jewish passengers, after being refused entry into Palestine, drown when the *S.S. Struma* sinks off of the Turkish coast

March 1: Extermination by gas begins at Sobibór

March 17: Killings begin at Bełżec extermination camp

June: First anti-Nazi resistance pamphlet published by the White Rose group of Hans and Sophie Scholl

June 1: Jews in France, Holland, Belgium, Croatia, Slovakia, and Romania ordered to wear yellow stars

June 1: Treblinka extermination camp begins operation

July 13: Eighteen hundred Jews are massacred in Jozefów, Poland, by German Reserve Police Battalion 101

July 14: Mass deportation of Dutch and Belgian Jews to Auschwitz begins

July 16: Over 4,000 children are taken from Paris and sent to Auschwitz; overall, some 12,887 Jews in Paris are sent through Drancy

July 22: Mass deportation of Jews from the Warsaw ghetto to Treblinka begins

July 23: Adam Czerniaków commits suicide in Warsaw

July 28: The Jewish Combat Organization is formed in the Warsaw ghetto

August 7: Dr. Janusz Korczak and 200 orphans under his care are gassed in Treblinka

August 17: Kurt Gerstein visits Bełżec death camp and witnesses the gassing of up to 3,000 Jews

August 29: The Riegner Telegram is sent

September 2–3: Revolt of the Łachwa ghetto, arguably the first ghetto revolt of the Holocaust

October 15: The SS slaughters 25,000 Jews near Brest-Litovsk

October 25: The deportation of Norwegian Jews begins

October 28: First transport of Jews sent from Terezín (Theresienstadt) to Auschwitz

December 24: Armed operations by the Jewish Combat Organization against German troops in Kraków

1943

January 18–21: Renewed deportations of Jews from the Warsaw ghetto begin following a visit from Himmler; Jewish resistance begins in the ghetto

February 22: Christoph Probst, Hans Scholl, and Sophie Scholl are executed after admitting to distributing White Rose pamphlets

February 26: The first Roma arrive at Auschwitz
March 13–14: Liquidation of the Kraków ghetto
March 23: Nazi deportation of Greek Jews begins
April 5: Approximately 4,000 Jews are massacred in the Ponary Forest,
outside Vilna
April 19: New deportations from the Warsaw ghetto; first day of
Warsaw Ghetto Uprising; Britain and the United States begin the
Bermuda Conference
May 1: Bermuda Conference ends
May 8: Nazi forces capture the Jewish Combat Organization's
command bunker at Miła 18; Mordecai Anielewicz is among the dead
found there
May 16: SS General Jürgen Stroop reports that the "Jewish quarter of
Warsaw is no more"
May 19: Nazis declare Berlin to be *Judenfrei* ("cleansed of Jews")
June 2: 3,000 Jews killed following resistance in Lvov (Lwów, Lviv);
another 7,000 are sent to the concentration camp at Janowska
June 11: Himmler orders liquidation of all ghettos in occupied Poland
August 2: Treblinka uprising
August 15–16: Uprising of the Białystok ghetto
October 1–2: German police begin deportations of Danish Jews; Danes
respond with a rescue effort that saves the lives of 90 percent of the
Jewish population
October 14: Sobibór uprising
October 16: Major Nazi raid and *razzia* (roundup) against the Jews of
Rome, who are sent to Auschwitz
October 21: Minsk ghetto liquidated

1944

January 22: US president Franklin D. Roosevelt creates the War Refugee
Board
March 19: Germany begins its occupation of Hungary; Adolf Eichmann
sent from Berlin to oversee the deportation of the Hungarian Jews
May 15: Beginning of the deportation of Jews from Hungary to
Auschwitz; Jews from Ruthenia and Transylvania are deported
May 16: Germans offer to free one million Jews in exchange for 10,000
trucks
July 9: Raoul Wallenberg arrives in Hungary, where he distributes
Swedish passports and sets up safe houses for Jews
July 11: Deportations from Hungary are halted by order of Regent
Miklós Horthy
July 24: Majdanek extermination camp is liberated by the Russians
August 1–October 4: Warsaw Revolt

August 2: Germany destroys the so-called Gypsy camp at Auschwitz, gassing some 3,000 in the process

August 6: Łódź, the last Jewish ghetto in Poland, is liquidated with 60,000 Jews sent to Auschwitz

October 7: *Sonderkommando* revolt at Auschwitz; one of the gas chambers is destroyed; 15 SS guards and 400 members of the *Sonderkommando* are killed

November 8: Deportations resume in Budapest

November 19: The Vatican and four other neutral powers in Budapest issue a collective protest to the Hungarian government calling for the suspension of Jewish deportations

November 28: Himmler orders the gas chambers at Auschwitz destroyed

December 24–9: Hungarian Arrow Cross fascists attack Jews in Budapest

1945

January 5: Roza Robota, Estusia Wajcblum, Ala Gertner, and Regina Safirsztajn, accused of supplying gunpowder to the Auschwitz *Sonderkommando*, are executed

January 18: The evacuation of Auschwitz begins

January 19: The Soviet army liberates Łódź

January 28: Soviet forces liberate Auschwitz

April 9: Evacuation of Mauthausen begins

April 11: American forces liberate Buchenwald

April 15: British forces liberate Bergen-Belsen

April 27: Soviet forces liberate Sachsenhausen

April 29: American forces liberate Dachau; Soviet forces liberate Ravensbrück

April 30: Hitler commits suicide

May 1: Joseph Goebbels kills his wife and children before shooting himself as Berlin is surrounded by the Soviet army

May 2: Soviet forces capture Berlin

May 3: Theresienstadt is surrendered to the International Committee of the Red Cross

May 5: American forces liberate Mauthausen

May 7: Germany surrenders to the Allies in Reims

May 9: Wilhelm Keitel signs surrender documents in Berlin

May 23: Heinrich Himmler commits suicide

September 1: Japan surrenders to the Allies after the United States detonates atomic bombs at Hiroshima and Nagasaki, ending the Second World War

October 18: The International Military Tribunal of major war criminals begins at Nuremberg

1946

July 4: Forty-two Jews are killed in a pogrom in Kielce, Poland
October 1: The International Military Tribunal ends
October 15: Hermann Göring commits suicide in his cell at Nuremberg
October 16: Death sentences carried out at Nuremberg, as those condemned are hanged

BIBLIOGRAPHY

The list that follows is intended as a starting point for all those interested in pursuing some of the themes introduced in this book. For students, it serves as a bare minimum of works that might be useful for you as you proceed with your work. It complements the Further Reading at the end of each of the histories in the book. It does not pretend to be a complete listing of all works relating to the Holocaust, nor could it be: there are tens of thousands of works on every aspect of the topic and new works are appearing literally every day. You are urged to be aware of the literature through constant screening of contemporary reviews, new book displays in bookstores, and online resources to ascertain how trends in the literature are developing. The works in this listing should be considered as the core of any research project.

Bar-Tov, Omer, *Germany's War and the Holocaust: Disputed Histories*, Ithaca: Cornell University Press, 2003.

Bartrop, Paul R., *Resisting the Holocaust: Upstanders, Partisans, and Survivors*, Santa Barbara: ABC-CLIO, 2016.

Bartrop, Paul R. (ed.), *Sources for Studying the Holocaust: A Guide*, Abingdon, UK: Routledge, 2023.

Bartrop, Paul R., and Eve E. Grimm, *Children of the Holocaust*, Santa Barbara: ABC-CLIO, 2019.

Bartrop, Paul R., and Eve E. Grimm, *The Holocaust: The Essential Reference Guide*, Santa Barbara: ABC-CLIO, 2022.

Bartrop, Paul R., and Eve E. Grimm, *Perpetrating the Holocaust: Leaders, Enablers, and Collaborators*, Santa Barbara: ABC-CLIO, 2019.

Bartrop, Paul R., and Michael Dickerman (ed.), *The Holocaust: An Encyclopedia and Document Collection* (4 vols.), Santa Barbara: ABC-CLIO, 2017.

Bauer, Yehuda, *A History of the Holocaust*, New York: Franklin Watts, 1982.

Beevor, Antony, *The Second World War*, London: Weidenfeld and Nicolson, 2012.

Berenbaum, Michael (ed.), *A Mosaic of Victims: Non-Jews Persecuted and Murdered by the Nazis*, New York: New York University Press, 1990.

Berenbaum Michael, and Abraham J. Peck (ed.), *The Holocaust and History: The Known, the Unknown, the Disputed, and the Reexamined*, Bloomington: Indiana University Press, 1998.

Bergen, Doris, *War and Genocide: A Concise History of the Holocaust* (3rd ed.), Lanham, MD: Rowman and Littlefield, 2016.

Bracher, Karl Dietrich, *The German Dictatorship: The Origins, Structure, and Effects of National Socialism*, New York: Praeger, 1970.

Burleigh, Michael, *The Third Reich: A New History*, New York: Hill and
    Wang, 2000.
Cesarani, David, *Final Solution: The Fate of the Jews, 1933–49*, London:
    Macmillan, 2016.
Cesarani, David (ed.), *The Final Solution: Origins and Implementation*,
    London: Routledge, 1994.
Childers, Thomas, *The Third Reich: A History of Nazi Germany*, New York: Simon
    and Schuster, 2017.
Cohn-Sherbok, Dan, *Understanding the Holocaust: An Introduction*, London:
    Cassell, 1999.
Dawidowicz, Lucy S., *The War against the Jews, 1933–1945*, New York: Holt,
    Rinehart and Winston, 1975.
Dwork, Debórah, and Robert Jan van Pelt, *Holocaust: A History*, New York:
    Norton, 2003.
Edelheit, Abraham J., and Hershel Edelheit, *History of the Holocaust: A Handbook
    and Dictionary*, Boulder: Westview Press, 1994.
Epstein, Eric Joseph, and Philip Rosen, *Dictionary of the Holocaust: Biography,
    Geography, and Terminology*, Westport: Greenwood Press, 1997.
Evans, Richard J., *The Coming of the Third Reich*, London: Penguin Books, 2003.
Evans, Richard J., *The Reich at War, 1939–1945*, London: Penguin Books, 2009.
Evans, Richard J., *The Third Reich in Power*, London: Penguin Books, 2005.
Fest, Joachim C., *The Face of the Third Reich: Portraits of the Nazi Leadership*,
    London: Weidenfeld and Nicolson, 1970.
Fischer, Klaus P., *Nazi Germany: A New History*, New York: Continuum, 1995.
Friedman, Jonathan C., *The Routledge History of the Holocaust*, Abingdon,
    UK: Routledge, 2011.
Friedländer, Saul, *Nazi Germany and the Jews, 1939–1945: The Years of
    Extermination*, New York: HarperCollins, 2007.
Friedländer, Saul, *Nazi Germany and the Jews, 1933–1939: The Years of
    Persecution*, New York: HarperCollins, 1997.
Gigliotti, Simone, and Berel Lang (ed.), *The Holocaust: A Reader*, Malden, MA:
    Blackwell, 2005.
Gilbert, Martin, *Holocaust: The Jewish Tragedy*, London: Collins, 1986.
Goda, Norman J. W., *The Holocaust: Europe, the World, and the Jews, 1918–1945*,
    Boston: Pearson, 2013.
Goeschel, Christian, and Nikolaus Wachsmann (ed.), *The Nazi Concentration
    Camps, 1933–1939: A Documentary History*, Lincoln: University of Nebraska
    Press, 2012.
Graml, Hermann, *Antisemitism in the Third Reich*, Oxford: Blackwell, 1992.
Griech-Polelle, Beth, *Anti-Semitism and the Holocaust: Language, Rhetoric, and
    the Traditions of Hatred*, London: Bloomsbury Academic, 2017.
Grunberger, Richard, *The Twelve-Year Reich: A Social History of Nazi Germany,
    1933–1945*, New York: Holt, Rinehart and Winston, 1971.
Gutman, Yisrael, and Michael Berenbaum (ed.), *Anatomy of the Auschwitz Death
    Camp*, Bloomington: Indiana University Press, 1994.
Hayes, Peter, *Why? Explaining the Holocaust*, New York: Norton, 2017.
Helig, Jocelyn, *The Holocaust and Antisemitism: A Short History*, Oxford:
    Oneworld, 2003.

Hilberg, Raul, *The Destruction of the European Jews* (3 vols.: rev. and definitive ed.), New York: Holmes and Meier, 1985.

Hilton, Laura, and Avinoam Patt, *Understanding and Teaching the Holocaust*, Madison: University of Wisconsin Press, 2020.

Kay, Alex J., *Empire of Destruction: A History of Nazi Mass Killing*, New Haven: Yale University Press, 2021.

Landau, Ronnie S., *Studying the Holocaust: Issues, Readings, and Documents*, London: Routledge, 1998.

Laqueur, Walter (ed.), *The Holocaust Encyclopedia*, New Haven: Yale University Press, 2001.

Lawson, Tom. *Debates on the Holocaust.* Manchester: Manchester University Press, 2010.

Levin, Nora, *The Holocaust: The Destruction of European Jewry, 1933–1945*, New York: Thomas Y. Crowell, 1968.

Lifton, Robert Jay. *The Nazi Doctors: Medical Killing and the Psychology of Genocide.* New York: Basic Books, 1986.

Longerich, Peter, *The Holocaust: Nazi Persecution and Murder of the Jews*, Oxford: Oxford University Press, 2010.

Paldiel, Mordecai. *Diplomat Heroes of the Holocaust.* New York: Yeshiva University/KTAV, 2007.

Paldiel, Mordecai. *The Path of the Righteous: Gentile Rescuers of Jews during the Holocaust.* Hoboken, NJ: KTAV, 1993.

Paldiel, Mordecai. *The Righteous among the Nations: Rescuers of Jews during the Holocaust.* New York: Harper and Row, 2007.

Paldiel, Mordecai. *Saving the Jews: Amazing Stories of Men and Women who Defied the "Final Solution."* Rockville, MD: Schreiber Publishing, 2000.

Rees, Laurence, *The Holocaust: A New History*, New York: PublicAffairs, 2017.

Rosenbaum, Alan S. (ed.), *Is the Holocaust Unique? Perspectives on Comparative Genocide* (3rd ed.), Boulder: Western Press, 2018.

Rozett, Robert, *Approaching the Holocaust: Texts and Contexts*, London: Vallentine Mitchell, 2005.

Shirer, William L., *The Rise and Fall of the Third Reich: A History of Nazi Germany*, New York: Simon and Schuster, 1960.

Stackelberg, Roderick, and Sally A. Winkle (ed.), *The Nazi Germany Sourcebook: An Anthology of Texts*, Abingdon, UK: Routledge, 2002.

Stone, Dan, *Histories of the Holocaust*, Manchester: Manchester University Press, 2010.

Vital, David, *A People Apart: The Jews in Europe, 1789–1939*, Oxford: Oxford University Press, 1999.

Weale, Adrian, *Army of Evil: A History of the SS*, New York: NAL Caliber, 2010.

Wistrich, Robert S., *A Lethal Obsession: Anti-Semitism from Antiquity to the Global Jihad*, New York: Random House, 2010.

Yahil, Leni. *The Holocaust: The Fate of European Jewry, 1932–1945.* New York: Oxford University Press, 1990.

Zentner, Christian, and Friedemann Bedürftig (ed.), *The Encyclopedia of the Third Reich* (2 vols.), New York: Macmillan, 1991.

Internet Resources

The internet is an extraordinarily rich repository for researching all forms of
resistance during the Holocaust, though a word of caution must be made. Not
all websites are trustworthy, accurate, or committed to historical accuracy. It is
intended that the following websites, arranged alphabetically, will provide a list
that is both authoritative and comprehensive. Researchers looking for more specific
information will in some instances need to move beyond these and in certain cases
be prepared to consult websites in languages other than English.

Beit Lohamei HaGetaot Ghetto Fighters' House Museum http://www.gfh.org.
    il/Eng/.
The European Holocaust Research Infrastructure http://www.ehri-project.eu/.
Holocaust Education and Archive Research Team http://www.holocaustresearch
    project.org/.
Jewish Foundation for the Righteous https://jfr.org/.
Jewish Virtual Library https://www.jewishvirtuallibrary.org/.
United States Holocaust Memorial Museum http://www.ushmm.org/.
Yad Vashem http://www.yadvashem.org/.
Yivo Institute for Jewish Research: Encyclopedia of Jews in Eastern Europe http://
    www.yivoencyclopedia.org/.

INDEX